THE AWAKENING

AN AUTHORITATIVE TEXT
BIOGRAPHICAL AND HISTORICAL CONTEXTS
CRITICISM

SECOND EDITION

Works Cited:

• Shakespeare, William. Julius Caesar. New York. Simon & Schuster Paperbacks. 1992.

• Chopin, Kate. The Awakening. New York. W. W. Norton & Company, Inc. 1994.

D0107034

W. W. NORTON & COMPANY, INC.
Also Publishes

For a complete list of Norton Critical Editions, visit
www.wwnorton.com/college/english/nce_home.htm

A NORTON CRITICAL EDITION

Kate Chopin
THE AWAKENING

AN AUTHORITATIVE TEXT
BIOGRAPHICAL AND HISTORICAL CONTEXTS
CRITICISM

SECOND EDITION

Edited by
MARGO CULLEY

UNIVERSITY OF MASSACHUSETTS AT AMHERST

W • W • NORTON & COMPANY • New York • London

The text of this book is composed in Electra with the display set in Bernhard
Modern. Composition by PennSet, Inc. Manufacturing by Courier.
Book design by Antonina Krass.

Library of Congress Cataloging-in-Publication Data
Chopin, Kate, 1851–1904.
The Awakening : an authoritative text, biography, contexts,
criticism / Kate Chopin ; edited by Margo Culley. — 2nd ed.
p.   cm.
Includes bibliographical references.
1. Chopin, Kate, 1851–1904. Awakening.   I. Culley, Margo.
II. Title.
PS1294.C63A6   1994
813'.4—dc20   92-40445
ISBN 0-393-96057-9

W. W. Norton & Company, Inc., 500 Fifth Avenue, New York, N.Y. 10110
www.wwnorton.com

W. W. Norton & Company Ltd., Castle House, 75/76 Wells Street,
London W1T 3QT

3 4 5 6 7 8 9 0

Contents

Criticism

Preface to the Second Edition

As we approach the one hundredth anniversary of the publication of Kate Chopin's *The Awakening*, the novel has at last claimed its rightful place as a classic of American literature. But for the first half-century after its publication, *The Awakening* languished in obscurity, out-of-print in America for almost sixty years. Widely condemned by early reviewers for its immoral or amoral sensibility, the novel continued to be ignored by all but a few important critics and shapers of the American literary tradition. (See "Editor's Note: History of the Criticism of *The Awakening*," p. 159.) Perhaps because of its "French connection," *The Awakening* first returned to print in France in 1953, translated with a long introduction by Cyrille Arnavon. Chopin thus joins a number of significant American writers, including Edgar Allen Poe and William Faulkner, whose work was particularly valued by French readers when it remained neglected at home. In this country, the novel returned to print in 1964, edited by Kenneth Eble. By 1969, the Norwegian scholar Per Seyersted (a student of Cyrille Arnavon) had published a biography of Kate Chopin and edited *The Complete Works of Kate Chopin* for Louisiana University Press. In the 1970s, the impact of feminist criticism and its focus on women writers brought Kate Chopin and her work to center stage. Today *The Awakening* is widely available in numerous paperback editions and is routinely included in major anthologies of American literature. In addition to French, the novel has been translated into German, Italian, and several Scandinavian languages. Robert Stone's novel *Children of Light* (1986) imagines a Hollywood production of *The Awakening*, and, indeed, two feature-length films, *The End of August* (1982) and *Grand Isle* (1992), have been based on Chopin's tale. The novel has been reprinted in *Redbook* magazine, filmed for educational television, and recorded on audio tape, and Kate Chopin's life has been adapted for the theater. In 1990, Emily Toth published what is the third full-length biography of Kate Chopin, an exhaustive study of the writer's life and world.

What would Kate Chopin—who earned less than $150 in royalties for *The Awakening* during her lifetime and who suffered widespread negative criticism for her bold novel—think of its late, great success?

In the preparation of this volume, I am particularly indebted to Emily Toth's extensive knowledge of Kate Chopin's life and its Louisiana context. Her detailed and generous suggestions guided my work on the second edition of the Norton Critical Edition of the novel. Any errors that persist are my own.

I would also like to thank the editor's editors: Carol Bemis for her expert guidance and her patience; Claudia Van der Heuval for her assistance in the final stages of the project; and Kathleen Swaim for two decades of cheerful and wholehearted support.

MARGO CULLEY
University of Massachusetts at Amherst

The Text of
THE AWAKENING

The page from a Chopin notebook where she recorded the original title of the novel, "A Solitary Soul." Used with permission of the Missouri Historical Society.

A green and yellow parrot, which hung in a cage outside the door, kept repeating over and over:

"*Allez vous-en! Allez vous-en! Sapristi!*[1] That's all right!"

He could speak a little Spanish, and also a language which nobody understood, unless it was the mocking-bird that hung on the other side of the door, whistling his fluty notes out upon the breeze with maddening persistence.

Mr. Pontellier, unable to read his newspaper with any degree of comfort, arose with an expression and an exclamation of disgust. He walked down the gallery and across the narrow "bridges" which connected the Lebrun cottages one with the other. He had been seated before the door of the main house. The parrot and the mocking-bird were the property of Madame Lebrun, and they had the right to make all the noise they wished. Mr. Pontellier had the privilege of quitting their society when they ceased to be entertaining.

He stopped before the door of his own cottage, which was the fourth one from the main building and next to the last. Seating himself in a wicker rocker which was there, he once more applied himself to the task of reading the newspaper. The day was Sunday; the paper was a day old. The Sunday papers had not yet reached Grand Isle.[2] He was already acquainted with the market reports, and he glanced restlessly over the editorials and bits of news which he had not had time to read before quitting New Orleans the day before.

Mr. Pontellier wore eye-glasses. He was a man of forty, of medium height and rather slender build; he stooped a little. His hair was brown and straight, parted on one side. His beard was neatly and closely trimmed.

Once in a while he withdrew his glance from the newspaper and looked about him. There was more noise than ever over at the house. The main building was called "the house," to distinguish it from the cottages. The chattering and whistling birds were still at it. Two young girls, the Farival twins, were playing a duet from "Zampa"[3] upon the piano. Madame Lebrun was bustling in and out, giving orders in a high key to a yard-boy whenever she got inside the house, and directions in an equally high voice to a dining-room servant whenever she got outside. She was a fresh, pretty woman, clad always in white with elbow sleeves.

1. "Go away! Go away! For God's sake!"
2. An island fifty miles south of New Orleans, between the Gulf of Mexico and Caminada Bay. The island was famed as the headquarters of Lafitte's pirates in the early nineteenth century, and toward the end of the century became a celebrated Creole resort. In 1893 a hurricane devastated the resort area. Chênière Caminada (see below) is an island between Grand Isle and the Louisiana coast.
3. A romantic opera by the French composer Ferdinand (Louis Joseph) Hérold (1791–1833). The plot involves a lover's death in the sea.

Her starched skirts crinkled as she came and went. Farther down, before one of the cottages, a lady in black was walking demurely up and down, telling her beads. A good many persons of the *pension* had gone over to the *Chênière Caminada* in Beaudelet's lugger[4] to hear mass. Some young people were out under the water-oaks playing croquet. Mr. Pontellier's two children were there—sturdy little fellows of four and five. A quadroon[5] nurse followed them about with a far-away, meditative air.

Mr. Pontellier finally lit a cigar and began to smoke, letting the paper drag idly from his hand. He fixed his gaze upon a white sunshade that was advancing at snail's pace from the beach. He could see it plainly between the gaunt trunks of the water-oaks and across the stretch of yellow camomile. The gulf looked far away, melting hazily into the blue of the horizon. The sunshade continued to approach slowly. Beneath its pink-lined shelter were his wife, Mrs. Pontellier, and young Robert Lebrun. When they reached the cottage, the two seated themselves with some appearance of fatigue upon the upper step of the porch, facing each other, each leaning against a supporting post.

"What folly! to bathe at such an hour in such heat!" exclaimed Mr. Pontellier. He himself had taken a plunge at daylight. That was why the morning seemed long to him.

"You are burnt beyond recognition," he added, looking at his wife as one looks at a valuable piece of personal property which has suffered some damage. She held up her hands, strong, shapely hands, and surveyed them critically, drawing up her lawn sleeves[6] above the wrists. Looking at them reminded her of her rings, which she had given to her husband before leaving for the beach. She silently reached out to him, and he, understanding, took the rings from his vest pocket and dropped them into her open palm. She slipped them upon her fingers; then clasping her knees, she looked across at Robert and began to laugh. The rings sparkled upon her fingers. He sent back an answering smile.

"What is it?" asked Pontellier, looking lazily and amused from one to the other. It was some utter nonsense; some adventure out there in the water, and they both tried to relate it at once. It did not seem half so amusing when told. They realized this, and so did Mr. Pontellier. He yawned and stretched himself. Then he got up, saying he had half a mind to go over to Klein's hotel[7] and play a game of billiards.

"Come go along, Lebrun," he proposed to Robert. But Robert admitted quite frankly that he preferred to stay where he was and talk to Mrs. Pontellier.

---

4. A small boat with a sail. *"Pension"*: boardinghouse.
5. A person with one-fourth black ancestry.
6. Sleeves made of lawn, a fine linen or sheer muslin.
7. Probably Krantz's Hotel, described by Catharine Cole in 1892: "An old, popular, well-known resort, built like a plantation quarters in a series of cottages along a grassy street. At one end a ballroom, at the other a dining room . . . out of the sight of the surf and the sea; but three times a day a tram car runs down to the beach where the bathhouses are. In the center of the island, rising above the clustered oaks, are the gray dormer windows of a huge unfinished hotel . . ." (*The Daily Picayune*, October 5, 1893).

"Well, send him about his business when he bores you, Edna," instructed her husband as he prepared to leave.

"Here, take the umbrella," she exclaimed, holding it out to him. He accepted the sunshade, and lifting it over his head descended the steps and walked away.

"Coming back to dinner?" his wife called after him. He halted a moment and shrugged his shoulders. He felt in his vest pocket; there was a ten-dollar bill there. He did not know; perhaps he would return for the early dinner and perhaps he would not. It all depended upon the company which he found over at Klein's and the size of "the game." He did not say this, but she understood it, and laughed, nodding goodby to him.

Both children wanted to follow their father when they saw him starting out. He kissed them and promised to bring them back bonbons and peanuts.

II

Mrs. Pontellier's eyes were quick and bright; they were a yellowish brown, about the color of her hair. She had a way of turning them swiftly upon an object and holding them there as if lost in some inward maze of contemplation or thought.

Her eyebrows were a shade darker than her hair. They were thick and almost horizontal, emphasizing the depth of her eyes. She was rather handsome than beautiful. Her face was captivating by reason of a certain frankness of expression and a contradictory subtle play of features. Her manner was engaging.

Robert rolled a cigarette. He smoked cigarettes because he could not afford cigars, he said. He had a cigar in his pocket which Mr. Pontellier had presented him with, and he was saving it for his after-dinner smoke. This seemed quite proper and natural on his part. In coloring he was not unlike his companion. A clean-shaved face made the resemblance more pronounced than it would otherwise have been. There rested no shadow of care upon his open countenance. His eyes gathered in and reflected the light and languor of the summer day.

Mrs. Pontellier reached over for a palmleaf fan that lay on the porch and began to fan herself, while Robert sent between his lips light puffs from his cigarette. They chatted incessantly: about the things around them; their amusing adventure out in the water—it had again assumed its entertaining aspect; about the wind, the trees, the people who had gone to the *Chênière*; about the children playing croquet under the oaks, and the Farival twins, who were now performing the overture to "The Poet and the Peasant."[8]

Robert talked a good deal about himself. He was very young, and did

8. An operetta by the Austrian composer Franz von Suppé (1819–95), known primarily for his overtures.

not know any better. Mrs. Pontellier talked a little about herself for the same reason. Each was interested in what the other said. Robert spoke of his intention to go to Mexico in the autumn, where fortune awaited him. He was always intending to go to Mexico, but some way never got there. Meanwhile he held on to his modest position in a mercantile house in New Orleans, where an equal familiarity with English, French and Spanish gave him no small value as a clerk and correspondent.

He was spending his summer vacation, as he always did, with his mother at Grand Isle. In former times, before Robert could remember, "the house" had been a summer luxury of the Lebruns. Now, flanked by its dozen or more cottages, which were always filled with exclusive visitors from the "*Quartier Français*,"[9] it enabled Madame Lebrun to maintain the easy and comfortable existence which appeared to be her birthright.

Mrs. Pontellier talked about her father's Mississippi plantation and her girlhood home in the old Kentucky blue-grass country. She was an American woman, with a small infusion of French which seemed to have been lost in dilution. She read a letter from her sister, who was away in the East, and who had engaged herself to be married. Robert was interested, and wanted to know what manner of girls the sisters were, what the father was like, and how long the mother had been dead.

When Mrs. Pontellier folded the letter it was time for her to dress for the early dinner.

"I see Léonce isn't coming back," she said, with a glance in the direction whence her husband had disappeared. Robert supposed he was not, as there were a good many New Orleans club men over at Klein's.

When Mrs. Pontellier left him to enter her room, the young man descended the steps and strolled over toward the croquet players, where, during the half-hour before dinner, he amused himself with the little Pontellier children, who were very fond of him.

III

It was eleven o'clock that night when Mr. Pontellier returned from Klein's hotel. He was in an excellent humor, in high spirits, and very talkative. His entrance awoke his wife, who was in bed and fast asleep when he came in. He talked to her while he undressed, telling her anecdotes and bits of news and gossip that he had gathered during the day. From his trousers pockets he took a fistful of crumpled bank notes and a good deal of silver coin, which he piled on the bureau indiscriminately with keys, knife, handkerchief, and whatever else happened to

---

9. The French Quarter, or Vieux Carré—the oldest part of New Orleans—settled by the French in the early 1700s and residence of most of the Creole population in the nineteenth century. See p. 10, n. 4.

be in his pockets. She was overcome with sleep, and answered him with little half utterances.

He thought it very discouraging that his wife, who was the sole object of his existence, evinced so little interest in things which concerned him and valued so little his conversation.

Mr. Pontellier had forgotten the bonbons and peanuts for the boys. Notwithstanding he loved them very much, and went into the adjoining room where they slept to take a look at them and make sure that they were resting comfortably. The result of his investigation was far from satisfactory. He turned and shifted the youngsters about in bed. One of them began to kick and talk about a basket full of crabs.

Mr. Pontellier returned to his wife with the information that Raoul had a high fever and needed looking after. Then he lit a cigar and went and sat near the open door to smoke it.

Mrs. Pontellier was quite sure Raoul had no fever. He had gone to bed perfectly well, she said, and nothing had ailed him all day. Mr. Pontellier was too well acquainted with fever symptoms to be mistaken. He assured her the child was consuming at that moment in the next room.

He reproached his wife with her inattention, her habitual neglect of the children. If it was not a mother's place to look after children, whose on earth was it? He himself had his hands full with his brokerage business. He could not be in two places at once; making a living for his family on the street, and staying at home to see that no harm befell them. He talked in a monotonous, insistent way.

Mrs. Pontellier sprang out of bed and went into the next room. She soon came back and sat on the edge of the bed, leaning her head down on the pillow. She said nothing, and refused to answer her husband when he questioned her. When his cigar was smoked out he went to bed, and in half a minute he was fast asleep.

Mrs. Pontellier was by that time thoroughly awake. She began to cry a little, and wiped her eyes on the sleeve of her *peignoir*. Blowing out the candle, which her husband had left burning, she slipped her bare feet into a pair of satin *mules* at the foot of the bed and went out on the porch, where she sat down in the wicker chair and began to rock gently to and fro.

It was then past midnight. The cottages were all dark. A single faint light gleamed out from the hallway of the house. There was no sound abroad except the hooting of an old owl in the top of a water-oak, and the everlasting voice of the sea, that was not uplifted at that soft hour. It broke like a mournful lullaby upon the night.

The tears came so fast to Mrs. Pontellier's eyes that the damp sleeve of her *peignoir* no longer served to dry them. She was holding the back of her chair with one hand; her loose sleeve had slipped almost to the shoulder of her uplifted arm. Turning, she thrust her face, steaming and wet, into the bend of her arm, and she went on crying there, not caring any longer to dry her face, her eyes, her arms. She could not have told why she was crying. Such experiences as the foregoing were not uncommon in her married life. They seemed never before to have weighed much against the abundance of her husband's kindness and a uniform devotion which had come to be tacit and self-understood.

An indescribable oppression, which seemed to generate in some unfamiliar part of her consciousness, filled her whole being with a vague anguish. It was like a shadow, like a mist passing across her soul's summer day. It was strange and unfamiliar; it was a mood. She did not sit there inwardly upbraiding her husband, lamenting at Fate, which had directed her footsteps to the path which they had taken. She was just having a good cry all to herself. The mosquitoes made merry over her, biting her firm, round arms and nipping at her bare insteps.

The little stinging, buzzing imps succeeded in dispelling a mood which might have held her there in the darkness half a night longer.

The following morning Mr. Pontellier was up in good time to take the rockaway[1] which was to convey him to the steamer at the wharf. He was returning to the city to his business, and they would not see him again at the Island till the coming Saturday. He had regained his composure, which seemed to have been somewhat impaired the night before. He was eager to be gone, as he looked forward to a lively week in Carondelet Street.[2]

Mr. Pontellier gave his wife half the money which he had brought away from Klein's hotel the evening before. She liked money as well as most women, and accepted it with no little satisfaction.

"It will buy a handsome wedding present for Sister Janet!" she exclaimed, smoothing out the bills as she counted them one by one.

"Oh! we'll treat Sister Janet better than that, my dear," he laughed, as he prepared to kiss her good-by.

The boys were tumbling about, clinging to his legs, imploring that numerous things be brought back to them. Mr. Pontellier was a great favorite, and ladies, men, children, even nurses, were always on hand to say good-by to him. His wife stood smiling and waving, the boys shouting, as he disappeared in the old rockaway down the sandy road.

A few days later a box arrived for Mrs. Pontellier from New Orleans. It was from her husband. It was filled with *friandises*,[3] with luscious and toothsome bits—the finest of fruits *patés*, a rare bottle or two, delicious syrups, and bonbons in abundance.

Mrs. Pontellier was always very generous with the contents of such a box; she was quite used to receiving them when away from home. The *patés* and fruit were brought to the dining-room; the bonbons were

---

1. A four-wheeled carriage with a high top and open sides, named for Rockaway, New Jersey, where it was manufactured.
2. New Orleans's equivalent of Wall Street, and the location of the Cotton Exchange. Chopin's husband, Oscar, a cotton factor (agent, broker, banker) had his office on Carondelet Street.
3. Delicacies.

passed around. And the ladies, selecting with dainty and discriminating fingers and a little greedily, all declared that Mr. Pontellier was the best husband in the world. Mrs. Pontellier was forced to admit that she knew of none better.

IV

It would have been a difficult matter for Mr. Pontellier to define to his own satisfaction or any one else's wherein his wife failed in her duty toward their children. It was something which he felt rather than perceived, and he never voiced the feeling without subsequent regret and ample atonement.

If one of the little Pontellier boys took a tumble whilst at play, he was not apt to rush crying to his mother's arms for comfort; he would more likely pick himself up, wipe the water out of his eyes and the sand out of his mouth, and go on playing. Tots as they were, they pulled together and stood their ground in childish battles with doubled fists and uplifted voices, which usually prevailed against the other mother-tots. The quadroon nurse was looked upon as a huge encumbrance, only good to button up waists and panties and to brush and part hair; since it seemed to be a law of society that hair must be parted and brushed.

In short, Mrs. Pontellier was not a mother-woman. The mother-women seemed to prevail that summer at Grand Isle. It was easy to know them, fluttering about with extended, protecting wings when any harm, real or imaginary, threatened their precious brood. They were women who idolized their children, worshiped their husbands, and esteemed it a holy privilege to efface themselves as individuals and grow wings as ministering angels.

Many of them were delicious in the rôle; one of them was the embodiment of every womanly grace and charm. If her husband did not adore her, he was a brute, deserving of death by slow torture. Her name was Adèle Ratignolle. There are no words to describe her save the old ones that have served so often to picture the bygone heroine of romance and the fair lady of our dreams. There was nothing subtle or hidden about her charms; her beauty was all there, flaming and apparent: the spun-gold hair that comb nor confining pin could restrain; the blue eyes that were like nothing but sapphires; two lips that pouted, that were so red one could only think of cherries or some other delicious crimson fruit in looking at them. She was growing a little stout, but it did not seem to detract an iota from the grace of every step, pose, gesture. One would not have wanted her white neck a mite less full or her beautiful arms more slender. Never were hands more exquisite than hers, and it was a joy to look at them when she threaded her needle or adjusted her gold thimble to her taper middle finger as she sewed away on the little night-drawers or fashioned a bodice or a bib.

Madame Ratignolle was very fond of Mrs. Pontellier, and often she took her sewing and went over to sit with her in the afternoons. She was sitting there the afternoon of the day the box arrived from New Orleans. She had possession of the rocker, and she was busily engaged in sewing upon a diminutive pair of night-drawers.

She had brought the pattern of the drawers for Mrs. Pontellier to cut out—a marvel of construction, fashioned to enclose a baby's body so effectually that only two small eyes might look out from the garment, like an Eskimo's. They were designed for winter wear, when treacherous drafts came down chimneys and insidious currents of deadly cold found their way through key-holes.

Mrs. Pontillier's mind was quite at rest concerning the present material needs of her children, and she could not see the use of anticipating and making winter night garments the subject of her summer meditations. But she did not want to appear unamiable and uninterested, so she had brought forth newspapers which she spread upon the floor of the gallery, and under Madame Ratignolle's directions she had cut a pattern of the impervious garment.

Robert was there, seated as he had been the Sunday before, and Mrs. Pontellier also occupied her former position on the upper step, leaning listlessly against the post. Beside her was a box of bonbons, which she held out at intervals to Madame Ratignolle.

That lady seemed at a loss to make a selection, but finally settled upon a stick of nugat, wondering if it were not too rich; whether it could possibly hurt her. Madame Ratignolle had been married seven years. About every two years she had a baby. At that time she had three babies, and was beginning to think of a fourth one. She was always talking about her "condition." Her "condition" was in no way apparent, and no one would have known a thing about it but for her persistence in making it the subject of conversation.

Robert started to reassure her, asserting that he had known a lady who had subsisted upon nugat during the entire—but seeing the color mount into Mrs. Pontellier's face he checked himself and changed the subject.

Mrs. Pontellier, though she had married a Creole,[4] was not thoroughly at home in the society of Creoles; never before had she been thrown so intimately among them. There were only Creoles that summer at Lebrun's. They all knew each other, and felt like one large family, among whom existed the most amicable relations. A characteristic which distinguished them and which impressed Mrs. Pontellier most forcibly was their entire absence of prudery. Their freedom of expression was at first incomprehensible to her, though she had no difficulty in reconciling it with a lofty chastity which in the Creole woman seems to be inborn and unmistakable.

Never would Edna Pontellier forget the shock with which she heard

4. As used in this novel, a person descended from the original French and Spanish settlers of New Orleans, an aristocrat.

Madame Ratignolle relating to old Monsieur Farival the harrowing story of one of her *accouchements*,[5] withholding no intimate detail. She was growing accustomed to like shocks, but she could not keep the mounting color back from her cheeks. Oftener than once her coming had interrupted the droll story with which Robert was entertaining some amused group of married women.

A book had gone the rounds of the *pension*. When it came her turn to read it, she did so with profound astonishment. She felt moved to read the book in secret and solitude, though none of the others had done so—to hide it from view at the sound of approaching footsteps. It was openly criticised and freely discussed at table. Mrs. Pontellier gave over being astonished, and concluded that wonders would never cease.

V

They formed a congenial group sitting there that summer afternoon —Madame Ratignolle sewing away, often stopping to relate a story or incident with much expressive gesture of her perfect hands; Robert and Mrs. Pontellier sitting idle, exchanging occasional words, glances or smiles which indicated a certain advanced stage of intimacy and *camaraderie*.

He had lived in her shadow during the past month. No one thought anything of it. Many had predicted that Robert would devote himself to Mrs. Pontellier when he arrived. Since the age of fifteen, which was eleven years before, Robert each summer at Grand Isle had constituted himself the devoted attendant of some fair dame or damsel. Sometimes it was a young girl, again a widow; but as often as not it was some interesting married woman.

For two consecutive seasons he lived in the sunlight of Mademoiselle Duvigné's presence. But she died between summers; then Robert posed as an inconsolable, prostrating himself at the feet of Madame Ratignolle for whatever crumbs of sympathy and comfort she might be pleased to vouchsafe.

Mrs. Pontellier liked to sit and gaze at her fair companion as she might look upon a faultless Madonna.

"Could any one fathom the cruelty beneath that fair exterior?" murmured Robert. "She knew that I adored her once, and she let me adore her. It was 'Robert, come; go; stand up; sit down; do this; do that; see if the baby sleeps; my thimble, please, that I left God knows where. Come and read Daudet[6] to me while I sew.' "

"*Par exemple!*[7] I never had to ask. You were always there under my feet, like a troublesome cat."

5. The birth of one of her children.
6. Alphonse Daudet (1840–87), French novelist of the naturalist school.
7. "For goodness sake!"

"You mean like an adoring dog. And just as soon as Ratignolle appeared on the scene, then it *was* like a dog. *'Passez! Adieu! Allez vous-en!'* "[8]

"Perhaps I feared to make Alphonse jealous," she interjoined, with excessive naïveté. That made them all laugh. The right hand jealous of the left! The heart jealous of the soul! But for that matter, the Creole husband is never jealous; with him the gangrene passion is one which has become dwarfed by disuse.

Meanwhile Robert, addressing Mrs. Pontellier, continued to tell of his one time hopeless passion for Madame Ratignolle; of sleepless nights, of consuming flames till the very sea sizzled when he took his daily plunge. While the lady at the needle kept up a little running, contemptuous comment:

"Blagueur—farceur—gros bête, va!"[9]

He never assumed this serio-comic tone when alone with Mrs. Pontellier. She never knew precisely what to make of it; at that moment it was impossible for her to guess how much of it was jest and what proportion was earnest. It was understood that he had often spoken words of love to Madame Ratignolle, without any thought of being taken seriously. Mrs. Pontellier was glad he had not assumed a similar rôle toward herself. It would have been unacceptable and annoying.

Mrs. Pontellier had brought her sketching materials, which she sometimes dabbled with in an unprofessional way. She liked the dabbling. She felt in it satisfaction of a kind which no other employment afforded her.

She had long wished to try herself on Madame Ratignolle. Never had that lady seemed a more tempting subject than at that moment, seated there like some sensuous Madonna, with the gleam of the fading day enriching her splendid color.

Robert crossed over and seated himself upon the step below Mrs. Pontellier, that he might watch her work. She handled her brushes with a certain ease and freedom which came, not from long and close acquaintance with them, but from a natural aptitude. Robert followed her work with close attention, giving forth little ejaculatory expressions of appreciation in French, which he addressed to Madame Ratignolle.

"Mais ce n'est pas mal! Elle s'y connait, elle a de la force, oui."[1]

During his oblivious attention he once quietly rested his head against Mrs. Pontellier's arm. As gently she repulsed him. Once again he repeated the offense. She could not but believe it to be thoughtlessness on his part; yet that was no reason she should submit to it. She did not remonstrate, except again to repulse him quietly but firmly. He offered no apology.

8. "Go on! Good-by! Go away!"
9. "Joker—comedian—silly, come off it!"
1. "Not bad at all! She knows what she's doing, she has talent."

The picture completed bore no resemblance to Madame Ratignolle. She was greatly disappointed to find that it did not look like her. But it was a fair enough piece of work, and in many respects satisfying. Mrs. Pontellier evidently did not think so. After surveying the sketch critically she drew a broad smudge of paint across its surface and crumpled the paper between her hands.

The youngsters came tumbling up the steps, the quadroon following at the respectful distance which they required her to observe. Mrs. Pontellier made them carry her paints and things into the house. She sought to detain them for a little talk and some pleasantry. But they were greatly in earnest. They had only come to investigate the contents of the bonbon box. They accepted without murmuring what she chose to give them, holding out two chubby hands scoop-like, in the vain hope that they might be filled; and then away they went.

The sun was low in the west, and the breeze soft and languorous that came up from the south, charged with the seductive odor of the sea. Children, freshly befurbelowed,[2] were gathering for their games under the oaks. Their voices were high and penetrating.

Madame Ratignolle folded her sewing, placing thimble, scissors and thread all neatly together in the roll, which she pinned securely. She complained of faintness. Mrs. Pontellier flew for the cologne water and a fan. She bathed Madame Ratignolle's face with cologne, while Robert plied the fan with unnecessary vigor.

The spell was soon over, and Mrs. Pontellier could not help wondering if there were not a little imagination responsible for its origin, for the rose tint had never faded from her friend's face.

She stood watching the fair woman walk down the long line of galleries with the grace and majesty which queens are sometimes supposed to possess. Her little ones ran to meet her. Two of them clung about her white skirts, the third she took from its nurse and with a thousand endearments bore it along in her own fond, encircling arms. Though, as everybody well knew, the doctor had forbidden her to lift so much as a pin!

"Are you going bathing?" asked Robert of Mrs. Pontellier. It was not so much a question as a reminder.

"Oh, no," she answered, with a tone of indecision. "I'm tired; I think not." Her glance wandered from his face away toward the Gulf, whose sonorous murmur reached her like a loving but imperative entreaty.

"Oh, come!" he insisted. "You mustn't miss your bath. Come on. The water must be delicious; it will not hurt you. Come."

He reached up for her big, rough straw hat that hung on a peg outside the door, and put it on her head. They descended the steps, and walked

2. Dressed, adorned, especially in petticoats or flounces.

away together toward the beach. The sun was low in the west and the breeze was soft and warm.

VI

Edna Pontellier could not have told why, wishing to go to the beach with Robert, she should in the first place have declined, and in the second place have followed in obedience to one of the two contradictory impulses which impelled her.

A certain light was beginning to dawn dimly within her,—the light which, showing the way, forbids it.

At that early period it served but to bewilder her. It moved her to dreams, to thoughtfulness, to the shadowy anguish which had overcome her the midnight when she had abandoned herself to tears.

In short, Mrs. Pontellier was beginning to realize her position in the universe as a human being, and to recognize her relations as an individual to the world within and about her. This may seem like a ponderous weight of wisdom to descend upon the soul of a young woman of twenty-eight—perhaps more wisdom than the Holy Ghost is usually pleased to vouchsafe to any woman.

But the beginning of things, of a world especially, is necessarily vague, tangled, chaotic, and exceedingly disturbing. How few of us ever emerge from such beginning! How many souls perish in its tumult!

The voice of the sea is seductive; never ceasing, whispering, clamoring, murmuring, inviting the soul to wander for a spell in abysses of solitude; to lose itself in mazes of inward contemplation.

The voice of the sea speaks to the soul. The touch of the sea is sensuous, enfolding the body in its soft, close embrace.

VII

Mrs. Pontellier was not a woman given to confidences, a characteristic hitherto contrary to her nature. Even as a child she had lived her own small life all within herself. At a very early period she had apprehended instinctively the dual life—that outward existence which conforms, the inward life which questions.

That summer at Grand Isle she began to loosen a little the mantle of reserve that had always enveloped her. There may have been—there must have been—influences, both subtle and apparent, working in their several ways to induce her to do this; but the most obvious was the influence of Adèle Ratignolle. The excessive physical charm of the Creole had first attracted her, for Edna had a sensuous susceptibility to beauty. Then the candor of the woman's whole existence, which every one might read, and which formed so striking a contrast to her own habitual reserve—this might have furnished a link. Who can tell what metals the gods use in forging the subtle bond which we call sympathy, which we might as well call love.

The two women went away one morning to the beach together, arm in arm, under the huge white sunshade. Edna had prevailed upon Madame Ratignolle to leave the children behind, though she could not induce her to relinquish a diminutive roll of needlework, which Adèle begged to be allowed to slip into the depths of her pocket. In some unaccountable way they had escaped from Robert.

The walk to the beach was no inconsiderable one, consisting as it did of a long, sandy path upon which a sporadic and tangled growth that bordered it on either side made frequent and unexpected inroads. There were acres of yellow camomile reaching out on either hand. Further away still, vegetable gardens abounded, with frequent small plantations of orange or lemon trees intervening. The dark green clusters glistened from afar in the sun.

The women were both of goodly height, Madame Ratignolle possessing the more feminine and matronly figure. The charm of Edna Pontellier's physique stole insensibly upon you. The lines of her body were long, clean and symmetrical; it was a body which occasionally fell into splendid poses; there was no suggestion of the trim, stereotyped fashion-plate about it. A casual and indiscriminating observer, in passing, might not cast a second glance upon the figure. But with more feeling and discernment he would have recognized the noble beauty of its modeling, and the graceful severity of poise and movement, which made Edna Pontellier different from the crowd.

She wore a cool muslin that morning—white, with a waving vertical line of brown running through it; also a white linen collar and the big straw hat which she had taken from the peg outside the door. The hat rested any way on her yellow-brown hair, that waved a little, was heavy, and clung close to her head.

Madame Ratignolle, more careful of her complexion, had twined a gauze veil about her head. She wore dogskin gloves, with gauntlets that protected her wrists. She was dressed in pure white, with a fluffiness of ruffles that became her. The draperies and fluttering things which she wore suited her rich, luxuriant beauty as a greater severity of line could not have done.

There were a number of bath-houses along the beach, of rough but solid construction, built with small, protecting galleries facing the water. Each house consisted of two compartments, and each family at Lebrun's possessed a compartment for itself, fitted out with all the essential paraphernalia of the bath and whatever other conveniences the owners might desire. The two women had no intention of bathing; they had just strolled down to the beach for a walk and to be alone and near the water. The Pontellier and Ratignolle compartments adjoined one another under the same roof.

Mrs. Pontellier had brought down her key through force of habit. Unlocking the door of her bath-room she went inside, and soon emerged, bringing a rug, which she spread upon the floor of the gallery, and two huge hair pillows covered with crash,[3] which she placed against the front of the building.

The two seated themselves there in the shade of the porch, side by side, with their backs against the pillows and their feet extended. Madame Ratignolle removed her veil, wiped her face with a rather delicate hand-kerchief, and fanned herself with the fan which she always carried suspended somewhere about her person by a long, narrow ribbon. Edna removed her collar and opened her dress at the throat. She took the fan from Madame Ratignolle and began to fan both herself and her companion. It was very warm, and for a while they did nothing but exchange remarks about the heat, the sun, the glare. But there was a breeze blowing, a choppy stiff wind that whipped the water into froth. It fluttered the skirts of the two women and kept them for a while engaged in adjusting, readjusting, tucking in, securing hair-pins and hat-pins. A few persons were sporting some distance away in the water. The beach was very still of human sound at that hour. The lady in black was reading her morning devotions on the porch of a neighboring bath-house. Two young lovers were exchanging their hearts' yearnings beneath the children's tent, which they had found unoccupied.

Edna Pontellier, casting her eyes about, had finally kept them at rest upon the sea. The day was clear and carried the gaze out as far as the blue sky went; there were a few white clouds suspended idly over the horizon. A lateen[4] sail was visible in the direction of Cat Island, and others to the south seemed almost motionless in the far distance.

"Of whom—of what are you thinking?" asked Adèle of her companion, whose countenance she had been watching with a little amused attention, arrested by the absorbed expression which seemed to have seized and fixed every feature into a statuesque repose.

"Nothing," returned Mrs. Pontellier, with a start, adding at once: "How stupid! But it seems to me it is the reply we make instinctively to such a question. Let me see," she went on, throwing back her head and narrowing her fine eyes till they shone like two vivid points of light. "Let me see. I was really not conscious of thinking of anything; but perhaps I can retrace my thoughts."

"Oh! never mind!" laughed Madame Ratignolle. "I am not quite so exacting. I will let you off this time. It is really too hot to think, especially to think about thinking."

"But for the fun of it," persisted Edna. "First of all, the sight of the water stretching so far away, those motionless sails against the blue sky, made a delicious picture that I just wanted to sit and look at. The hot

3. A heavy linen fabric.
4. Triangular

wind beating in my face made me think—without any connection that I can trace—of a summer day in Kentucky, of a meadow that seemed as big as the ocean to the very little girl walking through the grass, which was higher than her waist. She threw out her arms as if swimming when she walked, beating the tall grass as one strikes out in the water. Oh, I see the connection now!"

"Where were you going that day in Kentucky, walking through the grass?"

"I don't remember now. I was just walking diagonally across a big field. My sun-bonnet obstructed the view. I could see only the stretch of green before me, and I felt as if I must walk on forever, without coming to the end of it. I don't remember whether I was frightened or pleased. I must have been entertained.

"Likely as not it was Sunday," she laughed; "and I was running away from prayers, from the Presbyterian service, read in a spirit of gloom by my father that chills me yet to think of."

"And have you been running away from prayers ever since, *ma chère?*" asked Madame Ratignolle, amused.

"No! oh, no!" Edna hastened to say. "I was a little unthinking child in those days, just following a misleading impulse without question. On the contrary, during one period of my life religion took a firm hold upon me; after I was twelve and until—until—why, I suppose until now, though I never thought much about it—just driven along by habit. But do you know," she broke off, turning her quick eyes upon Madame Ratignolle and leaning forward a little so as to bring her face quite close to that of her companion, "sometimes I feel this summer as if I were walking through the green meadow again; idly, aimlessly, unthinking and unguided."

Madame Ratignolle laid her hand over that of Mrs. Pontellier, which was near her. Seeing that the hand was not withdrawn, she clasped it firmly and warmly. She even stroked it a little, fondly, with the other hand, murmuring in an undertone, *"Pauvre chérie."*

The action was at first a little confusing to Edna, but she soon lent herself readily to the Creole's gentle caress. She was not accustomed to an outward and spoken expression of affection, either in herself or in others. She and her younger sister, Janet, had quarreled a good deal through force of unfortunate habit. Her older sister, Margaret, was matronly and dignified, probably from having assumed matronly and housewifely responsibilities too early in life, their mother having died when they were quite young. Margaret was not effusive; she was practical. Edna had had an occasional girl friend, but whether accidentally or not, they seemed to have been all of one type—the self-contained. She never realized that the reserve of her own character had much, perhaps everything, to do with this. Her most intimate friend at school had been one of rather exceptional intellectual gifts, who wrote fine-sounding essays, which Edna admired and strove to imitate; and with her she talked and glowed over the English classics, and sometimes held religious and political controversies.

Edna often wondered at one propensity which sometimes had inwardly disturbed her without causing any outward show or manifestation on her part. At a very early age—perhaps it was when she traversed the ocean of waving grass—she remembered that she had been passionately enamored of a dignified and sad-eyed cavalry officer who visited her father in Kentucky. She could not leave his presence when he was there, nor remove her eyes from his face, which was something like Napoleon's, with a lock of black hair falling across the forehead. But the cavalry officer melted imperceptibly out of her existence.

At another time her affections were deeply engaged by a young gentleman who visited a lady on a neighboring plantation. It was after they went to Mississippi to live. The young man was engaged to be married to the young lady, and they sometimes called upon Margaret, driving over of afternoons in a buggy. Edna was a little miss, just merging into her teens; and the realization that she herself was nothing, nothing, nothing to the engaged young man was a bitter affliction to her. But he, too, went the way of dreams.

She was a grown young woman when she was overtaken by what she supposed to be the climax of her fate. It was when the face and figure of a great tragedian[5] began to haunt her imagination and stir her senses. The persistence of the infatuation lent it an aspect of genuineness. The hopelessness of it colored it with the lofty tones of a great passion.

The picture of the tragedian stood enframed upon her desk. Any one may possess the portrait of a tragedian without exciting suspicion or comment. (This was a sinister reflection which she cherished.) In the presence of others she expressed admiration for his exalted gifts, as she handed the photograph around and dwelt upon the fidelity of the likeness. When alone she sometimes picked it up and kissed the cold glass passionately.

Her marriage to Léonce Pontellier was purely an accident, in this respect resembling many other marriages which masquerade as the decrees of Fate. It was in the midst of her secret great passion that she met him. He fell in love, as men are in the habit of doing, and pressed his suit with an earnestness and an ardor which left nothing to be desired. He pleased her; his absolute devotion flattered her. She fancied there was a sympathy of thought and taste between them, in which fancy she was mistaken. Add to this the violent opposition of her father and her sister Margaret to her marriage with a Catholic, and we need seek no

---

5. Probably Edwin Booth (1833–93), the renowned Shakespearean actor particularly acclaimed for his Hamlet. Chopin was a fan of the actor and in 1894 published a review of his letters entitled "The Real Edwin Booth."

further for the motives which led her to accept Monsieur Pontellier for her husband.

The acme of bliss, which would have been a marriage with the tragedian, was not for her in this world. As the devoted wife of a man who worshiped her, she felt she would take her place with a certain dignity in the world of reality, closing the portals forever behind her upon the realm of romance and dreams.

But it was not long before the tragedian had gone to join the cavalry officer and the engaged young man and a few others; and Edna found herself face to face with the realities. She grew fond of her husband, realizing with some unaccountable satisfaction that no trace of passion or excessive and fictitious warmth colored her affection, thereby threatening its dissolution.

She was fond of her children in an uneven, impulsive way. She would sometimes gather them passionately to her heart; she would sometimes forget them. The year before they had spent part of the summer with their grandmother Pontellier in Iberville.[6] Feeling secure regarding their happiness and welfare, she did not miss them except with an occasional intense longing. Their absence was a sort of relief, though she did not admit this, even to herself. It seemed to free her of a responsibility which she had blindly assumed and for which Fate had not fitted her.

Edna did not reveal so much as all this to Madame Ratignolle that summer day when they sat with faces turned to the sea. But a good part of it escaped her. She had put her head down on Madame Ratignolle's shoulder. She was flushed and felt intoxicated with the sound of her own voice and the unaccustomed taste of candor. It muddled her like wine, or like a first breath of freedom.

There was the sound of approaching voices. It was Robert, surrounded by a troop of children, searching for them. The two little Pontelliers were with him, and he carried Madame Ratignolle's little girl in his arms. There were other children beside, and two nursemaids followed, looking disagreeable and resigned.

The women at once rose and began to shake out their draperies and relax their muscles. Mrs. Pontellier threw the cushions and rug into the bath-house. The children all scampered off to the awning, and they stood there in a line, gazing upon the intruding lovers, still exchanging their vows and sighs. The lovers got up, with only a silent protest, and walked slowly away somewhere else.

The children possessed themselves of the tent, and Mrs. Pontellier went over to join them.

Madame Ratignolle begged Robert to accompany her to the house; she complained of cramp in her limbs and stiffness of the joints. She leaned draggingly upon his arm as they walked.

6. A village northwest of New Orleans, near Baton Rouge; or the parish ("county") of the same name.

VIII

"Do me a favor, Robert," spoke the pretty woman at his side, almost as soon as she and Robert had started on their slow, homeward way. She looked up in his face, leaning on his arm beneath the encircling shadow of the umbrella which he had lifted.

"Granted; as many as you like," he returned, glancing down into her eyes that were full of thoughtfulness and some speculation.

"I only ask for one; let Mrs. Pontellier alone."

"*Tiens!*" he exclaimed, with a sudden, boyish laugh. "*Voilà que Madame Ratignolle est jalouse!*"[7]

"Nonsense! I'm in earnest; I mean what I say. Let Mrs. Pontellier alone."

"Why?" he asked; himself growing serious at his companion's solicitation.

"She is not one of us; she is not like us. She might make the unfortunate blunder of taking you seriously."

His face flushed with annoyance, and taking off his soft hat he began to beat it impatiently against his leg as he walked. "Why shouldn't she take me seriously?" he demanded sharply. "Am I a comedian, a clown, a jack-in-the-box? Why shouldn't she? You Creoles! I have no patience with you! Am I always to be regarded as a feature of an amusing programme? I hope Mrs. Pontellier does take me seriously. I hope she has discernment enough to find in me something besides the *blagueur*.[8] If I thought there was any doubt—"

"Oh, enough, Robert!" she broke into his heated outburst. "You are not thinking of what you are saying. You speak with about as little reflection as we might expect from one of those children down there playing in the sand. If your attentions to any married women here were ever offered with any intention of being convincing, you would not be the gentleman we all know you to be, and you would be unfit to associate with the wives and daughters of the people who trust you."

Madame Ratignolle had spoken what she believed to be the law and the gospel. The young man shrugged his shoulders impatiently.

"Oh! well! That isn't it," slamming his hat down vehemently upon his head. "You ought to feel that such things are not flattering to say to a fellow."

"Should our whole intercourse consist of an exchange of compliments? *Ma foi!*"[9]

"It isn't pleasant to have a woman tell you—" he went on, unheedingly, but breaking off suddenly: "Now if I were like Arobin—you remember Alcée Arobin and that story of the consul's wife at Biloxi?"[1]

7. "So! Madame Ratignolle is jealous!"
8. Joker, clown.
9. "For heaven's sake!"
1. A Mississippi coastal resort.

And he related the story of Alcée Arobin and the consul's wife; and another about the tenor of the French Opera,[2] who received letters, which should never have been written; and still other stories, grave and gay, till Mrs. Pontellier and her possible propensity for taking young men seriously was apparently forgotten.

Madame Ratignolle, when they had regained her cottage, went in to take the hour's rest which she considered helpful. Before leaving her, Robert begged her pardon for the impatience—he called it rudeness—with which he had received her well-meant caution.

"You made one mistake, Adèle," he said, with a light smile; "there is no earthly possibility of Mrs. Pontellier ever taking me seriously. You should have warned me against taking myself seriously. Your advice might then have carried some weight and given me subject for some reflection. Au revoir. But you look tired," he added, solicitously. "Would you like a cup of bouillon? Shall I stir you a toddy? Let me mix you a toddy with a drop of Angostura."

She acceded to the suggestion of bouillon, which was grateful and acceptable. He went himself to the kitchen, which was a building apart from the cottages and lying to the rear of the house. And he himself brought her the golden-brown bouillon, in a dainty Sèvres cup, with a flaky cracker or two on the saucer.

She thrust a bare, white arm from the curtain which shielded her open door, and received the cup from his hands. She told him he was a bon garçon,[3] and she meant it. Robert thanked her and turned away toward "the house."

The lovers were just entering the grounds of the pension. They were leaning toward each other as the water-oaks bent from the sea. There was not a particle of earth beneath their feet. Their heads might have been turned upside-down, so absolutely did they tread upon blue ether. The lady in black, creeping behind them, looked a trifle paler and more jaded than usual. There was no sign of Mrs. Pontellier and the children. Robert scanned the distance for any such apparition. They would doubtless remain away till the dinner hour. The young man ascended to his mother's room. It was situated at the top of the house, made up of odd angles and a queer, sloping ceiling. Two broad dormer windows looked out toward the Gulf, and as far across it as a man's eye might reach. The furnishings of the room were light, cool, and practical.

Madame Lebrun was busily engaged at the sewing-machine. A little black girl sat on the floor, and with her hands worked the treadle of the machine. The Creole woman does not take any chances which may be avoided of imperiling her health.

2. The French Opera in New Orleans was one of the most distinguished opera companies in nineteenth-century America.
3. A "nice fellow." Madame is making a pun, as in this context the phrase also means "good waiter."

Robert went over and seated himself on the broad sill of one of the dormer windows. He took a book from his pocket and began energetically to read it, judging by the precision and frequency with which he turned the leaves. The sewing-machine made a resounding clatter in the room; it was of a ponderous, by-gone make. In the lulls, Robert and his mother exchanged bits of desultory conversation.

"Where is Mrs. Pontellier?"

"Down at the beach with the children."

"I promised to lend her the Goncourt.[4] Don't forget to take it down when you go; it's there on the bookshelf over the small table." Clatter, clatter, clatter, bang! for the next five or eight minutes.

"Where is Victor going with the rockaway?"

"The rockaway? Victor?"

"Yes; down there in front. He seems to be getting ready to drive away somewhere."

"Call him." Clatter, clatter!

Robert uttered a shrill, piercing whistle which might have been heard back at the wharf.

"He won't look up."

Madame Lebrun flew to the window. She called "Victor!" She waved a handkerchief and called again. The young fellow below got into the vehicle and started the horse off at a gallop.

Madame Lebrun went back to the machine, crimson with annoyance. Victor was the younger son and brother—a *tête montée*,[5] with a temper which invited violence and a will which no ax could break.

"Whenever you say the word I'm ready to thrash any amount of reason into him that he's able to hold."

"If your father had only lived!" Clatter, clatter, clatter, clatter, bang! It was a fixed belief with Madame Lebrun that the conduct of the universe and all things pertaining thereto would have been manifestly of a more intelligent and higher order had not Monsieur Lebrun been removed to other spheres during the early years of their married life.

"What do you hear from Montel?" Montel was a middle-aged gentleman whose vain ambition and desire for the past twenty years had been to fill the void which Monsieur Lebrun's taking off had left in the Lebrun household. Clatter, clatter, bang, clatter!

"I have a letter somewhere," looking in the machine drawer and finding the letter in the bottom of the work-basket. "He says to tell you he will be in Vera Cruz the beginning of next month"—clatter, clatter!—"and if you still have the intention of joining him"—bang! clatter, clatter, bang!

"Why didn't you tell me so before, mother? You know I wanted—" Clatter, clatter, clatter!

4. A novel by French realist Edmond Goncourt (1822–96).
5. An impulsive character.

"Do you see Mrs. Pontellier starting back with the children? She will be in late to luncheon again. She never starts to get ready for luncheon till the last minute." Clatter, clatter! "Where are you going?" "Where did you say the Goncourt was?"

IX

Every light in the hall was ablaze; every lamp turned as high as it could be without smoking the chimney or threatening explosion. The lamps were fixed at intervals against the wall, encircling the whole room. Some one had gathered orange and lemon branches and with these fashioned graceful festoons between. The dark green of the branches stood out and glistened against the white muslin curtains which draped the windows, and which puffed, floated, and flapped at the capricious will of a stiff breeze that swept up from the Gulf.

It was Saturday night a few weeks after the intimate conversation held between Robert and Madame Ratignolle on their way from the beach. An unusual number of husbands, fathers, and friends had come down to stay over Sunday; and they were being suitably entertained by their families, with the material help of Madame Lebrun. The dining tables had all been removed to one end of the hall, and the chairs ranged about in rows and in clusters. Each little family group had had its say and exchanged its domestic gossip earlier in the evening. There was now an apparent disposition to relax; to widen the circle of confidences and give a more general tone to the conversation.

Many of the children had been permitted to sit up beyond their usual bedtime. A small band of them were lying on their stomachs on the floor looking at the colored sheets of the comic papers which Mr. Pontellier had brought down. The little Pontellier boys were permitting them to do so, and making their authority felt.

Music, dancing, and a recitation or two were the entertainments furnished, or rather, offered. But there was nothing systematic about the programme, no appearance of prearrangement nor even pre-meditation.

At an early hour in the evening the Farival twins were prevailed upon to play the piano. They were girls of fourteen, always clad in the Virgin's colors, blue and white, having been dedicated to the Blessed Virgin at their baptism. They played a duet from "Zampa," and at the earnest solicitation of every one present followed it with the overture to "The Poet and the Peasant."

"*Allez vous-en! Sapristi!*" shrieked the parrot outside the door. He was the only being present who possessed sufficient candor to admit that he was not listening to these gracious performances for the first time that summer. Old Monsieur Farival, grandfather of the twins, grew indignant over the interruption, and insisted upon having the bird removed and consigned to regions of darkness. Victor Lebrun objected; and his decrees were as immutable as those of Fate. The parrot fortunately offered no further interruption to the entertainment, the whole venom of his nature apparently having been cherished up and hurled against the twins in that one impetuous outburst.

Later a young brother and sister gave recitations, which every one present had heard many times at winter evening entertainments in the city.

A little girl performed a skirt dance in the center of the floor. The mother played her accompaniments and at the same time watched her daughter with greedy admiration and nervous apprehension. She need have had no apprehension. The child was mistress of the situation. She had been properly dressed for the occasion in black tulle[6] and black silk tights. Her little neck and arms were bare, and her hair, artifically crimped, stood out like fluffy black plumes over her head. Her poses were full of grace, and her little black-shod toes twinkled as they shot out and upward with a rapidity and suddenness which were bewildering.

But there was no reason why every one should not dance. Madame Ratignolle could not, so it was she who gaily consented to play for the others. She played very well, keeping excellent waltz time and infusing an expression into the strains which was indeed inspiring. She was keeping up her music on account of the children, she said; because she and her husband both considered it a means of brightening the home and making it attractive.

Almost every one danced but the twins, who could not be induced to separate during the brief period when one or the other should be whirling around the room in the arms of a man. They might have danced together, but they did not think of it.

The children were sent to bed. Some went submissively; others with shrieks and protests as they were dragged away. They had been permitted to sit up till after the ice-cream, which naturally marked the limit of human indulgence.

The ice-cream was passed around with cake—gold and silver cake arranged on platters in alternate slices; it had been made and frozen during the afternoon back of the kitchen by two black women, under the supervision of Victor. It was pronounced a great success—excellent if it had only contained a little less vanilla or a little more sugar, if it had been frozen a degree harder, and if the salt might have been kept out of portions of it. Victor was proud of his achievement, and went about recommending it and urging every one to partake of it to excess.

After Mrs. Pontellier had danced twice with her husband, once with Robert, and once with Monsieur Ratignolle, who was thin and tall and swayed like a reed in the wind when he danced, she went out on the

6. A thin, soft netting, usually silk.

gallery and seated herself on the low window-sill, where she commanded a view of all that went on in the hall and could look out toward the Gulf. There was a soft effulgence in the east. The moon was coming up, and its mystic shimmer was casting a million lights across the distant, restless water.

"Would you like to hear Mademoiselle Reisz play?" asked Robert, coming out on the porch where she was. Of course Edna would like to hear Mademoiselle Reisz play; but she feared it would be useless to entreat her.

"I'll ask her," he said. "I'll tell her that you want to hear her. She likes you. She will come." He turned and hurried away to one of the far cottages, where Mademoiselle Reisz was shuffling away. She was dragging a chair in and out of her room, and at intervals objecting to the crying of a baby, which a nurse in the adjoining cottage was endeavoring to put to sleep. She was a disagreeable little woman, no longer young, who had quarreled with almost every one, owing to a temper which was self-assertive and a disposition to trample upon the rights of others. Robert prevailed upon her without any too great difficulty.

She entered the hall with him during a lull in the dance. She made an awkward, imperious little bow as she went in. She was a homely woman, with a small weazened face and body and eyes that glowed. She had absolutely no taste in dress, and wore a batch of rusty black lace with a bunch of artificial violets pinned to the side of her hair.

"Ask Mrs. Pontellier what she would like to hear me play," she requested of Robert. She sat perfectly still before the piano, not touching the keys, while Robert carried her message to Edna at the window. A general air of surprise and genuine satisfaction fell upon every one as they saw the pianist enter. There was a settling down, and a prevailing air of expectancy everywhere. Edna was a trifle embarrassed at being thus signaled out for the imperious little woman's favor. She would not dare to choose, and begged that Mademoiselle Reisz would please herself in her selections.

Edna was what she herself called very fond of music. Musical strains, well rendered, had a way of evoking pictures in her mind. She sometimes liked to sit in the room of mornings when Madame Ratignolle played or practiced. One piece which that lady played Edna had entitled "Solitude."[7] It was a short, plaintive, minor strain. The name of the piece was something else, but she called it "Solitude." When she heard it there came before her imagination the figure of a man standing beside a desolate rock on the seashore. He was naked. His attitude was one of

---

7. Chopin's first biographer, Daniel Rankin, states that "A Solitary Soul" was the original title of *The Awakening* and that the title may have been changed by her publisher. In her notebook Chopin retained "A Solitary Soul" when she added the present title; and Per Seyersted, her second biographer, suggests she may have wished to retain "A Solitary Soul" as the subtitle. See the page from Chopin's notebook reproduced on p. 2. See also "Edna Pontellier: 'A Solitary Soul,' " p. 247.

hopeless resignation as he looked toward a distant bird winging its flight away from him.

Another piece called to her mind a dainty young woman clad in an Empire gown, taking mincing dancing steps as she came down a long avenue between tall hedges. Again, another reminded her of children at play, and still another of nothing on earth but a demure lady stroking a cat.

The very first chords which Mademoiselle Reisz struck upon the piano sent a keen tremor down Mrs. Pontellier's spinal column. It was not the first time she had heard an artist at the piano. Perhaps it was the first time she was ready, perhaps the first time her being was tempered to take an impress of the abiding truth.

She waited for the material pictures which she thought would gather and blaze before her imagination. She waited in vain. She saw no pictures of solitude, of hope, of longing, or of despair. But the very passions themselves were aroused within her soul, swaying it, lashing it, as the waves daily beat upon her splendid body. She trembled, she was choking, and the tears blinded her.

Mademoiselle had finished. She arose, and bowing her stiff, lofty bow, she went away, stopping for neither thanks nor applause. As she passed along the gallery she patted Edna upon the shoulder.

"Well, how did you like my music?" she asked. The young woman was unable to answer; she pressed the hand of the pianist convulsively. Mademoiselle Reisz perceived her agitation and even her tears. She patted her again upon the shoulder as she said:

"You are the only one worth playing for. Those others? Bah!" and she went shuffling and sidling on down the gallery toward her room.

But she was mistaken about "those others." Her playing had aroused a fever of enthusiasm. "What passion!" "What an artist!" "I have always said no one could play Chopin[8] like Mademoiselle Reisz!" "That last prelude! Bon Dieu! It shakes a man!"

It was growing late, and there was a general disposition to disband. But some one, perhaps it was Robert, thought of a bath at that mystic hour and under that mystic moon.

X

At all events Robert proposed it, and there was not a dissenting voice. There was not one but was ready to follow when he led the way. He did not lead the way, however, he directed the way; and he himself loitered behind with the lovers, who had betrayed a disposition to linger and hold themselves apart. He walked between them, whether with malicious or mischievous intent was not wholly clear, even to himself.

8. Frederic Chopin (1810–49), Polish-born composer who settled in Paris in 1832. He composed a large body of melodic piano music in the Romantic tradition.

The Pontelliers and Ratignolles walked ahead; the women leaning upon the arms of their husbands. Edna could hear Robert's voice behind them, and could sometimes hear what he said. She wondered why he did not join them. It was unlike him not to. Of late he had sometimes held away from her for an entire day, redoubling his devotion upon the next and the next, as though to make up for hours that had been lost. She missed him the days when some pretext served to take him away from her, just as one misses the sun on a cloudy day without having thought much about the sun when it was shining.

The people walked in little groups toward the beach. They talked and laughed; some of them sang. There was a band playing down at Klein's hotel, an the strains reached them faintly, tempered by the distance. There were strange, rare odors abroad—a tangle of the sea smell and of weeds and damp, new-plowed earth, mingled with the heavy perfume of a field of white blossoms somewhere near. But the night sat lightly upon the sea and the land. There was no weight of darkness; there were no shadows. The white light of the moon had fallen upon the world like the mystery and the softness of sleep.

Most of them walked into the water as though into a native element. The sea was quiet now, and smelled lazily in broad billows that melted into one another and did not break except upon the beach in little foamy crests that coiled back like slow, white serpents.

Edna had attempted all summer to learn to swim. She had received instructions from both the men and women; in some instances from the children. Robert had pursued a system of lessons almost daily; and he was nearly at the point of discouragement in realizing the futility of his efforts. A certain ungovernable dread hung about her when in the water, unless there was a hand near by that might reach out and reassure her.

But that night she was like the little tottering, stumbling, clutching child, who of a sudden realizes its powers, and walks for the first time alone, boldly and with over-confidence. She could have shouted for joy. She did shout for joy, as with a sweeping stroke or two she lifted her body to the surface of the water.

A feeling of exultation overtook her, as if some power of significant import had been given her soul. She grew daring and reckless, overestimating her strength. She wanted to swim far out, where no woman had swum before.

Her unlooked-for achievement was the subject of wonder, applause, and admiration. Each one congratulated himself that his special teachings had accomplished this desired end.

"How easy it is!" she thought. "It is nothing," she said aloud; "why did I not discover before that it was nothing Think of the time I have lost splashing about like a baby!" She would not join the groups in their sports and bouts, but intoxicated with her newly conquered power, she swam out alone.

She turned her face seaward to gather in an impression of space and
solitude, which the vast expanse of water, meeting and melting with the
moonlit sky, conveyed to her excited fancy. As she swam she seemed
to be reaching out for the unlimited in which to lose herself.

Once she turned and looked toward the shore, toward the people she
had left there. She had not gone any great distance—that is, what would
have been a great distance for an experienced swimmer. But to her
unaccustomed vision the stretch of water behind her assumed the aspect
of a barrier which her unaided strength would never be able to overcome.

A quick vision of death smote her soul, and for a second of time
appalled and enfeebled her senses. But by an effort she rallied her
staggering faculties and managed to regain the land.

She made no mention of her encounter with death and her flash of
terror, except to say to her husband, "I thought I should have perished
out there alone."

"You were not so very far, my dear; I was watching you," he told
her.

Edna went at once to the bath-house, and she had put on her dry
clothes and was ready to return home before the others had left the
water. She started to walk away alone. They all called to her and shouted
to her. She waved a dissenting hand, and went on, paying no further
heed to their renewed cries which sought to detain her.

"Sometimes I am tempted to think that Mrs. Pontellier is capricious"
said Madame Lebrun, who was amusing herself immensely and feared
that Edna's abrupt departure might put an end to the pleasure.

"I know she is," assented Mr. Pontellier; "sometimes, not often."

Edna had not traversed a quarter of the distance on her way home
before she was overtaken by Robert.

"Did you think I was afraid?" she asked him, without a shade of
annoyance.

"No; I knew you weren't afraid."

"Then why did you come? Why didn't you stay out there with the
others?"

"I never thought of it."

"Thought of what?"

"Of anything. What difference does it make?"

"I'm very tired," she uttered, complainingly.

"I know you are."

"You don't know anything about it. Why should you know? I never
was so exhausted in my life. But it isn't unpleasant. A thousand emotions
have swept through me to-night. I don't comprehend half of them.
Don't mind what I'm saying; I am just thinking aloud. I wonder if I
shall ever be stirred again as Mademoiselle Reisz's playing moved me
to-night. I wonder if any night on earth will ever again be like this one.
It is like a night in a dream. The people about me are like some uncanny,
half-human beings. There must be spirits abroad to-night."

"There are," whispered Robert. "Didn't you know this was the twenty-eighth of August?"

"The twenty-eighth of August?"

"Yes. On the twenty-eighth of August, at the hour of midnight, and if the moon is shining—the moon must be shining—a spirit that has haunted these shores for ages rises up from the Gulf. With its own penetrating vision the spirit seeks some one mortal worthy to hold him company, worthy of being exalted for a few hours into realms of the semi-celestials.[9] His search has always hitherto been fruitless, and he has sunk back, disheartened, into the sea. But tonight he found Mrs. Pontellier. Perhaps he will never wholly release her from the spell. Perhaps she will never again suffer a poor, unworthy earthling to walk in the shadow of her divine presence."

"Don't banter me," she said, wounded at what appeared to be his flippancy. He did not mind the entreaty, but the tone with its delicate note of pathos was like a reproach. He could not explain; he could not tell her that he had penetrated her mood and understood. He said nothing except to offer her his arm, for, by her own admission, she was exhausted. She had been walking alone with her arms hanging limp, letting her white skirts trail along the dewy path. She took his arm, but she did not lean upon it. She let her hand lie listlessly, as though her thoughts were elsewhere—somewhere in advance of her body, and she was striving to overtake them.

Robert assisted her into the hammock which swung from the post before her door out to the trunk of a tree.

"Will you stay out here and wait for Mr. Pontellier?" he asked.

"I'll stay out here. Good-night."

"Shall I get you a pillow?"

"There's one here," she said, feeling about, for they were in the shadow.

"It must be soiled; the children have been tumbling it about."

"No matter." And having discovered the pillow, she adjusted it beneath her head. She extended herself in the hammock with a deep breath of relief. She was not a supercilious or an over-dainty woman. She was not much given to reclining in the hammock, and when she did so it was with no cat-like suggestion of voluptuous ease, but with a beneficent repose which seemed to invade her whole body.

"Shall I stay with you till Mr. Pontellier comes?" asked Robert, seating himself on the outer edge of one of the steps and taking hold of the hammock rope which was fastened to the post.

"If you wish. Don't swing the hammock. Will you get my white shawl which I left on the window-sill over at the house?"

"Are you chilly?"

9. Beings who are partly divine.

"No; but I shall be presently."

"Presently?" he laughed. "Do you know what time it is? How long are you going to stay out here?"

"I don't know. Will you get the shawl?"

"Of course I will," he said, rising. He went over to the house, walking along the grass. She watched his figure pass in and out of the strips of moonlight. It was past midnight. It was very quiet. When he returned with the shawl she took it and kept it in her hand. She did not put it around her.

"Did you say I should stay till Mr. Pontellier came back?"

"I said you might if you wished to."

He seated himself again and rolled a cigarette, which he smoked in silence. Neither did Mrs. Pontellier speak. No multitude of words could have been more significant than those moments of silence, or more pregnant with the first-felt throbbings of desire.

When the voices of the bathers were heard approaching, Robert said good-night. She did not answer him. He thought she was asleep. Again she watched his figure pass in and out of the strips of moonlight as he walked away.

XI

"What are you doing out here, Edna? I thought I should find you in bed," said her husband, when he discovered her lying there. He had walked up with Madame Lebrun and left her at the house. His wife did not reply.

"Are you asleep?" he asked, bending down close to look at her.

"No." Her eyes gleamed bright and intense, with no sleepy shadows, as they looked into his.

"Do you know it is past one o'clock? Come on," and he mounted the steps and went into their room.

"Edna!" called Mr. Pontellier from within, after a few moments had gone by.

"Don't wait for me," she answered. He thrust his head through the door.

"You will take cold out there," he said, irritably. "What folly is this? Why don't you come in?"

"It isn't cold; I have my shawl."

"The mosquitoes will devour you."

"There are no mosquitoes."

She heard him moving about the room; every sound indicating impatience and irritation. Another time she would have gone in at his request. She would, through habit, have yielded to his desire; not with any sense of submission or obedience to his compelling wishes, but unthinkingly, as we walk, move, sit, stand, go through the daily treadmill of the life which has been portioned out to us.

"Edna, dear, are you not coming in soon?" he asked again, this time fondly, with a note of entreaty.

"No; I am going to stay out here."

"This is more than folly," he blurted out. "I can't permit you to stay out there all night. You must come in the house instantly."

With a writhing motion she settled herself more securely in the hammock. She perceived that her will had blazed up, stubborn and resistant. She could not at that moment have done other than denied and resisted. She wondered if her husband had ever spoken to her like that before, and if she had submitted to his command. Of course she had; she remembered that she had. But she could not realize why or how she should have yielded, feeling as she then did.

"Léonce, go to bed," she said. "I mean to stay out here. I don't wish to go in, and I don't intend to. Don't speak to me like that again; I shall not answer you."

Mr. Pontellier had prepared for bed, but he slipped on an extra garment. He opened a bottle of wine, of which he kept a small and select supply in a buffet of his own. He drank a glass of the wine and went out on the gallery and offered a glass to his wife. She did not wish any. He drew up the rocker, hoisted his slippered feet on the rail, and proceeded to smoke a cigar. He smoked two cigars; then he went inside and drank another glass of wine. Mrs. Pontellier again declined to accept a glass when it was offered to her. Mr. Pontellier once more seated himself with elevated feet, and after a reasonable interval of time smoked some more cigars.

Edna began to feel like one who awakens gradually out of a dream, a delicious, grotesque, impossible dream, to feel again the realities pressing into her soul. The physical need for sleep began to overtake her; the exuberance which had sustained and exalted her spirit left her helpless and yielding to the conditions which crowded her in.

The stillest hour of the night had come, the hour before dawn, when the world seems to hold its breath. The moon hung low, and had turned from silver to copper in the sleeping sky. The old owl no longer hooted, and the water-oaks had ceased to moan as they bent their heads.

Edna arose, cramped from lying so long and still in the hammock. She tottered up the steps, clutching feebly at the post before passing into the house.

"Are you coiming in, Léonce?" she asked, turning her face toward her husband.

"Yes, dear," he answered, with a glance following a misty puff of smoke. "Just as soon as I have finished my cigar."

XII

She slept but a few hours. They were troubled and feverish hours, disturbed with dreams that were intangible, that eluded her, leaving only an impression upon her half-awakened senses of something unattainable. She was up and dressed in the cool of the early morning. The air was invigorating and steadied somewhat her faculties. However, she was not seeking refreshment or help from any source, either external or from within. She was blindly following whatever impulse moved her, as if she had placed herself in alien hands for direction, and freed her soul of responsibility.

Most of the people at that early hour were still in bed and asleep. A few, who intended to go over to the *Chênière* for mass, were moving about. The lovers, who had laid their plans the night before, were already strolling toward the wharf. The lady in black, with her Sunday prayer book, velvet and gold-clasped, and her Sunday silver beads, was following them at no great distance. Old Monsieur Farival was up, and was more than half inclined to do anything that suggested itself. He put on his big straw hat, and taking his umbrella from the stand in the hall, followed the lady in black, never overtaking her.

The little negro girl who worked Madame Lebrun's sewing-machine was sweeping the galleries with long, absent-minded strokes of the broom. Edna sent her up into the house to awaken Robert.

"Tell him I am going to the *Chênière*. The boat is ready; tell him to hurry."

He had soon joined her. She had never sent for him before. She had never asked for him. She had never seemed to want him before. She did not appear conscious that she had done anything unusual in commanding his presence. He was apparently equally unconscious of anything extraordinary in the situation. But his face was suffused with a quiet glow when he met her.

They went together back to the kitchen to drink coffee. There was no time to wait for any nicety of service. They stood outside the window and the cook passed them their coffee and a roll, which they drank and ate from the window-sill. Edna said it tasted good. She had not thought of coffee nor of anything. He told her he had often noticed that she lacked forethought.

"Wasn't it enough to think of going to the *Chênière* and waking you up?" she laughed. "Do I have to think of everything?—as Léonce says when he's in a bad humor. I don't blame him; he'd never be in a bad humor if it weren't for me."

They took a short cut across the sands. At a distance they could see the curious procession moving toward the wharf—the lovers, shoulder to shoulder, creeping; the lady in black, gaining steadily upon them; old Monsieur Farival, losing ground inch by inch, and a young barefooted Spanish girl, with a red kerchief on her head and a basket on her arm, bringing up the rear.

Robert knew the girl, and he talked to her a little in the boat. No one present understood what they said. Her name was Mariequita. She had a round, sly, piquant face and pretty black eyes. Her hands were small, and she kept them folded over the handle of her basket. Her feet were broad and coarse. She did not strive to hide them. Edna looked at her feet, and noticed the sand and slime between her brown toes.

Beaudelet grumbled because Mariequita was there, taking up so much room. In reality he was annoyed at having old Monsieur Farival, who considered himself the better sailor of the two. But he would not quarrel with so old a man as Monsieur Farival, so he quarreled with Mariequita. The girl was deprecatory at one moment, appealing to Robert. She was saucy the next, moving her head up and down, making "eyes" at Robert and making "mouths" at Beaudelet.

The lovers were all alone. They saw nothing, they heard nothing. The lady in black was counting her beads for the third time. Old Monsieur Farival talked incessantly of what he knew about handling a boat, and of what Beaudelet did not know on the same subject.

Edna liked it all. She looked Mariequita up and down, from her ugly brown toes to her pretty black eyes, and back again.

"Why does she look at me like that?" inquired the girl of Robert.

"Maybe she thinks you are pretty. Shall I ask her?"

"No. Is she your sweetheart?"

"She's a married lady, and has two children."

"Oh! well! Francisco ran away with Sylvano's wife, who had four children. They took all his money and one of the children and stole his boat."

"Shut up!"

"Does she understand?"

"Oh, hush!"

"Are those two married over there—leaning on each other?"

"Of course not," laughed Robert.

"Of course not," echoed Mariequita, with a serious, confirmatory bob of the head.

The sun was high up and beginning to bite. The swift breeze seemed to Edna to bury the sting of it into the pores of her face and hands. Robert held his umbrella over her.

As they went cutting sidewise through the water, the sails bellied taut, with the wind filling and overflowing them. Old Monsieur Farival laughed sardonically at something as he looked at the sails, and Beaudelet swore at the old man under his breath.

Sailing across the bay to the *Chênière Caminada*, Edna felt as if she were being borne away from some anchorage which had held her fast, whose chains had been loosening—had snapped the night before when the mystic spirit was abroad, leaving her free to drift whithersoever she chose to set her sails. Robert spoke to her incessantly; he no longer noticed Mariequita. The girl had shrimps in her bamboo basket. They were covered with Spanish moss. She beat the moss down impatiently, and muttered to herself sullenly.

"Let us go to Grande Terre[1] to-morrow?" said Robert in a low voice.

"What shall we do there?"

"Climb up the hill to the old fort and look at the little wriggling gold snakes, and watch the lizards sun themselves."

She gazed away toward Grande Terre and thought she would like to be alone there with Robert, in the sun, listening to the ocean's roar and watching the slimy lizards writhe in and out among the ruins of the old fort.

"And the next day or the next we can sail to the Bayou Brulow,"[2] he went on.

"What shall we do there?"

"Anything—cast bait for fish."

"No; we'll go back to Grande Terre. Let the fish alone."

"We'll go wherever you like," he said. "I'll have Tonie come over and help me patch and trim my boat. We shall not need Beaudelet nor any one. Are you afraid of the pirogue?"[3]

"Oh, no."

"Then I'll take you some night in the pirogue when the moon shines. Maybe your Gulf spirit will whisper to you in which of these islands the treasures are hidden—direct you to the very spot, perhaps."

"And in a day we should be rich!" she laughed. "I'd give it all to you, the pirate gold and every bit of treasure we could dig up. I think you would know how to spend it. Pirate gold isn't a thing to be hoarded or utilized. It is something to squander and throw to the four winds, for the fun of seeing the golden specks fly."

"We'd share it, and scatter it together," he said. His face flushed.

They all went together up to the quaint little Gothic church of Our Lady of Lourdes, gleaming all brown and yellow with paint in the sun's glare.

Only Beaudelet remained behind, tinkering at his boat, and Marie-quita walked away with her basket of shrimps, casting a look of childish ill-humor and reproach at Robert from the corner of her eye.

XIII

A feeling of oppression and drowsiness overcame Edna during the service. Her head began to ache, and the lights on the altar swayed before her eyes. Another time she might have made an effort to regain her composure; but her one thought was to quit the stifling atmosphere

1. An island adjacent to Grand Isle.
2. Bayou Brulow (or Bruleau) was the nearest to Grand Isle of a series of villages built on stilts or platforms above the marshes of the bay.
3. A flat-bottomed boat designed for navigating shallow water, propelled by rowing or by sails, or (as used on p. 67) a dugout canoe.

of the church and reach the open air. She arose, climbing over Robert's feet with a muttered apology. Old Monsieur Farival, flurried, curious, stood up, but upon seeing that Robert had followed Mrs. Pontellier, he sank back into his seat. He whispered an anxious inquiry of the lady in black, who did not notice him or reply, but kept her eyes fastened upon the pages of her velvet prayer-book.

"I felt giddy and almost overcome," Edna said, lifting her hands instinctively to her head and pushing her straw hat up from her forehead. "I couldn't have stayed through the service." They were outside in the shadow of the church. Robert was full of solicitude.

"It was folly to have thought of going in the first place, let alone staying. Come over to Madame Antoine's; you can rest there." He took her arm and led her away, looking anxiously and continuously down into her face.

How still it was, with only the voice of the sea whispering through the reeds that grew in the salt-water pools! The long line of little gray, weather-beaten houses nestled peacefully among the orange trees. It must always have been God's day on that low, drowsy island, Edna thought. They stopped, leaning over a jagged fence made of sea-drift, to ask for water. A youth, a mild-faced Acadian,[4] was drawing water from the cistern, which was nothing more than a rusty buoy, with an opening on one side, sunk in the ground. The water which the youth handed to them in a tin pail was not cold to taste, but it was cool to her heated face, and it greatly revived and refreshed her.

Madame Antoine's cot[5] was at the far end of the village. She welcomed them with all the native hospitality, as she would have opened her door to let the sunlight in. She was fat, and walked heavily and clumsily across the floor. She could speak no English, but when Robert made her understand that the lady who accompanied him was ill and desired to rest, she was all eagerness to make Edna feel at home and to dispose of her comfortably.

The whole place was immaculately clean, and the big, four-posted bed, snow-white, invited one to repose. It stood in a small side room which looked out across a narrow grass plot toward the shed, where there was a disabled boat lying keel upward.

Madame Antoine had not gone to mass. Her son Tonie had, but she supposed he would soon be back, and she invited Robert to be seated and wait for him. But he went and sat outside the door and smoked. Madame Antoine busied herself in the large front room preparing dinner. She was boiling mullets[6] over a few red coals in the huge fireplace.

Edna, left alone in the little side room, loosened her clothes, removing

4. Descendant of the French Canadians who were expelled from Acadia, or Nova Scotia, by the British in 1755 and who made their way to other French colonies. Their settlements along the Louisiana coast remained French-speaking.
5. Cottage.
6. Fish.

the greater part of them. She bathed her face, her neck and arms in the basin that stood between the windows. She took off her shoes and stockings and stretched herself in the very center of the high, white bed. How luxurious it felt to rest thus in a strange, quaint bed, with its sweet country odor of laurel lingering about the sheets and mattress! She stretched her strong limbs that ached a little. She ran her fingers through her loosened hair for a while. She looked at her round arms as she held them straight up and rubbed them one after the other, observing closely, as if it were something she saw for the first time, the fine, firm quality and texture of her flesh. She clasped her hands easily above her head, and it was thus she fell asleep.

She slept lightly at first, half awake and drowsily attentive to the things about her. She could hear Madame Antoine's heavy, scraping tread as she walked back and forth on the sanded floor. Some chickens were clucking outside the windows, scratching for bits of gravel in the grass. Later she half heard the voices of Robert and Tonie talking under the shed. She did not stir. Even her eyelids rested numb and heavily over her sleepy eyes. The voices went on—Tonie's slow, Acadian drawl, Robert's quick, soft, smooth French. She understood French imperfectly unless directly addressed, and the voices were only part of the other drowsy, muffled sounds lulling her senses.

When Edna awoke it was with the conviction that she had slept long and soundly. The voices were hushed under the shed. Madame Antoine's step was no longer to be heard in the adjoining room. Even the chickens had gone elsewhere to scratch and cluck. The mosquito bar was drawn over her; the old woman had come in while she slept and let down the bar. Edna arose quietly from the bed, and looking between the curtains of the window, she saw by the slanting rays of the sun that the afternoon was far advanced. Robert was out there under the shed, reclining in the shade against the sloping keel of the overturned boat. He was reading from a book. Tonie was no longer with him. She wondered what had become of the rest of the party. She peeped out at him two or three times as she stood washing herself in the little basin between the windows.

Madame Antoine had laid some coarse, clean towels upon a chair, and had placed a box of *poudre de riz* within easy reach. Edna dabbed the powder upon her nose and cheeks as she looked at herself closely in the little distorted mirror which hung on the wall above the basin. Her eyes were bright and wide awake and her face glowed.

When she had completed her toilet she walked into the adjoining room. She was very hungry. No one was there. But there was a cloth spread upon the table that stood against the wall, and a cover was laid for one, with a crusty brown loaf and a bottle of wine beside the plate. Edna bit a piece from the brown loaf, tearing it with her strong, white teeth. She poured some of the wine into the glass and drank it down. Then she went softly out of doors, and plucking an orange from the low-hanging bough of a tree, threw it at Robert, who did not know she was awake and up.

An illumination broke over his whole face when he saw her and joined her under the orange tree.

"How many years have I slept?" she inquired. "The whole island seems changed. A new race of beings must have sprung up, leaving only you and me as past relics. How many ages ago did Madame Antoine and Tonie die? and when did our people from Grand Isle disappear from the earth?"

He familiarly adjusted a ruffle upon her shoulder.

"You have slept precisely one hundred years. I was left here to guard your slumbers; and for one hundred years I have been out under the shed reading a book. The only evil I couldn't prevent was to keep a broiled fowl from drying up."

"If it had turned to stone, still will I eat it," said Edna, moving with him into the house. "But really, what has become of Monsieur Farival and the others?"

"Gone hours ago. When they found that you were sleeping they thought it best not to awake you. Any way, I wouldn't have let them. What was I here for?"

"I wonder if Léonce will be uneasy!" she speculated, as she seated herself at table.

"Of course not; he knows you are with me," Robert replied, as he busied himself among sundry pans and covered dishes which had been left standing on the hearth.

"Where are Madame Antoine and her son?" asked Edna.

"Gone to Vespers,[7] and to visit some friends, I believe. I am to take you back in Tonie's boat whenever you are ready to go."

He stirred the smoldering ashes till the broiled fowl began to sizzle afresh. He served her with no mean repast, dripping the coffee anew and sharing it with her. Madame Antoine had cooked little else than the mullets, but while Edna slept Robert had foraged the island. He was childishly gratified to discover her appetite, and to see the relish with which she ate the food which he had procured for her.

"Shall we go right away?" she asked, after draining her glass and brushing together the crumbs of the crusty loaf.

"The sun isn't as low as it will be in two hours," he answered.

"The sun will be gone in two hours."

"Well, let it go; who cares!"

They waited a good while under the orange trees, till Madame Antoine came back, panting, waddling, with a thousand apologies to explain her absence. Tonie did not dare to return. He was shy, and would not willingly face any woman except his mother.

It was very pleasant to stay there under the orange trees, while the

7. An evening church service.

sun dipped lower and lower, turning the western sky to flaming copper and gold. The shadows lengthened and crept out like stealthy, grotesque monsters across the grass.

Edna and Robert both sat upon the ground—that is, he lay upon the ground beside her, occasionally picking at the hem of her muslin gown. Madame Antoine seated her fat body, broad and squat, upon a bench beside the door. She had been talking all the afternoon, and had wound herself up to the story-telling pitch.

But what stories she told them! But twice in her life she had left the *Chênière Caminada*, and then for the briefest span. All her years she had squatted and waddled there upon the island, gathering legends of the Baratarians[8] and the sea. The night came on, with the moon to lighten it. Edna could hear the whispering voices of dead men and the click of muffled gold.

When she and Robert stepped into Tonie's boat, with the red lateen sail, misty spirit forms were prowling in the shadows and among the reeds, and upon the water were phantom ships, speeding to cover.

XIV·

The youngest boy, Etienne, had been very naughty, Madame Ratignolle said, as she delivered him into the hands of his mother. He had been unwilling to go to bed and had made a scene; whereupon she had taken charge of him and pacified him as well as she could. Raoul had been in bed and asleep for two hours.

The youngster was in his long white nightgown, that kept tripping him up as Madame Ratignolle led him along by the hand. With the other chubby fist he rubbed his eyes, which were heavy with sleep and ill humor. Edna took him in her arms, and seating herself in the rocker, began to coddle and caress him, calling him all manner of tender names, soothing him to sleep.

It was not more than nine o'clock. No one had yet gone to bed but the children.

Léonce had been very uneasy at first, Madame Ratignolle said, and had wanted to start at once for the *Chênière*. But Monsieur Farival had assured him that his wife was only overcome with sleep and fatigue, that Tonie would bring her safely back later in the day; and he had thus been dissuaded from crossing the bay. He had gone over to Klein's, looking up some cotton broker whom he wished to see in regard to securities, exchanges, stocks, bonds, or something of the sort, Madame Ratignolle did not remember what. He said he would not remain away late. She herself was suffering from heat and oppression, she said. She

---

8. The pirates, especially Jean Lafitte, who operated in Barataria, an area of marshlands and islands stretching sixty miles south from New Orleans to Barataria Bay and the Gulf of Mexico. The area abounded with legends of pirateering, smuggling and buried treasure.

carried a bottle of salts and a large fan. She would not consent to remain with Edna, for Monsieur Ratignolle was alone, and he detested above all things to be left alone.

When Etienne had fallen asleep Edna bore him into the back room, and Robert went and lifted the mosquito bar that she might lay the child comfortably in his bed. The quadroon had vanished. When they emerged from the cottage Robert bade Edna good-night.

"Do you know we have been together the whole livelong day, Robert—since early this morning?" she said at parting.

"All but the hundred years when you were sleeping. Good-night."

He pressed her hand and went away in the direction of the beach. He did not join any of the others, but walked alone toward the Gulf.

Edna stayed outside, awaiting her husband's return. She had no desire to sleep or to retire; nor did she feel like going over to sit with the Ratignolles, or to join Madame Lebrun and a group whose animated voices reached her as they sat in conversation before the house. She let her mind wander back over her stay at Grand Isle; and she tried to discover wherein this summer had been different from any and every other summer of her life. She could only realize that she herself—her present self—was in some way different from the other self. That she was seeing with different eyes and making the acquaintance of new conditions in herself that colored and changed her environment, she did not yet suspect.

She wondered why Robert had gone away and left her. It did not occur to her to think he might have grown tired of being with her the livelong day. She was not tired, and she felt that he was not. She regretted that he had gone. It was so much more natural to have him stay, when he was not absolutely required to leave her.

As Edna waited for her husband she sang low a little song that Robert had sung as they crossed the bay. It began with "Ah! *Si tu savais,*" and every verse ended with "*si tu savais.*"[9]

Robert's voice was not pretentious. It was musical and true. The voice, the notes, the whole refrain haunted her memory.

XV

When Edna entered the dining-room one evening a little late, as was her habit, an unusually animated conversation seemed to be going on. Several persons were talking at once, and Victor's voice was predominating, even over that of his mother. Edna had returned late from her bath, had dressed in some haste, and her face was flushed. Her head, set off by her dainty white gown, suggested a rich, rare blossom. She

---

9. The Irish composer and baritone Michael William Balfe (1808–70) composed a song with this title ("Could Thou But Know"), but Chopin seems to have made up the words to the refrain.

took her seat at table between old Monsieur Farival and Madame Ratignolle.

As she seated herself and was about to begin to eat her soup, which had been served when she entered the room, several persons informed her simultaneously that Robert was going to Mexico. She laid her spoon down and looked about her bewildered. He had been with her, reading to her all the morning, and had never even mentioned such a place as Mexico. She had not seen him during the afternoon; she had heard some one say he was at the house, upstairs with his mother. This she had thought nothing of, though she was surprised when he did not join her later in the afternoon, when she went down to the beach.

She looked across at him, where he sat beside Madame Lebrun, who presided. Edna's face was a blank picture of bewilderment, which she never thought of disguising. He lifted his eyebrows with the pretext of a smile as he returned her glance. He looked embarrassed and uneasy.

"When is he going?" she asked of everybody in general, as if Robert were not there to answer for himself.

"To-night!" "This very evening!" "Did you ever!" "What possesses him!" were some of the replies she gathered, uttered simultaneously in French and English.

"Impossible!" she exlaimed. "How can a person start off from Grand Isle to Mexico at a moment's notice, as if he were going over to Klein's or to the wharf or down to the beach?"

"I said all along I was going to Mexico; I've been saying so for years!" cried Robert, in an excited and irritable tone, with the air of a man defending himself against a swarm of stinging insects.

Madame Lebrun knocked on the table with her knife handle.

"Please let Robert explain why he is going, and why he is going to-night," she called out. "Really, this table is getting to be more and more like Bedlam¹ every day, with everybody talking at once. Sometimes—I hope God will forgive me—but positively, sometimes I wish Victor would lose the power of speech."

Victor laughed sardonically as he thanked his mother for her holy wish, of which he failed to see the benefit to anybody, except that it might afford her a more ample opportunity and license to talk herself.

Monsieur Farival thought that Victor should have been taken out in mid-ocean in his earliest youth and drowned. Victor thought there would be more logic in thus disposing of old people with an established claim for making themselves universally obnoxious. Madame Lebrun grew a trifle hysterical; Robert called his brother some sharp, hard names.

"There's nothing much to explain, mother," he said; though he explained, nevertheless—looking chiefly at Edna—that he could only meet the gentleman whom he intended to join at Vera Cruz by taking

---

1. An insane asylum.

such and such a steamer, which left New Orleans on such a day; that Beaudelet was going out with his lugger-load of vegetables that night, which gave him an opportunity of reaching the city and making his vessel in time.

"But when did you make up your mind to all this?" demanded Monsieur Farival.

"This afternoon," returned Robert, with a shade of annoyance.

"At what time this afternoon?" persisted the old gentleman, with nagging determination, as if he were cross-questioning a criminal in a court of justice.

"At four o'clock this afternoon, Monsieur Farival," Robert replied, in a high voice and with a lofty air, which reminded Edna of some gentleman on the stage.

She had forced herself to eat most of her soup, and now she was picking the flaky bits of a *court bouillon*[2] with her fork.

The lovers were profiting by the general conversation on Mexico to speak in whispers of matters which they rightly considered were interesting to no one but themselves. The lady in black had once received a pair of prayer-beads of curious workmanship from Mexico, with very special indulgence[3] attached to them, but she had never been able to ascertain whether the indulgence extended outside the Mexican border. Father Fochel of the Cathedral had attempted to explain it; but he had not done so to her satisfaction. And she begged that Robert would interest himself, and discover, if possible, whether she was entitled to the indulgence accompanying the remarkably curious Mexican prayer-beads.

Madame Ratignolle hoped that Robert would exercise extreme caution in dealing with the Mexicans, who, she considered, were a treacherous people, unscrupulous and revengeful. She trusted she did them no injustice in thus condemning them as a race. She had known personally but one Mexican, who made and sold excellent tamales, and whom she would have trusted implicitly, so soft-spoken was he. One day he was arrested for stabbing his wife. She never knew whether he had been hanged or not.

Victor had grown hilarious, and was attempting to tell an anecdote about a Mexican girl who served chocolate one winter in a restaurant in Dauphine Street.[4] No one would listen to him but old Monsieur Farival, who went into convulsions over the droll story.

Edna wondered if they had all gone mad, to be talking and clamoring at that rate. She herself could think of nothing to say about Mexico or the Mexicans.

"At what time do you leave?" she asked Robert.

2. Fish broth.
3. Roman Catholic belief in the remission of punishment (time in Purgatory) for sins committed; attached to certain prayers and sacraments.
4. In the French Quarter.

"At ten," he told her. "Beaudelet wants to wait for the moon."

"Are you all ready to go?"

"Quite ready. I shall only take a handbag, and shall pack my trunk in the city."

He turned to answer some question put to him by his mother, and Edna, having finished her black coffee, left the table.

She went directly to her room. The little cottage was close and stuffy after leaving the outer air. But she did not mind; there appeared to be a hundred different things demanding her attention indoors. She began to set the toilet-stand to rights, grumbling at the negligence of the quadroon, who was in the adjoining room putting the children to bed. She gathered together stray garments that were hanging on the backs of chairs, and put each where it belonged in closet or bureau drawer. She changed her gown for a more comfortable and commodious wrapper. She rearranged her hair, combing and brushing it with unusual energy. Then she went in and assisted the quadroon in getting the boys to bed.

They were very playful and inclined to talk—to do anything but lie quiet and go to sleep. Edna sent the quadroon away to her supper and told her she need not return. Then she sat and told the children a story. Instead of soothing it excited them, and added to their wakefulness. She left them in heated argument, speculating about the conclusion of the tale which their mother promised to finish the following night.

The little black girl came in to say that Madame Lebrun would like to have Mrs. Pontellier go and sit with them over at the house till Mr. Robert went away. Edna returned answer that she had already undressed, that she did not feel quite well, but perhaps she would go over to the house later. She started to dress again, and got as far advanced as to remove her *peignoir*. But changing her mind once more she resumed the *peignoir*, and went outside and sat down before her door. She was overheated and irritable, and fanned herself energetically for a while. Madame Ratignolle came down to discover what was the matter.

"All that noise and confusion at the table must have upset me," replied Edna, "and moreover, I hate shocks and surprises. The idea of Robert starting off in such a ridiculously sudden and dramatic way! As if it were a matter of life and death! Never saying a word about it all morning when he was with me."

"Yes," agreed Madame Ratignolle. "I think it was showing us all— you especially—very little consideration. It wouldn't have surprised me in any of the others; those Lebruns are all given to heroics. But I must say I should never have expected such a thing from Robert. Are you not coming down? Come on, dear; it doesn't look friendly."

"No," said Edna, a little sullenly. "I can't go to the trouble of dressing again; I don't feel like it."

"You needn't dress; you look all right; fasten a belt around your waist. Just look at me!"

"No," persisted Edna; "but you go on. Madame Lebrun might be offended if we both stayed away."

Madame Ratignolle kissed Edna good-night, and went away, being in truth rather desirous of joining in the general and animated conversation which was still in progress concerning Mexico and the Mexicans. Somewhat later Robert came up, carrying his hand-bag.

"Aren't you feeling well?" he asked.

"Oh, well enough. Are you going right away?"

He lit a match and looked at his watch. "In twenty minutes," he said. The sudden and brief flare of the match emphasized the darkness for a while. He sat down upon a stool which the children had left out on the porch.

"Get a chair," said Edna.

"This will do," he replied. He put on his soft hat and nervously took it off again, and wiping his face with his handkerchief, complained of the heat.

"Take the fan," said Edna, offering it to him.

"Oh, no! Thank you. It does no good; you have to stop fanning some time, and feel all the more uncomfortable afterward."

"That's one of the ridiculous things which men always say. I have never known one of speak otherwise of fanning. How long will you be gone?"

"Forever, perhaps. I don't know. It depends upon a good many things."

"Well, in case it shouldn't be forever, how long will it be?"

"I don't know."

"This seems to me perfectly preposterous and uncalled for. I don't like it. I don't understand your motive for silence and mystery, never saying a word to me about it this morning." He remained silent, not offering to defend himself. He only said, after a moment:

"Don't part from me in an ill-humor. I never knew you to be out of patience with me before."

"I don't want to part in any ill-humor," she said. "But can't you understand? I've grown used to seeing you, to having you with me all the time, and your action seems unfriendly, even unkind. You don't even offer an excuse for it. Why, I was planning to be together, thinking of how pleasant it would be to see you in the city next winter."

"So was I," he blurted. "Perhaps that's the—" He stood up suddenly and held out his hand. "Good-by, my dear Mrs. Pontellier; good-by. You won't—I hope you won't completely forget me." She clung to his hand, striving to detain him.

"Write to me when you get there, won't you, Robert?" she entreated.

"I will, thank you. Good-by."

How unlike Robert! The merest acquaintance would have said something more emphatic than "I will, thank you; good-by," to such a request.

He had evidently already taken leave of the people over at the house, for he descended the steps and went to join Beaudelet, who was out there with an oar across his shoulder waiting for Robert. They walked away in the darkness. She could only hear Beaudelet's voice; Robert had apparently not even spoken a word of greeting to his companion.

Edna bit her handkerchief convulsively, striving to hold back and to hide, even from herself as she would have hidden from another, the emotion which was troubling—tearing—her. Her eyes were brimming with tears.

For the first time she recognized anew the symptoms of infatuation which she felt incipiently as a child, as a girl in her earliest teens, and later as a young woman. The recognition did not lessen the reality, the poignancy of the revelation by any suggestion or promise of instability. The past was nothing to her; offered no lesson which she was willing to heed. The future was a mystery which she never attempted to penetrate. The present alone was significant; was hers, to torture her as it was doing then with the biting conviction that she had lost that which she had held, that she had been denied that which her impassioned, newly awakened being demanded.

XVI

"Do you miss your friend greatly?" asked Mademoiselle Reisz one morning as she came creeping up behind Edna, who had just left her cottage on her way to the beach. She spent much of her time in the water since she had acquired finally the art of swimming. As their stay at Grand Isle drew near its close, she felt that she could not give too much time to a diversion which afforded her the only real pleasurable moments that she knew. When Mademoiselle Reisz came and touched her upon the shoulder and spoke to her, the woman seemed to echo the thought which was ever in Edna's mind; or, better, the feeling which constantly possessed her.

Robert's going had some way taken the brightness, the color, the meaning out of everything. The conditions of her life were in no way changed, but her whole existence was dulled, like a faded garment which seems to be no longer worth wearing. She sought him everywhere—in others whom she induced to talk about him. She went up in the mornings to Madame Lebrun's room, braving the clatter of the old sewing-machine. She sat there and chatted at intervals as Robert had done. She gazed around the room at the pictures and photographs hanging upon the wall, and discovered in some corner an old family album, which she examined with the keenest interest, appealing to Madame Lebrun for enlightenment concerning the many figures and faces which she discovered between its pages.

There was a picture of Madame Lebrun with Robert as a baby, seated

in her lap, a round-faced infant with a fist in his mouth. The eyes
alone in the baby suggested the man. And that was he also in kilts, at
the age of five, wearing long curls and holding a whip in his hand. It
made Edna laugh, and she laughed, too, at the portrait in his first long
trousers; while another interested her, taken when he left for college,
looking thin, long-faced, with eyes full of fire, ambition and great intentions. But there was no recent picture, none which suggested the
Robert who had gone away five days ago, leaving a void and wilderness
behind him.

"Oh, Robert stopped having his pictures taken when he had to pay
for them himself! He found wiser use for his money, he says," explained
Madame Lebrun. She had a letter from him, written before he left New
Orleans. Edna wished to see the letter, and Madame Lebrun told her
to look for it either on the table or the dresser, or perhaps it was on the
mantelpiece.

The letter was on the bookshelf. It possessed the greatest interest and
attraction for Edna; the envelope, its size and shape, the postmark, the
handwriting. She examined every detail of the outside before opening
it. There were only a few lines, setting forth that he would leave the
city that afternoon, that he had packed his trunk in good shape, that he
was well, and sent her his love and begged to be affectionately remembered to all. There was no special message to Edna except a postscript
saying that if Mrs. Pontellier desired to finish the book which he had
been reading to her, his mother would find it in his room, among other
books there on the table. Edna experienced a pang of jealousy because
he had written to his mother rather than to her.

Every one seemed to take for granted that she missed him. Even her
husband, when he came down the Saturday following Robert's departure, expressed regret that he had gone.

"How do you get on without him, Edna?" he asked.

"It's very dull without him," she admitted. Mr. Pontellier had seen
Robert in the city, and Edna asked him a dozen questions or more.
Where had they met? On Carondelet Street, in the morning. They had
gone "in" and had a drink and a cigar together. What had they talked
about? Chiefly about his prospects in Mexico, which Mr. Pontellier
thought were promising. How did he look? How did he seem—grave,
or gay, or how? Quite cheerful, and wholly taken up with the idea of
his trip, which Mr. Pontellier found altogether natural in a young fellow
about to seek fortune, and adventure in a strange, queer country.

Edna tapped her foot impatiently, and wondered why the children
persisted in playing in the sun when they might be under the trees. She
went down and led them out of the sun, scolding the quadroon for not
being more attentive.

It did not strike her as in the least grotesque that she should be making
of Robert the object of conversation and leading her husband to speak

of him. The sentiment which she entertained for Robert in no way resembled that which she felt for her husband, or had ever felt, or ever expected to feel. She had all her life long been accustomed to harbor thoughts and emotions which never voiced themselves. They had never taken the form of struggles. They belonged to her and were her own, and she entertained the conviction that she had a right to them and that they concerned no one but herself. Edna had once told Madame Ratignolle that she would never sacrifice herself for her children, or for any one. Then had followed a rather heated argument; the two women did not appear to understand each other or to be talking the same language. Edna tried to appease her friend, to explain.

"I would give up the unessential; I would give my money, I would give my life for my children; but I wouldn't give myself. I can't make it more clear; it's only something which I am beginning to comprehend, which is revealing itself to me."

"I don't know what you would call the essential, or what you mean by the unessential," said Madame Ratignolle, cheerfully; "but a woman who would give her life for her children could do no more than that— your Bible tells you so. I'm sure I couldn't do more than that."

"Oh, yes you could!" laughed Edna.

She was not surprised at Mademoiselle Reisz's question the morning that lady, following her to the beach, tapped her on the shoulder and asked if she did not greatly miss her young friend.

"Oh, good morning, Mademoiselle; it is you? Why, of course I miss Robert. Are you going down to bathe?"

"Why should I go down to bathe at the very end of the season when I haven't been in the surf all summer?" replied the woman, disagreeably.

"I beg your pardon," offered Edna, in some embarrassment, for she should have remembered that Mademoiselle Reisz's avoidance of the water had furnished a theme for much pleasantry. Some among them thought it was on account of her false hair, or the dread of getting the violets wet, while others attributed it to the natural aversion for water sometimes believed to accompany the artistic temperament. Mademoiselle offered Edna some chocolates in a paper bag, which she took from her pocket, by way of showing that she bore no ill feeling. She habitually ate chocolates for their sustaining quality; they contained much nutriment in small compass, she said. They saved her from starvation, as Madame Lebrun's table was utterly impossible; and no one save so impertinent a woman as Madame Lebrun could think of offering such food to people and requiring them to pay for it.

"She must feel very lonely without her son," said Edna, desiring to change the subject. "Her favorite son, too. It must have been quite hard to let him go."

Mademoiselle laughed maliciously.

"Her favorite son! Oh, dear! Who could have been imposing such a tale upon you? Aline Lebrun lives for Victor, and for Victor alone. She has spoiled him into the worthless creature he is. She worships him and the ground he walks on. Robert is very well in a way, to give up all the money he can earn to the family, and keep the barest pittance for himself. Favorite son, indeed! I miss the poor fellow myself, my dear. I liked to see him and to hear him about the place—the only Lebrun who is worth a pinch of salt. He comes to see me often in the city. I like to play to him. That Victor! hanging would be too good for him. It's a wonder Robert hasn't beaten him to death long ago."

"I thought he had great patience with his brother," offered Edna, glad to be talking about Robert, no matter what was said.

"Oh! he thrashed him well enough a year or two ago," said Mademoiselle. "It was about a Spanish girl, whom Victor considered that he had some sort of claim upon. He met Robert one day talking to the girl, or walking with her, or bathing with her, or carrying her basket—I don't remember what;—and he became so insulting and abusive that Robert gave him a thrashing on the spot that has kept him comparatively in order for a good while. It's about time he was getting another."

"Was her name Mariequita?" asked Edna.

"Mariequita—yes, that was it; Mariequita. I had forgotten. Oh, she's a sly one, and a bad one, that Mariequita!"

Edna looked down at Mademoiselle Reisz and wondered how she could have listened to her venom so long. For some reason she felt depressed, almost unhappy. She had not intended to go into the water; but she donned her bathing suit, and left Mademoiselle alone, seated under the shade of the children's tent. The water was growing cooler as the season advanced. Edna plunged and swam about with an abandon that thrilled and invigorated her. She remained a long time in the water, half hoping that Mademoiselle Reisz would not wait for her.

But Mademoiselle waited. She was very amiable during the walk back, and raved much over Edna's appearance in her bathing suit. She talked about music. She hoped that Edna would go to see her in the city, and wrote her address with the stub of a pencil on a piece of card which she found in her pocket.

"When do you leave?" asked Edna.

"Next Monday; and you?"

"The following week," answered Edna, adding, "It has been a pleasant summer, hasn't it, Mademoiselle?"

"Well," agreed Mademoiselle Reisz, with a shrug, "rather pleasant, if it hadn't been for the mosquitoes and the Farival twins."

XVII

The Pontelliers possessed a very charming home on Esplanade Street[5] in New Orleans. It was a large, double cottage, with a broad front

---

5. The most exclusive address of the Creole aristocracy. Called "Promenade Publique" in the 1830s, it was a street of palatial homes shaded by live oaks, palms, and magnolias.

veranda, whose round, fluted columns supported the sloping roof. The house was painted a dazzling white; the outside shutters, or jalousies, were green. In the yard, which was kept scrupulously neat, were flowers and plants of every description which flourishes in South Louisiana. Within doors the appointments were perfect after the conventional type. The softest carpets and rugs covered the floors; rich and tasteful draperies hung at doors and windows. There were paintings, selected with judgment and discrimination, upon the walls. The cut glass, the silver, the heavy damask which daily appeared upon the table were the envy of many women whose husbands were less generous than Mr. Pontellier.

Mr. Pontellier was very fond of walking about his house examining its various appointments and details, to see that nothing was amiss. He greatly valued his possessions, chiefly because they were his, and derived genuine pleasure from contemplating a painting, a statuette, a rare lace curtain—no matter what—after he had bought it and placed it among his household gods.

On Tuesday afternoons—Tuesday being Mrs. Pontellier's reception day[6]—there was a constant stream of callers—women who came in carriages or in the street cars, or walked when the air was soft and distance permitted. A light-colored mulatto boy, in dress coat and bearing a diminutive silver tray for the reception of cards, admitted them. A maid, in white fluted cap, offered the callers liqueur, coffee, or chocolate, as they might desire. Mrs. Pontellier, attired in a handsome reception gown, remained in the drawing-room the entire afternoon receiving her visitors. Men sometimes called in the evening with their wives.

This had been the programme which Mrs. Pontellier had religiously followed since her marriage, six years before. Certain evenings during the week she and her husband attended the opera or sometimes the play.

Mr. Pontellier left his home in the mornings between nine and ten o'clock, and rarely returned before half-past six or seven in the evening—dinner being served at half-past seven.

He and his wife seated themselves at table on Tuesday evening, a few weeks after their return from Grand Isle. They were alone together. The boys were being put to bed; the patter of their bare, escaping feet could be heard occasionally, as well as the pursuing voice of the quadroon, lifted in mild protest and entreaty. Mrs. Pontellier did not wear her usual Tuesday reception gown; she was in ordinary house dress. Mr. Pontellier, who was observant about such things, noticed it, as he served the soup and handed it to the boy in waiting.

"Tired out, Edna? Whom did you have? Many callers?" he asked. He tasted his soup and began to season it with pepper, salt, vinegar, mustard—everything within reach.

6. A day once a week when a woman was expected to be "at home" to receive visitors. See below, p. 123.

"There were a good many," replied Edna, who was eating her soup with evident satisfaction. "I found their cards when I got home; I was out."

"Out!" exclaimed her husband, with something like genuine consternation in his voice as he laid down the vinegar cruet and looked at her through his glasses. "Why, what could have taken you out on Tuesday? What did you have to do?"

"Nothing. I simply felt like going out, and I went out."

"Well, I hope you left some suitable excuse," said her husband, somewhat appeased, as he added a dash of cayenne pepper to the soup.

"No, I left no excuse. I told Joe to say I was out, that was all."

"Why, my dear, I should think you'd understand by this time that people don't do such things; we've got to observe *les convenances*[7] if we ever expect to get on and keep up with the procession. If you felt that you had to leave home this afternoon, you should have left some suitable explanation for your absence.

"This soup is really impossible; it's strange that woman hasn't learned yet to make a decent soup. Any free-lunch stand in town serves a better one. Was Mrs. Belthrop here?"

"Bring the tray with the cards, Joe. I don't remember who was here."

The boy retired and returned after a moment, bringing the tiny silver tray, which was covered with ladies' visiting cards. He handed it to Mrs. Pontellier.

"Give it to Mr. Pontellier," she said.

Joe offered the tray to Mr. Pontellier, and removed the soup.

Mr. Pontellier scanned the names of his wife's callers, reading some of them aloud, with comments as he read.

" 'The Misses Delasidas.' I worked a big deal in futures[8] for their father this morning; nice girls; it's time they were getting married. 'Mrs. Belthrop.' I tell you what it is, Edna; you can't afford to snub Mrs. Belthrop. Why, Belthrop could buy and sell us ten times over. His business is worth a good, round sum to me. You'd better write her a note. 'Mrs. James Highcamp.' Hugh! the less you have to do with Mrs. Highcamp, the better. 'Madame Laforcé.' Came all the way from Carrolton,[9] too, poor old soul. 'Miss Wiggs,' 'Mrs. Eleanor Boltons.' " He pushed the cards aside.

"Mercy!" exclaimed Edna, who had been fuming. "Why are you taking the thing so seriously and making such a fuss over it?"

"I'm not making any fuss over it. But it's just such seeming trifles that we've got to take seriously; such things count."

The fish was scorched. Mr. Pontellier would not touch it. Edna said

7. Proprieties, social conventions.
8. Items bought and sold for delivery at a future time; a form of speculation in stocks or commodities.
9. A village to the west of New Orleans, later absorbed by the city.

she did not mind a little scorched taste. The roast was in some way not to his fancy, and he did not like the manner in which the vegetables were served.

"It seems to me," he said, "we spend money enough in this house to procure at least one meal a day which a man could eat and retain his self-respect."

"You used to think the cook was a treasure," returned Edna, indifferently.

"Perhaps she was when she first came; but cooks are only human. They need looking after, like any other class of persons that you employ. Suppose I didn't look after the clerks in my office, just let them run things their own way; they'd soon make a nice mess of me and my business."

"Where are you going?" asked Edna, seeing that her husband arose from table without having eaten a morsel except a taste of the highly-seasoned soup.

"I'm going to get my dinner at the club. Good night." He went into the hall, took his hat and stick from the stand, and left the house.

She was somewhat familiar with such scenes. They had often made her very unhappy. On a few previous occasions she had been completely deprived of any desire to finish her dinner. Sometimes she had gone into the kitchen to administer a tardy rebuke to the cook. Once she went to her room and studied the cookbook during an entire evening, finally writing out a menu for the week, which left her harassed with a feeling that, after all, she had accomplished no good that was worth the name.

But that evening Edna finished her dinner alone, with forced deliberation. Her face was flushed and her eyes flamed with some inward fire that lighted them. After finishing her dinner she went to her room, having instructed the boy to tell any other callers that she was indisposed.

It was a large, beautiful room, rich and picturesque in the soft, dim light which the maid had turned low. She went and stood at an open window and looked out upon the deep tangle of the garden below. All the mystery and witchery of the night seemed to have gathered there amid the perfumes and the dusky and tortuous outlines of flowers and foliage. She was seeking herself and finding herself in just such sweet, half-darkness which met her moods. But the voices were not soothing that came to her from the darkness and the sky above and the stars. They jeered and sounded mournful notes without promise, devoid even of hope. She turned back into the room and began to walk to and fro down its whole length, without stopping, without resting. She carried in her hands a thin handkerchief, which she tore into ribbons, rolled into a ball, and flung from her. Once she stopped, and taking off her wedding ring, flung it upon the carpet. When she saw it lying there, she stamped her heel upon it, striving to crush it. But her small boot heel did not make an indenture, not a mark upon the little glittering circlet.

In a sweeping passion she seized a glass vase from the table and flung it upon the tiles of the hearth. She wanted to destroy something. The crash and clatter were what she wanted to hear.

A maid, alarmed at the din of breaking glass, entered the room to discover what was the matter.

"A vase fell upon the hearth," said Edna. "Never mind; leave it till morning."

"Oh! you might get some of the glass in your feet, ma'am," insisted the young woman, picking up bits of the broken vase that were scattered upon the carpet. "And here's your ring, ma'am, under the chair."

Edna held out her hand, and taking the ring, slipped it upon her finger.

XVIII

The following morning Mr. Pontellier, upon leaving for his office, asked Edna if she would not meet him in town in order to look at some new fixtures for the library.

"I hardly think we need new fixtures, Léonce. Don't let us get anything new; you are too extravagant. I don't believe you ever think of saving or putting by."

"The way to become rich is to make money, my dear Edna, not to save it," he said. He regretted that she did not feel inclined to go with him and select new fixtures. He kissed her good-bye, and told her she was not looking well and must take care of herself. She was unusually pale and very quiet.

She stood on the front veranda as he quitted the house, and absently picked a few sprays of jessamine[1] that grew upon a trellis near by. She inhaled the odor of the blossoms and thrust them into the bosom of her white morning gown. The boys were dragging along the banquette[2] a small "express wagon," which they had filled with blocks and sticks. The quadroon was following them with little quick steps, having assumed a fictitious animation and alacrity for the occasion. A fruit vender was crying his wares in the street.

Edna looked straight before her with a self-absorbed expression upon her face. She felt no interest in anything about her. The street, the children, the fruit vender, the flowers growing there under her eyes, were all part and parcel of an alien world which had suddenly become antagonistic.

She went back into the house. She had thought of speaking to the cook concerning her blunders of the previous night; but Mr. Pontellier

1. Jasmine.
2. A raised platform serving as a sidewalk.

had saved her that disagreeable mission, for which she was so poorly fitted. Mr. Pontellier's arguments were usually convincing with those whom he employed. He left home feeling quite sure that he and Edna would sit down that evening, and possibly a few subsequent evenings, to a dinner deserving of the name.

Edna spent an hour or two in looking over some of her old sketches. She could see their shortcomings and defects, which were glaring in her eyes. She tried to work a little, but found she was not in the humor. Finally she gathered together a few of the sketches—those which she considered the least discreditable; and she carried them with her when, a little later, she dressed and left the house. She looked handsome and distinguished in her street gown. The tan of the seashore had left her face, and her forehead was smooth, white, and polished beneath her heavy, yellow-brown hair. There were a few freckles on her face, and a small, dark mole near the under lip and one on the temple, half-hidden in her hair.

As Edna walked along the street she was thinking of Robert. She was still under the spell of her infatuation. She had tried to forget him, realizing the inutility of remembering. But the thought of him was like an obsession, ever pressing itself upon her. It was not that she dwelt upon details of their acquaintance, or recalled in any special or peculiar way his personality; it was his being, his existence, which dominated her thought, fading sometimes as if it would melt into the mist of the forgotten, reviving again with an intensity which filled her with an incomprehensible longing.

Edna was on her way to Madame Ratignolle's. Their intimacy, begun at Grand Isle, had not declined, and they had seen each other with some frequency since their return to the city. The Ratignolles lived at no great distance from Edna's home, on the corner of a side street, where Monsieur Ratignolle owned and conducted a drug store which enjoyed a steady and prosperous trade. His father had been in the business before him, and Monsieur Ratignolle stood well in the community and bore an enviable reputation for integrity and clear-headedness. His family lived in commodious apartments over the store, having an entrance on the side within the *porte cochère*.[3] There was something which Edna thought very French, very foreign, about their whole manner of living. In the large and pleasant salon which extended across the width of the house, the Ratignolles entertained their friends once a fortnight with a *soirée musicale*,[4] sometimes diversified by card-playing. There was a friend who played upon the 'cello. One brought his flute and another his violin, while there were some who sang and a number who performed upon the piano with various degrees of taste and agility. The Ratignolles'

3. In America, a porch under which a carriage is driven in order to protect travelers alighting or boarding.
4. An evening of music.

soirées musicales were widely known, and it was considered a privilege to be invited to them.

Edna found her friend engaged in assorting the clothes which had returned that morning from the laundry. She at once abandoned her occupation upon seeing Edna, who had been ushered without ceremony into her presence.

" 'Cité can do it as well as I; it is really her business," she explained to Edna, who apologized for interrupting her. And she summoned a young black woman, whom she instructed, in French, to be very careful in checking off the list which she handed her. She told her to notice particularly if a fine linen handkerchief of Monsieur Ratignolle's, which was missing last week, had been returned; and to be sure to set to one side such pieces as required mending and darning.

Then placing an arm around Edna's waist, she led her to the front of the house, to the salon, where it was cool and sweet with the odor of great roses that stood upon the hearth in jars.

Madame Ratignolle looked more beautiful than ever there at home, in a negligé which left her arms almost wholly bare and exposed the rich, melting curves of her white throat.

"Perhaps I shall be able to paint your picture some day," said Edna with a smile when they were seated. She produced the roll of sketches and started to unfold them. "I believe I ought to work again. I feel as if I wanted to be doing something. What do you think of them? Do you think it worth while to take it up again and study some more? I might study for a while with Laidpore."[5]

She knew that Madame Ratignolle's opinion in such a matter would be next to valueless, that she herself had not alone decided, but determined; but she sought the words and praise and encouragement that would help her to put heart into her venture.

"Your talent is immense, dear!"

"Nonsense!" protested Edna, well pleased.

"Immense, I tell you," persisted Madame Ratignolle, surveying the sketches one by one, at close range, then holding them at arm's length, narrowing her eyes, and dropping her head on one side. "Surely, this Bavarian peasant is worthy of framing; and this basket of apples! never have I seen anything more lifelike. One might almost be tempted to reach out a hand and take one."

Edna could not control a feeling which bordered upon complacency at her friend's praise, even realizing, as she did, its true worth. She retained a few of the sketches, and gave all the rest to Madame Ratignolle, who appreciated the gift far beyond its value and proudly exhibited the pictures to her husband when he came up from the store a little later for his midday dinner.

5. No such painter was known to be active in New Orleans. The name was invented by Chopin, perhaps with satiric intent, as in French *laid* means "ugly."

Mr. Ratignolle was one of those men who are called the salt of the earth. His cheerfulness was unbounded, and it was matched by his goodness of heart, his broad charity, and common sense. He and his wife spoke English with an accent which was only discernible through its un-English emphasis and a certain carefulness and deliberation. Edna's husband spoke English with no accent whatever. The Ratignolles understood each other perfectly. If ever the fusion of two human beings into one has been accomplished on this sphere it was surely in their union.

As Edna seated herself at table with them she thought, "Better a dinner of herbs,"[6] though it did not take her long to discover that was no dinner of herbs, but a delicious repast, simple, choice, and in every way satisfying.

Monsieur Ratignolle was delighted to see her, though he found her looking not so well as at Grand Isle, and he advised a tonic. He talked a good deal on various topics, a little politics, some city news and neighborhood gossip. He spoke with an animation and earnestness that gave an exaggerated importance to every syllable he uttered. His wife was keenly interested in everything he said, laying down her fork the better to listen, chiming in, taking the words out of his mouth.

Edna felt depressed rather than soothed after leaving them. The little glimpse of domestic harmony which had been offered her, gave her no regret, no longing. It was not a condition of life which fitted her, and she could see in it but an appalling and hopeless ennui. She was moved by a kind of commiseration for Madame Ratignolle,—a pity for that colorless existence which never uplifted its possessor beyond the region of blind contentment, in which no moment of anguish ever visited her soul, in which she would never have the taste of life's delirium. Edna vaguely wondered what she meant by "life's delirium." It had crossed her thought like some unsought, extraneous impression.

XIX

Edna could not help but think that it was very foolish, very childish, to have stamped upon her wedding ring and smashed the crystal vase upon the tiles. She was visited by no more outbursts, moving her to such futile expedients. She began to do as she liked and to feel as she liked. She completely abandoned her Tuesdays at home, and did not return the visits of those who had called upon her. She made no ineffectual efforts to conduct her household *en bonne ménagère*,[7] going and coming as it suited her fancy, and, so far as she was able, lending herself to any passing caprice.

6. "Better a dinner of herbs where love is, than a stalled ox [that is, one fattened in a stall for killing] and hatred therewith" (Proverbs 15.17).
7. As a good housewife.

Mr. Pontellier had been a rather courteous husband so long as he met a certain tacit submissiveness in his wife. But her new and unexpected line of conduct completely bewildered him. It shocked him. Then her absolute disregard for her duties as a wife angered him. When Mr. Pontellier became rude, Edna grew insolent. She had resolved never to take another step backward.

"It seems to me the utmost folly for a woman at the head of a household, and the mother of children, to spend in an atelier[8] days which would be better employed contriving for the comfort of her family."

"I feel like painting," answered Edna. "Perhaps I shan't always feel like it."

"Then in God's name paint! but don't let the family go to the devil. There's Madame Ratignolle; because she keeps up her music, she doesn't let everything else go to chaos. And she's more of a musician than you are a painter."

"She isn't a musician, and I'm not a painter. It isn't on account of painting that I let things go."

"On account of what, then?"

"Oh! I don't know. Let me alone; you bother me."

It sometimes entered Mr. Pontellier's mind to wonder if his wife were not growing a little unbalanced mentally. He could see plainly that she was not herself. That is, he could not see that she was becoming herself and daily casting aside that fictitious self which we assume like a garment with which to appear before the world.

Her husband let her alone as she requested, and went away to his office. Edna went up to her atelier—a bright room in the top of the house. She was working with great energy and interest, without accomplishing anything, however, which satisfied her even in the smallest degree. For a time she had the whole household enrolled in the service of art. The boys posed for her. They thought it amusing at first, but the occupation soon lost its attractiveness when they discovered that it was not a game arranged especially for their entertainment. The quadroon sat for hours before Edna's palette, patient as a savage, while the housemaid took charge of the children, and the drawing-room went undusted. But the house-maid, too, served her term as model when Edna perceived that the young woman's back and shoulders were molded on classic lines, and that her hair, loosened from its confining cap, became an inspiration. While Edna worked she sometimes sang low the little air, "Ah! si tu savais!"

It moved her with recollections. She could hear again the ripple of the water, the flapping sail. She could see the glint of the moon upon the bay, and could feel the soft, gusty beating of the hot south wind. A

8. Studio.

subtle current of desire passed through her body, weakening her hold upon the brushes and making her eyes burn.

There were days when she was very happy without knowing why. She was happy to be alive and breathing, when her whole being seemed to be one with the sunlight, the color, the odors, the luxuriant warmth of some perfect Southern day. She liked then to wander alone into strange and unfamiliar places. She discovered many a sunny, sleepy corner, fashioned to dream in. And she found it good to dream and to be alone and unmolested.

There were days when she was unhappy, she did not know why,— when it did not seem worth while to be glad or sorry, to be alive or dead; when life appeared to her like a grotesque pandemonium and humanity like worms struggling blindly toward inevitable annihilation. She could not work on such a day, nor weave fancies to stir her pulses and warm her blood.

XX

It was during such a mood that Edna hunted up Mademoiselle Reisz. She had not forgotten the rather disagreeable impression left upon her by their last interview; but she nevertheless felt a desire to see her— above all, to listen while she played upon the piano. Quite early in the afternoon she started upon her quest for the pianist. Unfortunately she had mislaid or lost Mademoiselle Reisz's card, and looking up her address in the city directory, she found that the woman lived on Bienvilles Street,[9] some distance away. The directory which fell into her hands was a year or more old, however, and upon reaching the number indicated, Edna discovered that the house was occupied by a respectable family of mulattoes who had *chambres garnies*[1] to let. They had been living there for six months, and knew absolutely nothing of a Mademoiselle Reisz. In fact, they knew nothing of any of their neighbors; their lodgers were all people of the highest distinction, they assured Edna. She did not linger to discuss class distinctions with Madame Pouponne, but hastened to a neighboring grocery store, feeling sure that Mademoiselle would have left her address with the proprietor.

He knew Mademoiselle Reisz a good deal better than he wanted to know her, he informed his questioner. In truth, he did not want to know her at all, anything concerning her—the most disagreeable and unpopular woman who ever lived in Bienville Street. He thanked heaven she had left the neighborhood, and was equally thankful that he did not know where she had gone.

Edna's desire to see Mademoiselle Reisz had increased tenfold since

9. On the opposite side of the French Quarter from the Pontelliers' house, the street runs down to the shipyards.
1. Furnished rooms.

these unlooked-for obstacles had arisen to thwart it. She was wondering who could give her the information she sought, when it suddenly occured to her that Madame Lebrun would be the one most likely to do so. She knew it was useless to ask Madame Ratignolle, who was on the most distant terms with the musician, and preferred to know nothing concerning her. She had once been almost as emphatic in expressing herself upon the subject as the corner grocer.

Edna knew that Madame Lebrun had returned to the city, for it was the middle of November. And she also knew where the Lebruns lived, on Chartres Street.[2]

Their home from the outside looked like a prison, with iron bars before the door and lower windows. The iron bars were a relic of the old *régime*,[3] and no one had ever thought of dislodging them. At the side was a high fence enclosing the garden. A gate or door opening upon the street was locked. Edna rang the bell at this side garden gate, and stood upon the banquette, waiting to be admitted.

It was Victor who opened the gate for her. A black woman, wiping her hands upon her apron, was close at his heels. Before she saw them Edna could hear them in altercation, the woman—plainly an anomaly—claiming the right to be allowed to perform her duties, one of which was to answer the bell.

Victor was surprised and delighted to see Mrs. Pontellier, and he made no attempt to conceal either his astonishment or his delight. He was a dark-browed, good-looking youngster of nineteen, greatly resembling his mother, but with ten times her impetuosity. He instructed the black woman to go at once and inform Madame Lebrun that Mrs. Pontellier desired to see her. The woman grumbled a refusal to do part of her duty when she had not been permitted to do it all, and started back to her interrupted task of weeding the garden. Whereupon Victor administered a rebuke in the form of a volley of abuse, which owing to its rapidity and incoherence, was all but incomprehensible to Edna. Whatever it was, the rebuke was convincing, for the woman dropped her hoe and went mumbling into the house.

Edna did not wish to enter. It was very pleasant there on the side porch, where there were chairs, a wicker lounge, and a small table. She seated herself, for she was tired from her long tramp; and she began to rock gently and smooth out the folds of her silk parasol. Victor drew up his chair beside her. He at once explained that the black woman's offensive conduct was all due to imperfect training, as he was not there to take her in hand. He had only come up from the island the morning before, and expected to return next day. He stayed all winter at the island; he lived there, and kept the place in order and got things ready for the summer visitors.

2. In the heart of the French Quarter.
3. The Spanish regime (1766–1803).

But a man needed occasional relaxation, he informed Mrs. Pontellier, and every now and again he drummed up a pretext to bring him to the city. My! but he had had a time of it the evening before! He wouldn't want his mother to know, and he began to talk in a whisper. He was scintillant with recollections. Of course, he couldn't think of telling Mrs. Pontellier all about it, she being a woman and not comprehending such things. But it all began with a girl peeping and smiling at him through the shutters as he passed by. Oh! but she was a beauty! Certainly he smiled back, and went up and talked to her. Mrs. Pontellier did not know him if she supposed he was one to let an opportunity like that escape him. Despite herself, the youngster amused her. She must have betrayed in her look some degree of interest or entertainment. The boy grew more daring, and Mrs. Pontellier might have found herself, in a little while, listening to a highly colored story but for the timely appearance of Madame Lebrun.

That lady was still clad in white, according to her custom of the summer. Her eyes beamed an effusive welcome. Would not Mrs. Pontellier go inside? Would she partake of some refreshment? Why had she not been there before? How was that dear Mr. Pontellier and how were those sweet children? Has Mrs. Pontellier ever known such a warm November?

Victor went and reclined on the wicker lounge behind his mother's chair, where he commanded a view of Edna's face. He had taken her parasol from her hands while he spoke to her, and he now lifted it and twirled it above him as he lay on his back. When Madame Lebrun complained that it was so dull coming back to the city; that she saw so few people now; that even Victor, when he came up from the island for a day or two, had so much to occupy him and engage his time; then it was that the youth went into contortions on the lounge and winked mischievously at Edna. She somehow felt like a confederate in crime, and tried to look severe and disapproving.

There had been but two letters from Robert, with little in them, they told her. Victor said it was really not worth while to go inside for the letters, when his mother entreated him to go in search of them. He remembered the contents, which in truth he rattled off very glibly when put to the test.

One letter was written from Vera Cruz and the other from the City of Mexico. He had met Montel, who was doing everything toward his advancement. So far, the financial situation was no improvement over the one he had left in New Orleans, but of course the prospects were vastly better. He wrote of the City of Mexico, the buildings, the people and their habits, the conditions of life which he found there. He sent his love to the family. He inclosed a check to his mother, and hoped she would affectionately remember him to all his friends. That was about the substance of the two letters. Edna felt that if there had been a message for her, she would have received it. The despondent frame of mind in which she had left home began again to overtake her, and she remembered that she wished to find Mademoiselle Reisz. Madame Lebrun knew where Mademoiselle Reisz lived. She gave Edna the address, regretting that she would not consent to stay and spend the remainder of the afternoon, and pay a visit to Mademoiselle Reisz some other day. The afternoon was already well advanced.

Victor escorted her out upon the banquette, lifted her parasol, and held it over her while he walked to the car with her. He entreated her to bear in mind that the disclosures of the afternoon were strictly confidential. She laughed and bantered him a little, remembering too late that she should have been dignified and reserved.

"How handsome Mrs. Pontellier looked!" said Madame Lebrun to her son.

"Ravishing!" he admitted. "The city atmosphere has improved her. Some way she doesn't seem like the same woman."

XXI

Some people contended that the reason Mademoiselle Reisz always chose apartments up under the roof was to discourage the approach of beggars, peddlars and callers. There were plenty of windows in her little front room. They were for the most part dingy, but as they were nearly always open it did not make so much difference. They often admitted into the room a good deal of smoke and soot; but at the same time all the light and air that there was came through them. From her windows could be seen the crescent of the river, the masts of ships and the big chimneys of the Mississippi steamers. A magnificent piano crowded the apartment. In the next room she slept, and in the third and last she harbored a gasoline stove on which she cooked her meals when disinclined to descend to the neighboring restaurant. It was there also that she ate, keeping her belongings in a rare old buffet, dingy and battered from a hundred years of use.

When Edna knocked at Mademoiselle Reisz's front room door and entered, she discovered that person standing beside the window, engaged in mending or patching an old prunella gaiter.[4] The little musician laughed all over when she saw Edna. Her laugh consisted of a contortion of the face and all the muscles of the body. She seemed strikingly homely, standing there in the afternoon light. She still wore the shabby lace and the artificial bunch of violets on the side of her head.

"So you remembered me at last," said Mademoiselle. "I had said to myself, 'Ah, bah! she will never come.' "

"Did you want me to come?" asked Edna with a smile.

"I had not thought much about it," answered Mademoiselle. The

---

4. A button shoe with a cloth upper section.

two had seated themselves on a little bumpy sofa which stood against the wall. "I am glad, however, that you came. I have the water boiling back there, and was just about to make some coffee. You will drink a cup with me. And how is *la belle dame?*[5] Always handsome! always healthy! always contented!" She took Edna's hand between her strong wiry fingers, holding it loosely without warmth, and executing a sort of double theme upon the back and palm.

"Yes," she went on; "I sometimes thought: 'She will never come. She promised as those women in society always do, without meaning it. She will not come.' For I really don't believe you like me, Mrs. Pontellier."

"I don't know whether I like you or not," replied Edna, gazing down at the little woman with a quizzical look.

The candor of Mrs. Pontellier's admission greatly pleased Mademoiselle Reisz. She expressed her gratification by repairing forthwith to the region of the gasoline stove and rewarding her guest with the promised cup of coffee. The coffee and the biscuit accompanying it proved very acceptable to Edna, who had declined refreshment at Madame Lebrun's and was now beginning to feel hungry. Mademoiselle set the tray which she brought in upon a small table near at hand, and seated herself once again on the lumpy sofa.

"I have had a letter from your friend," she remarked, as she poured a little cream into Edna's cup and handed it to her.

"My friend?"

"Yes, your friend Robert. He wrote to me from the City of Mexico."

"Wrote to *you?*" repeated Edna in amazement, stirring her coffee absently.

"Yes, to me. Why not? Don't stir all the warmth out of your coffee; drink it. Though the letter might as well have been sent to you; it was nothing but Mrs. Pontellier from beginning to end."

"Let me see it," requested the young woman, entreatingly.

"No, a letter concerns no one but the person who writes it and the one to whom it is written."

"Haven't you just said it concerned me from beginning to end?"

"It was written about you, not to you. 'Have you seen Mrs. Pontellier? How is she looking?' he asks. 'As Mrs. Pontellier says,' or 'as Mrs. Pontellier once said.' 'If Mrs. Pontellier should call upon you, play for her that Impromptu of Chopin's,[6] my favorite. I heard it here a day or two ago, but not as you play it. I should like to know how it affects her,' and so on, as if he supposed we were constantly in each other's society."

"Let me see the letter."

"Oh, no."

"Have you answered it?"

<hr />

5. "The beautiful woman."
6. Chopin composed three works with this title during the years of his passionate liaison with George Sand.

"No."

"Let me see the letter."

"No, and again, no."

"Then play the Impromptu for me."

"It is growing late; what time do you have to be home?"

"Time doesn't concern me. Your question seems a little rude. Play the Impromptu."

"But you have told me nothing of yourself. What are you doing?"

"Painting!" laughed Edna. "I am becoming an artist. Think of it!"

"Ah! an artist! You have pretensions, Madame."

"Why pretensions? Do you think I could not become an artist?"

"I do not know you well enough to say. I do not know your talent or your temperament. To be an artist includes much; one must possess many gifts—absolute gifts—which have not been acquired by one's own effort. And, moreover, to succeed, the artist must possess the courageous soul."

"What do you mean by the courageous soul?"

"Courageous, ma foi![7] The brave soul. The soul that dares and defies."

"Show me the letter and play for me the Impromptu. You see that I have persistence. Does that quality count for anything in art?"

"It counts with a foolish old woman whom you have captivated," replied Mademoiselle, with her wriggling laugh.

The letter was right there at hand in the drawer of the little table upon which Edna had just placed her coffee cup. Mademoiselle opened the drawer and drew forth the letter, the topmost one. She placed it in Edna's hands, and without further comment arose and went to the piano.

Mademoiselle played a soft interlude. It was an improvisation. She sat low at the instrument, and the lines of her body settled into ungraceful curves and angles that gave it an appearance of deformity. Gradually and imperceptibly the interlude melted into the soft opening minor chords of the Chopin Impromptu.

Edna did not know when the Impromptu began or ended. She sat in the sofa corner reading Robert's letter by the fading light. Mademoiselle had glided from the Chopin into the quivering love-notes of Isolde's song,[8] and back again to the Impromptu with its soulful and poignant longing.

The shadows deepened in the little room. The music grew strange and fantastic—turbulent, insistent, plaintive and soft with entreaty. The shadows grew deeper. The music filled the room. It floated out upon the night, over the housetops, the crescent of the river, losing itself in the silence of the upper air.

7. "Indeed!"
8. From Wagner's opera *Tristan und Isolde*, based on a medieval legend of ill-fated love. Isolde's song, known as her *Liebestod* ("Love-death"), is sung as she bids her dead lover farewell and falls dead herself in his arms.

Edna was sobbing, just as she had wept one midnight at Grand Isle when strange, new voices awoke in her. She arose in some agitation to take her departure. "May I come again, Mademoiselle?" she asked at the threshold.

"Come whenever you feel like it. Be careful; the stairs and landings are dark; don't stumble."

Mademoiselle reëntered and lit a candle. Robert's letter was on the floor. She stooped and picked it up. It was crumpled and damp with tears. Mademoiselle smoothed the letter out, restored it to the envelope, and replaced it in the table drawer.

XXII

One morning on his way into town Mr. Pontellier stopped at the house of his old friend and family physician, Doctor Mandelet. The Doctor was a semi-retired physician, resting, as the saying is, upon his laurels. He bore a reputation for wisdom rather than skill—leaving the active practice of medicine to his assistants and younger comtemporaries—and was much sought for in matters of consultation. A few families, united to him by bonds of friendship, he still attended when they required the services of a physician. The Pontelliers were among these.

Mr. Pontellier found the Doctor reading at the open window of his study. His house stood rather far back from the street, in the center of a delightful garden, so that it was quiet and peaceful at the old gentleman's study window. He was a great reader. He stared up disapprovingly over his eye-glasses as Mr. Pontellier entered, wondering who had the temerity to disturb him at that hour of the morning.

"Ah, Pontellier! Not sick, I hope. Come and have a seat. What news do you bring this morning?" He was quite portly, with a profusion of gray hair, and small blue eyes which age had robbed of much of their brightness but none of their penetration.

"Oh! I'm never sick, Doctor. You know that I come of tough fiber —of that old Creole race of Pontelliers that dry up and finally blow away. I came to consult—no, not precisely to consult—to talk to you about Edna. I don't know what ails her."

"Madame Pontellier not well?" marveled the Doctor. "Why, I saw her—I think it was a week ago—walking along Canal Street,[9] the picture of health, it seemed to me."

"Yes, yes; she seems quite well," said Mr. Pontellier, leaning forward and whirling his stick between his two hands; "but she doesn't act well. She's odd, she's not like herself. I can't make her out, and I thought perhaps you'd help me."

9. The main street of downtown New Orleans, separating the old French city from the newer American section.

"How does she act?" inquired the doctor.

"Well, it isn't easy to explain," said Mr. Pontellier, throwing himself back in his chair. "She lets the housekeeping go to the dickens."

"Well, well; women are not all alike, my dear Pontellier. We've got to consider—"

"I know that; I told you I couldn't explain. Her whole attitude—toward me and everybody and everything—has changed. You know I have a quick temper, but I don't want to quarrel or be rude to a woman, especially my wife; yet I'm driven to it, and feel like ten thousand devils after I've made a fool of myself. She's making it devilishly uncomfortable for me," he went on nervously. "She's got some sort of notion in her head concerning the eternal rights of women; and—you understand—we meet in the morning at the breakfast table."

The old gentleman lifted his shaggy eyebrows, protruded his thick nether lip, and tapped the arms of his chair with his cushioned fingertips.

"What have you been doing to her, Pontellier?"

"Doing! *Parbleu!*"

"Has she," asked the Doctor, with a smile, "has she been associating of late with a circle of pseudo-intellectual women[1]—super-spiritual superior beings? My wife has been telling me about them."

"That's the trouble," broke in Mr. Pontellier, "she hasn't been associating with any one. She has abandoned her Tuesdays at home, has thrown over all her acquaintances, and goes tramping about by herself, moping in the street-cars, getting in after dark. I tell you she's peculiar. I don't like it; I feel a little worried over it."

This was a new aspect for the Doctor. "Nothing hereditary?" he asked, seriously. "Nothing peculiar about her family antecedents, is there?"

"Oh, no, indeed! She comes of sound old Presbyterian Kentucky stock. The old gentleman, her father, I have heard, used to atone for his week-day sins with his Sunday devotions. I know for a fact, that his race horses literally ran away with the prettiest bit of Kentucky farming land I had ever laid eyes upon. Margaret—you know Margaret—she has all the Presbyterianism undiluted. And the youngest is something of a vixen. By the way, she gets married in a couple of weeks from now."

"Send your wife up to the wedding," exclaimed the Doctor, foreseeing a happy solution. "Let her stay among her own people for a while; it will do her good."

"That's what I want her to do. She won't go to the marriage. She says a wedding is one of the most lamentable spectacles on earth. Nice thing for a woman to say to her husband!" exclaimed Mr. Pontellier, fuming anew at the recollection.

"Pontellier," said the Doctor, after a moment's reflection, "let your

---

1. Women's clubs flourished during the late nineteenth century in America. They were a source of education for women as well as an arena for political organization. As the doctor's remark indicates, the club movement was met with scorn in some quarters.

wife alone for a while. Don't bother her, and don't let her bother you. Woman, my dear friend, is a very peculiar and delicate organism—a sensitive and highly organized woman, such as I know Mrs. Pontellier to be, is especially peculiar. It would require an inspired psychologist to deal successfully with them. And when ordinary fellows like you and me attempt to cope with their idiosyncrasies the result is bungling. Most women are moody and whimsical. This is some passing whim of your wife, due to some cause or causes which you and I needn't try to fathom. But it will pass happily over, especially if you let her alone. Send her around to see me."[2]

"Oh! I couldn't do that; there'd be no reason for it," objected Mr. Pontellier.

"Then I'll go around and see her," said the Doctor. "I'll drop in to dinner some evening *en bon ami*."[3]

"Do! by all means," urged Mr. Pontellier. "What evening will you come? Say Thursday. Will you come Thursday?" he asked, rising to take his leave.

"Very well; Thursday. My wife may possibly have some engagement for me Thursday. In case she has, I shall let you know. Otherwise, you may expect me."

Mr. Pontellier turned before leaving to say:

"I am going to New York on business very soon. I have a big scheme on hand, and want to be on the field proper to pull the ropes and handle the ribbons.[4] We'll let you in on the inside if you say so, Doctor," he laughed.

"No, I thank you, my dear sir," returned the Doctor. "I leave such ventures to you younger men with the fever of life still in your blood."

"What I wanted to say," continued Mr. Pontellier, with his hand on the knob; "I may have to be absent a good while. Would you advise me to take Edna along?"

"By all means, if she wishes to go. If not, leave her here. Don't contradict her. The mood will pass, I assure you. It may take a month, two, three months—possibly longer, but it will pass; have patience."

"Well, good-by, *à jeudi*,"[5] said Mr. Pontellier, as he let himself out.

The Doctor would have liked during the course of conversation to ask, "Is there any man in the case?" but he knew his Creole too well to make such a blunder as that.

He did not resume his book immediately, but sat for a while meditatively looking out into the garden.

---

2. See Ann Douglas Wood, "The Fashionable Diseases: Women's Complaints and Their Treatment in Nineteenth-Century America," *Journal of Interdisciplinary History* 4 (Summer 1973): 25–52, for a discussion of upper-class women's "nervous" disorders. See also John S. Haller, Jr., and Robin M. Haller, *The Physician and Sexuality in Victorian America* (New York: Norton, 1977), and Elaine Showalter, *The Female Malady: Women, Madness and English Culture, 1830–1980* (New York: Pantheon, 1985).
3. "As a friend."
4. Handle the reins—that is, be in charge.
5. "Until Thursday."

XXIII

Edna's father was in the city, and had been with them several days. She was not very warmly or deeply attached to him, but they had certain tastes in common, and when together they were companionable. His coming was in the nature of a welcome disturbance; it seemed to furnish a new direction for her emotions.

He had come to purchase a wedding gift for his daughter, Janet, and an outfit for himself in which he might make a creditable appearance at her marriage. Mr. Pontellier had selected the bridal gift, as every one immediately connected with him always deferred to his taste in such matters. And his suggestions on the question of dress—which too often assumes the nature of a problem—were of inestimable value to his father-in-law. But for the past few days the old gentleman had been upon Edna's hands, and in his society she was becoming acquainted with a new set of sensations. He had been a colonel in the Confederate army, and still maintained, with the title, the military bearing which had always accompanied it. His hair and mustache were white and silky, emphasizing the rugged bronze of his face. He was tall and thin, and wore his coats padded, which gave a fictitious breadth and depth to his shoulders and chest. Edna and her father looked very distinguished together, and excited a good deal of notice during their perambulations. Upon his arrival she began by introducing him to her atelier and making a sketch of him. He took the whole matter very seriously. If her talent had been ten-fold greater than it was, it would not have surprised him, convinced as he was that he had bequeathed to all of his daughters the germs of a masterful capability, which only depended upon their own efforts to be directed toward successful achievement.

Before her pencil he sat rigid and unflinching, as he had faced the cannon's mouth in days gone by. He resented the intrusion of the children, who gaped with wondering eyes at him, sitting so stiff up there in their mother's bright atelier. When they drew near he motioned them away with an expressive action of the foot, loath to disturb the fixed lines of his countenance, his arms, or his rigid shoulders.

Edna, anxious to entertain him, invited Mademoiselle Reisz to meet him, having promised him a treat in her piano playing; but Mademoiselle declined the invitation. So together they attended a *soirée musicale* at the Ratignolles'. Monsieur and Madame Ratignolle made much of the Colonel, installing him as the guest of honor and engaging him at once to dine with them the following Sunday, or any day which he might select. Madame coquetted with him in the most captivating and naïve manner, with eyes, gestures, and a profusion of compliments, till the Colonel's old head felt thirty years younger on his padded shoulders. Edna marveled, not comprehending. She herself was almost devoid of coquetry.

There were one or two men whom she observed at the *soirée musicale*; but she would never have felt moved to any kittenish display to attract their notice—to any feline or feminine wiles to express herself toward them. Their personality attracted her in an agreeable way. Her fancy selected them, and she was glad when a lull in the music gave them an opportunity to meet her and talk with her. Often on the street the glance of strange eyes had lingered in her memory, and sometimes had disturbed her.

Mr. Pontellier did not attend these *soirées musicales*. He considered them *bourgeois*,[6] and found more diversion at the club. To Madame Ratignolle he said the music dispensed at her *soirées* was too "heavy," too far beyond his untrained comprehension. His excuse flattered her. But she disapproved of Mr. Pontellier's club, and she was frank enough to tell Edna so.

"It's a pity Mr. Pontellier doesn't stay home more in the evenings. I think you would be more—well, if you don't mind my saying it—more united, if he did."

"Oh! dear no!" said Edna, with a blank look in her eyes. "What should I do if he stayed home? We wouldn't have anything to say to each other."

She had not much of anything to say to her father, for that matter; but he did not antagonize her. She discovered that he interested her, though she realized that he might not interest her long; and for the first time in her life she felt as if she were thoroughly acquainted with him. He kept her busy serving him and ministering to his wants. It amused her to do so. She would not permit a servant or one of the children to do anything for him which she might do herself. Her husband noticed, and thought it was the expression of a deep filial attachment which he had never suspected.

The Colonel drank numerous "toddies" during the course of the day, which left him, however, imperturbed. He was an expert at concocting strong drinks. He had even invented some, to which he had given fantastic names, and for whose manufacture he required diverse ingredients that it devolved upon Edna to procure for him.

When Doctor Mandelet dined with the Pontelliers on Thursday he could discern in Mrs. Pontellier no trace of that morbid condition which her husband had reported to him. She was excited and in a manner radiant. She and her father had been to the race course, and their thoughts when they seated themselves at table were still occupied with the events of the afternoon, and their talk was still of the track. The Doctor had not kept pace with turf affairs. He had certain recollections of racing in what he called "the good old times" when the Lecompte stables[7] flourished, and he drew upon this fund of memories so that he

---

6. Middle-class, common.
7. New Orleans was a celebrated racing center before the Civil War, boasting four racetracks. Chopin uses the name of the most famous Louisiana racehorse before the Civil War.

might not be left out and seem wholly devoid of the modern spirit. But he failed to impose upon the Colonel, and was even far from impressing him with this trumped-up knowledge of bygone days. Edna had staked her father on his last venture, with the most gratifying results to both of them. Besides, they had met some very charming people, according to the Colonel's impressions. Mrs. Mortimer Merriman and Mrs. James Highcamp, who were there with Alcée Arobin, had joined them and had enlivened the house in a fashion that warmed him to think of.

Mr. Pontellier himself had no particular leaning toward horse-racing, and was even rather inclined to discourage it as a pastime, especially when he considered the fate of that blue-grass farm in Kentucky. He endeavored, in a general way, to express a particular disapproval and only succeeded in arousing the ire and opposition of his father-in-law. A pretty dispute followed, in which Edna warmly espoused her father's cause and the Doctor remained neutral.

He observed his hostess attentively from under his shaggy brows, and noted a subtle change which had transformed her from the listless woman he had known into a being who, for the moment, seemed palpitant with the forces of life. Her speech was warm and energetic. There was no repression in her glance or gesture. She reminded him of some beautiful, sleek animal waking up in the sun.

The dinner was excellent. The claret was warm and the champagne was cold, and under their beneficent influence the threatened unpleasantness melted and vanished with the fumes of the wine.

Mr. Pontellier warmed up and grew reminiscent. He told some amusing plantation experiences, recollections of old Iberville and his youth, when he hunted 'possum in company with some friendly darky; thrashed the pecan trees, shot the grosbec,[8] and roamed the woods and fields in mischievous idleness.

The Colonel, with little sense of humor and of the fitness of things, related a somber episode of those dark and bitter days, in which he had acted a conspicious part and always formed a central figure. Nor was the Doctor happier in his selection, when he told the old, ever new and curious story of the waning of a woman's love, seeking strange, new channels, only to return to its legitimate source after days of fierce unrest. It was one of the many little human documents which had been unfolded to him during his long career as a phsycian. The story did not seem especially to impress Edna. She had one of her own to tell, of a woman who paddled away with her lover one night in a pirogue and never came back. They were lost amid the Baratarian Islands, and no one ever heard of them or found trace of them from that day to this. It was a pure invention. She said that Madame Antoine had related it to her. That, also, was an invention. Perhaps it was a dream she had had. But every glowing word seemed real to those who listened. They could feel the

8. Grosbeak, birds distinguished by their large bills.

hot breath of the Southern night; they could hear the long sweep of the pirogue through the glistening moonlit water, the beating of birds' wings, rising startled from among the reeds in the salt-water pools; they could see the faces of the lovers, pale, close together, rapt in oblivious forgetfulness, drifting into the unknown.

The champagne was cold, and its subtle fumes played fantastic tricks with Edna's memory that night.

Outside, away from the glow of the fire and the soft lamplight, the night was chill and murky. The Doctor doubled his old-fashioned cloak across his breast as he strode home through the darkness. He knew his fellow-creatures better than most men; knew that inner life which so seldom unfolds itself to unanointed eyes. He was sorry he had accepted Pontellier's invitation. He was growing old, and beginning to need rest and an imperturbed spirit. He did not want the secrets of other lives thrust upon him.

"I hope it isn't Arobin," he muttered to himself as he walked. "I hope to heaven it isn't Alcée Arobin."

XXIV

Edna and her father had a warm, and almost violent dispute upon the subject of her refusal to attend her sister's wedding. Mr. Pontellier declined to interfere, to interpose either his influence or his authority. He was following Doctor Mandelet's advice, and letting her do as she liked. The Colonel reproached his daughter for her lack of filial kindness and respect, her want of sisterly affection and womanly consideration. His arguments were labored and unconvincing. He doubted if Janet would accept any excuse—forgetting that Edna had offered none. He doubted if Janet would ever speak to her again, and he was sure Margaret would not.

Edna was glad to be rid of her father when he finally took himself off with his wedding garments and his bridal gifts, with his padded shoulders, his Bible reading, his "toddies" and ponderous oaths.

Mr. Pontellier followed him closely. He meant to stop at the wedding on his way to New York and endeavor by every means which money and love could devise to atone somewhat for Edna's incomprehensible action.

"You are too lenient, too lenient by far, Léonce," asserted the Colonel. "Authority, coercion are what is needed. Put your foot down good and hard; the only way to manage a wife. Take my word for it."

The Colonel was perhaps unaware that he had coerced his own wife into her grave. Mr. Pontellier had a vague suspicion of it which he thought it needless to mention at that late day.

Edna was not so consciously gratified at her husband's leaving home as she had been over the departure of her father. As the day approached when he was to leave her for a comparatively long stay, she grew melting and affectionate, remembering his many acts of consideration and his repeated expressions of an ardent attachment. She was solicitous about his health and his welfare. She bustled around, looking after his clothing, thinking about heavy underwear, quite as Madame Ratignolle would have done under similar circumstances. She cried when he went away, calling him her dear, good friend, and she was quite certain she would grow lonely before very long and go to join him in New York.

But after all, a radiant peace settled upon her when she at last found herself alone. Even the children were gone. Old Madame Pontellier had come herself and carried them off to Iberville with their quadroon. The old madame did not venture to say she was afraid they would be neglected during Léonce's absence; she hardly ventured to think so. She was hungry for them—even a little fierce in her attachment. She did not want them to be wholly "children of the pavement," she always said when begging to have them for a space. She wished them to know the country, with its streams, its fields, its woods, its freedom, so delicious to the young. She wished them to taste something of the life their father had lived and known and loved when he, too, was a little child.

When Edna was at last alone, she breathed a big, genuine sigh of relief. A feeling that was unfamiliar but very delicious came over her. She walked all through the house, from one room to another, as if inspecting it for the first time. She tried the various chairs and lounges, as if she had never sat and reclined upon them before. And she perambulated around the outside of the house, investigating, looking to see if windows and shutters were secure and in order. The flowers were like new acquaintances; she approached them in a familiar spirit, and made herself at home among them. The garden walks were damp, and Edna called to the maid to bring out her rubber sandals. And there she stayed, and stooped, digging around the plants, trimming, picking dead, dry leaves. The children's little dog came out, interfering, getting in her way. She scolded him, laughing at him, played with him. The garden smelled so good and looked so pretty in the afternoon sunlight. Edna plucked all the bright flowers she could find, and went into the house with them, she and the little dog.

Even the kitchen assumed a sudden interesting character which she had never before perceived. She went in to give directions to the cook, to say that the butcher would have to bring much less meat, that they would require only half their usual quantity of bread, of milk and groceries. She told the cook that she herself would be greatly occupied during Mr. Pontellier's absence, and she begged her to take all thought and responsibility of the larder upon her own shoulders.

That night Edna dined alone. The candelabra, with a few candles in the center of the table, gave all the light she needed. Outside the circle of light in which she sat, the large dining-room looked solemn and shadowy. The cook, placed upon her mettle, served a delicious repast —a luscious tenderloin broiled à point. The wine tasted good; the marron glace[9] seemed to be just what she wanted. It was so pleasant, too, to dine in a comfortable peignoir.

She thought a little sentimentally about Léonce and the children, and wondered what they were doing. As she gave a dainty scrap or two to the doggie, she talked intimately to him about Etienne and Raoul. He was beside himself with astonishment and delight over these companionable advances, and showed his appreciation by his little quick, snappy barks and a lively agitation.

Then Edna sat in the library after dinner and read Emerson[1] until she grew sleepy. She realized that she had neglected her reading, and determined to start anew upon a course of improving studies, now that her time was completely her own to do with as she liked.

After a refreshing bath, Edna went to bed. And as she snuggled comfortably beneath the eiderdown a sense of restfulness invaded her, such as she had not known before.

XXV

When the weather was dark and cloudy Edna could not work. She needed the sun to mellow and temper her mood to the sticking point. She had reached a stage when she seemed to be no longer feeling her way, working, when in the humor, with sureness and ease. And being devoid of ambition, and striving not toward accomplishment, she drew satisfaction from the work in itself.

On rainy or melancholy days Edna went out and sought the society of the friends she had made at Grand Isle. Or else she stayed indoors and nursed a mood with which she was becoming too familiar for her own comfort and peace of mind. It was not despair; but it seemed to her as if life were passing by, leaving its promise broken and unfulfilled. Yet there were other days when she listened, was led on and deceived by fresh promises which her youth held out to her.

She went again to the races, and again. Alcée Arobin and Mrs. Highcamp called for her one bright afternoon in Arobin's drag.[2] Mrs. Highcamp was a worldly but unaffected, intelligent, slim, tall blonde woman in the forties, with an indifferent manner and blue eyes that stared. She had a daughter who served her as a pretext for cultivating the society of young men of fashion. Alcée Arobin was one of them. He was a familiar figure at the race course, the opera, the fashionable clubs. There was a perpetual smile in his eyes, which seldom failed to

---

9. Chestnuts glazed with sugar.
1. Ralph Waldo Emerson (1803–82), American philosopher, essayist, and poet of the transcendental school.
2. A heavy coach with seats on top drawn by four horses.

awaken a corresponding cheerfulness in any one who looked into them and listened to his good-humored voice. His manner was quiet, and at times a little insolent. He possessed a good figure, a pleasing face, not overburdened with depth of thought or feeling; and his dress was that of the conventional man of fashion.

He admired Edna extravagantly, after meeting her at the races with her father. He had met her before on other occasions, but she had seemed to him unapproachable until that day. It was at his instigation that Mrs. Highcamp called to ask her to go with them to the Jockey Club[3] to witness the turf event of the season.

There were possibly a few track men out there who knew the race horse as well as Edna, but there was certainly none who knew it better. She sat between her two companions as one having authority to speak. She laughed at Arobin's pretensions, and deplored Mrs. Highcamp's ignorance. The race horse was a friend and intimate associate of her childhood. The atmosphere of the stables and the breath of the blue grass paddock revived in her memory and lingered in her nostrils. She did not perceive that she was talking like her father as the sleek geldings ambled in review before them. She played for very high stakes, and fortune favored her. The fever of the game flamed in her cheeks and eyes, and it got into her blood and into her brain like an intoxicant. People turned their heads to look at her, and more than one lent an attentive ear to her utterances, hoping thereby to secure the elusive but ever-desired "tip." Arobin caught the contagion of excitement which drew him to Edna like a magnet. Mrs. Highcamp remained, as usual, unmoved, with her indifferent stare and uplifted eyebrows.

Edna stayed and dined with Mrs. Highcamp upon being urged to do so. Arobin also remained and sent away his drag.

The dinner was quiet and uninteresting, save for the cheerful efforts of Arobin to enliven things. Mrs. Highcamp deplored the absence of her daughter from the races, and tried to convey to her what she had missed by going to the "Dante[4] reading" instead of joining them. The girl held a geranium leaf up to her nose and said nothing, but looked knowing and noncommittal. Mr. Highcamp was a plain, bald-headed man, who only talked under compulsion. He was unresponsive. Mrs. Highcamp was full of delicate courtesy and consideration toward her husband. She addressed most of her conversation to him at table. They sat in the library after dinner and read the evening papers together under the drop-light.[5] while the younger people went into the drawing-room near by and talked. Miss Highcamp played some selections from Grieg[6]

3. The New Louisiana Jockey Club, a social club with membership limited to several hundred of the most prominent and wealthy citizens of New Orleans.
4. Dante Alighieri (1265–1321), Italian poet, author of *The Divine Comedy*.
5. Portable gas lamp attached to chandelier or wall fixture.
6. Edvard Grieg (1843–1907), Norwegian composer and conductor during the Romantic-nationalist period, known for his *Peer Gynt Suite*.

upon the piano. She seemed to have apprehended all of the composer's coldness and none of his poetry. While Edna listened she could not help wondering if she had lost her taste for music. When the time came for her to go home, Mr. Highcamp grunted a lame offer to escort her, looking down at his slippered feet with tactless concern. It was Arobin who took her home. The car ride was long, and it was late when they reached Esplanade Street. Arobin asked permission to enter for a second to light his cigarette—his match safe[7] was empty. He filled his match safe, but did not light his cigarette until he left her, after she had expressed her willingness to go to the races with him again.

Edna was neither tired nor sleepy. She was hungry again, for the Highcamp dinner, though of excellent quality, had lacked abundance. She rummaged in the larder and brought forth a slice of "Gruyère" and some crackers. She opened a bottle of beer which she found in the ice-box. Edna felt extremely restless and excited. She vacantly hummed a fantastic tune as she poked at the wood embers on the hearth and munched a cracker.

She wanted something to happen—something, anything; she did not know what. She regretted that she had not made Arobin stay a half hour to talk over the horses with her. She counted the money she had won. But there was nothing else to do, so she went to bed, and tossed there for hours in a sort of monotonous agitation.

In the middle of the night she remembered that she had forgotten to write her regular letter to her husband; and she decided to do so next day and tell him about her afternoon at the Jockey Club. She lay wide awake composing a letter which was nothing like the one which she wrote next day. When the maid awoke her in the morning Edna was dreaming of Mr. Highcamp playing the piano at the entrance of a music store on Canal Street, while his wife was saying to Alcée Arobin, as they boarded an Esplanade Street car:

"What a pity that so much talent has been neglected! but I must go."

When, a few days later, Alcée Arobin again called for Edna in his drag, Mrs. Highcamp was not with him. He said they would pick her up. But as that lady had not been apprised of his intention of picking her up, she was not at home. The daughter was just leaving the house to attend the meeting of a branch Folk Lore Society,[8] and regretted that she could not accompany them. Arobin appeared nonplused, and asked Edna if there were any one else she cared to ask.

She did not deem it worth while to go in search of any of the fashionable acquaintances from whom she had withdrawn herself. She thought of Madame Ratignolle, but knew that her fair friend did not leave the house, except to take a languid walk around the block with

7. Box of noncombustible material made for holding friction matches.
8. The New Orleans Association of the American Folklore Society, founded in 1892 by Alcée Fortier of Tulane University, was very active from 1892 to 1895.

her husband after nightfall. Mademoiselle Reisz would have laughed at such a request from Edna. Madame Lebrun might have enjoyed the outing, but for some reason Edna did not want her. So they went alone, she and Arobin.

The afternoon was intensely interesting to her. The excitement came back upon her like a remittent fever. Her talk grew familiar and confidential. It was no labor to become intimate with Arobin. His manner invited easy confidence. The preliminary stage of becoming acquainted was one which he always endeavored to ignore when a pretty and engaging woman was concerned.

He stayed and dined with Edna. He stayed and sat beside the wood fire. They laughed and talked; and before it was time to go he was telling her how different life might have been if he had known her years before. With ingenuous frankness he spoke of what a wicked, ill-disciplined boy he had been, and impulsively drew up his cuff to exhibit upon his wrist the scar from a saber cut which he had received in a duel outside of Paris when he was nineteen. She touched his hand as she scanned the red cicatrice[9] on the inside of his white wrist. A quick impulse that was somewhat spasmodic impelled her fingers to close in a sort of clutch upon his hand. He felt the pressure of her pointed nails in the flesh of his palm.

She arose hastily and walked toward the mantel.

"The sight of a wound or scar always agitates and sickens me," she said. "I shouldn't have looked at it."

"I beg your pardon," he entreated, following her; "it never occurred to me that it might be repulsive."

He stood close to her, and the effrontery in his eyes repelled the old, vanishing self in her, yet drew all her awakening sensuousness. He saw enough in her face to impel him to take her hand and hold it while he said his lingering good night.

"Will you go to the races again?" he asked.

"No," she said. "I've had enough of the races. I don't want to lose all the money I've won, and I've got to work when the weather is bright, instead of—"

"Yes; work; to be sure. You promised to show me your work. What morning may I come up to your atelier? To-morrow?"

"No!"

"Day after?"

"No, no."

"Oh, please don't refuse me! I know something of such things. I might help you with a stray suggestion or two."

"No. Good night. Why don't you go after you have said good night? I don't like you," she went on in a high, excited pitch, attempting to

9. Scar.

draw away her hand. She felt that her words lacked dignity and sincerity, and she knew that he felt it.

"I'm sorry you don't like me. I'm sorry I offended you. How have I offended you? What have I done? Can't you forgive me?" And he bent and pressed his lips upon her hand as if he wished never more to withdraw them.

"Mr. Arobin," she complained, "I'm greatly upset by the excitement of the afternoon; I'm not myself. My manner must have misled you in some way. I wish you to go, please." She spoke in a monotonous, dull tone. He took his hat from the table, and stood with eyes turned from her, looking into the dying fire. For a moment or two he kept an impressive silence.

"Your manner has not misled me, Mrs. Pontellier," he said finally. "My own emotions have done that. I couldn't help it. When I'm near you, how could I help it? Don't think anything of it, don't bother, please. You see, I go when you command me. If you wish me to stay away, I shall do so. If you let me come back, I—oh! you will let me come back?"

He cast one appealing glance at her, to which she made no response. Alcée Arobin's manner was so genuine that it often deceived even himself.

Edna did not care or think whether it were genuine or not. When she was alone she looked mechanically at the back of her hand which he had kissed so warmly. Then she leaned her head down on the mantelpiece. She felt somewhat like a woman who in a moment of passion is betrayed into an act of infidelity, and realizes the significance of the act without being wholly awakened from its glamour. The thought was passing vaguely through her mind, "What would he think?"

She did not mean her husband; she was thinking of Robert Lebrun. Her husband seemed to her now like a person whom she had married without love as an excuse.

She lit a candle and went up to her room. Alcée Arobin was absolutely nothing to her. Yet his presence, his manners, the warmth of his glances, and above all the touch of his lips upon her hand had acted like a narcotic upon her.

She slept a languorous sleep, interwoven with vanishing dreams.

XXVI

Alcée Arobin wrote Edna an elaborate note of apology, palpitant with sincerity. It embarrassed her; for in a cooler, quieter moment it appeared to her absurd that she should have taken his action so seriously, so dramatically. She felt sure that the significance of the whole occurrence had lain in her own self-consciousness. If she ignored his note it would give undue importance to a trivial affair. If she replied to it in a serious spirit it would still leave in his mind the impression that she had in a susceptible moment yielded to his influence. After all, it was no great matter to have one's hand kissed. She was provoked at his having written the apology. She answered in as light and bantering a spirit as she fancied it deserved, and said she would be glad to have him look in upon her at work whenever he felt the inclination and his business gave him the opportunity.

He responded at once by presenting himself at her home with all his disarming naïveté. And then there was scarcely a day which followed that she did not see him or was not reminded of him. He was prolific in pretexts. His attitude became one of good-humored subservience and tacit adoration. He was ready at all times to submit to her moods, which were as often kind as they were cold. She grew accustomed to him. They became intimate and friendly by imperceptible degrees, and then by leaps. He sometimes talked in a way that astonished her at first and brought the crimson into her face; in a way that pleased her at last, appealing to the animalism that stirred impatiently within her.

There was nothing which so quieted the turmoil of Edna's senses as a visit to Mademoiselle Reisz. It was then, in the presence of that personality which was offensive to her, that the woman, by her divine art, seemed to reach Edna's spirit and set it free.

It was misty, with heavy, lowering atmosphere, one afternoon, when Edna climbed the stairs to the pianist's apartments under the roof. Her clothes were dripping with moisture. She felt chilled and pinched as she entered the room. Mademoiselle was poking at a rusty stove that smoked a little and warmed the room indifferently. She was endeavoring to heat a pot of chocolate on the stove. The room looked cheerless and dingy to Edna as she entered. A bust of Beethoven,[1] covered with a hood of dust, scowled at her from the mantelpiece.

"Ah! here comes the sunlight!" exclaimed Mademoiselle, rising from her knees before the stove. "Now it will be warm and bright enough; I can let the fire alone."

She closed the stove door with a bang, and approaching, assisted in removing Edna's dripping mackintosh.

"You are cold; you look miserable. The chocolate will soon be hot. But would you rather have a taste of brandy? I have scarcely touched the bottle which you brought me for my cold." A piece of red flannel was wrapped around Mademoiselle's throat; a stiff neck compelled her to hold her head on one side.

"I will take some brandy," said Edna, shivering as she removed her gloves and overshoes. She drank the liquor from the glass as a man would have done. Then flinging herself upon the uncomfortable sofa

---

1. Ludwig von Beethoven (1770–1827), German composer, most admired musical figure of the nineteenth century, best known for his nine symphonies and the opera *Fidelio*.

she said, "Mademoiselle, I am going to move away from my house on Esplanade Street."

"Ah!" ejaculated the musician, neither surprised nor especially interested. Nothing ever seemed to astonish her very much. She was endeavoring to adjust the bunch of violets which had become loose from its fastening in her hair. Edna drew her down upon the sofa, and taking a pin from her own hair, secured the shabby artificial flowers in their accustomed place.

"Aren't you astonished?"

"Passably. Where are you going? To New York? to Iberville? to your father in Mississippi? where?"

"Just two steps away," laughed Edna, "in a little four-room house around the corner. It looks so cozy, so inviting and restful, whenever I pass by; and it's for rent. I'm tired looking after that big house. It never seemed like mine, anyway—like home. It's too much trouble. I have to keep too many servants. I am tired bothering with them."

"That is not your true reason, ma belle. There is no use in telling me lies. I don't know your reason, but you have not told me the truth." Edna did not protest or endeavor to justify herself.

"The house, the money that provides for it, are not mine. Isn't that enough reason?"

"They are your husband's," returned Mademoiselle, with a shrug and a malicious elevation of the eyebrows.

"Oh! I see there is no deceiving you. Then let me tell you: It is a caprice. I have a little money of my own from my mother's estate, which my father sends me by driblets. I won a large sum this winter on the races, and I am beginning to sell my sketches. Laidpore is more and more pleased with my work; he says it grows in force and individuality. I cannot judge of that myself, but I feel that I have gained in ease and confidence. However, as I said, I have sold a good many through Laidpore. I can live in the tiny house for little or nothing, with one servant. Old Celestine, who works occasionally for me, says she will come stay with me and do my work. I know I shall like it, like the feeling of freedom and independence."

"What does your husband say?"

"I have not told him yet. I only thought of it this morning. He will think I am demented, no doubt. Perhaps you think so."

Mademoiselle shook her head slowly. "Your reason is not yet clear to me," she said.

Neither was it quite clear to Edna herself; but it unfolded itself as she sat for a while in silence. Instinct had prompted her to put away her husband's bounty in casting off her allegiance. She did not know how it would be when he returned. There would have to be an understanding, an explanation. Conditions would some way adjust themselves, she felt; but whatever came, she had resolved never again to belong to another than herself.

"I shall give a grand dinner before I leave the old house!" Edna exclaimed. "You will have to come to it, Mademoiselle. I will give you everything that you like to eat and to drink. We shall sing and laugh and be merry for once." And she uttered a sigh that came from the very depths of her being.

If Mademoiselle happened to have received a letter from Robert during the interval of Edna's visits, she would give her the letter unsolicited. And she would seat herself at the piano and play as her humor prompted her while the young woman read the letter.

The little stove was roaring; it was red-hot, and the chocolate in the tin sizzled and sputtered. Edna went forward and opened the stove door, and Mademoiselle rising, took a letter from under the bust of Beethoven and handed it to Edna.

"Another! so soon!" she exclaimed, her eyes filled with delight. "Tell me, Mademoiselle, does he know that I see his letters?"

"Never in the world! He would be angry and would never write to me again if he thought so. Does he write to you? Never a line. Does he send you a message? Never a word. It is because he loves you, poor fool, and is trying to forget you, since you are not free to listen to him or to belong to him."

"Why do you show me his letters, then?"

"Haven't you begged for them? Can I refuse you anything? Oh! you cannot deceive me," and Mademoiselle approached her beloved instrument and began to play. Edna did not at once read the letter. She sat holding it in her hand, while the music penetrated her whole being like an effulgence, warming and brightening the dark places of her soul. It prepared her for joy and exultation.

"Oh!" she exclaimed, letting the letter fall to the floor. "Why did you not tell me?" She went and grasped Mademoiselle's hands up from the keys. "Oh! unkind! malicious! Why did you not tell me?"

"That he was coming back? No great news, *ma foi*. I wonder he did not come long ago."

"But when, when?" cried Edna, impatiently. "He does not say when."

"He says 'very soon.' You know as much about it as I do; it is all in the letter."

"But why? Why is he coming? Oh, if I thought—" and she snatched the letter from the floor and turned the pages this way and that way, looking for the reason, which was left untold.

"If I were young and in love with a man," said Mademoiselle, turning on the stool and pressing her wiry hands between her knees as she looked down at Edna, who sat on the floor holding the letter, "it seems to me he would have to be some *grand esprit*; a man with lofty aims and ability to reach them; one who stood high enough to attract the notice of his fellow-men. It seems to me if I were young and in love I should never deem a man of ordinary caliber worthy of my devotion."

"Now it is you who are telling lies and seeking to deceive me, Mademoiselle; or else you have never been in love, and know nothing about it. Why," went on Edna, clasping her knees and looking up into Mademoiselle's twisted face, "do you suppose a woman knows why she loves? Does she select? Does she say to herself: 'Go to! Here is a distinguished statesman with presidential possibilities; I shall proceed to fall in love with him.' Or, 'I shall set my heart upon this musician, whose fame is on every tongue?' Or, 'This financier, who controls the world's money markets?' "

"You are purposely misunderstanding me, *ma reine*.[2] Are you in love with Robert?"

"Yes," said Edna. It was the first time she had admitted it, and a glow overspread her face, blotching it with red spots.

"Why?" asked her companion. "Why do you love him when you ought not to?"

Edna, with a motion or two, dragged herself on her knees before Mademoiselle Reisz, who took the glowing face between her two hands.

"Why? Because his hair is brown and grows away from his temples; because he opens and shuts his eyes, and his nose is a little out of drawing; because he has two lips and a square chin, and a little finger which he can't straighten from having played baseball too energetically in his youth. Because—"

"Because you do, in short," laughed Mademoiselle. "What will you do when he comes back?" she asked.

"Do? Nothing, except feel glad and happy to be alive."

She was already glad and happy to be alive at the mere thought of his return. The murky, lowering sky, which had depressed her a few hours before, seemed bracing and invigorating as she splashed through the streets on her way home.

She stopped at a confectioner's and ordered a huge box of bonbons for the children in Iberville. She slipped a card in the box, on which she scribbled a tender message and sent an abundance of kisses.

Before dinner in the evening Edna wrote a charming letter to her husband, telling him of her intention to move for a while into the little house around the block, and to give a farewell dinner before leaving, regretting that he was not there to share it, to help her out with the menu and assist her in entertaining the guests. Her letter was brilliant and brimming with cheerfulness.

XXVII

"What is the matter with you?" asked Arobin that evening. "I never found you in such a happy mood." Edna was tired by that time, and was reclining on the lounge before the fire.

2. "My love" (literally, "my queen").

"Don't you know the weather prophet has told us we shall see the sun pretty soon?"

"Well, that ought to be reason enough," he acquiesced. "You wouldn't give me another if I sat here all night imploring you." He sat close to her on a low tabouret,[3] and as he spoke his fingers lightly touched the hair that fell a little over her forehead. She liked the touch of his fingers through her hair, and closed her eyes sensitively.

"One of these days," she said, "I'm going to pull myself together for a while and think—try to determine what character of a woman I am; for, candidly, I don't know. By all the codes which I am acquainted with, I am a devilishly wicked specimen of the sex. But some way I can't convince myself that I am. I must think about it."

"Don't. What's the use? Why should you bother thinking about it when I can tell you what manner of woman you are." His fingers strayed occasionally down to her warm, smooth cheeks and firm chin, which was growing a little full and double.

"Oh, yes! You will tell me that I am adorable; everything that is captivating. Spare yourself the effort."

"No; I shan't tell you anything of the sort, though I shouldn't be lying if I did."

"Do you know Mademoiselle Reisz?" she asked irrelevantly.

"The pianist? I know her by sight. I've heard her play."

"She says queer things sometimes in a bantering way that you don't notice at the time and you find yourself thinking about afterward."

"For instance?"

"Well, for instance, when I left her today, she put her arms around me and felt my shoulder blades, to see if my wings were strong, she said. 'The bird that would soar above the level plain of tradition and prejudice must have strong wings. It is a sad spectacle to see the weaklings bruised, exhausted, fluttering back to earth.' "

"Whither would you soar?"

"I'm not thinking of any extraordinary flights. I only half comprehend her."

"I've heard she's partially demented," said Arobin.

"She seems to me wonderfully sane," Edna replied.

"I'm told she's extremely disagreeable and unpleasant. Why have you introduced her at a moment when I desired to talk of you?"

"Oh! talk of me if you like," cried Edna, clasping her hands beneath her head; "but let me think of something else while you do."

"I'm jealous of your thoughts to-night. They're making you a little kinder than usual; but some way I feel as if they were wandering, as if they were not here with me." She only looked at him and smiled. His eyes were very near. He leaned upon the lounge with an arm extended across her, while the other hand still rested upon her hair. They con-

3. A low stool.

tinued silently to look into each other's eyes. When he leaned forward and kissed her, she clasped his head, holding his lips to hers.

It was the first kiss of her life to which her nature had really responded. It was a flaming torch that kindled desire.

sex XXVIII

Edna cried a little that night after Arobin left her. It was only one phase of the multitudinous emotions which had assailed her. There was with her an overwhelming feeling of irresponsibility. There was the shock of the unexpected and the unaccustomed. There was her husband's reproach looking at her from the external things around her which he had provided for her external existence. There was Robert's reproach making itself felt by a quicker, fiercer, more overpowering love, which had awakened within her toward him. Above all, there was understanding. She felt as if a mist had been lifted from her eyes, enabling her to look upon and comprehend the significance of life, that monster made up of beauty and brutality. But among the conflicting sensations which assailed her, there was neither shame nor remorse. There was a dull pang of regret because it was not the kiss of love which had inflamed her, because it was not love which had held this cup of life to her lips.

XXIX

Without even waiting for an answer from her husband regarding his opinion or wishes in the matter, Edna hastened her preparations for quitting her home on Esplanade Street and moving into the little house around the block. A feverish anxiety attended her every action in that direction. There was no moment of deliberation, no interval of repose between the thought and its fulfillment. Early upon the morning following those hours passed in Arobin's society, Edna set about securing her new abode and hurrying her arrangements for occupying it. Within the precincts of her home she felt like one who has entered and lingered within the portals of some forbidden temple in which a thousand muffled voices bade her begone.

Whatever was her own in the house, everything which she had acquired aside from her husband's bounty, she caused to be transported to the other house, supplying simple and meager deficiencies from her own resources.

Arobin found her with rolled sleeves, working in company with the house-maid when he looked in during the afternoon. She was splendid and robust, and had never appeared handsomer than in the old blue gown, with a red silk handkerchief knotted at random around her head to protect her hair from the dust. She was mounted upon a high step-ladder, unhooking a picture from the wall when he entered. He had found the front door open, and had followed his ring by walking in unceremoniously.

"Come down!" he said. "Do you want to kill yourself?" She greeted him with affected carelessness, and appeared absorbed in her occupation.

If he had expected to find her languishing, reproachful, or indulging in sentimental tears, he must have been greatly surprised.

He was no doubt prepared for any emergency, ready for any one of the foregoing attitudes, just as he bent himself easily and naturally to the situation which confronted him.

"Please come down," he insisted, holding the ladder and looking up at her.

"No," she answered; "Ellen is afraid to mount the ladder. Joe is working over at the 'pigeon house'—that's the name Ellen gives it, because it's so small and looks like a pigeon house[4]—and some one has to do this."

Arobin pulled off his coat, and expressed himself ready and willing to tempt fate in her place. Ellen brought him one of her dust-caps, and went into contortions of mirth, which she found it impossible to control, when she saw him put it on before the mirror as grotesquely as he could. Edna herself could not refrain from smiling when she fastened it at his request. So it was he who in turn mounted the ladder, unhooking pictures and curtains, and dislodging ornaments as Edna directed. When he had finished he took off his dust-cap and went out to wash his hands.

Edna was sitting on the tabouret, idly brushing the tips of a feather duster along the carpet when he came in again.

"Is there anything more you will let me do?" he asked.

"That is all," she answered. "Ellen can manage the rest." She kept the young woman occupied in the drawing-room, unwilling to be left alone with Arobin.

"What about the dinner?" he asked; "the grand event, the *coup d'état?*"

"It will be day after to-morrow. Why do you call it the '*coup d'état?*' Oh! it will be very fine; all my best of everything—crystal, silver and gold, Sèvres, flowers, music, and champagne to swim in. I'll let Léonce pay the bills. I wonder what he'll say when he sees the bills."

"And you ask me why I call it a *coup d'état?*" Arobin had put on his coat, and he stood before her and asked if his cravat was plumb. She told him it was, looking no higher than the tip of his collar.

"When do you go to the 'pigeon house?'—with all due acknowledgment to Ellen."

"Day after to-morrow, after the dinner. I shall sleep there."

"Ellen, will you very kindly get me a glass of water?" asked Arobin. "The dust in the curtains, if you will pardon me for hinting such a thing, has parched my throat to a crisp."

---

4. A house or dovecot for the domesticated birds kept for show or sport. The breeds kept by these fashionable hobbyists were elegantly colored, little resembling the drab street pigeon.

"While Ellen gets the water," said Edna, rising, "I will say good-by and let you go. I must get rid of this grime, and I have a million things to do and think of."

"When shall I see you?" asked Arobin, seeking to detain her, the maid having left the room.

"At the dinner, of course. You are invited."

"Not before?—not to-night or to-morrow morning or to-morrow noon or night? or the day after morning or noon? Can't you see yourself, without my telling you, what an eternity it is?"

He had followed her into the hall and to the foot of the stairway, looking up at her as she mounted with her face half turned to him.

"Not an instant sooner," she said. But she laughed and looked at him with eyes that at once gave him courage to wait and made it torture to wait.

XXX

Though Edna had spoken of the dinner as a very grand affair, it was in truth a very small affair and very select, in so much as the guests invited were few and were selected with discrimination. She had counted upon an even dozen seating themselves at her round mahogany board, forgetting for the moment that Madame Ratignolle was to the last degree *souffrante*[5] and unpresentable, and not foreseeing that Madame Lebrun would send a thousand regrets at the last moment. So there were only ten, after all, which made a cozy, comfortable number.

There were Mr. and Mrs. Merriman, a pretty, vivacious little woman in the thirties; her husband, a jovial fellow, something of a shallow-pate,[6] who laughed a good deal at other people's witticisms, and had thereby made himself extremely popular. Mrs. Highcamp had accompanied them. Of course, there was Alcée Arobin; and Mademoiselle Reisz had consented to come. Edna had sent her a fresh bunch of violets with black lace trimmings for her hair. Monsieur Ratignolle brought himself and his wife's excuses. Victor Lebrun, who happened to be in the city, bent upon relaxation, had accepted with alacrity. There was a Miss Mayblunt, no longer in her teens, who looked at the world through lorgnettes and with the keenest interest. It was thought and said that she was intellectual; it was suspected of her that she wrote under a *nom de guerre*.[7] She had come with a gentleman by the name of Gouvernail, connected with one of the daily papers, of whom nothing special could be said, except that he was observant and seemed quiet and inoffensive. Edna herself made the tenth, and at half-past eight they seated themselves at table, Arobin and Monsieur Ratignolle on either side of their hostess.

Mrs. Highcamp sat between Arobin and Victor Lebrun. Then came

5. Ill.
6. A person of limited intellect.
7. Pseudonym.

Mrs. Merriman, Mr. Gouvernail, Miss Mayblunt, Mr. Merriman, and Mademoiselle Reisz next to Monsieur Ratignolle.

There was something extremely gorgeous about the appearance of the table, an effect of splendor conveyed by a cover of pale yellow satin under strips of lace-work. There were wax candles in massive brass candelabra, burning softly under yellow silk shades; full, fragrant roses, yellow and red, abounded. There were silver and gold, as she had said there would be, and crystal which glittered like the gems which the women wore.

The ordinary stiff dining chairs had been discarded for the occasion and replaced by the most commodious and luxurious which could be collected throughout the house. Mademoiselle Reisz, being exceedingly diminutive, was elevated upon cushions, as small children are sometimes hoisted at table upon bulky volumes.

"Something new, Edna?" exclaimed Miss Mayblunt, with lorgnette directed toward a magnificent cluster of diamonds that sparkled, that almost sputtered, in Edna's hair, just over the center of her forehead.

"Quite new; 'brand' new, in fact; a present from my husband. It arrived this morning from New York. I may as well admit that this is my birthday, and that I am twenty-nine. In good time I expect you to drink my health. Meanwhile, I shall ask you to begin with this cocktail, composed—would you say 'composed?' " with an appeal to Miss Mayblunt—"composed by my father in honor of Sister Janet's wedding."

Before each guest stood a tiny glass that looked and sparkled like a garnet gem.

"Then, all things considered," spoke Arobin, "it might not be amiss to start out by drinking the Colonel's health in the cocktail which he composed, on the birthday of the most charming of women—the daughter whom he invented."

Mr. Merriman's laugh at this sally was such a genuine outburst and so contagious that it started the dinner with an agreeable swing that never slackened.

Miss Mayblunt begged to be allowed to keep her cocktail untouched before her, just to look at. The color was marvelous! She could compare it to nothing she had ever seen, and the garnet lights which it emitted were unspeakably rare. She pronounced the Colonel an artist, and stuck to it.

Monsieur Ratignolle was prepared to take things seriously; the *mets*, the *entre-mets*,[8] the service, the decorations, even the people. He looked up from his pompono[9] and inquired of Arobin if he were related to the gentleman of that name who formed one of the firm of Laitner and Arobin, lawyers. The young man admitted that Laitner was a warm personal friend, who permitted Arobin's name to decorate the firm's

8. The main courses, the side dishes.
9. Fish, usually spelled *pompano*.

letterheads and to appear upon a shingle that graced Perdido Street.[1]

"There are so many inquisitive people and institutions abounding," said Arobin, "that one is really forced as a matter of convenience these days to assume the virtue of an occupation if he has it not."

Monsieur Ratignolle stared a little, and turned to ask Mademoiselle Reisz if she considered the symphony concerts up to the standard which had been set the previous winter. Mademoiselle Reisz answered Monsieur Ratignolle in French, which Edna thought a little rude, under the circumstances, but characteristic. Mademoiselle had only disagreeable things to say of the symphony concerts, and insulting remarks to make of all the musicians of New Orleans, singly and collectively. All her interest seemed to be centered upon the delicacies placed before her.

Mr. Merriman said that Mr. Arobin's remark about inquisitive people reminded him of a man from Waco[2] the other day at the St. Charles Hotel—but as Mr. Merriman's stories were always lame and lacking point, his wife seldom permitted him to complete them. She interrupted him to ask 'if he remembered the name of the author whose book she had bought the week before to send to a friend in Geneva. She was talking "books" with Mr. Gouvernail and trying to draw from him his opinion upon current literary topics. Her husband told the story of the Waco man privately to Miss Mayblunt, who pretended to be greatly amused and to think it extremely clever.

Mrs. Highcamp hung with languid but unaffected interest upon the warm and impetuous volubility of her left-hand neighbor, Victor Lebrun. Her attention was never for a moment withdrawn from him after seating herself at table; and when he turned to Mrs. Merriman, who was prettier and more vivacious than Mrs. Highcamp, she waited with easy indifference for an opportunity to reclaim his attention. There was the occasional sound of music, of mandolins, sufficiently removed to be an agreeable accompaniment rather than an interruption to the conversation. Outside the soft, monotonous splash of a fountain could be heard; the sound penetrated into the room with the heavy odor of jessamine that came through the open windows.

The golden shimmer of Edna's satin gown spread in rich folds on either side of her. There was a soft fall of lace encircling her shoulders. It was the color of her skin, without the glow, the myriad living tints that one may sometimes discover in vibrant flesh. There was something in her attitude, in her whole appearance when she leaned her head against the high-backed chair and spread her arms, which suggested the regal woman, the one who rules, who looks on, who stands alone.

But as she sat there amid her guests, she felt the old ennui overtaking her; the hopelessness which so often assailed her, which came upon her like an obsession, like something extraneous, independent of volition.

1. From *perdido*, the Spanish word for "lost," because the street ends in a cypress swamp where by legend travelers have strayed.
2. Waco, Texas.

It was something which announced itself; a chill breath that seemed to issue from some vast cavern wherein discords wailed. There came over her the acute longing which always summoned into her spiritual vision the presence of the beloved one, overpowering her at once with a sense of the unattainable.

The moments glided on, while a feeling of good fellowship passed around the circle like a mystic cord, holding and binding these people together with jest and laughter. Monsieur Ratignolle was the first to break the pleasant charm. At ten o'clock he excused himself. Madame Ratignolle was waiting for him at home. She was *bien souffrante*,[3] and she was filled with vague dread, which only her husband's presence could allay.

Mademoiselle Reisz arose with Monsieur Ratignolle, who offered to escort her to the car. She had eaten well; she had tasted the good, rich wines, and they must have turned her head, for she bowed pleasantly to all as she withdrew from table. She kissed Edna upon the shoulder, and whispered: *"Bonne nuit, ma reine; soyez sage."*[4] She had been a little bewildered upon rising, or rather, descending from her cushions, and Monsieur Ratignolle gallantly took her arm and led her away.

Mrs. Highcamp was weaving a garland of roses, yellow and red. When she had finished the garland, she laid it lightly upon Victor's black curls. He was reclining far back in the luxurious chair, holding a glass of champagne to the light.

As if a magician's wand had touched him, the garland of roses transformed him into a vision of Oriental beauty. His cheeks were the color of crushed grapes, and his dusky eyes glowed with a languishing fire.

"Sapristi!" exclaimed Arobin.

But Mrs. Highcamp had one more touch to add to the picture. She took from the back of her chair a white silken scarf, with which she had covered her shoulders in the early part of the evening. She draped it across the boy in graceful folds, and in a way to conceal his black, conventional evening dress. He did not seem to mind what she did to him, only smiled, showing a faint gleam of white teeth, while he continued to gaze with narrowing eyes at the light through his glass of champagne.

"Oh! to be able to paint in color rather than in words!" exclaimed Miss Mayblunt, losing herself in a rhapsodic dream as she looked at him.

> " 'There was a graven image of Desire
> Painted with red blood on a ground of gold.' "[5]

murmured Gouvernail, under his breath.

The effect of the wine upon Victor was to change his accustomed

---

3. Very ill.
4. "Good night, my love; be good."
5. Lines from a sonnet by A. C. Swinburne (1837–1909) called "A Cameo." See below, p. 250.

volubility into silence. He seemed to have abandoned himself to a reverie, and to be seeing pleasing visions in the amber bead.

"Sing," entreated Mrs. Highcamp. "Won't you sing to us?"

"Let him alone," said Arobin.

"He's posing," offered Mr. Merriman; "let him have it out."

"I believe he's paralyzed," laughed Mrs. Merriman. And leaning over the youth's chair, she took the glass from his hand and held it to his lips. He sipped the wine slowly, and when he had drained the glass she laid it upon the table and wiped his lips with her little filmy handkerchief.

"Yes, I'll sing for you," he said, turning in his chair toward Mrs. Highcamp. He clasped his hands behind his head, and looking up at the ceiling began to hum a little, trying his voice like a musician tuning an instrument. Then, looking at Edna, he began to sing:

"Ah! si tu savais!"

"Stop!" she cried, "don't sing that. I don't want you to sing it," and she laid her glass so impetuously and blindly upon the table as to shatter it against a caraffe. The wine spilled over Arobin's legs and some of it trickled down upon Mrs. Highcamp's black gauze gown. Victor had lost all idea of courtesy, or else he thought his hostess was not in earnest, for he laughed and went on:

"Ah! si tu savais
Ce que tes yeux me disent"—6

"Oh! you mustn't! you mustn't," exclaimed Edna, and pushing back her chair she got up, and going behind him placed her hand over his mouth. He kissed the soft palm that pressed upon his lips.

"No, no, I won't, Mrs. Pontellier. I didn't know you meant it," looking up at her with caressing eyes. The touch of his lips was like a pleasing sting to her hand. She lifted the garland of roses from his head and flung it across the room.

"Come, Victor; you've posed long enough. Give Mrs. Highcamp her scarf."

Mrs. Highcamp undraped the scarf from about him with her own hands. Miss Mayblunt and Mr. Gouvernail suddenly conceived the notion that it was time to say good night. And Mr. and Mrs. Merriman wondered how it could be so late.

Before parting from Victor, Mrs. Highcamp invited him to call upon her daughter, who she knew would be charmed to meet him and talk French and sing French songs with him. Victor expressed his desire

6. "Ah! If you knew / What your eyes are saying to me."

and intention to call upon Miss Highcamp at the first opportunity which presented itself. He asked if Arobin were going his way. Arobin was not.

The mandolin players had long since stolen away. A profound stillness had fallen upon the broad, beautiful street. The voices of Edna's disbanding guests jarred like a discordant note upon the quiet harmony of the night.

XXXI

"Well?" questioned Arobin, who had remained with Edna after the others had departed.

"Well," she reiterated, and stood up, stretching her arms, and feeling the need to relax her muscles after having been so long seated.

"What next?" he asked.

"The servants are all gone. They left when the musicians did. I have dismissed them. The house has to be closed and locked, and I shall trot around to the pigeon house, and shall send Celestine over in the morning to straighten things up."

He looked around, and began to turn out some of the lights.

"What about upstairs?" he inquired.

"I think it is all right; but there may be a window or two unlatched. We had better look; you might take a candle and see. And bring me my wrap and hat on the foot of the bed in the middle room."

He went up with the light, and Edna began closing doors and windows. She hated to shut in the smoke and the fumes of the wine. Arobin found her cape and hat, which he brought down and helped her to put on.

When everything was secured and the lights put out, they left through the front door, Arobin locking it and taking the key, which he carried for Edna. He helped her down the steps.

"Will you have a spray of jessamine?" he asked, breaking off a few blossoms as he passed.

"No; I don't want anything."

She seemed disheartened, and had nothing to say. She took his arm, which he offered her, holding up the weight of her satin train with the other hand. She looked down, noticing the black line of his leg moving in and out so close to her against the yellow shimmer of her gown. There was the whistle of a railway train somewhere in the distance, and the midnight bells were ringing. They met no one in their short walk.

The "pigeon-house" stood behind a locked gate, and a shallow *parterre*[7] that had been somewhat neglected. There was a small front porch, upon which a long window and the front door opened. The door opened directly into the parlor; there was no side entry. Back in the yard was a room for servants, in which old Celestine had been ensconced.

7. Garden.

Edna had left a lamp burning low upon the table. She had succeeded in making the room look habitable and homelike. There were some books on the table and a lounge near at hand. On the floor was a fresh matting, covered with a rug or two; and on the walls hung a few tasteful pictures. But the room was filled with flowers. These were a surprise to her. Arobin had sent them, and had had Celestine distribute them during Edna's absence. Her bedroom was adjoining, and across a small passage were the dining-room and kitchen.

Edna seated herself with every appearance of discomfort.

"Are you tired?" he asked.

"Yes, and chilled, and miserable. I feel as if I had been wound up to a certain pitch—too tight—and something inside of me had snapped." She rested her head against the table upon her bare arm.

"You want to rest," he said, "and to be quiet. I'll go; I'll leave you and let you rest."

"Yes," she replied.

He stood up beside her and smoothed her hair with his soft, magnetic hand. His touch conveyed to her a certain physical comfort. She could have fallen quietly asleep there if he had continued to pass his hand over her hair. He brushed the hair upward from the nape of her neck.

"I hope you will feel better and happier in the morning," he said. "You have tried to do too much in the past few days. The dinner was the last straw; you might have dispensed with it."

"Yes," she admitted; "it was stupid."

"No, it was delightful; but it has worn you out." His hand had strayed to her beautiful shoulders, and he could feel the response of her flesh to his touch. He seated himself beside her and kissed her lightly upon the shoulder.

"I thought you were going away," she said, in an uneven voice.

"I am, after I have said good night."

"Good night," she murmured.

He did not answer, except to continue to caress her. He did not say good night until she had become supple to his gentle, seductive entreaties.

XXXII

When Mr. Pontellier learned of his wife's intention to abandon her home and take up her residence elsewhere, he immediately wrote her a letter of unqualified disapproval and remonstrance. She had given reasons which he was unwilling to acknowledge as adequate. He hoped she had not acted upon her rash impulse; and he begged her to consider first, foremost, and above all else, what people would say. He was not dreaming of scandal when he uttered this warning; that was a thing which would never have entered into his mind to consider in connection with his wife's name or his own. He was simply thinking of his financial integrity. It might get noised about that the Pontelliers had met with reverses, and were forced to conduct their *ménage*[8] on a humbler scale than heretofore. It might do incalculable mischief to his business prospects.

But remembering Edna's whimsical turn of mind of late, and foreseeing that she had immediately acted upon her impetuous determination, he grasped the situation with his usual promptness and handled it with his well-known business tact and cleverness.

The same mail which brought to Edna his letter of disapproval carried instructions—the most minute instructions—to a well-known architect concerning the remodeling of his home, changes which he had long contemplated, and which he desired carried forward during his temporary absence.

Expert and reliable packers and movers were engaged to convey the furniture, carpets, pictures—everything movable, in short—to places of security. And in an incredibly short time the Pontellier house was turned over to the artisans. There was to be an addition—a small snuggery; there was to be frescoing, and hardwood flooring was to be put into such rooms as had not yet been subjected to this improvement.

Furthermore, in one of the daily papers appeared a brief notice to the effect that Mr. and Mrs. Pontellier were contemplating a summer sojourn abroad, and that their handsome residence on Esplanade Street was undergoing sumptuous alterations, and would not be ready for occupancy until their return. Mr. Pontellier had saved appearances!

Edna admired the skill of his maneuver, and avoided any occasion to balk his intentions. When the situation as set forth by Mr. Pontellier was accepted and taken for granted, she was apparently satisfied that it should be so.

The pigeon-house pleased her. It at once assumed the intimate character of a home, while she herself invested it with a charm which it reflected like a warm glow. There was with her a feeling of having descended in the social scale, with a corresponding sense of having risen in the spiritual. Every step which she took toward relieving herself from obligations added to her strength and expansion as an individual. She began to look with her own eyes; to see and to apprehend the deeper undercurrents of life. No longer was she content to "feed upon opinion" when her own soul had invited her.

After a little while, a few days, in fact, Edna went up and spent a week with her children in Iberville. They were delicious February days, with all the summer's promise hovering in the air.

How glad she was to see the children! She wept for very pleasure when she felt their little arms clasping her; their hard, ruddy cheeks

---

8. Household.

pressed against her own glowing cheeks. She looked into their faces with hungry eyes that could not be satisfied with looking. And what stories they had to tell their mother! About the pigs, the cows, the mules! About riding to the mill behind Gluglu; fishing back in the lake with their Uncle Jasper; picking pecans with Lidie's little black brood, and hauling chips in their express wagon. It was a thousand times more fun to haul real chips for old lame Susie's real fire than to drag painted blocks along the banquette on Esplanade Street!

She went with them herself to see the pigs and the cows, to look at the darkies laying the cane, to thrash the pecan trees, and catch fish in the back lake. She lived with them a whole week long, giving them all of herself, and gathering and filling herself with their young existence. They listened, breathless, when she told them the house in Esplanade Street was crowded with workmen, hammering, nailing, sawing, and filling the place with clatter. They wanted to know where their bed was; what had been done with their rocking-horse; and where did Joe sleep, and where had Ellen gone, and the cook? But, above all, they were fired with a desire to see the little house around the block. Was there any place to play? Were there any boys next door? Raoul, with pessimistic foreboding, was convinced that there were only girls next door. Where would they sleep, and where would papa sleep? She told them the fairies would fix it all right.

The old Madame was charmed with Edna's visit, and showered all manner of delicate attentions upon her. She was delighted to know that the Esplanade Street house was in a dismantled condition. It gave her the promise and pretext to keep the children indefinitely.

It was with a wrench and a pang that Edna left her children. She carried away with her the sound of their voices and the touch of their cheeks. All along the journey homeward their presence lingered with her like the memory of a delicious song. But by the time she had regained the city the song no longer echoed in her soul. She was again alone.

XXXIII

It happened sometimes when Edna went to see Mademoiselle Reisz that the little musician was absent, giving a lesson or making some small necessary household purchase. The key was always left in a secret hiding-place in the entry, which Edna knew. If Mademoiselle happened to be away, Edna would usually enter and wait for her return.

When she knocked at Mademoiselle Reisz's door one afternoon there was no response; so unlocking the door, as usual, she entered and found the apartment deserted, as she had expected. Her day had been quite filled up, and it was for a rest, for a refuge, and to talk about Robert, that she sought out her friend.

She had worked at her canvas—a young Italian character study—all the morning, completing the work without the model; but there had been many interruptions, some incident to her modest housekeeping, and others of a social nature.

Madame Ratignolle had dragged herself over, avoiding the too public thoroughfares, she said. She complained that Edna had neglected her much of late. Besides, she was consumed with curiosity to see the little house and the manner in which it was conducted. She wanted to hear all about the dinner party; Monsieur Ratignolle had left so early. What had happened after he left? The champagne and grapes which Edna sent over were *too* delicious. She had so little appetite; they had refreshed and toned her stomach. Where on earth was she going to put Mr. Pontellier in that little house, and the boys? And then she made Edna promise to go to her when her hour of trial overtook her.

"At any time—any time of the day or night, dear," Edna assured her.

Before leaving Madame Ratignolle said:

"In some way you seem to me like a child, Edna. You seem to act without a certain amount of reflection which is necessary in this life. That is the reason I want to say you mustn't mind if I advise you to be a little careful while you are living here alone. Why don't you have some one come and stay with you? Wouldn't Mademoiselle Reisz come?"

"No; she wouldn't wish to come, and I shouldn't want her always with me."

"Well, the reason—you know how evil-minded the world is—some one was talking of Alcée Arobin visiting you. Of course, it wouldn't matter if Mr. Arobin had not such a dreadful reputation. Monsieur Ratignolle was telling me that his attentions alone are considered enough to ruin a woman's name."

"Does he boast of his successes?" asked Edna, indifferently, squinting at her picture.

"No, I think not. I believe he is a decent fellow as far as that goes. But his character is so well known among the men. I shan't be able to come back and see you; it was very, very imprudent today."

"Mind the step!" cried Edna.

"Don't neglect me," entreated Madame Ratignolle; "and don't mind what I said about Arobin, or having some one to stay with you."

"Of course not," Edna laughed. "You may say anything you like to me." They kissed each other good-bye. Madame Ratignolle had not far to go, and Edna stood on the porch a while watching her walk down the street.

Then in the afternoon Mrs. Merriman and Mrs. Highcamp had made their "party call."[9] Edna felt that they might have dispensed with the formality. They had also come to invite her to play *vingt-et-un*[1] one

9. "Within the next week, you should call upon your hostess, if it is the first party you have attended at her house. If she is an intimate friend, the call should be made within a fortnight" (Florence Hartley, *The Ladies' Book of Etiquette and Manual of Politeness* [Philadelphia: Evans, 1860] 59). For more advice on etiquette, see below, pp. 122–30.

1. Twenty-one: a card game.

evening at Mrs. Merriman's. She was asked to go early, to dinner, and Mr. Merriman or Mr. Arobin would take her home. Edna accepted in a half-hearted way. She sometimes felt very tired of Mrs. Highcamp and Mrs. Merriman.

Late in the afternoon she sought refuge with Mademoiselle Reisz, and stayed there alone, waiting for her, feeling a kind of repose invade her with the very atmosphere of the shabby, unpretentious little room. Edna sat at the window, which looked out over the house-tops and across the river. The window frame was filled with pots of flowers, and she sat and picked the dry leaves from a rose geranium. The day was warm, and the breeze which blew from the river was very pleasant. She removed her hat and laid it on the piano. She went on picking the leaves and digging around the plants with her hat pin. Once she thought she heard Mademoiselle Reisz approaching. But it was a young black girl, who came in, bringing a small bundle of laundry, which she deposited in the adjoining room, and went away.

Edna seated herself at the piano, and softly picked out with one hand the bars of a piece of music which lay open before her. A half-hour went by. There was the occasional sound of people going and coming in the lower hall. She was growing interested in her occupation of picking out the aria, when there was a second rap at the door. She vaguely wondered what these people did when they found Mademoiselle's door locked.

"Come in," she called, turning her face toward the door. And this time it was Robert Lebrun who presented himself. She attempted to rise; she could not have done so without betraying the agitation which mastered her at sight of him, so she fell back upon the stool, only exclaiming, "Why, Robert!"

He came and clasped her hand, seemingly without knowing what he was saying or doing.

"Mrs. Pontellier! How do you happen—oh! how well you look! Is Mademoiselle Reisz not here? I never expected to see you."

"When did you come back?" asked Edna in an unsteady voice, wiping her face with her handkerchief. She seemed ill at ease on the piano stool, and he begged her to take the chair by the window. She did so, mechanically, while he seated himself on the stool.

"I returned day before yesterday," he answered, while he leaned his arm on the keys, bringing forth a crash of discordant sound.

"Day before yesterday!" she repeated, aloud; and went on thinking to herself, "day before yesterday," in a sort of an uncomprehending way. She had pictured him seeking her at the very first hour, and he had lived under the same sky since day before yesterday; while only by accident had he stumbled upon her. Mademoiselle must have lied when she said, "Poor fool, he loves you."

"Day before yesterday," she repeated, breaking off a spray of Mademoiselle's geranium; "then if you had not met me here to-day you wouldn't—when—that is, didn't you mean to come and see me?"

"Of course, I should have gone to see you. There have been so many things—" he turned the leaves of Mademoiselle's music nervously. "I started in at once yesterday with the old firm. After all there is as much chance for me here as there was there—that is, I might find it profitable some day. The Mexicans were not very congenial."

So he had come back because the Mexicans were not congenial; because business was as profitable here as there; because of any reason, and not because he cared to be near her. She remembered the day she sat on the floor, turning the pages of his letter, seeking the reason which was left untold.

She had not noticed how he looked—only feeling his presence; but she turned deliberately and observed him. After all, he had been absent but a few months, and was not changed. His hair—the color of hers— waved back from his temples in the same way as before. His skin was not more burned than it had been at Grand Isle. She found in his eyes, when he looked at her for one silent moment, the same tender caress, with an added warmth and entreaty which had not been there before —the same glance which had penetrated to the sleeping places of her soul and awakened them.

A hundred times Edna had pictured Robert's return, and imagined their first meeting. It was usually at her home, whither he had sought her out at once. She always fancied him expressing or betraying in some way his love for her. And here, the reality was that they sat ten feet apart, she at the window, crushing geranium leaves in her hand and smelling them, he twirling around on the piano stool, saying:

"I was very much surprised to hear of Mr. Pontellier's absence; it's a wonder Mademoiselle Reisz did not tell me; and your moving—mother told me yesterday. I should think you would have gone to New York with him, or to Iberville with the children, rather than be bothered here with housekeeping. And you are going abroad, too, I hear. We shan't have you at Grand Isle next summer; it won't seem—do you see much of Mademoiselle Reisz? She often spoke of you in the few letters she wrote."

"Do you remember that you promised to write to me when you went away?" A flush overspread his whole face.

"I couldn't believe that my letters would be of any interest to you."

"That is an excuse; it isn't the truth." Edna reached for her hat on the piano. She adjusted it, sticking the hat pin through the heavy coil of hair with some deliberation.

"Are you not going to wait for Mademoiselle Reisz?" asked Robert.

"No; I have found when she is absent this long, she is liable not to come back till late." She drew on her gloves, and Robert picked up his hat.

"Won't you wait for her?" asked Edna.

"Not if you think she will not be back till late," adding, as if suddenly aware of some discourtesy in his speech, "and I should miss the pleasure of walking home with you." Edna locked the door and put the key back in its hiding-place.

They went together, picking their way across muddy streets and sidewalks encumbered with the cheap display of small tradesmen. Part of the distance they rode in the car, and after disembarking, passed the Pontellier mansion, which looked broken and half torn asunder. Robert had never known the house, and looked at it with interest.

"I never knew you in your home," he remarked.

"I am glad you did not."

"Why?" She did not answer. They went on around the corner, and it seemed as if her dreams were coming true after all, when he followed her into the little house.

"You must stay and dine with me, Robert. You see I am all alone, and it is so long since I have seen you. There is so much I want to ask you."

She took off her hat and gloves. He stood irresolute, making some excuse about his mother who expected him; he even muttered something about an engagement. She struck a match and lit the lamp on the table; it was growing dusk. When he saw her face in the lamplight, looking pained, with all the soft lines gone out of it, he threw his hat aside and seated himself.

"Oh! you know I want to stay if you will let me!" he exclaimed. All the softness came back. She laughed, and went and put her hand on his shoulder.

"This is the first moment you have seemed like the old Robert. I'll go tell Celestine." She hurried away to tell Celestine to set an extra place. She even sent her off in search of some added delicacy which she had not thought of for herself. And she recommended great care in dripping the coffee and having the omelet done to a proper turn.

When she reëntered, Robert was turning over magazines, sketches, and things that lay upon the table in great disorder. He picked up a photograph, and exclaimed:

"Alcée Arobin! What on earth is his picture doing here?"

"I tried to make a sketch of his head one day," answered Edna, "and he thought the photograph might help me. It was at the other house. I thought it had been left there. I must have packed it up with my drawing materials."

"I should think you would give it back to him if you have finished with it."

"Oh! I have a great many such photographs. I never think of returning them. They don't amount to anything." Robert kept on looking at the picture.

"It seems to me—do you think his head worth drawing? Is he a friend of Mr. Pontellier's? You never said you knew him."

"He isn't a friend of Mr. Pontellier's; he's a friend of mine. I always knew him—that is, it is only of late that I know him pretty well. But I'd rather talk about you, and know what you have been seeing and doing and feeling out there in Mexico." Robert threw aside the picture.

"I've been seeing the waves and the white beach of Grand Isle; the quiet, grassy street of the *Chênière*; the old fort at Grande Terre. I've been working like a machine, and feeling like a lost soul. There was nothing interesting."

She leaned her head upon her hand to shade her eyes from the light.

"And what have you been seeing and doing and feeling all these days?" he asked.

"I've been seeing the waves and the white beach of Grand Isle; the quiet, grassy street of the *Chênière Caminada*; the old sunny fort at Grande Terre. I've been working with little more comprehension than a machine, and still feeling like a lost soul. There was nothing interesting."

"Mrs. Pontellier, you are cruel," he said, with feeling, closing his eyes and resting his head back in his chair. They remained in silence till old Celestine announced dinner.

XXXIV

The dining-room was very small. Edna's round mahogany would have almost filled it. As it was there was but a step or two from the little table to the kitchen, to the mantel, the small buffet, and the side door that opened out on the narrow brick-paved yard.

A certain degree of ceremony settled upon them with the announcement of dinner. There was no return to personalities. Robert related incidents of his sojourn in Mexico, and Edna talked of events likely to interest him, which had occurred during his absence. The dinner was of ordinary quality, except for the few delicacies which she had sent out to purchase. Old Celestine, with a bandana *tignon*[2] twisted about her head, hobbled in and out, taking a personal interest in everything; and she lingered occasionally to talk patois[3] with Robert, whom she had known as a boy.

He went out to a neighboring cigar stand to purchase cigarette papers, and when he came back he found that Celestine had served the black coffee in the parlor.

"Perhaps I shouldn't have come back," he said. "When you are tired of me, tell me to go."

---

2. Creole form of the word *chignon*, a "coil of hair," a "bun." She has her hair tied up with a scarf.
3. A dialect of archaic French mixed with English, Spanish, German, and American Indian words spoken by the descendants of the Acadians.

"You never tire me. You must have forgotten the hours and hours at Grand Isle in which we grew accustomed to each other and used to being together."

"I have forgotten nothing at Grand Isle," he said, not looking at her, but rolling a cigarette. His tobacco pouch, which he laid upon the table, was a fantastic embroidered silk affair, evidently the handiwork of a woman.

"You used to carry your tobacco in a rubber pouch," said Edna, picking up the pouch and examining the needlework.

"Yes; it was lost."

"Where did you buy this one? In Mexico?"

"It was given to me by a Vera Cruz girl; they are very generous," he replied, striking a match and lighting his cigarette.

"They are very handsome, I suppose, those Mexican women; very picturesque, with their black eyes and their lace scarfs."

"Some are; other are hideous. Just as you find women everywhere."

"What was she like—the one who gave you the pouch? You must have known her very well."

"She was very ordinary. She wasn't of the slightest importance. I knew her well enough."

"Did you visit at her house? Was it interesting? I should like to know and hear about the people you met, and the impressions they made on you."

"There are some people who leave impressions not so lasting as the imprint of an oar upon the water."

"Was she such a one?"

"It would be ungenerous for me to admit that she was of that order and kind." He thrust the pouch back in his pocket, as if to put away the subject with the trifle which had brought it up.

Arobin dropped in with a message from Mrs. Merriman, to say that the card party was postponed on account of the illness of one of her children.

"How do you do, Arobin?" said Robert, rising from the obscurity.

"Oh! Lebrun. To be sure! I heard yesterday you were back. How did they treat you down in Mexique?"

"Fairly well."

"But not well enough to keep you there. Stunning girls, though, in Mexico. I thought I should never get away from Vera Cruz when I was down there a couple of years ago."

"Did they embroider slippers and tobacco pouches and hat-bands and things for you?" asked Edna.

"Oh! my! no! I didn't get so deep in their regard. I fear they made more impression on me than I made on them.

"You were less fortunate than Robert, then."

"I am always less fortunate than Robert. Has he been imparting tender confidences?"

"I've been imposing myself long enough," said Robert, rising, and shaking hands with Edna. "Please convey my regards to Mr. Pontellier when you write."

He shook hands with Arobin and went away.

"Fine fellow, that Lebrun," said Arobin when Robert had gone. "I never heard you speak of him."

"I knew him last summer at Grand Isle," she replied. "Here is that photograph of yours. Don't you want it?"

"What do I want with it? Throw it away." She threw it back on the table.

"I'm not going to Mrs. Merriman's," she said. "If you see her, tell her so. But perhaps I had better write. I think I shall write now, and say that I am sorry her child is sick, and tell her not to count on me."

"It would be a good scheme," acquiesced Arobin. "I don't blame you; stupid lot!"

Edna opened the blotter, and having procured paper and pen, began to write the note. Arobin lit a cigar and read the evening paper, which he had in his pocket.

"What is the date?" she asked. He told her.

"Will you mail this for me when you go out?"

"Certainly." He read to her little bits out of the newspaper, while she straightened things on the table.

"What do you want to do?" he asked, throwing aside the paper. "Do you want to go out for a walk or a drive or anything? It would be a fine night to drive."

"No; I don't want to do anything but just be quiet. You go away and amuse yourself. Don't stay."

"I'll go away if I must; but I shan't amuse myself. You know that I only live when I am near you."

He stood up to bid her good night.

"Is that one of the things you always say to women?"

"I have said it before, but I don't think I ever came so near meaning it," he answered with a smile. There were no warm lights in her eyes; only a dreamy, absent look.

"Good night. I adore you. Sleep well," he said, and he kissed her hand and went away.

She stayed alone in a kind of reverie—a sort of stupor. Step by step she lived over every instant of the time she had been with Robert after he had entered Mademoiselle Reisz's door. She recalled his words, his looks. How few and meager they had been for her hungry heart! A vision—a transcendently seductive vision of a Mexican girl arose before her. She writhed with a jealous pang. She wondered when he would come back. He had not said he would come back. She had been with

him, had heard his voice and touched his hand. But some way he had
seemed nearer to her off there in Mexico.

XXXV

The morning was full of sunlight and hope. Edna could see before
her no denial—only the promise of excessive joy. She lay in bed awake,
with bright eyes full of speculation. "He loves you, poor fool." If she
could but get that conviction firmly fixed in her mind, what mattered
about the rest? She felt she had been childish and unwise the night
before in giving herself over to despondency. She recapitulated the motives which no doubt explained Robert's reserve. They were not insur-
mountable; they would not hold if he really loved her; they could not
hold against her own passion, which he must come to realize in time.
She pictured him going to his business that morning. She even saw how
he was dressed; how he walked down one street, and turned the corner
of another; saw him bending over his desk, talking to people who entered
the office, going to his lunch, and perhaps watching for her on the
street. He would come to her in the afternoon or evening, sit and roll
his cigarette, talk a little, and go away as he had done the night before.
But how delicious it would be to have him there with her! She would
have no regrets, nor seek to penetrate his reserve if he still chose to wear
it.

Edna ate her breakfast only half dressed. The maid brought her a
delicious printed scrawl from Raoul, expressing his love, asking her to
send him some bonbons, and telling her they had found that morning
ten tiny white pigs all lying in a row beside Lidie's big white pig.

A letter also came from her husband, saying he hoped to be back
early in March, and then they would get ready for that journey abroad
which he had promised her so long, which he felt now fully able to
afford; he felt able to travel as people should, without any thought of
small economies—thanks to his recent speculations in Wall Street.

Much to her surprise she received a note from Arobin, written at
midnight from the club. It was to say good morning to her, to hope that
she had slept well, to assure her of his devotion, which he trusted she
in some faintest manner returned.

All these letters were pleasing to her. She answered the children in
a cheerful frame of mind, promising them bonbons, and congratulating
them upon their happy find of the little pigs.

She answered her husband with friendly evasiveness,—not with any
fixed design to mislead him, only because all sense of reality had gone
out of her life; she had abandoned herself to Fate, and awaited the
consequences with indifference.

To Arobin's note she made no reply. She put it under Celestine's
stove-lid.

Edna worked several hours with much spirit. She saw no one but a picture dealer, who asked her if it were true that she was going abroad to study in Paris.

She said possibly she might, and he negotiated with her for some Parisian studies to reach him in time for the holiday trade in December.

Robert did not come that day. She was keenly disappointed. He did not come the following day, nor the next. Each morning she awoke with hope, and each night she was a prey to despondency. She was tempted to seek him out. But far from yielding to the impulse, she avoided any occasion which might throw her in his way. She did not go to Mademoiselle Reisz's nor pass by Madame Lebrun's, as she might have done if he had still been in Mexico.

When Arobin, one night, urged her to drive with him, she went— out to the lake, on the Shell Road.[4] His horses were full of mettle, and even a little unmanageable. She liked the rapid gait at which they spun along, and the quick, sharp sound of the horses' hoofs on the hard road. They did not stop anywhere to eat or to drink. Arobin was not needlessly imprudent. But they ate and they drank when they regained Edna's little dining-room—which was comparatively early in the evening.

It was late when he left her. It was getting to be more than a passing whim with Arobin to see her and be with her. He had detected the latent sensuality, which unfolded under his delicate sense of her nature's requirements like a torpid, torrid, sensitive blossom.

There was no despondency when she fell asleep that night; nor was there hope when she awoke in the morning.

XXXVI

There was a garden out in the suburbs; a small, leafy corner, with a few green tables under the orange trees. An old cat slept all day on the stone step in the sun, and an old *mulatresse*[5] slept her idle hours away in her chair at the open window, till some one happened to knock on one of the green tables. She had milk and cream cheese to sell, and bread and butter. There was no one who could make such excellent coffee or fry a chicken so golden brown as she.

The place was too modest to attract the attention of people of fashion, and so quiet as to have escaped the notice of those in search of pleasure and dissipation. Edna had discovered it accidentally one day when the high-board gate stood ajar. She caught sight of a little green table, blotched with the checkered sunlight that filtered through the quivering leaves overhead. Within she had found the slumbering *mulatresse*, the drowsy cat, and a glass of milk which reminded her of the milk she had tasted in Iberville.

4. Bordering Lake Pontchartrain, the road was a favorite to test the speed of one's horses.
5. A woman of mixed racial ancestry, black and white. See also below, p. 309, n. 1.

She often stopped there during her perambulations; sometimes taking a book with her, and sitting an hour or two under the trees when she found the place deserted. Once or twice she took a quiet dinner there alone, having instructed Celestine beforehand to prepare no dinner at home. It was the last place in the city where she would have expected to meet any one she knew.

Still she was not astonished when, as she was partaking of a modest dinner late in the afternoon, looking into an open book, stroking the cat, which had made friends with her—she was not greatly astonished to see Robert come in at the tall garden gate.

"I am destined to see you only by accident," she said, shoving the cat off the chair beside her. He was surprised, ill at ease, almost embarrassed at meeting her thus so unexpectedly.

"Do you come here often?" he asked.

"I almost live here," she said.

"I used to drop in very often for a cup of Catiche's good coffee. This is the first time since I came back."

"She'll bring you a plate, and you will share my dinner. There's always enough for two—even three." Edna had intended to be indifferent and as reserved as he when she met him; she had reached the determination by a laborious train of reasoning, incident to one of her despondent moods. But her resolve melted when she saw him before her, seated there beside her in the little garden, as if a designing Providence had led him into her path.

"Why have you kept away from me, Robert?" she asked, closing the book that lay open upon the table.

"Why are you so personal, Mrs. Pontellier? Why do you force me to idiotic subterfuges?" he exclaimed with sudden warmth. "I suppose there's no use telling you I've been very busy, or that I've been sick, or that I've been to see you and not found you at home. Please let me off with any one of these excuses."

"You are the embodiment of selfishness," she said. "You save yourself something—I don't know what—but there is some selfish motive, and in sparing yourself you never consider for a moment what I think, or how I feel your neglect and indifference. I suppose this is what you would call unwomanly; but I have got into a habit of expressing myself. It doesn't matter to me, and you may think me unwomanly if you like."

"No; I only think you cruel, as I said the other day. Maybe not intentionally cruel; but you seem to be forcing me into disclosures which can result in nothing; as if you would have me bare a wound for the pleasure of looking at it, without the intention or power of healing it."

"I'm spoiling your dinner, Robert; never mind what I say. You haven't eaten a morsel."

"I only came in for a cup of coffee." His sensitive face was all disfigured with excitement.

"Isn't this a delightful place?" she remarked. "I am so glad it has never actually been discovered. It is so quiet, so sweet, here. Do you notice there is scarcely a sound to be heard? It's so out of the way; and a good walk from the car. However, I don't mind walking. I always feel so sorry for women who don't like to walk; they miss so much—so many rare little glimpses of life; and we women learn so little of life on the whole. "Catiche's coffee is always hot. I don't know how she manages it, here in the open air. Celestine's coffee gets cold bringing it from the kitchen to the dining-room. Three lumps! How can you drink it so sweet? Take some of the cress with your chop; it's so biting and crisp. Then there's the advantage of being able to smoke with your coffee out here. Now, in the city—aren't you going to smoke?"

"After a while," he said, laying a cigar on the table.

"Who gave it to you?" she laughed.

"I bought it. I suppose I'm getting reckless; I bought a whole box."

She was determined not to be personal again and make him uncomfortable.

The cat made friends with him, and climbed into his lap when he smoked his cigar. He stroked her silky fur, and talked a little about her. He looked at Edna's book, which he had read; and he told her the end, to save her the trouble of wading through it, he said.

Again he accompanied her back to her home; and it was after dusk when they reached the little "pigeon-house." She did not ask him to remain, which he was grateful for, as it permitted him to stay without the discomfort of blundering through an excuse which he had no intention of considering. He helped her to light the lamp; then she went into her room to take off her hat and to bathe her face and hands.

When she came back Robert was not examining the pictures and magazines as before; he sat off in the shadow, leaning his head back on the chair as if in a reverie. Edna lingered a moment beside the table, arranging the books there. Then she went across the room to where he sat. She bent over the arm of his chair and called his name.

"Robert," she said, "are you asleep?"

"No," he answered, looking up at her.

She leaned over and kissed him—a soft, cool, delicate kiss, whose voluptuous sting penetrated his whole being—then she moved away from him. He followed, and took her in his arms, just holding her close to him. She put her hand up to his face and pressed his cheek against her own. The action was full of love and tenderness. He sought her lips again. Then he drew her down upon the sofa beside him and held her hand in both of his.

"Now you know," he said, "now you know what I have been fighting against since last summer at Grand Isle; what drove me away and drove me back again."

"Why have you been fighting against it?" she asked. Her face glowed with soft lights.

"Why? Because you were not free; you were Léonce Pontellier's wife.

I couldn't help loving you if you were ten times his wife; but so long as I went away from you and kept away I could help telling you so." She put her free hand up to his shoulder, and then against his cheek, rubbing it softly. He kissed her again. His face was warm and flushed.

"There in Mexico I was thinking of you all the time, and longing for you."

"But not writing to me," she interrupted.

"Something put into my head that you cared for me; and I lost my senses. I forgot everything but a wild dream of your some way becoming my wife."

"Your wife!"

"Religion, loyalty, everything would give way if only you cared."

"Then you must have forgotten that I was Léonce Pontellier's wife."

"Oh! I was demented, dreaming of wild, impossible things, recalling men who had set their wives free, we have heard of such things."

"Yes, we have heard of such things."

"I came back full of vague, mad intentions. And when I got here—"

"When you got here you never came near me!" She was still caressing his cheek.

"I realized what a cur I was to dream of such a thing, even if you had been willing."

She took his face between his hands and looked into it as if she would never withdraw her eyes more. She kissed him on the forehead, the eyes, the cheeks, and the lips.

"You have been a very, very foolish boy, wasting your time dreaming of impossible things when you speak of Mr. Pontellier setting me free! I am no longer one of Mr. Pontellier's possessions to dispose of or not. I give myself where I choose. If he were to say, 'Here, Robert, take her and be happy; she is yours,' I should laugh at you both."

His face grew a little white. "What do you mean?" he asked.

There was a knock at the door. Old Celestine came in to say that Madame Ratignolle's servant had come around the back way with a message that Madame had been taken sick and begged Mrs. Pontellier to go to her immediately.

"Yes, yes," said Edna, rising; "I promised. Tell her yes—to wait for me. I'll go back with her."

"Let me walk over with you," offered Robert.

"No," she said; "I will go with the servant." She went into her room to put on her hat, and when she came in again she sat once more upon the sofa beside him. He had not stirred. She put her arms about his neck.

"Good-by, my sweet Robert. Tell me good-by." He kissed her with a degree of passion which had not before entered into his caress, and strained her to him.

"I love you," she whispered, "only you; no one but you. It was you who awoke me last summer out of a life-long, stupid dream. Oh! you have made me so unhappy with your indifference. Oh! I have suffered, suffered! Now you are here we shall love each other, my Robert. We shall be everything to each other. Nothing else in the world is of any consequence. I must go to my friend; but you will wait for me? No matter how late; you will wait for me, Robert?"

"Don't go; don't go! Oh! Edna, stay with me," he pleaded. "Why should you go? Stay with me, stay with me."

"I shall come back as soon as I can; I shall find you here." She buried her face in his neck, and said good-by again. Her seductive voice, together with his great love for her, had enthralled his senses, had deprived him of every impulse but the longing to hold her and keep her.

XXXVII

Edna looked in at the drug store. Monsieur Ratignolle was putting up a mixture himself, very carefully, dropping a red liquid into a tiny glass. He was grateful to Edna for having come; her presence would be a comfort to his wife. Madame Ratignolle's sister, who had always been with her at such trying times, had not been able to come up from the plantation, and Adèle had been inconsolable until Mrs. Pontellier so kindly promised to come to her. The nurse had been with them at night for the past week, as she lived a great distance away. And Dr. Mandelet had been coming and going all the afternoon. They were then looking for him any moment.

Edna hastened upstairs by a private stairway that led from the rear of the store to the apartments above. The children were all sleeping in a back room. Madame Ratignolle was in the salon, whither she had strayed in her suffering impatience. She sat on the sofa, clad in an ample white *peignoir*, holding a handkerchief tight in her hand with a nervous clutch. Her face was drawn and pinched, her sweet blue eyes haggard and unnatural. All her beautiful hair had been drawn back and plaited. It lay in a long braid on the sofa pillow, coiled like a golden serpent. The nurse, a comfortable looking *Griffe*[6] woman in white apron and cap, was urging her to return to her bedroom.

"There is no use, there is no use," she said at once to Edna. "We must get rid of Mandelet; he is getting too old and careless. He said he would be here at half-past seven; now it must be eight. See what time it is, Joséphine."

The woman was possessed of a cheerful nature, and refused to take any situation too seriously, especially a situation with which she was so familiar. She urged Madame to have courage and patience. But Madame only set her teeth hard into her under lip, and Edna saw the sweat gather

---

6. A term designating racial identity in the complex caste system based on color in Louisiana. A *Griffe* was "three fourths Negro," or had one "Negro" parent and one who was a "mulatto." See also below, p. 309, n. 1.

in beads on her white forehead. After a moment or two she uttered a profound sigh and wiped her face with the handkerchief rolled in a ball. She appeared exhausted. The nurse gave her a fresh handkerchief, sprinkled with cologne water.

"This is too much!" she cried. "Mandelet ought to be killed! Where is Alphonse? Is it possible I am to be abandoned like this—neglected by every one?"

"Neglected, indeed!" exclaimed the nurse. Wasn't she there? And here was Mrs. Pontellier leaving, no doubt, a pleasant evening at home to devote to her? And wasn't Monsieur Ratignolle coming that very instant through the hall? And Joséphine was quite sure she had heard Doctor Mandelet's coupé. Yes, there it was, down at the door.

Adèle consented to go back to her room. She sat on the edge of a little low couch next to her bed.

Doctor Mandelet paid no attention to Madame Ratignolle's upbraidings. He was accustomed to them at such times, and was too well convinced of her loyalty to doubt it.

He was glad to see Edna, and wanted her to go with him into the salon and entertain him. But Madame Ratignolle would not consent that Edna should leave her for an instant. Between agonizing moments, she chatted a little, and said it took her mind off her sufferings.

Edna began to feel uneasy. She was seized with a vague dread. Her own like experiences seemed far away, unreal, and only half remembered. She recalled faintly an ecstasy of pain, the heavy odor of chloroform, a stupor which had deadened sensation, and an awakening to find a little new life to which she had given being, added to the great unnumbered multitude of souls that come and go.

She began to wish she had not come; her presence was not necessary. She might have invented a pretext for staying away; she might even invent a pretext now for going. But Edna did not go. With an inward agony, with a flaming, outspoken revolt against the ways of Nature, she witnessed the scene [of] torture.

She was still stunned and speechless with emotion when later she leaned over her friend to kiss her and softly say good-by. Adèle, pressing her cheek, whispered in an exhausted voice: "Think of the children. Edna. Oh think of the children! Remember them!"

XXXVIII

Edna still felt dazed when she got outside in the open air. The Doctor's coupé had returned for him and stood before the *porte cochère*. She did not wish to enter the coupé, and told Doctor Mandelet she would walk; she was not afraid, and would go alone. He directed his carriage to meet him at Mrs. Pontellier's, and he started to walk home with her.

Up—away up, over the narrow street between the tall houses, the stars were blazing. The air was mild and caressing, but cool with the breath of spring and the night. They walked slowly, the Doctor with a heavy, measured tread and his hands behind him; Edna, in an absent-minded way, as she had walked one night at Grand Isle, as if her thoughts had gone ahead of her and she was striving to overtake them.

"You shouldn't have been there, Mrs. Pontellier," he said. "That was no place for you. Adèle is full of whims at such times. There were a dozen women she might have had with her, unimpressionable women. I felt that it was cruel, cruel. You shouldn't have gone."

"Oh, well!" she answered, indifferently. "I don't know that it matters after all. One has to think of the children some time or other; the sooner the better."

"When is Léonce coming back?"

"Quite soon. Some time in March."

"And you are going abroad?"

"Perhaps—no, I am not going. I'm not going to be forced into doing things. I don't want to go abroad. I want to be let alone. Nobody has any right—except childen, perhaps—and even then, it seems to me— or it did seem—" She felt that her speech was voicing the incoherency of her thoughts, and stopped abruptly.

"The trouble is," sighed the Doctor, grasping her meaning intui-tively, "that youth is given up to illusions. It seems to be a provision of Nature; a decoy to secure mothers for the race. And Nature takes no account of moral consequences, of arbitrary conditions which we create, and which we feel obliged to maintain at any cost."

"Yes," she said. "The years that are gone seem like dreams—if one might go on sleeping and dreaming—but to wake up and find—oh! well! perhaps it is better to wake up after all, even to suffer, rather than to remain a dupe to illusions all one's life."

"It seems to me, my dear child," said the Doctor at parting, holding her hand, "you seem to be in trouble. I am not going to ask for your confidence. I will only say that if ever you feel moved to give it to me, perhaps I might help you. I know I would understand, and I tell you there are not many who would—not many, my dear."

"Some way I don't feel moved to speak of things that trouble me. Don't think I am ungrateful or that I don't appreciate your sympathy. There are periods of despondency and suffering which take possession of me. But I don't want anything but my own way. That is wanting a good deal, of course, when you have to trample upon the lives, the hearts, the prejudices of others—but no matter—still, I shouldn't want to trample upon the little lives. Oh! I don't know what I'm saying, Doctor. Good night. Don't blame me for anything."

"Yes, I will blame you if you don't come and see me soon. We will talk of things you never have dreamt of talking about before. It will do us both good. I don't want you to blame yourself, whatever comes. Good night, my child."

She let herself in at the gate, but instead of entering she sat upon the step of the porch. The night was quiet and soothing. All the tearing emotion of the last few hours seemed to fall away from her like a somber, uncomfortable garment, which she had but to loosen to be rid of. She went back to that hour before Adèle had sent for her; and her senses kindled afresh in thinking of Robert's words, the pressure of his arms, and the feeling of his lips upon her own. She could picture at that moment no greater bliss on earth than possession of the beloved one. His expression of love had already given him to her in part. When she thought that he was there at hand, waiting for her, she grew numb with the intoxication of expectancy. It was so late; he would be asleep perhaps. She would awaken him with a kiss. She hoped he would be asleep that she might arouse him with her caresses.

Still, she remembered Adèle's voice whispering. "Think of the children; think of them." She meant to think of them; that determination had driven into her soul like a death wound—but not to-night. To-morrow would be time to think of everything.

Robert was not waiting for her in the little parlor. He was nowhere at hand. The house was empty. But he had scrawled on a piece of paper that lay in the lamplight:

"I love you. Good-by—because I love you."

Edna grew faint when she read the words. She went and sat on the sofa. Then she stretched herself out there, never uttering a sound. She did not sleep. She did not go to bed. The lamp sputtered and went out. She was still awake in the morning, when Celestine unlocked the kitchen door and came in to light the fire.

XXXIX

Victor, with hammer and nails and scraps of scantling, was patching a corner of one of the galleries. Mariequita sat near by, dangling her legs, watching him work, and handing him nails from the tool-box. The sun was beating down upon them. The girl had covered her head with her apron folded into a square pad. They had been talking for an hour or more. She was never tired of hearing Victor describe the dinner at Mrs. Pontellier's. He exaggerated every detail, making it appear a veritable Lucillean[7] feast. The flowers were in tubs, he said. The champagne was quaffed from huge golden goblets. Venus rising from the foam[8] could have presented no more entrancing a spectacle than Mrs. Pontellier, blazing with beauty and diamonds at the head of the board, while the other women were all of them youthful houris[9] possessed of incomparable charms.

---

7. After the first-century Roman general Lucius Licinius Lucullus, who was noted for his banquets.
8. Roman goddess of love and beauty, daughter of Jupiter and Dione, sprung from the foam at birth. In a version of the myth about Aphrodite, her Greek counterpart, she attempts to drown herself, ashamed of her love affair with a beautiful young man, but she is changed instead into a fish with a human face.
9. Virgin nymphs, everlastingly young and beautiful.

She got it into her head that Victor was in love with Mrs. Pontellier, and he gave her evasive answers, framed so as to confirm her belief. She grew sullen and cried a little, threatening to go off and leave him to his fine ladies. There were a dozen men crazy about her at the Chênière; and since it was the fashion to be in love with married people, why, she could run away any time she liked to New Orleans with Célina's husband.

Célina's husband was a fool, a coward, and a pig, and to prove it to her, Victor intended to hammer his head into a jelly the next time he encountered him. This assurance was very consoling to Mariequita. She dried her eyes, and grew cheerful at the prospect.

They were still talking of the dinner and the allurements of city life when Mrs. Pontellier herself slipped around the corner of the house. The two youngsters stayed dumb with amazement before what they considered to be an apparition. But it was really she in flesh and blood, looking tired and a little travel-stained.

"I walked up from the wharf," she said, "and heard the hammering. I supposed it was you, mending the porch. It's a good thing. I was always tripping over those loose planks last summer. How dreary and deserted everything looks!"

It took Victor some little time to comprehend that she had come in Beaudelet's lugger, that she had come alone, and for no purpose but to rest.

"There's nothing fixed up yet, you see. I'll give you my room; it's the only place."

"Any corner will do," she assured him.

"And if you can stand Philomel's cooking," he went on, "though I might try to get her mother while you are here. Do you think she would come?" turning to Mariequita.

Mariequita thought that perhaps Philomel's mother might come for a few days, and money enough.

Beholding Mrs. Pontellier make her appearance, the girl had at once suspected a lovers' rendezvous. But Victor's astonishment was so genuine, and Mrs. Pontellier's indifference so apparent, that the disturbing notion did not lodge long in her brain. She contemplated with the greatest interest this woman who gave the most sumptuous dinners in America, and who had all the men in New Orleans at her feet.

"What time will you have dinner?" asked Edna. "I'm very hungry; but don't get anything extra."

"I'll have it ready in little or no time," he said, bustling and packing away his tools. "You may go to my room to brush up and rest yourself. Mariequita will show you."

"Thank you," said Edna. "But, do you know, I have a notion to go down to the beach and take a good wash and even a little swim, before dinner?"

"The water is too cold!" they both exclaimed. "Don't think of it."

"Well, I might go down and try—dip my toes in. Why, it seems to me the sun is hot enough to have warmed the very depths of the ocean. Could you get me a couple of towels? I'd better go right away, so as to be back in time. It would be a little too chilly if I waited till this afternoon."

Mariequita ran over to Victor's room, and returned with some towels, which she gave to Edna.

"I hope you have fish for dinner," said Edna, as she started to walk away; "but don't do anything extra if you haven't."

"Run and find Philomel's mother," Victor instructed the girl. "I'll go to the kitchen and see what I can do. By Gimminy! Women have no consideration! She might have sent me word."

Edna walked on down to the beach rather mechanically, not noticing anything special except that the sun was hot. She was not dwelling upon any particular train of thought. She had done all the thinking which was necessary after Robert went away, when she lay awake upon the sofa till morning.

She had said over and over to herself: "To-day it is Arobin; to-morrow it will be some one else. It makes no difference to me, it doesn't matter about Léonce Pontellier—but Raoul and Etienne!" She understood now clearly what she had meant long ago when she said to Adèle Ratignolle that she would give up the unessential, but she would never sacrifice herself for her children.

Despondency had come upon her there in the wakeful night, and had never lifted. There was no one thing in the world that she desired. There was no human being whom she wanted near her except Robert; and she even realized that the day would come when he, too, and the thought of him would melt out of her existence, leaving her alone. The children appeared before her like antagonists who had overcome her; who had overpowered and sought to drag her into the soul's slavery for the rest of her days. But she knew a way to elude them. She was not thinking of these things when she walked down to the beach.

The water of the Gulf stretched out before her, gleaming with the million lights of the sun. The voice of the sea is seductive, never ceasing, whispering, clamoring, murmuring, inviting the soul to wander in abysses of solitude. All along the white beach, up and down, there was no living thing in sight. A bird with a broken wing was beating the air above, reeling, fluttering, circling disabled down, down to the water.

Edna had found her old bathing suit still hanging, faded, upon its accustomed peg.

She put it on, leaving her clothing in the bath-house. But when she was there beside the sea, absolutely alone, she cast the unpleasant, pricking garments from her, and for the first time in her life she stood naked in the open air, at the mercy of the sun, the breeze that beat upon her, and the waves that invited her.

How strange and awful it seemed to stand naked under the sky! how delicious! She felt like some new-born creature, opening its eyes in a familiar world that it had never known.

The foamy wavelets curled up to her white feet, and coiled like serpents about her ankles. She walked out. The water was chill, but she walked on. The water was deep, but she lifted her white body and reached out with a long, sweeping stroke. The touch of the sea is sensuous, enfolding the body in its soft, close embrace.

She went on and on. She remembered the night she swam far out, and recalled the terror that seized her at the fear of being unable to regain the shore. She did not look back now, but went on and on, thinking of the blue-grass meadow that she had traversed when a little child, believing that it had no beginning and no end.

Her arms and legs were growing tired.

She thought of Léonce and the children. They were a part of her life. But they need not have thought that they could possess her, body and soul. How Mademoiselle Reisz would have laughed, perhaps sneered, if she knew! "And you call yourself an artist! What pretensions, Madame! The artist must possess the courageous soul that dares and defies."

Exhaustion was pressing upon and over-powering her.

"Good-by—because, I love you." He did not know; he did not understand. He would never understand. Perhaps Doctor Mandelet would have understood if she had seen him—but it was too late; the shore was far behind her, and her strength was gone.

She looked into the distance, and the old terror flamed up for an instant, then sank again. Edna heard her father's voice and her sister Margaret's. She heard the barking of an old dog that was chained to the sycamore tree. The spurs of the cavalry officer clanged as he walked across the porch. There was the hum of bees, and the musky odor of pinks filled the air.

BIOGRAPHICAL AND
HISTORICAL CONTEXTS

Editor's Note: Biography

Kate Chopin has been the subject of three full-length biographies. In 1932, Daniel S. Rankin published *Kate Chopin and Her Creole Stories*, which, as the title suggests, treats Chopin as a "regional" writer. Rankin interviewed a number of people who had known Kate Chopin, and he was instrumental in preserving major Chopin manuscript material. Per Seyersted, in his work *Kate Chopin: A Critical Biography* (1969), discovered additional manuscript material, including unpublished pieces of short fiction. Seyersted identifies Chopin as a pioneer American realist in her treatment of "women's urge for an existential authenticity" and her capacity for sexual passion, both subjects that made Chopin's earlier biographer uneasy. The most recent biography, *Kate Chopin* (1990) by Emily Toth, is an exhaustive study providing important new information about Chopin's life and challenging a number of persistent myths of Chopin scholarship. Toth argues that Kate Chopin was born on February 8, 1850, not 1851 as earlier biographers maintained. She identifies Albert Sampite, a wealthy Creole planter, as a likely romantic interest in Kate Chopin's life. Toth argues that no evidence exists that *The Awakening* was ever banned or withdrawn from St. Louis libraries (nor was its author refused membership in any St. Louis clubs), as was once widely believed. Toth also demonstrates that although Chopin was deeply hurt by negative criticism of *The Awakening*, she did not lapse into complete artistic silence as many commentators have suggested. Though her literary production was indeed slowed by numerous personal difficulties, she did continue to write until the end of her life.

EMILY TOTH

A New Biographical Approach†

> If it were possible for my husband and my mother to come back to earth, I feel that I would unhesitatingly give up every thing that has come into my life since they left it and join my existence again with theirs. To do that, I would have to forget the past ten years of my growth—my real growth.
>
> Kate Chopin's diary, 22 May 1894[1]

Kate Chopin never expected us to read her diary—nor, most likely, did she expect us to read *The Awakening*. But my students are always intrigued by Kate Chopin. They want to know about her life and "real growth": How independent *was* she? Did she earn a living from her writing? (No; she lived on real estate investments.) What really went on in her marriage? And how did she know all that in 1899?

---

† Reprinted by permission of the Modern Language Association from *Approaches to Teaching Kate Chopin's "The Awakening,"* ed. Bernard Koloski (New York: 1988) 60–66.
1. Per Seyersted and Emily Toth, eds., *A Kate Chopin Miscellany* (Oslo: Universitetsforlaget; Natchitoches: Northwestern State UP of Louisiana, 1979) 92.

Literary critics have long presented Kate Chopin as a detached, objective observer who rarely wrote from personal experience—but as I show in my biography,[2] she drew on real life for most of her inspiration. In short stories, Chopin used the names of real people and revealed their secrets with only the thinnest of disguises. She also was not above using fiction for satire and revenge. Even the plot of *The Awakening* is not a total invention; according to Chopin's brother-in-law Phanor Breazeale, with whom she enjoyed playing cards and arguing religion, *The Awakening* was inspired by the true story of a New Orleans woman, well-known to French Quarter residents.[3]

But *The Awakening* also has its roots in Kate Chopin's own life, especially her pursuit of solitude, independence, and an identity apart from her children—and apart from the men who always admired her. Like Edna Pontellier, Kate Chopin knew "the outward existence which conforms, the inward life which questions." From an early age, she developed both "a keen sense of humor," in her daughter's words, and "a rather sad nature," because of her many early losses.[4]

Kate O'Flaherty, born in St. Louis in 1850, was the third of five children, but her sisters died as babies and her brothers died in their twenties—so that Kate was the only one to live past the age of twenty-five.[5] But Kate had also been sent from the family nest much earlier than the others: she was barely five and a half when her parents enrolled her in boarding school, at the Sacred Heart Academy in St. Louis. Then, just two months after Kate began school in 1855, her father was one of the civic leaders riding the first train over the newly built Gasconade River bridge. The bridge collapsed, Thomas O'Flaherty was killed, and for the next two years Kate lived at home with her mother, grandmother, and great grandmother—all of them widows. (Nearly forty years later, Kate Chopin created a railroad acident in "The Story of an Hour," in which a woman newly widowed revels in her independence and freedom.)

Kate's great grandmother Victoria Verdon Charleville took charge of Kate's education, emphasizing French, music, clear thinking, and scan-

2. *Kate Chopin* (New York: Morrow, 1990).
3. Interview with Julia ("July") Breazeale Waters, Kate Chopin's niece, August 1984; Daniel S. Rankin, *Kate Chopin and Her Creole Stories* (Philadelphia: U of Pennsylvania P, 1932) 92. [Toth's full-length biography explores real-life parallels in much greater detail—*Editor.*]
4. Rankin 35; Per Seyersted, *Kate Chopin: A Critical Biography* (Baton Rouge: Louisiana State UP, 1969) 48.
5. Maryhelen Wilson, "Kate Chopin's Family: Fallacies and Facts, Including Kate's True Birthdate," *Kate Chopin Newsletter* 2 (1976–77): 25–31; interview with Wilson, May 1985.
   The 1850 census lists "Cath. 7/12" among the O'Flaherty's, meaning that "Cath." was seven months old as of the census date, June 1850—but Kate Chopin's tombstone and other biographies give her birthday as 8 February 1851. The definitive evidence, however, comes from Jean Bardot, who has recovered the baptismal record at the St. Louis Cathedral, showing that Kate O'Flaherty was born 8 February 1850. Kate's sisters Jane and Marie Therese died in infancy; her brother Tom was killed in a buggy accident at age twenty-five (U.S. Census, 1850; Jean Bardot, *L'influence française dans la vie et l'oeuvre de Kate Chopin,*" Thèse de doctorat, Université de Paris-IV [1985–86] 18; Wilson, "Kate Chopin's Family," interview).

dalous gossip about St. Louis women of the past. Charleville's own mother had obtained the first legal separation in colonial St. Louis— after which she'd raised five children while running a highly profitable shipping business on the Mississippi. But Mme Charleville's daughter, Kate's grandmother, had married a man whose every financial venture turned to dross, and when he disappeared, he left his wife with no money and eight children.[6]

And so the eldest child, Eliza, barely sixteen, did the one thing she could do to save her family: she married. Eliza brought to her marriage the Charleville name and social standing, and her husband, Thomas O'Flaherty, a thirty-nine-year-old Irish immigrant, brought money, financial acumen, and a son from his first marriage. No "excessive and fictitious warmth colored her affection," Kate Chopin writes of Edna and Léonce Pontellier in *The Awakening*—and it is unlikely that the O'Flahertys had any particular community of interests. Once Thomas died, Eliza—like her mother and grandmother—did not remarry.

Kate O'Flaherty attended school irregularly and lived in a house full of people. Besides her mother, grandmother, great grandmother, and brothers, there were aunts and uncles and cousins and servants and boarders. But there were no married couples in the house until Kate was sixteen, after the Civil War (1850 and 1860 censuses, St. Louis city directories). Kate O'Flaherty grew up surrounded by single and very independent women, both at home and at the Sacred Heart Academy, where the sisters were famous for their intellectual rigor.

Then, at the academy, Kate found a soulmate: Kitty Garesché, a classmate who also loved climbing trees, sharing candy, and laughing and weeping over popular novels—but their idyllic friendship was shattered by war.[7] The O'Flahertys and Gareschés were slaveholders and rebel supporters in a Union city, and when both girls were thirteen, Kitty's family was banished from St. Louis. The Gareschés spent the next four years in South Carolina.[8] Kitty did return and their friendship resumed until she entered a convent, but Kate seems never to have been as close to another girl—a fact reflected in Edna Pontellier's girlhood memories. All Edna's friends had been "of one type—the self-contained," and her "most intimate friend at school had been one of rather exceptional intellectual gifts" with whom Edna "sometimes held religious and political controversies."

Kitty was exiled in 1863, the same year Kate's great grandmother and mentor, Mme Charleville, died, three weeks after Christmas. Less than

6. Rankin 35–36; Elizabeth Shown Mills, *Chauvin dit Charleville* (Mississippi State: Mississippi State UP, 1976) 51, 56–57; Seyersted, *Kate Chopin* 13–21; Wilson, "Kate Chopin's Family," and "Woman's Lib in Old St. Louis: 'La Verdon,'" *St. Louis Genealogical Society* 14.4 (n.d.): 139–40.
7. Seyersted and Toth 104; Rankin 37.
8. Dorothy Garesché Holland, *The Garesché, De Bauduy, and Des Chapelles Families: History and Genealogy* (St. Louis: Schneider Printing, 1963).

a month later, Kate's half-brother George, a rebel soldier, died of typhoid on Mardi Gras Day. Their father had been killed on All Saints' Day, eight years earlier, and Kate grew more than a little skeptical about the consolations of religion: even the Presbyterian Edna, in *The Awakening*, finds church suffocating and races outside for air and freedom.

Most college students reading *The Awakening* have questioned their own religious upbringings; most also understand the social pressures that make young women deny their intellectual achievements. Although Kate Chopin claimed, much later, to have been "undistinguished" at the Sacred Heart Academy after the war, in fact she was an honor student. She was elected to the elite Children of Mary Society, she won medals, and she delivered a commencement address, an original composition called "National Peculiarities."[9]

Kate O'Flaherty was also a youthful cynic, and today's students enjoy her musings. Fawned over as a society belle, admired for her cleverness and musical talent, Kate wrote what she really thought in her diary: "I dance with people I despise; amuse myself with men whose only talent is in their feet." She wrote advice about how to flirt (just keep asking, "What do *you* think?" and you'll be praised everywhere for your intelligence), and she was desperate to spend more time with "my dear reading and writing that I love so well."[1]

Then, in 1870, she married "the right man." Oscar Chopin was twenty-five, handsome, from a wealthy cotton-growing family in Louisiana. (The name is pronounced "show-pan," like the composer's.) Both French Catholic by ancestry, Kate and Oscar spoke French and evidently had that kinship of tastes and values Edna hopes for but never finds.[2] Kate used their European honeymoon to emancipate heself: she smoked cigarettes publicly, walked about alone, and drank beer; she learned to row and got herself a sunburn (probably, like Edna, she threw off the hats and gloves and veils that separated women from sensual experiences). Kate and Oscar also skipped mass—and that seems to have become a habit by the time they settled in New Orleans.[3]

During the New Orleans years, 1870–79, Kate Chopin was abruptly separated from her community of women. She took long walks and streetcar rides alone, exploring the city and enjoying her own company. ("I always feel sorry for women who don't like to walk; they miss so much—so many rare little glimpses of life; and we women learn so little of life on the whole," Edna says in ch. 36.) Still, Kate Chopin was also constantly pregnant—and therefore not to be seen in public. Forced to

9. William Schuyler, "Kate Chopin," *Writer* 7 (August 1894): 116. Rpt. in Seyersted and Toth 115–19. "St. Louis Convents," *Missouri Republican* 30 June 1868: 2.
1. Seyersted and Toth 62, 63, 60.
2. Interview with Lucille Tinker Carnahan, former curator of the Kate Chopin/Bayou Folk Museum, Cloutierville, Louisiana; Seyersted and Toth 67; Rankin 58, 81, 82, 89; Seyersted 31, 38, 39. Waters interview.
3. Seyersted and Toth 75, 78, 81, 82, 85.

stay indoors except for Grand Isle vacations, Kate became a talented mimic, a keen observer, and even more a social critic.[4]

By the time she was twenty-eight, Kate Chopin had given birth to five sons, with her mother by her side. (After the first birth, in 1871, Oscar departed on a summer-long European trip.) Still, Oscar was evidently a loving, jolly father but a failure as a breadwinner. After several disastrous seasons, he closed up shop as a cotton factor, and the Chopins moved to his old home in Cloutierville, Natchitoches Parish, northwest Louisiana. (The names are pronounced "Cloochy-ville" and "NACK-it-tush"; Louisiana has "parishes" instead of counties.)

For the first time Kate would be living in a small town—and when she arrived, she was pregnant with her last child, the daughter they named Lélia, born 31 December 1879.[5] In Cloutierville—a tiny French village that became the site of many of her short stories— Kate Chopin shocked the longtime residents. She would lift her skirts too high, deliberately revealing her ankles, when she crossed the town's one street; she smoked Cuban cigarettes and wore fancy riding habits from New Orleans, and many local people tut-tutted. But after Lélia's birth, Kate was finally freed from constant pregnancy and able to listen much more to her own needs.[6]

After Oscar Chopin died suddenly of "swamp fever" in December 1882, Kate ran his general store and plantation for more than a year. An attractive local planter, a married man, pursued her, and Kate was more than a little responsive—but she made a choice: in 1884 she sold her furniture and returned to St. Louis to live with her mother. (That choice is echoed in *The Awakening*, when Edna leaves a man—Robert—to be with a woman: the "mother-woman" Adèle, who is about to give birth.)[7] But when Eliza O'Flaherty died the following year, leaving Kate with a modest income and sole responsibility for six children, Kate turned to writing. Her first published story, "Wiser Than a God" (1889), tells the story of a woman who becomes a great artistic success, but only after her mother's death.

By almost any standards, Kate Chopin was an immediate literary success. Within four years she was appearing in the most prestigious national magazines. Her first short story collection, *Bayou Folk*—mostly local-color stories of Cloutierville-area people—gained nationwide acclaim; her second, *A Night in Acadie*, was well-received. She was also one of the most popular and sought-after writers in St. Louis's literary colony. She held salons at her home, with visiting writers; she was friendly with journalists, poets, and editors of both sexes. She had numerous admirers and suitors, including an editor at the St. Louis *Post-*

---

4. Rankin 82.
5. Rankin 89–90; Seyersted 38.
6. Rankin 103; Carnahan interview.
7. Interviews with Carnahan; Ivy DeLouche, former resident of Cloutierville, Louisiana; and Leona Sampite [granddaughter of Albert Sampite, the wealthy Louisiana planter whom Toth (*Kate Chopin* 164–72) argues was Chopin's lover—*Editor*].

Dispatch, which published her son Oscar's sketch of his mother's study.[8]

In the 1890s Kate Chopin also retained her ties with Louisiana friends and relatives, although some bristled when they recognized her characters. In her first novel, *At Fault* (1890), and in several short stories, she portrayed the Cloutierville priest Father Jean Marie Beaulieu ("Père Antoine") as obtuse and ineffectual—but in "Dr. Chevalier's Lie" (1893) she published a sympathetic portrait of her New Orleans obstetrician and anticipated the character of Dr. Mandelet. For several rakish characters, she drew on the Louisiana planter who had pursued her, and she named one story for his wife.

During her prime, Kate Chopin also wrote "The Storm" (1898), about a young Louisiana mother and a planter—both married to others—who take refuge in her house during a thunderstorm. The storm outside inspires a different sensual storm inside, which is described with a startling explicitness for the 1890s: "When he touched her breasts they gave themselves up in quivering ecstasy, inviting his lips. . . ."[9] The enthusiasm in the story—and its lack of moral condemnation—suggests a personal experience, which may be why Kate Chopin never attempted to publish "The Storm."

Then, in *The Awakening*, Chopin reconsidered her years in New Orleans, the years of pregnancy and motherhood. The action takes place over nine months, the space of Adèle's pregnancy; *The Awakening*'s image of womanly beauty is a radiantly pregnant woman—perhaps the only one described in novels of the 1890s. Though Adèle, the traditional woman, prefers to give birth in pain, Edna (like her creator) took chloroform during her deliveries—and *The Awakening* is Edna's protest against physical and spiritual confinement and pain. Most of Edna's awakenings take place in the unconfined outdoors, in the sensual tropical paradise of Grand Isle.[1]

The Awakening, of course, generated a storm of hostile criticism, but there is no documentary evidence that the book was actually banned or withdrawn from St. Louis library shelves. The story that it was kept from the public stems mainly from Kate Chopin's own ironic statement: "The libraries! Oh, no, they don't keep it."[2] Nor was Kate Chopin totally ostracized in St. Louis: women wrote her warm letters full of praise for *The Awakening*.[3] They also invited her to give a reading at the Wednesday Club, the most prestigious intellectual women's club in St. Louis. Of the two women who reviewed *The Awakening*—Willa Cather in

8. Waters interview; "St. Louis Woman Who Has Won Fame in Literature," [St. Louis] *Post-Dispatch* 26 November 1899: 4.1.
9. Per Seyersted, ed., *The Complete Works of Kate Chopin* (Baton Rouge: Louisiana State UP, 1969) 2.595.
1. Emily Toth, "Timely and Timeless: The Treatment of Time in *The Awakening* and *Sister Carrie*," *Southern Studies* 16 (Fall 1977): 271–76; Seyersted and Toth 93.
2. *Works* 2.722. Librarians Erik Stocker of the St. Louis Public Library and Robert Behra and John Neal Hoover of the St. Louis Mercantile Library can find no evidence that the book was ever banned or withdrawn.
3. Seyersted and Toth 133–34, 137–39.

Pittsburgh and Frances Porcher in St. Louis—both had questions about the theme, but both warmly praised the book's artistry.[4] It was the male critics, editors, and gatekeepers in St. Louis and around the nation who condemned *The Awakening* and cut short Kate Chopin's writing career. She was stung by the negative reviews—some of them from men she knew well—and afterward wrote only a few more short stories. At the turn of the century, she was in failing health (her symptoms suggest diabetes); many of her close friends were dying; and her son Jean's young wife died in childbirth, along with Kate's first grandchild. Though Chopin rallied with enthusiasm for the St. Louis World's Fair in 1904, the August heat brought on a cerebral hemorrhage, and she died on 22 August. She was buried in St. Louis's Calvary Cemetery (sec. 17, lot 47) and virtually forgotten for half a century, until Per Seyersted rediscovered her in the 1960s and American feminists embraced her.

My students like to know that Kate Chopin did not walk into the sea and that long after her death, she has been resurrected for us. They are also fascinated by the unconventional streak that seems to run through her entire life—including her refusal to remarry: obviously she preferred her freedom, her writing, and her solitude. Like Edna, she was "the regal woman, the one who rules, who looks on, who stands alone." She was her own woman.

Editor's Note: Contexts of *The Awakening*

The 1890s in America was a decade of social change and social tension. The depression of 1893–96 accentuated class divisions, and urbanization and industrialization continued to challenge traditional ways of life. The World's Columbian Exposition in Chicago in 1893 announced the fact of the machine age in a dramatic, public fashion. Darwinism and higher criticism of the Bible threatened established ways of thinking about human origins and destiny. The 1890s also brought legalized segregation, or Jim Crow laws, to the South. In Louisiana after the Civil War, African-American men had voted in large numbers, held public office, served on juries, and worked on the railroad. But between 1890 and 1900, the number of registered black voters in Louisiana dropped from 127,923 to 5,320.[1] It is not surprising that in a decade of such social and intellectual ferment, reaction and resistance to change took the form of a particular Puritan-American brand of Victorian moralism.

By 1890 "the woman question" had been a matter of public discussion in America for over fifty years. In that year, the two national suffrage organizations merged for the final push for the vote—which would not come, however, for another thirty years. Upper-class white women were attending college in record numbers, entering professions previously barred to them, and beginning to reap the benefits of improved medical care and dress reform. They formed innumerable women's organizations:

4. See below, pp. 170 and 162 [*Editor*].
1. Henry C. Dethloff and Robert R. Jones, "Race Relations in Louisiana, 1877–98," *Louisiana History* 9.4 (Fall 1968): 316.

social, intellectual, political, and philanthropic. Lower-class white women came together to work long hours for low wages, and the organizing they did was to combat working conditions in the textile mills and sweatshops where they were employed. African-American women, who continued to work overwhelmingly in agriculture and as domestics, organized to combat, among other things, the rising tide of lynching. Women black and white, north and south, were active in attempts to better their lot.

Women's independence became a central theme in the fiction of Kate Chopin, though she herself was never active in any suffrage organization and was even known to make fun of women's clubs. Strongly committed to personal freedom, Chopin defied social convention in numerous ways, including smoking cigarettes, riding horseback in bright-colored costume, walking about the village and city alone, running her husband's business for a time after his death, refusing to remarry, and likely taking lovers. Her diary records that she met one of the Claflin sisters while on her honeymoon and assured her that she would never fall into "the useless degrading life of most married ladies."[2]

Most married women in Louisiana, where *The Awakening* is set, were the legal property of their husbands. In the late nineteenth century, the Napoleonic code was still the basis of state law governing the marriage contract. Though she might retain control over any inheritances she had received prior to her marriage, all of a wife's "accumulations" after marriage were the property of her husband, including any money she might earn and the clothes she wore. The husband was the legal guardian of the children and until 1888 was granted custody of the children in the event of a divorce. The wife was "bound to live with her husband, and follow him wherever he [chose] to reside." A wife could not sign any legal contract (with the exception of her will) without the consent of her husband, nor could she institute a lawsuit, appear in court, hold public office, or make a donation to a living person. The woman's position in the eyes of the law is well captured in Article 1591 of the laws of Louisiana: "The following persons are absolutely incapable of bearing witness to testaments: 1. Woman of any age whatsoever. 2. Male children who have not attained the age of sixteen years complete. 3. Persons who are insane, deaf, dumb or blind. 4. Persons whom the criminal laws declare incapable of exercising civil functions." Though divorce laws in Louisiana were somewhat more liberal than those in other parts of the country—divorce could be granted on the grounds of abandonment after one year of separation—divorce rates were much lower than in other states. Louisiana was a largely Catholic state, and divorce was a scandalous and rather rare occurrence (twenty-nine divorces granted per one hundred thousand members of the population in 1890). In any case, Chopin's Edna Pontellier had no legal grounds for divorce, though her husband undoubtedly did.

Upper-class southern white women, raised with a particular sense of "woman's place" derived from some mythic age of chivalry, and then drawn by the Civil War into arenas of activity previously unknown and forbidden to them, came relatively late to the women's movement. The 1880s brought the first stirrings of the suffrage movement to New Orleans, and Susan B. Anthony addressed large audiences when she visited the city in 1885 to attend the Cotton Exposition. In 1892 the first suffrage organization, the Portia Club, was formed by Caroline Merrick and Elizabeth Saxon,

2. Per Seyersted, *Kate Chopin: A Critical Biography* (Baton Rouge: Louisiana State UP, 1969) 33. The woman Chopin met was either Victoria Claflin Woodhull (1838–1927) or her sister Tennessee Claflin Cook (1845–1923), journalists, businesswomen, spiritualists, advocates of women's rights including suffrage, dress reform, legalized prostitution, and "free love." In 1872 Victoria Woodhull ran for president of the United States as the nominee of the People's Party.

and later that year, a second suffrage organization, the Era Club (Equal Rights Association), joined efforts with the Portia Club. Before the end of the decade, New Orleans women had won the right to vote on matters of local taxation. Though this concession was undoubtedly in part to assure white supremacy, women's political influence was felt in two important reform efforts: the antilottery campaign of 1891 and later a major campaign to improve sewage and drainage in a city especially subject to epidemic disease.

The New Orleans *Daily Picayune* was the first major American newspaper edited by a woman, and its pages supported a variety of women's causes in the 1890s. Reference to "the New Woman," the late-nineteenth-century equivalent of "the liberated woman," appeared often in its pages. A June 1897 article recounts the occupations that women in the city were pursuing: "Among other things gleaned from [the city directory] of our own city, is the fact that there are two women barbers, following the hirsute tradition in the Crescent City. There are also importers of cigars among the fair sex, six women undertakers, one embalmer, a real estate agent (it is true in partnership with a man), insurance solicitors, several practicing physicians, a box manufacturer, three drummers, a steamboat captain, several florists and a number of liquor dealers." The national census of 1890 showed that in only 9 of the 369 professions listed for the city were women not represented.

These social changes serve as the broad backdrop to *The Awakening* and, in part, explain the avalanche of hostile criticism that the novel received. When Kate Chopin created a fictional hero who would test the limits of freedom for a woman of her social class, she touched a very raw nerve of the body politic. Though Kate Chopin had not lived in New Orleans for twenty years when she wrote *The Awakening*, her visits to Louisiana had made her very aware of change. When she strategically placed her Edna Pontellier in an aristocratic Creole society, she knew it to be much under seige from the newer entrepreneurial society of "American" New Orleans. Chopin also knew, as did her readers, that the privileged, leisured world of Grand Isle where the novel opens had been literally destroyed by a hurricane in 1893, a nice image of "the storm" of social ferment that was leaving America and American women forever changed.[3] When she published her bold novel, Chopin should not have been surprised to find herself caught in the eye of that storm.

The selections that follow are intended to frame *The Awakening* in the variety of its social and cultural contexts. In her novel, Chopin richly references the structures and details of everyday life in a very particular world. Attention to food, costume, reading, visiting, entertaining, leisure activities and the like fill the novel's pages. The documents included here, all roughly contemporary with the novel, ground and extend that reference. It is difficult for a modern reader, for example, to understand the extent to which Edna Pontellier flouts social convention on almost every page. But a glance at etiquette books of the period shows Edna consistently disregarding her "duties" to her husband, her children, and her "station" in life. She does not "manage" the servants; she forms questionable cross-class friendships; she ignores her reception day to walk about the city alone; she attends public places of amusement (the races) with a "gentleman" other than her husband and without a chaperone; she

---

3. See Helen Taylor, *Gender, Race and Region in the Writings of Grace King, Ruth McEnery Stuart, and Kate Chopin* (Baton Rouge: Louisiana State UP, 1989) 177–78. Also, Frederick Stielow, "Grand Isle, Louisiana, and the 'New' Leisure, 1866–1893," *Louisiana History* 23 (1982): 239–57.

hosts an elaborate dinner party in her husband's absence; she rents and moves into a small house of her own; and she has taken a lover. Similarly, it is hard to appreciate the significance of "for the first time in her life she stood naked in the open air," without a picture of what the bathing costume Edna has just cast aside would have been like.[4] More broadly, two examples of white southern chauvinism, the essays by Mary L. Shaffter and Wilbur Fisk Tillett, give glimpses of the ways class and race constructed gender in the period. The advice columns of Dorothy Dix and the social theory of Charlotte Perkins Stetson (Gilman) and Thorstein Veblen demonstrate that in her day Kate Chopin was not the only one challenging the prevailing gender ideology of the period.

An Etiquette/Advice Book Sampler

Duties of the Wife[1]

On the wife especially devolves the privilege and pleasure of rendering home happy. We shall, therefore, speak of such duties and observances as pertain to her. * * *

Avoid All Causes for Complaint

Never let your husband have cause to complain that you are more agreeable abroad than at home; nor permit him to see in you an object of admiration as respects your dress and manners, when in company, while you are negligent of both in the domestic circle. Many an unhappy marriage has been occasioned by neglect in these particulars. Nothing can be more senseless than the conduct of a young woman, who seeks to be admired in general society for her politeness and engaging manners, or skill in music, when, at the same time, she makes no effort to render her home attractive; and yet that home whether a palace or a cottage, is the very centre of her being—the nucleus around which her affections should revolve, and beyond which she has comparatively small concern.

Beware of Confidants

Beware of intrusting any individual whatever with small annoyances, or misunderstandings, between your husband and yourself, if they unhappily occur. Confidants are dangerous persons, and many seek to obtain an ascendency in families by gaining the good opinion of young married women. Be on your guard, and reject every overture that may lead to undesirable intimacy. Should any one presume to offer you

---

4. See below, pp. 135–36.
1. From Richard A. Wells, *Decorum: A Practical Treatise on Etiquette and Dress of the Best American Society* (New York: Union Publishing House, 1886) 248–49. Etiquette books of the period often appeared in numerous editions, and identical text may appear in books with different titles and even different authors.

advice with regard to your husband, or seek to lessen him by insinuations, shun that person as you would a serpent. * * *

Influence of Mothers[2]

* * * What the child needs pre-eminently above playthings, books, clothes, and every other earthly thing, is *the presence and influence of mother.* No other woman in the world can take her place. Many mothers farm their children out to nurses, and then give themselves to household duties, social pleasures, or possibly to duties which may be important in themselves, but which, after all, can only be secondary to the discharge of the all-important duties of motherhood.

Many otherwise excellent women find the nursery a prison, and the care of their own children irksome, simply because they have a perverted mother-sense. The mother should have proper relief from the care of her children, but if she has the true mother-heart the companionship of her children will be the society which she will prefer above that of all others.

Reception Days[3]

Let nothing, but the most imperative duty, call you out upon your reception day. Your callers are, in a measure, invited guests, and it will be an insulting mark of rudeness to be out when they call. Neither can you be excused, except in case of sickness.

Having appointed the day when you will be at home to see your friends, you must, for that day, prepare to give your time wholly to them. The usual hours for morning receptions are from twelve to three, and you should be dressed, and ready for callers, at least half an hour before that time.

Rules for Summer Resorts[4]

At places of summer resort, those who own their cottages, call first upon those who rent them, and those who rent, in turn, call upon each other, according to priority of arrival. In all these cases there are exceptions; as, where there is any great difference in ages, the younger then calling upon the older, if there has been a previous acquaintance or exchange of calls. If there has been no previous acquaintance or exchange of calls, the older lady pays the first call, unless she takes the initiative by inviting the younger to call upon her, or by sending her an

2. From Sylvanus Stall, *What A Young Husband Ought to Know* (Philadelphia: Vir Publishing, 1897) 293.
3. From Florence Hartley, *The Ladies Book of Etiquette and Manual of Politeness* (Philadelphia: Evans, 1860) 76–77.
4. From John H. Young, *Our Deportment, Or the Manners, Conduct and Dress of the Most Refined Society* (Springfield, MA, 1882) 56.

invitation to some entertainment, which she is about to give. When the occupants of two villas, who have arrived the same season, meet at the house of a common friend, and the older of the two uses her privilege of inviting the other to call, it would be a positive rudeness not to call; and the sooner the call is made, the more civil will it be considered. It is equally rude, when one lady asks permission of another to bring a friend to call, and then neglects to do it, after permission has been given. If the acquaintance is not desired, the first call can be the last.

Flirtation and Increasing Fastness of Manner[5]

Flirtation is more openly indulged in by married women, even those who are old enough to have grown-up daughers, than ever before, and *fastness of manner* is certainly rapidly on the increase.

* * * we may not be surprised to see the woman of fifty assuming the graces of sixteen, and occupying the corridors and piazzas of watering-place hotels with feeble attendant swains. It is a melancholy spectacle to those who desire to respect or love the woman, particularly to her sons and daughters. But her end is gained if somebody says: "Oh, Mrs. Feathercap is such a very fascinating woman to gentlemen!" She dresses, poses, and lives painfully, to reach this goal, and becomes the worst model for her young countrywomen to follow.

Flirtation among the young is forgiven, because it is very like the best and noblest event of human life—a true and honest love affair. It is a very good artificial rose—very like a real one; therefore we prefer it. Youth and high spirits being good things to have, we forgive their excesses and pardon their follies. There is no doubt that a coquettish and flirtatious girl, however, although she may become very fashionable, the reigning belle and the *toast*, is dangerously periling her chances for a good marriage by her habits of freebootery. No man cares to marry a free lance. Let her catch her fish, land him safely, and then, as a young married woman, let her go in and win as a married flirt. She will gain a fashionable position and a detestable reputation.

Musicales[6]

The character of the music and the length of the programme are decided upon by the lady giving the musicale, and it is supposed that a cultivated knowledge of music and some consideration for the known tastes of her guests govern this part of the preparations. Classical selections receive positions of honor in the list, but lighter melodies should not be obstracized altogether, as even in an audience selected for its profound music-lore there are sure to be some who will appreciate a

5. From *The American Code of Manners: a Study of the Usages, Laws and Observances which govern Intercourse in the Best Social Circles* . . . (New York: Andrews, 1880) 194, 196–97.
6. From [Eliza Lavin], *Good Manners*, 3rd ed. (New York: Butterick Publishing Company, 1889) 229.

ballad or a popular instrumental piece which suggests heroic reminiscences. The opening selection is usually instrumental, and the performer has quite as much right to expect respectful silence during instrumental as vocal music. It is downright rudeness to withhold it. A fashionable musicale may be given with only the piano for instrumental music and with a soprano and tenor of exceptional note for vocalists, an accompanist being also provided; but very often the piano is reinforced by the violin, a mandolin quartette is included, the singers number four or more, and solos, trios and duets vary the programme.

The Street Manners of a Lady[7]

The true lady walks the street, wrapped in a mantle of proper reserve, so impenetrable that insult and coarse familiarity shrink from her, while she, at the same time, carries with her a congenial atmosphere which attracts all, and puts all at their ease.

A lady walks quietly through the streets, seeing and hearing nothing that she ought not to see and hear, recognizing acquaintances with a courteous bow, and friends with words of greeting. She is always unobtrusive, never talks loudly, or laughs boisterously, or does anything to attract the attention of the passers-by. She walks along in her own quiet, lady-like way, and by her pre-occupation is secure from any annoyance to which a person of less perfect breeding might be subjected.

Places of Amusement[8]

Do not accept an invitation to visit any place of public amusement, with a gentleman with whom you are but slightly acquainted, unless there is another lady also invited. You may, as a young lady, go with a relative or your fiancée, without a chaperon, but not otherwise.

Formal Dinner Parties[9]

It is needless to say to aspirants for social honors, who really wish to "entertain," that dinner-giving is a serious expense, and entails all sorts of obligations upon the embarkers in such an enterprise. * * *

Suppose you start with a dinner of eight, which is the most comfortable, genial—and expensive—number. You have a moderate-sized dining-room, and a large acquaintance. You are happy in the possession of a reliable cook, and a fair table-waitress. If the latter has a head, and table-sense, she may be able to wait on eight, but certainly not, of course, if you have champagne. That requires an expert's whole time. Let us suppose you do not have champagne, and that your one woman

7. Young 145–46.
8. Hartley 172.
9. From *Etiquette for Americans by a Woman of Fashion* (Chicago: Herbert S. Stone, 1898) 74–79, 85.

is expected to take entire care of the guests. They are formal, consisting of two august couples, middle-aged; an engaged pair, youthful; besides yourselves. Your *menu* is by no means the greatest care. You write that out, and give it to your cook. It consists of caviare sandwiches and vermouth cocktails; oysters and sherry; lobster cutlets and sauterne; mushrooms on toast, claret for the ladies, Scotch whisky and aërated water of some kind for the men—these two kept up through the dinner; joint with two or three vegetables; salad and game, biscuits and perhaps a compote next; a pudding, hot or cold; fruit, cheese and coffee. Sweets must be on the table, and condiments, olives, etc. Flowers may be omitted (but never are) if you have a handsome dish of fruit, candelabra, and plenty of small things about. But the dishes mentioned are the fewest possible at a formal first dinner.

* * * After dinner come liqueurs, carefully prepared with pounded ice; coffee in the drawing-room, cigarettes and lights for the men; and half an hour after dinner, aërated water again, for there is an almost inevitable after-dinner-party thirst. * * *

Dinners of ten, twelve and fourteen cannot be managed without three, four and six servants, in any sort of order, and are absolutely forbidden to any but the well-to-do. * * *

Your husband must be near you; for although the dinner is the hostess' affair, the invitations are given out in the names of both; and only a very informal dinner permits him to be absent.

Dress to Suit the Occasion[1]

The dress should always be adapted to the occasion. Nothing is more proper for the morning than a loosely made dress, high in the neck, with sleeves fastened at the wrist with a band, and belt. It looks well, and is convenient. For a walking dress, the skirt should be allowed only just to touch the ground; for while a train looks well in the drawing-room, and is inconspicuous in a carriage or opera-box, it serves a very ignoble purpose in sweeping the street. Ladies' shoes for walking should be substantial, to keep the feet dry and warm. If neatly made and well fitted, they need not be clumsy.

Hats are now fashionable for morning walks, and they are both pretty and convenient.

Dress for Receiving Calls[2]

If a lady has a special day for the reception of calls, her dress must be of silk, or other goods suitable to the season, or to her position, but

1. Wells 327.
2. Young 327–28, 326.

must be of quiet colors and plainly worn. Lace collars and cuffs should be worn with this dress, and a certain amount of jewelry is also admissible. A lady whose mornings are devoted to the superintendence of her domestic affairs, may receive a casual caller in her ordinary morning dress, which must be neat, yet plain, with white plain linen collars and cuffs. For New Year's, or other calls of special significance, the dress should be rich, and may be elaborately trimmed. If the parlors are closed and the gas lighted, full evening dress is required.

Carriage Dress

The material for a dress for a drive through the public streets of a city, or along a fashionable drive or park, cannot be too rich. Silks, velvets and laces, are all appropriate, with rich jewelry and costly furs in cold weather. If the fashion require it, the carriage dress may be long enough to trail, or it may be of the length of a walking dress, which many prefer. For driving in the country, a different style of dress is required, as the dust and mud would soil rich material.

The Full Dinner Dress

The full dinner dress for guests admits of great splendor. It may be of any thick texture of silk or velvet for winter, or light rich goods for summer, and should be long and sweeping. Every trifle in a lady's costume should be, as far as she can afford it, faultless. The fan should be perfect in its way, and the gloves should be quite fresh. Diamonds are used in broaches, pendants, ear-rings and bracelets. If artificial flowers are worn in the hair, they should be of the choicest description. All the light neutral tints, and black, dark blue, purple, dark green, garnet, brown and fawn are suited for dinner wear.

Costumes for Country and Sea-side[3]

We cannot give a full description of the wardrobe which the lady of fashion desires to take with her to the country or sea-side. But there are a few general rules which apply to many things, and which all must more or less observe. Let the wardrobe be ever so large there must be a certain number of costumes suited for ordinary wear. Thus, dresses, while they may be somewhat brighter in tint than good taste would justify in the streets of a city, must yet be durable in quality and of material which can be washed. The brim of the hat should be broad to protect the face from the sun. The fashion of making hats of shirred muslin is a very sensible one, as it enables them to be done up when

3. Wells 341.

they are soiled. The boots should be strong and durable. A waterproof is an indispensable article to the sojourner at country resorts.

Bathing Dresses[4]

The problem of bathing dresses is always one that is rather perplexing, for while, in a general way, the style does not change, there are always little points of difference from year to year.

There is no longer any question about the length of a skirt or of the trousers that are worn, for it is now some years since the law went forth that it was not necessary to wear long ungainly trousers fastened in at the ankles and skirts as scant as possible, so that a jaunty smart effect is perfectly possible, even in the plainest of dresses. Most women know how to swim, or are learning to, so that also has to be considered, for their dress must then be made to allow as much freedom of the limbs as possible, and there must be nothing to hamper the circulation in any way.

The material which stays in favor the longest for bathing dresses is serge. There have been a great many innovations of late years, and other materials are extensively used; but serge seems to be the prime favorite. A rough heavy serge, that does not retain the moisture, will wear well for two or three seasons without losing its color or shrinking. It is not well to buy too expensive a one, for it does not seem to wear as well as the coarser varieties, and the fine twill is never as effective.

The best way to make up a bathing suit is with full short trousers or knickerbockers gartered above the knee, and a short skirt made with gored front breadth, a little fulness over the hips, and considerable fulness in the back. This skirt should be finished with a deep hem, and the seams should be stitched with silk, for even the best cotton loses its color quickly in salt water, and the suit will look shabby long before the material shows the slightest sign of wear. The waist must be made to have the appearance of fit—the back with a little fulness drawn in under the belt; the front slightly bloused, cut in sailor-blouse fashion with wide open revers;[5] sleeves, short puffs reaching only half-way down the arm, this to give full play to the arms when swimming. As many stout women object to the full knickerbockers, it is quite possible to have them made with only sufficient fulness to prevent their drawing tightly over the leg. One design has the waist and trousers all in one piece, and then the skirt buttoned on at the waist line under the belt. The other plan is to have the waist and the skirt in one piece, and the trousers separate.

Mohair is another favorite material for bathing suits. It sheds the water quite as well as serge, and when wet has a silky look that is attractive. There is no difference in the style for the different materials, but there

4. From "New York Fashions," *Harper's Bazar* 25 June 1898: 551.
5. Part of a garment folded over to show the inside, as a lapel [*Editor*].

is a great deal of difference in the way in which the waists are trimmed. The revers are faced with some bright color, and there are a sailor collar and belt which match the revers. These can be made of blue, red, black, or white, and trimmed with bands of braid or left plain. The different kinds of duck are used to face them, as is also turkey-red cotton, and on many expensive ones silk is used, and silk does retain its color marvellously.

Of course where the blouse opens at the throat there must needs be a piece shaped like a vest buttoned underneath, exactly on the plan of the children's sailor suits. These vest pieces are made to match the revers and other trimmings. They must be cut well up in the neck, for, although at the fashionable watering-places last year bathing suits were worn open a little at the throat, it is never good style, and lacks a certain smartness that a trim high-cut waist always possesses.

Many of the mohair skirts are trimmed with bands of some bright color. Black is more used for the body material than anything else, although there are many made of red. The disadvantage of red is that it loses its bright color very quickly. White mohair suits are often seen, but must always be made of the heaviest qualities, for white is too transparent to be modest. It is very pretty, particularly when the trimmings are effective.

Some of the most effective bathing suits seen this year are made of ticking or canvas cloth. This material has its excellent points, and also its very objectionable ones. Its good points are that it sheds the water well, and also retains its stiffness, and of course does not cling to the figure as the others sometimes do. When thoroughly wet it will look just as smart as when it was prefectly dry. It comes in the different stripes we have always been accustomed to see, and can be made more effective by trimmings of bright red, bright blue, or white.

Silk bathing dresses are a little conspicuous, and hardly in good style. They shed the water well, but require a great deal of trimming, and then look overdone and not quite appropriate. Black silk and dark blue silk are the only possible colors, and these are made and trimmed just like the others that have been described.

Mohair, silk, ticking, and all other materials, excepting serge and flannel, require to have the yoke lined with a light flannel, as they are otherwise quite too cool.

What to wear on the head and on the feet is a most important question in a bathing costume. Excepting on rocky beaches, shoes are not worn. Bathing stockings must be long enough to garter well above the knee, and must have good stout soles. As the bathing skirts are all short, the stockings are very much in evidence, and require to be a good shape and well fitted.

There are many different kinds of fancy bathing stockings, but it is not always well to buy them. A heavy ribbed silk, while expensive to start with, wears so well, that the expense is worth while. As a rule black stockings are worn, but some women like to have them match the trimming on their suits. It looks gayer, and is certainly more conspicuous.

Very few embroidered stockings are worn. Some few have clocks, which are supposed to be becoming and make the ankle look more slender. The ribbed ones, however, are the most becoming and the most suitable.

There are many different opinions as to whether salt water is good for the hair or not. It is certainly not pleasant to have long hair soaked in sea-water every other day, or every day, as the case may be; consequently women who are particular wear a rubber cap, and over this a bright handkerchief tied in turban fashion, with the ends in front sticking up very smartly and becomingly. Women who do not wet their hair while bathing have it arranged as high and quite as elaborately as if they were going out to dinner.

The old-fashioned big straw hat tied down over the ears is no longer seen, but there are some smaller bathing hats very much on the same plan, and these prevent the terrible tanning which is part of the sea-bath, and which cannot be anything but injurious to a delicate skin. A bow of bright turkey-red, or flowers that will resist wind, water, and sun, are put on these hats.

Fashion Plates from *Harper's Bazar*

Demi-saison gowns from Félix. August 20, 1898.

Watering-place costume—Paris model from the Maison Weille. July 30, 1898.

Paris costume for the races—Worth Collet and Virot hat. July 13, 1895.

Paris costume for the races. May 15, 1897.

Bathing suit of dull red serge with trimmings of white serge or braid; white canvas belt. April 6, 1901.

Ladies' bathing suits. June 11, 1898.

MARY L. SHAFFTER

Creole Women†

Creoles are the descendants of French or Spanish, born in Louisiana. Incorrectly the term is applied to any one born and living in New Orleans or its vicinity. Indeed there is a broader misapplication common in some parts of the state, where fresh eggs, Louisiana cows, horses, and chickens are called creole eggs, creole ponies, etc.

New Orleans, in reality, is two cities, the dividing line being a broad, tree-bordered avenue, running east and west from Lake Pontchartrain to the Mississippi River. "Up town," or the south side of this avenue, which is called Canal Street, is the home of the American population, while "down town," the north side, is the French or Creole Quarter. Up town the streets and the houses and many of the residents are new. It is a progressive, a self-made, a new city. Down town is the old town, with little improvement since the days when the houses were first built. Occasionally, a creole family crosses the line, as it were, and goes to live up town, but they rarely become Americanized, for, above all things the creole is conservative.

To-day the wealth of the city is in the American portion: thirty or forty years ago its wealth and refinement were centered in the French Quarter. Not much wealth remains there, but the people still possess what money cannot buy—the chivalry of their men and the grace and beauty of their women.

The women are called beautiful, and justly so. It is true that as the years creep on apace, they incline to *embonpoint*[1] and the down on their upper lips often darkens and deepens into a very perceptible line. Despite these facts, a creole woman grows old gracefully, she never becomes coarse looking, and her hands never lose their distinctive marks of refinement.

There live no lovelier girls than those one meets in creole society in New Orleans. Such figures, lithe yet full, such shapely heads, with crowns of glossy black hair, such a clear olive complexion, and great dark eyes, which speak before the arched red lips,—who can condemn the heart that is taken captive by the bewitching beauty of *la belle creole?*[2]

Creole women are artistic by nature; they paint and play and sing. They talk well and are good at repartee. They usually speak several languages, French being their mother tongue. They emphasize with

† Originally appeared in *The Chautauquan* 15 (June 1892): 346–47. Footnotes are by the editor of this Norton Critical Edition.
1. Stoutness, plumpness.
2. The beautiful creole.

gesture, and occasionally surprise the listener with a *Mondieu!* or *O ciel!*[3] which, with them, is no profanity.

As wives, creole women are without superiors; loving and true, they seldom figure in domestic scandals.

The creole woman entertains beautifully. Her salon, her toilet, show the refinement of her taste. In her manner there is none of the American "gush"; she receives with unaffected cordiality, which has the true ring. She is careful in the selection of her friends, for down in the *vieux carré*[4] of New Orleans money cannot purchase an entrance into society.

Creole women, as a rule, are good housekeepers, are economical and industrious. When one pauses to think that these women were reared as princesses, with slaves at their command, one realizes that noble blood has made noble women. They never speak of their poverty, or proclaim their ingenuity in supplying a dainty table from a slender larder. They have accepted their lot, they attend to their homes, they make their cheap dresses with their French taste and wear them with the grace of a *grande dame*.[5] There are many creole women who have striven hard with pride, and have wished to die rather than to acknowledge their poverty, but whose better nature conquered, and they now hold honored places among the bread winners of to-day.

Creole women have large families. This they do not regard as a misfortune, after the manner of some of their more progressive sisters. Their babies are made welcome and tenderly reared. Especially are the girls the object of much solicitude. Above all their beauty must be preserved, their hands and feet, their glossy hair and white teeth must be cared for. They must learn to dance, to sing, and to embroider. Their religion, too, must not be neglected. At ten or twelve they must go, arrayed as brides, to take their first communion. The next few years are spent at a convent, and at sixteen or seventeen the girl is ready for society. She receives with *maman*, visits with *maman*, shops with *maman*, goes to balls, the opera, and to church with *maman*. Sometimes it happens that a gentleman visits the house say five or six times; if so *papa* asks his intentions. If he expresses friendship only, he is then requested to discontinue his coming; but if, on the other hand, he declares his love, all things being desirable, the visitor becomes a suitor, the engagement is announced, the girl wears the honors as a *fiancée* but a short time, and then becomes a wife.

While there is about creole women that refinement that one admires, a *noblesse oblige*[6] that one respects, a dependence that attracts love, it must be acknowledged that as a class they are not progressive. They are tender, loving mothers, they care for the health and beauty of their children, but they know nothing of the beauty and development that

3. "My God!" or "Heavens!"
4. The French Quarter or "old city." See above, p. 6, n. 9.
5. Great lady.
6. Literally, "nobility obligates"—the benevolent or charitable behavior regarded as the obligation of those born to privilege.

come from physical culture. They train the little feet to dance bewitch-ingly, but are horrified at the suggestion of a thick-soled, broad-heeled boot and a five-mile walk.

They are accomplished rather than intellectual. Women's rights, for them, are the right to love and be loved, and to name the babies rather than the next president or city officials.

Musically gifted, they prefer a gay *chansonette* to the intricate passages of one of Bach's fugues, and they would rather wander through the realms of poesie than to venture into the shadowy region of metaphysical laws.

They are not club women, they do not aspire to fame, and it is true that the average creole woman cannot compete, in some respects, with her American sisters.

When the pictures in books do not make creole women proud and pure and loving, capable of great development morally and mentally, women of whom Louisiana should be proud, then it is simply because the painters painted without a model and the writers never knew the password by which to gain admittance into the society of creole women.

WILBUR FISK TILLETT

[Southern Womanhood]†

Among the many changes that have taken place in the Southern States and among Southern people within the past thirty years, some of which are the direct result of war, and others the simple and natural devel-opment of the times, there is none more significant and worthy of notice than the change that has taken place in the condition, the life and the labor of Southern women.

* * *

We might conveniently divide our subject into these three heads: (1) the Southern woman before the war; (2) the Southern woman during the war; (3) the Southern woman since the war. Were this our mode of presenting the subject, it would be to give three pictures of the same woman, and not of three different women. The virtues that adorn and ennoble the Southern woman of to-day find their explanation and origin

---

† From "Southern Womanhood as Affected by the Civil War," *The Century Magazine* 43 (November 1891): 5–16. For a more recent discussion of ideologies of southern womanhood, see Elizabeth Fox-Genovese, *Within the Plantation Household* (Chapel Hill: U of North Carolina P, 1988).

  Kate O'Flaherty was eleven years old when the Civil War broke out. She lost a beloved stepbrother, who died of disease when returning from the Confederate Army. The O'Flaherty family was staunchly anti-Union; the Chopin family left Louisiana when the war broke out and spent those years in France. Emily Toth comments that for Kate O'Flaherty the war meant "street violence, constant fear, and sudden death" (*Kate Chopin* [New York: Morrow, 1990] 70).

largely in that womanhood which for the last fifty years and more has been the product and the pride of the Southern people. No matter what may be one's sympathy with or prejudice against the institution of slavery, there is no denying the fact that American civilization has nowhere produced a purer and loftier type of refined and cultured womanhood than existed in the South before the war. Nowhere else in America have hospitality and social intercourse among the better classes been so cultivated or have constituted so large a part of life as in what is called the old South. These large and constant social demands upon Southern women, growing out of the hospitable customs of the old plantation life, made the existing conditions very favorable for developing women of rare social gifts and accomplishments. In native womanly modesty, in neatness, grace, and beauty of person, in ease and freedom without boldness of manner, in refined and cultivated minds, in gifts and qualities that shone brilliantly in the social circle, in spotless purity of thought and character, in laudable pride of family and devotion to home, kindred, and loved ones—these were the qualities for which Southern women were noted and in which they excelled. That the Southern woman of ante-bellum times lacked those stronger qualities of character and mind that are born only of trials and hardships and poverty and adversity may be granted. That she contributed less in labor, especially manual labor, to the support and economy of the household than women in like financial condition elsewhere may also be granted. But this was not because she was unable or unwilling to work, but simply because it was unnecessary. Before the Southern woman had passed through the four years' fiery ordeal of war, the virtues of character, of head and heart, that are born of adversity were all richly hers.

But the Southern woman's most trying period came only after the war, terminating as it did in the loss of nearly all property, in the entire breaking up of the old home life, and in the emancipation of the slaves, who had always relieved white women of the more unpleasant duties that would otherwise have long fallen to their lot in the economy of domestic life. Thousands upon thousands of delicate and cultivated women who had never done any of the harder and more disagreeable duties of domestic and home life, universally performed by the slaves, were now compelled to enter upon a life of drudgery and hardship for which nothing in their previous training had prepared them. If in prosperity, wealth, and luxury woman is weaker and frailer than man, when adversity comes she is stronger than man, stronger in heart and purpose, stronger to adapt herself to unfortunate circumstances and to make the best of them. Indeed, it is not until adversity comes that we know how strong a creature woman is. Many a trouble that utterly crushes strong man transforms weak woman into a tower of strength. Never did woman have a better opportunity to show this strength than at the close of the war, and right nobly did she meet the emergency and set herself to her work, encouraging and inspiring with hope Southern men, too many of whom had lost heart with their lost cause. It was the heart, the hope, the faith of Southern womanhood that set Southern men to working when the war was over, and in this work they led the way, filling the stronger sex with utter amazement at the readiness and power with which they began to perform duties to which they had never been used before. The wonderful recuperative energies of the Southern people since the war, as manifested in the present wide-spread prosperity of the Southern States, is recognized and admired by all; but who can tell how largely this is due to Southern womanhood? Was it not the brave-hearted wife that inspired the despairing husband when the war had ended to go to work and redeem his lost fortune, happy enough herself that she had a living husband to work with her, since so many of her sisters had to fight the battle with labor and poverty alone, while their husbands slept in the soldier's grave? Was it not the ambitious and hopeful sister that inspired her soldier brother, the unconquered and unconquerable maiden that inspired her disheartened lover, when the war was over? And was not this womanly inspiration the most potent factor that entered the problem of the white man's immediate future in the South? Nor has woman's part in the up-building of the South been one of inspiration simply. It is the work which her own head and hands have acomplished that we wish to speak of more particularly in this paper; not her influence upon other things, but the influence upon her of the changes of the last thirty years. How then has Southern womanhood been affected by these great changes?

* * *

[The author then puts this question to a number of his women correspondents, whose answers follow.]

There is no point perhaps wherein the Southern ideal of woman has changed so much as in the nobility of helplessness in woman. Before the war, so far as I have been able to learn from contact and conversation with those whose knowledge and experience, antedate my own by many years, self-support was a last resort with respectable women in the South, and such a thought was never entertained so long as there was any male relative to look to for support, and men felt responsible for the support of even remote female relatives. So deeply embedded in Southern ideas and feeling was this sentiment of the nobility of dependence and help-lessness in woman, and the degradation of labor, even for self-support, in the sex, that I have heard of instances where refined and able-bodied women would allow themselves to be supported by the charity of their friends rather than resort to work for self-support—and this not because they had any reluctance to work, but because livelihood by charity seemed to them to be the more respectable and honorable alternative of the two. Such instances may not have been very numerous, but they were at least of frequent enough occurrence to show the strong prejudice that existed in the South before the war with reference to white women working. Of course this does not mean that the thousands of wives, mothers, and housekeepers throughout the South did not perform the duties incident to their situation. It was single ladies, and those who had no means of support within their own homes, whom public sentiment forbade to work for self-support; or if they did, it was at the expense of injuring or entirely forfeiting their social standing, and hence was to compromise themselves and their families. Now, on the contrary, a woman is respected and honored in the South for earning her own living, and would lose respect if, as an able-bodied woman, she settled herself as a burden on a brother, or even on a father, working hard for a living, while looking to more-distant male relatives for support is now quite out of the question. As a woman is now respected and honored, rather than discounted socially, for earning her own living when necessary, the field of labor for women is constantly widening. While she would not injure her social position by earning a living at any calling open to her sex, yet, socially, teaching and other forms of literary work have the advantage, and are to be preferred. Other callings, though not exactly tabooed by the sex, yet have such objections to them as would cause a young woman's friends to ask, "What makes her do that? Couldn't she get a place to teach?" This increasing tendency among women to earn their own living by teaching has raised the standard of thoroughness in female education to some extent, though much is still to be desired, especially in the larger schools, where girls are too often sent to be "graduated" rather than to be educated. Southern people, having passed through the financial reverses of the war, now realize as never before that a daughter's bread may some day depend upon herself, and so they want her well educated. And as a thorough knowledge of a few things is a better foundation for self-support than a mere smattering of many accomplishments, there is more tendency toward specialties in woman's education than before the war.

* * *

Woman's opportunities for work have increased. The number of single women who support themselves, and of married women who help their husbands in supporting their families, is much larger than before the war, and this class of women is more respected than in ante-bellum times. The number of vocations open to women is of course much larger than before the war, but the value in money of woman's work is shamefully depreciated. No matter what work a woman does, men will not pay her its full value, not half what they would pay a man for the very same work. There is proof of this unjust discrimination in almost every female college in the South where men and women are employed to do the same or equal work as teachers, not to speak of other callings where they are performing exactly the same work for very unequal wages.

If then we look at this question concerning Southern womanhood in the light of the present and of the more hopeful future, rather than of the past succeeding the war, I can say that in my judgment the freeing of the slaves and the changed conditions of life resulting from the war have proved a blessing to the white women of the South. It has taught them the value of actual labor with their own hands; it has taught them that the hardships and trials of life teach useful lessons, and have their rewards. It has proved to them that poverty does not necessarily degrade, that culture and refinement may preside in the kitchen, mold the biscuit and watch the griddle, turn the steak and bake the cake, but that wisdom and economy must be constantly exercised or there will be little time for anything but these homely duties.

* * *

The growing respectability of self-support in woman is everywhere recognized as one of the healthiest signs of the times. The number of vocations open to women is constantly on the increase. Some modes of self-support are, and always will be, socially more respectable than others. In the report of 1888 of the Commissioner of Labor concerning the number and condition of working-women in the large cities is the following concerning Charleston, South Carolina:

> In no other Southern city has the exclusion of women from business been so rigid and the tradition that respectability is forfeited by manual labor so influential and powerful. Proud and well-born women have practised great self-denial at ill-paid conventional pursuits in preference to independence in untrodden paths. The embargo against self-support, however, has to some extent been lifted, and were there a larger number of remunerative occupations open to women, the rush to avail of them would show how ineffectual the old traditions have become.

A similar report of 1890 would show rapid changes and advances in public sentiment concerning the respectability of self-support in women, and would reveal that the "embargo" had, in most parts of the South at least, been entirely removed.

If we look at the South as a whole, and not at individual portions of it, it is unquestionably true that the great changes which the past thirty years have witnessed have wrought most favorably upon the intellectual life of Southern womanhood. The conditions under which Southern women now live are far more favorable for developing literary women than those existing in the days of slavery. In 1869 a volume was published by Mr. James Wood Davidson entitled "The Living Writers of the South," in which 241 writers are noticed, of which number 75 are women and 166 are men. Of the 241 named, 40 had written only for newspapers and magazines, while 201 had published one or more volumes, aggregating 739 in all. Although this book was published only four years after the close of the war, it was even then true that from two thirds to three fourths of the volumes mentioned in it as having been published by women—not to speak of the others—had been written and published after the opening of the war. They had been called forth by the war and the trying experiences following it. Whether the changed conditions under which we live have anything to do with it, it is nevertheless certainly true that there have been more literary women developed in the South in the thirty years since the war than in all our previous history.

* * *

It is Victor Hugo who has called this "the century of woman." It is certainly an age that has witnessed great changes in the life, education, and labor of women everywhere; and these changes have all been in the direction of enlarging the sphere of woman's activities, increasing her liberties, and opening up possibilities to her life hitherto restricted to man. It is a movement limited to no land and to no race. So far as this movement may have any tendency to take woman out of her true place in the home, to give her man's work to do and to develop masculine qualities in her, it finds no sympathy in the South. The Southern woman loves the retirement of home, and shrinks from everything that would tend to bring her into the public gaze.

DOROTHY DIX

Are Women Growing Selfish?†

Women have been extolled for their unselfishness so long that it comes with a shock of surprise to learn that their pet virtue has at last been called into question. Nay, it has been more than questioned. It has been positively asserted that woman is the very quintessence of selfishness. It is boldly charged that she thinks of nothing but her own pleasures, amusements and interest. She is accused of belonging to clubs that are neither more nor less than mutual admiration societies, where women meet together to glorify their own sex and formulate plans for its advancement. Worse than that, she goes off in summer to the mountains or seaside, leaving her poor down-trodden husband to swelter in the city, without even the reward of a cool smile or a frozen glance when he returns home at night after his arduous day's work. If this is not ingrained, hopeless, conscienceless selfishness, the critics would just like to know what is, that's all.

From time immemorial it has been the custom of woman to sacrifice heself whenever she got a chance, and any deflection from the course she was expected to pursue must necessarily occasion a deal of comment.

† Dorothy Dix (Elizabeth Gilmer, 1861–1951) was the first advice-to-women columnist in America. Beginning in 1895 she wrote for the major newspaper in New Orleans, *The Daily Picayune*. The items here are from her column, which was entitled "Dorothy Dix Speaks." This first item is from *The Daily Picayune* 15 Aug. 1897.

Unselfishness with her has been a cult. She has worn it ostentatiously, and flaunted it in the face of the world with a feeling that it would make good any other deficiencies or shortcomings. She has courted persecution, and gone out of her way to become a martyr. She has accounted it unto herself for righteousness to do those things she did not wish to do, and to leave undone those things she was dying to do. On the platform of pure and unadulterated unselfishness she has taken a stand, and defied competition, and now when she wishes to climb down and off, and give other people a chance to practice the virtue they admire so much, she is cruelly misjudged and assailed.

It must be admitted in all fairness that this attitude of perfect self-abnegation is one which men have never failed to praise, but seldom emulated. Men have always taken a saner view of life than women. A woman sacrifices herself in a thousand needless little ways which do no one any good, but when a man makes a sacrifice it is big with heroism, and counts. A woman thinks she is being good when she is uncomfortable. A man knows people are much more apt to be good when they are comfortable. No man with a full purse and a full stomach was ever an anarchist.

The truth of the matter simply is that women have awakened to the fact that they have been overdoing the self-sacrifice business. A reasonable amount of unselfishness is all right. It is the sense of justice with which we recognize other people's rights; it is the love that makes us prefer another to ourselves; it is the adorable grace and sweetness that softens a strong and independent character, and is as far different as possible from the lack of backbone that weakly gives away before everything and everybody.

* * *

The same thing may be said of the attitude of one's husband. The woman who makes a slave of herself, gets a slave's pay in contemptuous indifference. No man ever cared for the thing that groveled at his feet, and those women have been best loved who have stood up for their rights, and at every stage of the matrimonial journey have demanded upon courteous treatment, and a fair divide of the pleasures and perquisites of their joint partnership. It is a theory of the perfectly unselfish woman that she must bear everything without complaint. She must put up with drunkenness, and ill-temper, and abuse, and not a murmur must cross her lips. I have often wondered how much these evils were encouraged by this supineness, and that if women had the courage to kick, like men would, if they couldn't remedy them. You never catch a man bearing a thing until he has made a vigorous protest against it. A drunken woman, reeling home, is no more disgusting than a drunken man, yet nobody would expect a man to put up with such a state of affairs for a moment. A woman knows very well she isn't going to be pitied and forgiven, and the result is she keeps sober. I have known a man who browbeat and bullied a meek, little, self-sacrificing wife into the grave, called down and terrorized into a decent and considerate husband by a determined second wife. Undoubtedly the woman who is imposed upon has only herself to blame.

Are women growing selfish? I answer, no. They are beginning to realize that there is a middle ground between being a monster of selfishness and a door mat for everybody to walk over and on that middle ground they propose to take their stand. But wherever there is a clarion call to duty, wherever love lies wounded and bleeding, and in want of succor, wherever there is need of tender nursing or pitying tears, there in the future, as in the past, will women be found, last at the cross, and earliest at the tomb.[1]

The American Wife[2]

* * * It always seems to the American woman that the wives of other countries, who are held up for her admiration and imitation, have rather the easiest time of it. It would be comparatively simple to make yourself a decorative object to adorn a man's house, if that were all that was expected of you. It would be simple enough to accomplish marvels of cooking and housekeeping if that were the chief end of life. It is when one attempts to combine the useful and the ornamental—to be a Dresden statuette in the parlor and a reliable range in the kitchen—that the situation becomes trying, and calls for genuine ability. Yet this is what we expect of the average American wife, merely as a matter of course. She must be a paragon of domesticity, an ornament in society, a wonder in finance and a light in the literary circle to which she belongs.

In our curious social system, many things are left to her that the men attend to in other countries. For one thing, her husband expects her to assume all authority and management of the home and family. He doesn't want to be bothered about it. When he makes the money he feels he has done his whole duty, and he leaves the rest to her. When he comes home, tired out, after a day's work, he wants to rest, to read his paper, to think out some scheme in which he is interested. If his wife has any idea of leaning on his superior judgment and asking his advice about domestic problems she is very soon undeceived. "Great Scotts, Mary," is the impatient reply, "can't you manage your own affairs? I haven't got time to see about it. Settle it yourself."

It is the same way about the children. The American father is generally a devoted parent, but he wants his wife to do the managing and disciplining. In the brief hours he is at home, the little ones are his playthings, and he spoils them, and indulges them with a happy sense that he has

---

1. A reference to the women (including Mary Magdalene) who were present at the Crucifixion and Resurrection of Jesus. See Matthew 27.56 and 28.1; Mark 15.40 and 16.1; Luke 23.55 and 24.10; and John 20.1 [*Editor*].
2. *The Daily Picayune* 23 Jan. 1898.

no responsibility about it and that their mother will have to do the subsequent disciplining . She is responsible for their mental and physical well-being. She decides on the schools, and what they shall study, what colleges they shall attend, and all the rest of it. The average American John has a well-founded belief that his Mary is the smartest woman in the world, and knows what she is about, and so, at last, when she announces that the children need to go to Europe to study this or that, he consents through mere force of habit. He is so much in the way of letting her decide things it doesn't occur to him he could raise a dissenting voice.

To her, too, her leaves the matter of society. She dominates it, and runs it, and an American married man's social position depends entirely on his wife. If she is ambitious he climbs meekly up the social ladder in her wake; if she is not ambitious, they sit comfortably and contentedly down on the lower rungs, and stay there. He feels that he would be a bungler in the game of society, and he simply backs her hand for all it is worth. He pays for the house in the fashionable neighborhood of her choice, and for her entertainments, but he leaves all the rest to "mother and the girls." They must attend to the intricate social machinery, that he admits is a necessity, and is perfectly willing to support with anything but his own presence. * * *

Summer Flirtations[3]

* * * But did you ever think that among all the inexplicable vagaries of human nature there is none so peculiar as the latitude we lend ourselves in the summer? Is dignity, common sense and even plain decency a matter of the thermometer? You see women such prudes they will hardly raise their frocks two inches to keep them out of the mud in the winter, posing around on the beach at the seaside in summer in clothes that would bring a blush to the cheek of a wooden Indian. You see women who are the pink of propriety at home drinking mixed drinks in public places that are none too proper, and you see women noted for exclusiveness, recklessly making acquaintances with strangers of whose antecedents they know absolutely nothing. What, one might ask, has brought about such a revolution? Nothing at all. It is merely summer, and we have let ourselves go. With the first cold weather madame will resume her stiff tailor-made frock, and with it her perfectly correct ideas of deportment. She will also resume her previous attitude towards the church and society, and when she meets the pleasant, though socially undesirable men and women with whom she was on such delightful terms of bon commaradie during the summer, she will simply look through them as if she was gazing at vacancy, with nothing to intercept her view. We have all seen it a hundred times, and we will see it again

3. *The Daily Picayune* 13 Aug. 1899.

as long as summer follies and winter repentance continue to follow each
other.

But by far the most amazing part of the whole thing is the summer
flirtation. Why summer should be given over to sentiment more than
other seasons of the year is one of the things nobody understands. That
it is, is a fact no one will deny, and it is probably the reason that we
call the summer season the silly season. The summer flirtation, at any
rate, is a recognized institution, and an accessory just as much as the
hop and tennis courts, and golf links, and no matter what other diversions
a girl had during her summer outing she would consider the whole thing
a dead failure if it did not include a flirtation. It is this that makes the
presence of man such an event. Of course, we all recognize that at times
everywhere man is a necessity, and at all seasons a convenience to have
about the house, but at a summer resort he becomes a gilt-edged luxury.

*   *   *

The married flirt—the woman who has achieved a kind of temporary
widowhood by going off for the summer—is even more dangerous. Like
the widow, she knows all the ropes and possesses all the advantage that
the professional always has over the amateur, with this further point in
her favor, that there is a definite time limit to the flirtation. She knows,
and the man knows, that when the vacation is over and the time comes
to part, he will look down upon her and sigh, and she will look up
and sigh, and both will murmur, "If we had only met sooner," and that
will end it. No tears, no future making good of reckless promises and
vows, no scenes, nothing more expected of either one, nothing to sneak
out of and feel mean about, which men hate. It was a game played on
top of the table between evenly matched players, and it ends in a draw.

*   *   *

A Strike for Liberty[4]

There comes a time in the life of almost every woman when she has
to choose between a species of slavery and freedom, and when, if she
ever expects to enjoy any future liberty, she must hoist the red flag of
revolt and make a fight for her rights. It counts for nothing that the
oppressor is generally of her own household and is blissfully unconscious
of being a tyrant. One may be bound just as securely and as fatally with
silken cords as with iron fetters, and the fact that our jailer happens to
love us does not offer adequate compensation for being in prison. No
amount of gilding ever made a cage attractive to the poor wretch within.

All of us have sufficient spirit to repel the attacks of the enemy from
without. We are armed and prepared for them, and their first act of
aggression rouses our fighting blood, but there is nothing else on earth

4. *The Daily Picayune* 29 Oct. 1899.

that takes so much cool nerve and determination and courage as to make a stand against those we love and whom we dread to wound. The thought that we will hurt them or anger them, makes cowards of us, and we keep giving in, and giving in, to their demands and whims and caprices until some fine day we find out that we have not a vestige of personal liberty left, and are nothing more than bond slaves to the tyrant on our hearth.

Chief and foremost among these oppressors are children. In her desire to be a good mother, and to do everything possible for her child's welfare, the average mother permits herself to be made a martyr before she realizes it. It doesn't take a baby but three days to develop all the amiable traits and the despotic power of a Nero and a Caligula,[5] and there are plenty of women who never draw a single breath of freedom after their first child is born. They may have the very best of nurses, but angel Freddy howls like a Commanche unless his mother sits by his side and holds his hand until he goes to sleep, or darling Mary won't let the nurse undress her, and so no matter how interesting the conversation downstairs, or how important the guest, the poor mother has to leave it all, and spend her evening in solitary confinement in a dark room to gratify the whims of a selfish and unreasonable little creature.

* * *

Sometimes—and it is one of the cruelest situations of untoward fate—it is against her husband that a woman must make a stand, unless her whole married life is to degenerate into a kind of purgatory. She loves him and is sure of his affection for her. She respects all the sterling worth of his character, his honor, his honesty, his truth and goodness. She appreciates all his hard work and his sacrifices to support his family in comfort. For a long time it has made her bear many things with patience. She has made the excuse of "overwork" and "nerves," those convenient packhorses on which we lay too much ill-temper and brutality, hoping that time would cure the fault. It may be that he has fallen into a way of petty nagging. She cannot express an opinion without having him sneer it down. He ridicules her efforts at self-improvement, and derides her church and clubs, and she feels insulted and outraged before her children and servants; or he flashes out impatient speeches that sear her heart like a redhot iron. Often and often it is the money question. He doles out a quarter here and there, and grumbles over the bills until she feels herself as much a mendicant as the very beggar that asks alms on the street corner.

A woman in such a position, and her name is Mrs. Legion, feels that she is the most helpless creature living. There's no question of divorce for her. With all his faults she loves her tyrant still for the good and the lovableness that is in him. She wouldn't leave him if she could, but

<hr>

5. Emperors of Rome: Nero from A.D. 54 to 68, Caligula from A.D. 37 to 41 [Editor].

none the less the bitterness of death is in her soul, all the crueler and more desperate that she sees nothing for it but endurance. My dear sisters, if you have got the courage to make a fight, you can conquer. Make your stand on your right to be treated with the courtesy your husband would show a lady, and you take an unassailable position. Assert your right to a share in the finances of the partnership of matrimony. Refuse to be any longer a beggar. Ninety-nine times out of a hundred a woman has only to make one stand against oppression to gain a victory that lasts a life time, and she not only wins for herself decent treatment, but respect and admiration, for it is one of the unalterable principles of human nature that we despise those who permit us to impose on them. Contemporary history does not show one single meek woman whose husband treated her with ordinary civility. * * *

Women and Suicide[6]

The claim recently put boldly forth by a distinguished lawyer that a person has a right to die, when by means of disease or misfortune life becomes a burden, has provoked renewed discussion of the suicide question, and it is interesting, in this connection, to note that by far the larger number of suicides are among men. Women seldom take their own lives, and so we have the curious and contradictory spectacle of the sex that is universally accounted the braver and stronger, flinging themselves out of the world to avoid its troubles, while the weaklings patiently bear theirs on to the bitter end.

Nothing is more common than for the man who has speculated with other people's money and lost, and so brought ruin and disgrace on his family, to commit suicide. In fact, after reading of the trusted cashier going wrong, in one column, we almost expect to read in the next that he shot himself. No thought apparently comes to him of having any duty to stay and help lift the misery he brought on innocent people. In times of great financial stress, when a rich man has everything swept away, he, too, often solves the question of the future for himself by suicide, leaving his wife and little children to face a situation for which they are wholly unprepared. You never hear of a woman committing suicide and leaving her little children to the cruel mercies of the world, because she has lost her property. Instead, she feels more than ever that they need her care, and her help, and that she would be incapable of the unmentionable baseness of deserting them in such a crisis.

Yet if suicide is ever justifiable, it is for woman far more than men. She is always handicapped in the race of life. Sometimes with bodily infirmities, sometimes with mental idiosyncrasies, always by lack of training and business experience. Hard as poverty is for a man, it is

6. *The Daily Picayune* 8 Oct. 1899. Appeared unsigned on the woman's page, which was under the editorship of Dorothy Dix.

harder still for a woman. Desperate as the struggle for existence is for him, it is still more desperate for her, limited by narrower opportunities, and rewarded with lesser pay. Terrible as are the tortures suffered by many a poor wretch, they are no worse than the life-long martyrdom that many a woman endures with never a thought of doing anything but bearing them with Christian fortitude and resignation until God's own hand sets her free.

There are many reasons why this state of affairs should exist. Woman's whole life is one long lesson in patience and submission. She must always give in. Men feel that they are born to command, to force circumstances to their will, and when circumstances can no longer be forced or bent, and they must yield to untoward fate, too many yield to the desire to avoid the misery they see before them by sneaking out of life. It is always a coward's deed. The babe salutes life with a wail, and the dying man takes leave of it with a groan. Between there is no time that has not its own troubles, and cares, and sorrows, and it is our part to bear them with courage, and it should be part of our pride in our sex that so many women sustain this brave attitude towards life under circumstances that might well tempt them to play the coward's part.

CHARLOTTE PERKINS STETSON (GILMAN)

From *Women and Economics*†

* * * Our thrones have been emptied, and turned into mere chairs for passing presidents. Our churches have been opened to the light of modern life, and the odor of sanctity has been freshened with sweet sunny air. We can see room for change in these old sanctuaries, but none in the sanctuary of the home. And this temple, with its rights, is so closely interwound with the services of subject woman, its altar so demands her ceaseless sacrifices, that we find it impossible to conceive of any other basis of human living. We are chilled to the heart's core by the fear of losing any of these ancient and hallowed associations. Without this blessed background of all our memories and foreground of all our hopes, life seems empty indeed. In homes we were all born. In homes we all die or hope to die. In homes we all live or want to live. For homes we all labor, in them or out of them. The home is the centre and circumference, the start and the finish, of most of our lives. We love it with a love older than the human race. We reverence it with the blind obeisance of those crouching centuries when its cult began. We cling to it with the tenacity of every inmost, oldest instinct of our

† From *Women and Economics: A Study of the Economic Relation Between Men and Women as a Factor in Social Evolution* (Boston: Small, Maynard, 1899).

animal natures, and with the enthusiasm of every latest word in the unbroken chant of adoration which we have sung to it since first we learned to praise.

And since we hold that our home life, just as we have it, is the best thing on earth, and that our home life plainly demands one whole woman at the least to each home, and usually more, it follows that anything which offers to change the position of woman threatens to "undermine the home," "strikes at the root of the family," and we will have none of it. If, in honest endeavor to keep up to the modern standard of free thought and free speech, we do listen,—turning from our idol for a moment, and saying to the daring iconoclast, "Come, show us anything better!"—with what unlimited derision do we greet his proposed substitute! Yet everywhere about us to-day this inner tower, this castle keep of vanishing tradition, is becoming more difficult to defend or even to keep in repair. We buttress it anew with every generation; we love its very cracks and crumbling corners; we hang and drape it with endless decorations; we hide the looming dangers overhead with fresh clouds of incense; and we demand of the would-be repairers and rebuilders that they prove to us the desirability of their wild plans before they lift a hammer. But, when they show their plans, we laugh them to scorn.

* * *

Worse than the check set upon the physical activities of women has been the restriction of their power to think and judge for themselves. The extended use of the human will and its decisions is conditioned upon free, voluntary action. In her rudimentary position, woman was denied the physical freedom which underlies all knowledge, she was denied the mental freedom which is the path to further wisdom, she was denied the moral freedom of being mistress of her own action and of learning by the merciful law of consequences what was right and what was wrong; and she has remained, perforce, undeveloped in the larger judgment of ethics.

Her moral sense is large enough, morbidly large, because in this tutelage she is always being praised or blamed for her conduct. She lives in a forcing-bed of sensitiveness to moral distinctions, but the broad judgment that alone can guide and govern this sensitiveness she has not. Her contribution to moral progress has added to the anguish of the world the fierce sense of sin and shame, the desperate desire to do right, the fear of wrong; without giving it the essential help of a practical wisdom and a regulated will. Inheriting with each generation the accumulating forces of our social nature, set back in each generation by the conditions of the primitive human female, women have become vividly self-conscious centres of moral impulse, but poor guides as to the conduct which alone can make that impulse useful and build the habit of morality into the constitution of the race.

Recognizing her intense feeling on moral lines, and seeing in her the rigidly preserved virtues of faith, submission, and self-sacrifice,—qualities which in the Dark Ages were held to be the first of virtues,—we have agreed of late years to call woman the moral superior of man. But the ceaseless growth of human life, social life, has developed in him new virtues, later, higher, more needful; and the moral nature of woman, as maintained in this rudimentary stage by her economic dependence, is a continual check to the progress of the human soul. The main feature of her life—the restriction of her range of duty to the love and service of her own immediate family—acts upon us continually as a retarding influence, hindering the expansion of the spirit of social love and service on which our very lives depend. It keeps the moral standard of the patriarchal era still before us, and blinds our eyes to the full duty of man.

An intense self-consciousness, born of the ceaseless contact of close personal relation; an inordinate self-interest, bred by the constant personal attention and service of this relation; a feverish, torturing, moral sensitiveness, without the width and clarity of vision of a full-grown moral sense; a thwarted will, used to meek surrender, cunning evasion, or futile rebellion; a childish, wavering, short-range judgment, handicapped by emotion; a measureless devotion to one's own sex relatives, and a maternal passion swollen with the full strength of the great social heart, but denied social expression,—such psychic qualities as these, born in us all, are the inevitable result of the sexuo-economic relation.

It is not alone upon woman, and, through her, upon the race, that the ill-effects may be observed. Man, as master, has suffered from his position also. The lust for power and conquest, natural to the male of any species, has been fostered in him to an enormous degree by this cheap and easy lordship. His dominance is not that of one chosen as best fitted to rule or of one ruling by successful competition with "foemen worthy of his steel"; but it is a sovereignty based on the accident of sex, and holding over such helpless and inferior dependants as could not question or oppose. The easy superiority that needs no striving to maintain it; the temptation to cruelty always begotten by irresponsible power; the pride and self-will which surely accompany it,—these qualities have been bred into the souls of men by their side of the relation. When man's place was maintained by brute force, it made him more brutal: when his place was maintained by purchase, by the power of economic necessity, then he grew into the merciless use of such power as distinguishes him to-day.

Another giant evil engendered by this relation is what we call selfishness. Social life tends to reduce this feeling, which is but a belated individualism; but the sexuo-economic relation fosters and developes it. To have a whole human creature consecrated to his direct personal service, to pleasing and satisfying him in every way possible,—this has kept man selfish beyond the degree incidental to our stage of social growth. Even in our artificial society life men are more forbearing and considerate, more polite and kind, than they are at home. Pride, cruelty, and selfishness are the vices of the master; and these have been kept strong in the bosom of the family through the false position of woman. And every human soul is born, an impressionable child, into the close presence of these conditions. Our men must live in the ethics of a civilized free, industrial, democratic age; but they are born and trained in the moral atmosphere of a primitive patriarchate. No wonder that we are all somewhat slow to rise to the full powers and privileges of democracy, to feel full social honor and social duty, while every soul of us is reared in this stronghold of ancient and outgrown emotions,—the economically related family.

So we may trace from the sexuo-economic relation of our species not only definite evils in psychic development, bred severally in men and women, and transmitted indifferently to their offspring, but the innate perversion of character resultant from the moral miscegenation of two so diverse souls,—the unfailing shadow and distortion which has darkened and twisted the spirit of man from its beginnings. We have been injured in body and in mind by the too dissimilar traits inherited from our widely separated parents, but nowhere is the injury more apparent than in its ill effects upon the moral nature of the race.

Yet here, as in the other evil results of the sexuo-economic relation, we can see the accompanying good that made the condition necessary in its time; and we can follow the beautiful results of our present changes with comforting assurance. A healthy, normal moral sense will be ours, freed from its exaggerations and contradictions; and, with that clear perception, we shall no longer conceive of the ethical process as something outside of and against nature, but as the most natural thing in the world.

Where now we strive and agonize after impossible virtues, we shall then grow naturally and easily into those very qualities; and we shall not even think of them as especially commendable. Where our progress hitherto has been warped and hindered by the retarding influence of surviving rudimentary forces, it will flow on smoothly and rapidly when both men and women stand equal in economic relation. When the mother of the race is free, we shall have a better world, by the easy right of birth and by the calm, slow, friendly forces of social evolution. * * *

THORSTEIN VEBLEN

[Conspicuous Consumption and the Servant-Wife]†

* * * In what has been said of the evolution of the vicarious leisure class and its differentiation from the general body of the working classes,

† From *The Theory of the Leisure Class: An Economic Study in the Evolution of Institutions* (New York and London: Macmillan, 1899).

reference has been made to a further division of labour,—that between different servant classes. One portion of the servant class, chiefly those persons whose occupation is vicarious leisure, come to undertake a new, subsidiary range of duties—the vicarious consumption of goods. The most obvious form in which this consumption occurs is seen in the wearing of liveries and the occupation of spacious servants' quarters. Another, scarcely less obtrusive or less effective form of vicarious consumption, and a much more widely prevalent one, is the consumption of food, clothing, dwelling, and furniture by the lady and the rest of the domestic establishment.

* * *

With the disappearance of servitude, the number of vicarious consumers attached to any one gentleman tends, on the whole, to decrease. The like is of course true, and perhaps in a still higher degree, of the number of dependants who peform vicarious leisure for him. In a general way, though not wholly nor consistently, these two groups coincide. The dependent who was first delegated for these duties was the wife, or the chief wife; and, as would be expected, in the later development of the institution, when the number of persons by whom these duties are customarily performed gradually narrows, the wife remains the last. In the higher grades of society a large volume of both these kinds of service is required; and here the wife is of course still assisted in the work by a more or less numerous corps of menials. But as we descend the social scale, the point is presently reached where the duties of vicarious leisure and consumption devolve upon the wife alone. In the communities of the Western culture, this point is at present found among the lower middle class.

And here occurs a curious inversion. It is a fact of common observation that in this lower middle class there is no pretence of leisure on the part of the head of the household. Through force of circumstances it has fallen into disuse. But the middle-class wife still carries on the business of vicarious leisure, for the good name of the household and its master. In descending the social scale in any modern industrial community, the primary fact—the conspicuous leisure of the master of the household—disappears at a relatively high point. The head of the middle-class household has been reduced by economic circumstances to turn his hand to gaining a livelihood by occupations which often partake largely of the character of industry, as in the case of the ordinary business man of to-day. But the derivative fact—the vicarious leisure and consumption rendered by the wife, and the auxiliary vicarious performance of leisure by menials—remains in vogue as a conventionality which the demands of reputability will not suffer to be slighted. It is by no means an uncommon spectacle to find a man applying himself to work with the utmost assiduity, in order that his wife may in due form render for him that degree of vicarious leisure which the common sense of the time demands.

The leisure rendered by the wife in such cases is, of course, not a simple manifestation of idleness or indolence. It almost invariably occurs disguised under some form of work or household duties or social amenities, which prove on analysis to serve little or no ulterior end beyond showing that she does not and need not occupy herself with anything that is gainful or that is of substantial use. As has already been noticed under the head of manners, the greater part of the customary round of domestic cares to which the middleclass housewife gives her time and effort is of this character. Not that the results of her attention to household matters, of a decorative and mundificatory character, are not pleasing to the sense of men trained in middle-class proprieties; but the taste to which these effects of household adornment and tidiness appeal is a taste which has been formed under the selective guidance of a canon of propriety that demands just these evidences of wasted effort. The effects are pleasing to us chiefly because we have been taught to find them pleasing. There goes into these domestic duties much solicitude for a proper combination of form and colour, and for other ends that are to be classed as æsthetic in the proper sense of the term; and it is not denied that effects having some substantial æsthetic value are sometimes attained. Pretty much all that is here insisted on is that, as regards these amenities of life, the housewife's efforts are under the guidance of traditions that have been shaped by the law of conspicuously wasteful expenditure of time and substance. If beauty or comfort is achieved,— and it is a more or less fortuitous circumstance if they are,—they must be achieved by means and methods that commend themselves to the great economic law of wasted effort. The more reputable, "presentable" portion of middle-class household paraphernalia are, on the one hand, items of conspicuous consumption, and on the other hand, apparatus for putting in evidence the vicarious leisure rendered by the housewife.

The requirement of vicarious consumption at the hands of the wife continues in force even at a lower point in the pecuniary scale than the requirement of vicarious leisure. At a point below which little if any pretence of wasted effort, in ceremonial cleanness and the like, is observable, and where there is assuredly no conscious attempt at ostensible leisure, decency still requires the wife to consume some goods conspicuously for the reputability of the household and its head. So that, as the latter-day outcome of this evolution of an archaic institution, the wife, who was at the outset the drudge and chattel of the man, both in fact and in theory,—the producer of goods for him to consume,—has become the ceremonial consumer of goods which he produces. But she still quite unmistakably remains his chattel in theory; for the habitual rendering of vicarious leisure and consumption is the abiding mark of the unfree servant. * * *

CRITICISM

Editor's Note: History of the Criticism of *The Awakening*†

Early reviewers of *The Awakening* whose moral sensibilities were affronted by the novel's themes of sex and suicide gave testimony to the power of the novel in their vigorous condemnations of it. Charles L. Deyo, one reviewer who praised the book in 1899, wrote, "It is sad and mad and bad, but it is all consummate art." The artistic power of the novel was precisely what made it such a dangerous book in the opinions of most early reviewers. Kate Chopin did not seem to use her talent to condemn Edna Pontellier as Flaubert had condemned Emma in *Madame Bovary*, the novel to which *The Awakening* was most often compared.

Hostile early reactions to the novel, combined with the fact that it was written by a woman who was considered a "regional" writer (something of which a Hawthorne or a Faulkner is never accused), contributed to the half-century of neglect the novel endured and which it has most emphatically survived. Revival of interest in the novel began slowly in this country in the 1950s. In 1952, Van Wyck Brooks wrote, "But there is one small novel of the nineties in the South that should have been remembered, one small perfect book that mattered more than the whole life-work of many a prolific writer."[1] In 1953, the novel came back into print in France, translated by Cyrille Arnavon (*Edna*). In 1956, Kenneth Eble and Robert Cantwell each wrote appreciative essays and gave the novel the first extended attention it had received in this country since its publication. Cantwell argued that the novel "seems to me to be the finest novel of its sort written by an American, and to rank among the world's masterpieces of short fiction."[2] In 1962, Edmund Wilson argued for its place in the American canon when he wrote of a novel "quite uninhibited and beautifully written, which anticipates D. H. Lawrence in its treatment of infidelity."[3] More than a decade after the French translation and fifty-eight years after it was last published in America (second edition, 1906), Kenneth Eble edited a paperback, facsimile edition in 1964.[4] In response, a chorus of influential (male) critics of American literature joined in praise of the book, focusing on its themes of sexual transgression. Larzer Ziff called the novel "the most important piece of fiction about the sexual life of a woman written to date in America"; and Stanley Kauffmann termed it "an excellent and prodigiously courageous study of marital infidelity [that] deserves a place in the line of major American fiction."[5]

The watershed year in assuring Kate Chopin's place as an American writer of enduring significance was 1969, the year in which Per Seyersted, a Norwegian Americanist, published both *Kate Chopin: A Critical Biography* and *The Complete Works of Kate Chopin*. With Chopin's work and a new biography now widely available, critics gave her fiction the serious attention it had long deserved. Articles traced influences upon Chopin and placed her in relation to other writers, exploring, among other issues, whether Chopin belongs in the realist (Seyersted) or romantic (Ringe) tradition. Scholars asked: does she most resemble Flaubert, Tolstoy, Emerson, Whitman, Dreiser, Mary Wilkins Freeman, or Sarah Orne Jewett? Critics with a bent

---

† Footnotes refer only to materials not included in this Norton Critical Edition.
1. Van Wyck Brooks, *The Confident Years, 1885–1915* (New York: Dutton, 1952) 341.
2. Robert Cantwell, "*The Awakening* by Kate Chopin," *Georgia Review* 10 (1956): 489–94.
3. Edmund Wilson, *Patriotic Gore: Studies in the Literature of the American Civil War* (New York: Oxford, 1962) 590.
4. Published in New York by Capricorn.
5. Stanley Kauffmann, "The Really Lost Generation," *New Republic* 155 (3 Dec. 1966) 37.

toward "new criticism" explored the rich detail of the novel: its imagery, structure, irony, and narrative point of view. Those with an interest in psychoanalytic and/or myth criticism also found productive textual terrain here.

Seyersted's work coincided with, and was influenced by, the beginnings of feminist criticism and its transformation of the literary canon. Early articles by Marie Fletcher (1966) and Joan Zlotnik (1968)[6] anticipated what was to be an avalanche of feminist criticism of *The Awakening* in the 1970s and 1980s. Interestingly, these critics focused on a number of the issues that had preoccupied early reviewers of the novel—the meaning of the ending and Kate Chopin's perspective on her fictional hero. Analyses of the ending ranged from reading it as triumphant (Fryer)[7] to reading it as regressive (Wolff) and every possibility in between. The novel became a text through which scholars wrote of patriarchy, marriage and motherhood, woman's independence, friendship, desire, sexuality, and language. Recently, critics using a social history and/or history of ideas approach (Kate Chopin and Charles Darwin, Kate Chopin and "voluntary motherhood")[8], as well as those using methods of linguistic/psychoanalytic criticism, have found much to reward them in the text. Studies continue to explore Chopin's "place" in relation to other writers and artists of the nineteenth century, while important commentary has deepened our understanding of how race and class construct gender identity in the novel.

The recent biography of Kate Chopin (Toth, 1990) will surely stimulate additional Chopin scholarship. Analysis of the place of Kate Chopin in the history of feminist criticism and of the academy's current fondness for this text would tell us much about both the 1890s and the 1990s.[9] Such a project would not deny Kate Chopin "her day"—long overdue and richly deserved—but it would shed welcome light on our unarticulated needs and agendas as critics, teachers, and readers.

6. Joan Zlotnik, "A Woman's Will: Kate Chopin on Selfhood, Wifehood, and Motherhood," *Markham Review* 3 (1968): 1–5.
7. Judith Fryer, *The Faces of Eve: Women in the Nineteenth-Century American Novel* (New York: Oxford UP, 1976).
8. Bert Bender, "The Teeth of Desire: *The Awakening* and *The Descent of Man*," *American Literature* 63.3 (September 1991): 459–73. And Margit Stange, "Personal Property: Exchange Value and the Female Self in *The Awakening*," *Genders* 5 (Summer 1989): 106–19.
9. See Susan S. Lanser, "Feminist Criticism, 'The Yellow Wallpaper,' and the Politics of Color in America," *Feminist Studies* 15.3 (Fall 1989): 415–41.

Contemporary Reviews

From *Book News*†

["A *remarkable novel* . . ."]

A remarkable novel will come out of the West[1] about the first of March, a novel so keen in its analysis of character, so subtle in its presentation of emotional effects that it seems to reveal life as well as to represent it. In reading it you have the impression of being in the very heart of things, you feel the throb of the machinery, you see and understand the slight transitions of thought, the momentary impulses, the quick sensations of the hardness of life, which govern so much of our action. It is an intimate thing, which in studying the nature of one woman reveals something which brings her in touch with all women— something larger than herself. This it is which justifies the audacity of "The Awakening" and makes it big enough to be true. The author has shown herself an artist in the manipulation of a complex character, and faulty as the woman is, she has the magnetism which is essential to the charm of a novel. It is a quality hard to analyze, for it does not seem to be in what she says or does; it is rather, as in life, in what she is. The novel pictures, too, with extraordinary vividness, the kind of silent sympathy which is sometimes the expression of the love that goes deep. The men in the book are capital, with the exception perhaps of Robert, who is a bit wooden; and Edna's husband especially is drawn to the life. In construction, in the management of movement and climaxes, the thing shows a very subtle and brilliant kind of art.

---

† Lucy Monroe, "Chicago's New Books," *Book News* (March 1899): 387. The first review of *The Awakening* appeared a month before the novel was published and was written by a reader and editor for the publisher Herbert S. Stone. See Emily Toth, *Kate Chopin* (New York: Morrow, 1990) 328–29.
1. *The Awakening* was first published in Chicago [*Editor*].

From *The Mirror*†

["... what an ugly, cruel, loathsome monster Passion can be ..."]

Of an already successful writer's first novel one should not write, perhaps, while the spell of the book is upon one; it is something to be "dreamed upon," like a piece of wedding-cake for luck on one's first marriage-proposal, or anything upon which hangs some importance of decision. And so, because we admire Kate Chopin's other work immensely and delight in her evergrowing fame and are proud that she is "one-of-us St. Louisans," one dislikes to acknowledge a wish that she had not written her novel.

Not because it is not bright with her own peculiar charm of style, not because there is missing any touch of effect or lacking any beauty of description—but—well, it is one of the books of which we feel *"cui bono?"*[1] It absorbs and interests, then makes one wonder, for the moment, with a little sick feeling, if all women are like the one, and that isn't a pleasant reflection after you have thoroughly taken in this character study whose "awakening" gives title to Mrs. Chopin's novel.

One would fain beg the gods, in pure cowardice, for sleep unending rather than to know what an ugly, cruel, loathsome monster Passion can be when, like a tiger, it slowly stretches its graceful length and yawns and finally awakens. This is the kind of an awakening that impresses the reader in Mrs. Chopin's heroine. I do not believe it impressed the heroine herself that way. I think, like the tiger, she hated to be balked of her desire and that was about the worst of it to her.

*   *   *

It is not a pleasant picture of soul-dissection, take it anyway you like; and so, though she finally kills herself, or rather lets herself drown to death, one feels that it is not in the desperation born of an over-burdened heart, torn by complicating duties but rather because she realizes that something is due to her children, that she cannot get away from, and she is too weak to face the issue. Besides which, and this is the stronger feeling, she has offered herself wholly to the man, who loves her too well to take her at her word; "she realizes that the day would come when he, too, and the thought of him, would melt out of her existence," she has awakened to know the shifting, treacherous, fickle deeps of her own soul in which lies, alert and strong and cruel, the fiend called Passion that is all animal and all of the earth, earthy. It is better to lie down in the green waves and sink down in close embraces of old ocean, and so she does.

There is no fault to find with the telling of the story, there are no

† Frances Porcher, "Kate Chopin's Novel," *The Mirror* 9 (4 May 1899): 6.
1. "What's the use?" [*Editor*].

blemishes in its art, but it leaves one sick of human nature and so one feels—*cui bono!*

From the *St. Louis Daily Globe-Democrat*†

[*"It is not a healthy book . . ."*]

The appearance of a new novel by Kate Chopin, of St. Louis, is an event of interest to St. Louisans. The appearance of a book such as "The Awakening" by this St. Louis lady, is fraught with especial interest, and that interest carries with it surprise. Whether that surprise is pleasant or the reverse depends largely on the view point of the reader. It is hardly the kind of a book some people would look for from her. It is preeminently a romance of to-day—a love story with one woman as the central figure, around which several male characters revolve; and thoughts of the proverbial moth and the traditional candle force themselves on the reader in almost every chapter. At the very outset of the story one feels that the heroine should pray for deliverance from temptation, and in the very closing paragraph, when, having removed every vestige of clothes she "stands naked in the sun" and then walks out into the water until she can walk no farther, and then swims on into eternity, one thinks that her very suicide is in itself a prayer for deliverance from the evils that beset her, all of her own creating.

It is not a healthy book; if it points any particular moral or teaches any lesson, the fact is not apparent. But there is no denying the fact that it deals with existent conditions, and without attempting a solution, handles a problem that obtrudes itself only too frequently in the social life of people with whom the question of food and clothing is not the all absorbing one. Mrs. Pontellier does not love her husband. The poison of passion seems to have entered her system, with her mother's milk.

*   *   *

There are some pretty bits of description of Louisiana Creole life, and there are two or three minor characters in the book that are drawn with a deft hand. After reading the whole story, it can not be said that either of the principal characters claims admiration or sympathy. It is a morbid book, and the thought suggests itself that the author herself would probably like nothing better than to "tear it to pieces" by criticism if only some other person had written it.

---

† From "Notes from Bookland," *St. Louis Daily Globe-Democrat* 13 May 1899: 5.

From the *St. Louis Post-Dispatch*†

[" . . . *flawless art.*"]

There may be many opinions touching other aspects of Mrs. Chopin's novel "The Awakening," but all must concede its flawless art. The delicacy of touch of rare skill in construction, the subtle understanding of motive, the searching vision into the recesses of the heart—these are known to readers of "Bayou Folk" and "A Night in Acadie." But in this new work power appears, power born of confidence. There is no uncertainty in the lines, so surely and firmly drawn. Complete mastery is apparent on every page. Nothing is wanting to make a complete artistic whole. In delicious English, quick with life, never a word too much, simple and pure, the story proceeds with classic severity through a labyrinth of doubt and temptation and dumb despair.

It is not a tragedy, for it lacks the high motive of tragedy. The woman, not quite brave enough, declines to a lower plane and does not commit a sin ennobled by love. But it is terribly tragic. Compassion, not pity, is excited, for pity is for those who sin, and Edna Pontellier only offended—weakly, passively, vainly offended.

"The Awakening" is not for the young person; not because the young person would be harmed by reading it, but because the young person wouldn't understand it, and everybody knows that the young person's understanding should be scrupulously respected. It is for seasoned souls, for those who have lived, who have ripened under the gracious or ungracious sun of experience and learned that realities do not show themselves on the outside of things where they can be seen and heard, weighed, measured and valued like the sugar of commerce, but treasured within the heart, hidden away, never to be known perhaps save when exposed by temptation or called out by occasions of great pith and moment. No, the book is not for the young person, nor, indeed, for the old person who has no relish for unpleasant truths. For such there is much that is very improper in it, not to say positively unseemly. A fact, no matter how essential, which we have all agreed shall not be acknowledged, is as good as no fact at all. And it is disturbing—even indelicate—to mention it as something which, perhaps, does play an important part in the life behind the mask.

It is the life and not the mask that is the subject of the story. One day Edna Pontellier, whose husband has vaguely held her dear as a bit of decorative furniture, a valuable piece of personal property, suddenly becomes aware she is a human being. It was her husband's misfortune that he did not make this interesting discovery himself, but he had his brokerage business to think about and brokers deal in stocks, not hearts. It was Mrs. Pontellier's misfortune that another man revealed her to

† C. L. Deyo, "The Newest Books," *St. Louis Post-Dispatch* 20 May 1899: 4.

herself, and when the knowledge came it produced profound dissatisfaction, as often happens when love is born in a cage not of its own building. In the beginning she had no thought of wrong-doing, but resentment was hot and made her sullen. Robert Lebrun, whose heart was ensnared before he realized it, went away to Mexico to make money, which was quite the proper thing to do. It would have been the right thing had he gone before it was too late, for then he might have been only a shadowy dream in Edna's life, instead of a consuming reality. This made the poor woman still more discontented. She took to all sorts of foolish fancies to divert her mind. Her children did not help her, for she was not a mother woman and didn't feel that loving babies was the whole duty of a woman. She loved them, but said that while she was willing to die for them she couldn't give up anything essential for them. This sounded clever because it was paradoxical, but she didn't quite know what it meant. She dabbled with brush and canvas. Mademoiselle Reisz told her that to be an artist one must be courageous, to dare and defy. But, unhappily, Mrs. Pontellier was not courageous. So she was not an artist. Mademoiselle Reisz, who was a witch, and knew Robert and Edna better than they knew themselves, did not add, what was really in her mind, that to be a great sinner a woman must be courageous, for great sinners are those who sin for a pure, howbeit unlawful, motive. Edna was not courageous. So she was not a great sinner, but by and by she became a poor, helpless offender, which is the way of such persons—not good enough for heaven, not wicked enough for hell.

Mrs. Pontellier was prepared by unlawful love for unholy passion. Her husband was extinct so far as she was concerned, and the man she loved was beyond her power. She had no anchor and no harbor was in sight. She was a derelict in a moral ocean, whose chart she had never studied, and one of the pirates who cruise in that sea made her his prize. Robert might have saved her from ignoble temptation by supplying a motive for a robust sin, but he was in Mexico and the thought of him only deepened her discontent. The moment came and with it the man. There is always a man for the moment, sometimes two or three. So thought Mrs. Pontellier, and she grew dull with despair. Passion without love was not to her liking and she feared the future. If she had been a courageous woman she would have put away passion and waited for love, but she was not courageous. She let sensation occupy a vacant life, knowing the while that it only made it emptier and more hopeless.

So because she could not forget her womanhood, and to save the remnants of it, she swam out into the sunkissed gulf and did not come back.

It is sad and mad and bad, but it is all consummate art. The theme is difficult, but it is handled with a cunning craft. The work is more than unusual. It is unique. The integrity of its art is that of well-knit individuality at one with itself, with nothing superfluous to weaken the impression of a perfect whole.

From the *Chicago Times-Herald*†

["*. . . sex fiction.*"]

Kate Chopin, author of those delightful sketches, "A Night in Acadie," has made a new departure in her long story, "The Awakening." The many admirers whom she has won by her earlier work will be surprised—perhaps disagreeably—by this latest venture. That the book is strong and that Miss Chopin has a keen knowledge of certain phases of feminine character will not be denied. But it was not necessary for a writer of so great refinement and poetic grace to enter the overworked field of sex fiction.

* * * This is not a pleasant story, but the contrast between the heroine and another character who is devoted to her husband and family saves it from utter gloom, and gives the reader a glimpse of the real Miss Chopin, who is at her best as a creator of sweet and loveable characters.

From *The Outlook*‡

["*. . . disagreeable glimpses of sensuality . . .*"]

The Awakening is a decidedly unpleasant study of a temperament. The author, Kate Chopin, is known as the writer of several faithful stories of Louisiana life. This, too, is faithful enough in its presentation of certain phases of human passion and downward drift of character, but the story was not really worth telling, and its disagreeable glimpses of sensuality are repellent.

From the *Providence Sunday Journal**

["*The purport of the story can hardly be described in language fit for publication.*"]

* * * Miss Kate Chopin is another clever woman, but she has put her cleverness to a very bad use in writing "The Awakening." The purport of the story can hardly be described in language fit for publication. We are fain to believe that Miss Chopin did not herself realize what she was doing when she wrote it. With a bald realism that fairly out Zolas Zola,[1] she describes the result upon a married woman who lives amiably with

† From "Books of the Day," *Chicago Times-Herald* 1 June 1899: 9.
‡ From "Novels and Tales," *The Outlook* 3 June 1899: 314.
* From "Books of the Week," *Providence Sunday Journal* 4 June 1899: 15.
1. Émile Zola (1840–1902), French naturalistic novelist whose work is known for its frank, realistic detail [*Editor*].

her husband without caring for him, of a slowly growing admiration for another man. He is too honorable to speak and goes away; but her life is spoiled already, and she falls with a merely animal instinct into the arms of the first man she meets. The worst of such stories is that they will fall into the hands of youth, leading them to dwell on things that only matured persons can understand, and promoting unholy imaginations and unclean desires. It is nauseating to remember that those who object to the bluntness of our older writers will excuse and justify the gilded dirt of these latter days. * * *

From the *New Orleans Times-Democrat*†

["... an undercurrent of sympathy for Edna ..."]

* * * By the way, "The Awakening" does not strike one as a very happy title for the story Mrs. Chopin tells. A woman of twenty-eight, a wife and twice a mother who in pondering upon her relations to the world around her, fails to perceive that the relation of a mother to her children is far more important than the gratification of a passion which experience has taught her is, by its very nature, evanescent, can hardly be said to be fully awake. This unhappy Edna's awakening seems to have been confined entirely to the senses, while reason, judgment, and all the higher faculties and perceptions, whose office it is to weigh and criticise, impulse and govern conduct, fell into slumber deep as that of the seven sleepers. It gives one a distinct shock to see Edna's crude mental operations, of which we are compelled to judge chiefly by results—characterized as "perhaps more wisdom than the Holy Ghost is usually pleased to vouchsafe to any woman." The assumption that such a course as that pursued by Edna has any sort of divine sanction cannot be too strongly protested against. In a civilized society the right of the individual to indulge all his caprices is, and must be, subject to many restrictive clauses, and it cannot for a moment be admitted that a woman who has willingly accepted the love and devotion of a man, even without an equal love on her part—who has become his wife and the mother of his chidren—has not incurred a moral obligation which peremptorily forbids her from wantonly severing her relations with him, and entering openly upon the independent existence of an unmarried woman. It is not altogether clear that this is the doctrine Mrs. Chopin intends to teach, but neither is it clear that it is not. Certainly there is throughout the story an undercurrent of sympathy for Edna, and nowhere a single note of censure of her totally unjustifiable conduct.

† "New Publications," *New Orleans Times-Democrat* 18 June 1899: 15.

From *Public Opinion*†

[" . . . *we are well satisfied when Mrs. Pontellier deliberately swims out to her death . . ."*]

* * * "The Awakening," by Kate Chopin, is a feeble reflection of Bourget,[1] theme and manner of treatment both suggesting the French novelist. We very much doubt the possibility of a woman of "solid old Presbyterian Kentucky stock" being at all like Mrs. Edna Pontellier who has a long list of lesser loves, and one absorbing passion, but gives herself only to the man for whom she did not feel the least affection. If the author had secured our sympathy for this unpleasant person it would not have been a small victory, but we are well satisfied when Mrs. Pontellier deliberately swims out to her death in the waters of the gulf.
* * *

From *Literature*‡

[" . . . *an essentially vulgar story."*]

* * * One cannot refrain from regret that so beautiful a style and so much refinement of taste have been spent by Miss Chopin on an essentially vulgar story. The peculiarities of Creole life and temperament, and the sensuous atmosphere of life in New Orleans and at summer resorts on the Gulf, are happily sketched and outlined in this dramatic tale, and emphasis is laid upon the freedom of the Creole from false modesty and the pleasant social relations which inhere among Creole circles. A Creole husband as a rule entirely trusts his wife and is incapable of jealousy, for the reason that the right hand is not jealous of the left nor the head of the heart. Nevertheless, Léonce Pontellier, the Creole husband in the story, having married a beautiful Kentuckian, is less fortunate than most of his compatriots in having excellent reason for jealousy. His wife, having married him in a reaction from a fancied love affair of her girlhood, does not find marriage and motherhood a cable strong enough to keep her from forming other attachments, and the story of these and of her final awakening has little to redeem it from the commonplace, nor is it strong enough to condone the character of its revelations. The awakening itself is tragic, as might have been anticipated, and the waters of the gulf close appropriately over one who has drifted from all right moorings, and has not the grace to repent.
* * *

From the *New York Times*†

["... pity for the most unfortunate of her sex."]

Would it have been better had Mrs. Kate Chopin's heroine slept on forever and never had an awakening? Does that sudden condition of change from sleep to consciousness bring with it happiness? Not always, and particularly poignant is the woman's awakening, as Mrs. Chopin tells it. The author has a clever way of managing a difficult subject, and wisely tempers the emotional elements found in the situation. Such is the cleverness in the handling of the story that you feel pity for the most unfortunate of her sex.

From the *Los Angeles Sunday Times*‡

["... unhealthily introspective and morbid ..."]

It is rather difficult to decide whether Mrs. Kate Chopin, the author of "The Awakening," tried in that novel merely to make an intimate, analytical study of the character of a selfish, capricious woman, or whether she wanted to preach the doctrine of the right of the individual to have what he wants, no matter whether or not it may be good for him. It is true that the woman in the book who wanted her own way comes to an untimely end in the effort to get what she wants, or rather, in the effort to gratify every whim that moves her capricious soul, but there are sentences here and there through the book that indicate the author's desire to hint her belief that her heroine had the right of the matter and that if the woman had only been able to make other people "understand" things as she did she would not have had to drown herself in the blue waters of the Mexican Gulf. The scene of the story is laid in New Orleans and in a summer resort on the coast of the Gulf, and the book is concerned mainly with the mental and moral development of Edna, wife of Leonce Pontellier, a Kentucky woman, married to a creole, after she discovers that she has fallen in love with Robert Lebrun, another creole. And as the biography of one individual out of that large section of femininity which may be classified as "fool women," the book is a strong and graceful piece of work. It is like one of Aubrey Beardsley's[1] hideous but haunting pictures with their disfiguring leer of sensuality, but yet carrying a distinguishing strength and grace and individuality. The book shows a searching insight into the motives of the "fool woman" order of being, the woman who learns nothing by experience and has

---

† From "100 Books for Summer," *New York Times* 24 June 1899: 408.
‡ From "Fresh Literature," *Los Angeles Sunday Times* 25 June 1899: 12.
1. Aubrey Vincent Beardsley (1872–98), English artist whose black-and-white line compositions were widely criticized in the 1890s as gloomy and unwholesome [*Editor*].

not a large enough circle of vision to see beyond her own immediate desires. In many ways, it is unhealthily introspective and morbid in feeling, as the story of that sort of woman must inevitably be. The evident powers of the author are employed on a subject that is unworthy of them, and when she writes another book it is to be hoped that she will choose a theme more healthful and sweeter of smell.

From the *Pittsburgh Leader*†

["A *Creole* Bovary . . ."]

A Creole *Bovary* is this little novel of Miss Chopin's.[1] Not that the heroine is a Creole exactly, or that Miss Chopin is a Flaubert—save the mark!—but the theme is similar to that which occupied Flaubert. There was, indeed, no need that a second *Madame Bovary* should be written, but an author's choice of themes is frequently as inexplicable as his choice of a wife. It is governed by some innate temperamental bias that cannot be diagrammed. This is particularly so in women who write, and I shall not attempt to say why Miss Chopin has devoted so exquisite and sensitive, well-governed a style to so trite and sordid a theme. She writes much better than it is ever given to most people to write, and hers is a genuinely literary style; of no great elegance or solidity; but light, flexible, subtle, and capable of producing telling effects directly and simply. The story she has to tell in the present instance is new neither in matter nor treatment. Edna Pontellier, a Kentucky girl, who, like Emma Bovary, had been in love with innumerable dream heroes before she was out of short skirts, married Leonce Pontellier as a sort of reaction from a vague and visionary passion for a tragedian whose unresponsive picture she used to kiss. She acquired the habit of liking her husband in time, and even of liking her children. Though we are not justified in presuming that she ever threw articles from her dressing table at them, as the charming Emma had a winsome habit of doing. We are told that "she would sometimes gather them passionately to her heart; she would sometimes forget them." At a Creole watering place, which is admirably and deftly sketched by Miss Chopin, Edna met Robert Lebrun, son of the landlady, who dreamed of a fortune awaiting him in Mexico while he occupied a petty clerical position in New Orleans. Robert made it his business to be agreeable to his mother's boarders, and Edna, not being a Creole, much against his wish and will, took him seriously. . . . The lover of course disappointed her, was a coward and ran away from his responsibilities before they began. He was

---

† From "Books and Magazines," *Pittsburgh Leader* 8 July 1899: 6. Signed "Sibert" [Willa Cather]. Footnotes are by the editor of this Norton Critical Edition.
1. Cather is the first of a number of critics to compare the novel to *Madame Bovary* (1856) by Gustave Flaubert (1821–80), French realist novelist.

afraid to begin a chapter with so serious and limited a woman. She remembered the sea where she had first met Robert. Perhaps from the same motive which threw Anna Karenina under the engine wheels,[2] she threw herself into the sea, swam until she was tired and then let go. . . . Edna Pontellier and Emma Bovary are studies in the same feminine type; one a finished and complete portrayal, the other a hasty sketch, but the theme is essentially the same. Both women belong to a class, not large, but forever clamoring in our ears, that demands more romance out of life than God put into it. Mr. G. Bernard Shaw would say that they are the victims of the over-idealization of love.[3] They are the spoil of the poets, the Iphigenias of sentiment.[4] The unfortunate feature of their disease is that it attacks only women of brains, at least of rudimentary brains, but whose development is one-sided; women of strong and fine intuitions, but without the faculty of observation, comparison, reasoning about things. Probably, for emotional people, the most convenient thing about being able to think is that it occasionally gives them a rest from feeling. Now with women of the Bovary type, this relaxation and recreation is impossible. They are not critics of life, but, in the most personal sense, partakers of life. They receive impressions through the fancy. With them everything begins with fancy, and passions rise in the brain rather than in the blood, the poor, neglected, limited one-sided brain that might do so much better things than badgering itself into frantic endeavors to love. For these are the people who pay with their blood for the fine ideals of the poets, as Marie Delclasse paid for Dumas' great creation, Marguerite Gauthier.[5] These people really expect the passion of love to fill and gratify every need of life, whereas nature only intended that it should meet one of many demands. They insist upon making it stand for all the emotional pleasures of life and art; expecting an individual and self-limited passion to yield infinite variety, pleasure, and distraction, to contribute to their lives what the arts and the pleasurable exercise of the intellect gives to less limited and less intense idealists. So this passion, when set up against Shakespeare, Balzac, Wagner, Raphael,[6] fails them. They have staked everything on one hand, and they lose. They have driven the blood until it will drive no further, they

---

2. A reference to the ending of *Anna Karenina* (1875–76), by Leo Tolstoy (1828–1910).
3. George Bernard Shaw (1856–1950), Irish playwright, known for his satiric criticism of romantic love in several plays, among them *Man and Superman* (1903).
4. Sacrificial victims. Iphigenia, daugher of Agamemnon and Clytemnestra, was sacrificed to the gods in order to obtain favorable winds for the Greek fleet on its way to Troy.
5. Cather means Marie Duplessis, a Paris courtesan with whom playwright Alexander Dumas, the younger (1824–1895), lived for one year before she died of consumption. Marguerite Gauthier is the main character in Dumas's *Camille* (1848), based on the life of Marie Duplessis.
6. Master painter and architect of the Italian Renaissance (1483–1520): the leading painter of his day in Rome, Raphael's many renderings of the Madonna and Child are particularly famous, "Balzac": Honoré de Balzac (1799–1850), French author of the monumental *Comedie Humaine* (1842–48), a seventeen-volume collection of his novels and tales; a precursor of realism, his work offers a panoramic view of French society. "Wagner": Richard Wagner (1813–83), German composer of elaborate operas based on Nordic and Teutonic mythology.

have played their nerves up to the point where any relaxation short of absolute annihilation is impossible. Every idealist abuses his nerves, and every sentimentalist brutually abuses them. And in the end, the nerves get even. Nobody ever cheats them, really. Then "the awakening" comes. Sometimes it comes in the form of arsenic, as it came to Emma Bovary, sometimes it is carbolic acid taken covertly in the police station, a goal to which unbalanced idealism not infrequently leads. Edna Pontellier, fanciful and romantic to the last, chose the sea on a summer night and went down with the sound of her first lover's spurs in her ears, and the scent of pinks about her. And next time I hope that Miss Chopin will devote that flexible iridescent style of hers to a better cause.

From *The Dial*†

[" . . . *not altogether wholesome in its tendency.*"]

"The Awakening," by Mrs. Chopin, is a story in which, with no other accessories than the trivial details of everyday life in and about New Orleans, there is worked out a poignant spiritual tragedy. The story is familiar enough. A woman is married without knowing what it is to love. Her husband is kind but commonplace. He cares overmuch for the conventions of life; she, finding them a bar to the free development of her wayward personality, casts them off when "the awakening" comes to her, and discovers, too late, that she has cast off the anchor which alone could have saved her from shipwreck. It is needless to say that the agency by which she becomes awakened is provided by another man. But he proves strong enough to resist temptation, while she is too weak to think of atoning for her fault. To her distraught thinking, self-destruction is the only way out, and the tragedy is accomplished in picturesque fashion. The story is a simple one, not without charm, but not altogether wholesome in its tendency.

From *The Nation*‡

[" . . . *one more clever author gone wrong.*"]

"The Awakening" is the sad story of a Southern lady who wanted to do what she wanted to. From wanting to, she did, with disastrous consequences; but as she swims out to sea in the end, it is to be hoped that her example may lie for ever undredged. It is with high expectation that we open the volume, remembering the author's agreeable short stories,

† William Morton Payne, "Recent Fiction," *The Dial* 37 (1 Aug. 1899): 75.
‡ From "Recent Novels," *The Nation* 69 (3 Aug. 1899): 96.

and with real disappointment that we close it. The recording reviewer drops a tear over one more clever author gone wrong. Mrs. Chopin's accustomed fine workmanship is here, the hinted effects, the well-expended epithet, the pellucid style; and, so far as construction goes, the writer shows herself as competent to write a novel as a sketch. The tint and air of Creole New Orleans and the Louisiana seacoast are conveyed to the reader with subtle skill, and among the secondary characters are several that are lifelike. But we cannot see that literature or the criticism of life is helped by the detailed history of the manifold and contemporary love affairs of a wife and mother. Had she lived by Prof. William James's[1] advice to do one thing a day one does not want to do (in Creole society, two would perhaps be better), flirted less and looked after her children more, or even assisted at more *accouchements*—her *chef d'œuvre* in self-denial—we need not have been put to the unpleasantness of reading about her and the temptations she trumped up for herself.

From *The Congregationalist*†

["... *unwholesome in its influence.*"]

* * * It is a languorous, passionate story of New Orleans and vicinity, hinging on the gradual yielding of a wife to the attractions of other men than her husband. It is a brilliant piece of writing, but unwholesome in its influence. We cannot commend it.

* * *

Letters from "Lady Janet Scammon Young" and "Dr. Dunrobin Thomson"‡

8 *Newman Street*
Oxford St. W.
London

"Kate Chopin":

I feel sure I ought to send you the inclosed letter from the great consulting physician of England, who is also one of the purest and best

---

1. American philosopher (1842–1910), known as a "radical pragmatist," author of influential books on religion and psychology, brother of the novelist Henry James.
† From "Literature," *The Congregationalist* 24 Aug. 1899: 256.
‡ One of the mysteries of Chopin scholarship is the origin of these letters. The existence of the persons who wrote them has never been established. Scholars have suggested that they may have been fabricated by friends of Kate Chopin aware of the negative publicity the book had received. Emily Toth notes that the handwriting of "Lady Janet's" letter "resembles" Kate Chopin's handwriting. The text of these letters is from *A Kate Chopin Miscellany*, eds. Per Seyersted and Emily Toth (Oslo: Universitetsforlaget; Natchitoches: Northwestern State UP, 1979) 142–47. Footnotes are by the editor of this Norton Critical Edition.

of men, and who has been said by a great editor to be "the soundest critic since Matthew Arnold."[1]

Your book has deeply stirred some other noble souls to whom I have lent it. Like Doctor T—— I assume that it is to be republished over here. Maarten Maartens,[2] who was here last week, said "The Awakening" ought to be translated into Dutch. Scandinavian and Russian— so at least he was reported to me.

But great as is my interest in this book I confess to a still deeper interest in one which you ought to write—which you alone among living novelists *could* write. Evidently like all of us you believe *Edna* to have been worth saving—believe her to have been too noble to go to her death as she did. I quite bow to Doctor T's better sense of art. The conventions required her to die. But suppose her husband had been conceived on higher lines? Suppose Dr. Mandelet had said other things to him—had said, for example: "Pontellier, like most men you fancy that because you have possessed your wife hundreds of times she necessarily long ago came to entire womanly self knowledge—that your embraces have as a matter of course aroused whatever of passion she may be endowed with. You are mistaken. She is just becoming conscious of sex—is just finding herself compelled to take account of masculinity *as such*. You cannot *arrest* that process whatever you do; you should not wish to do so. Assist this birth of your wife's deeper womanliness. Be tender, let her know that you see how *Robert, Arobin* affect her. Laugh with her over the evident influence of her womanhood over them. Tell her how, *in itself* it is *natural*, that is divinely made & therefore innocent and pure and the very basis of social life—else why is true society absolutely nonexistent without *both* sexes. There is no *society* in Turkey. Show her the nonsense of ascribing all this interinfluence to "the feminine mind acting upon the masculine mind"—a saying that so severe a thinker as Herbert Spencer[3] ridicules. Above all *trust* her, let her see that you do. Only the inherently base woman betrays a *trust*. Leave her with *Robert*, with *Arobin*. *Trusted* she will never fail you—distrusted, ignored, left in ignorance of what her new unrest really means she will fall. Follow my advice and in a year you will have a new wife with whom you will fall in love again; & you will be a new husband, manlier, more virile and impassioned with whom she will fall in love again."

Suppose Dr. *Mandelet* had thus spoken, and *Pontellier* had thus acted?

Of course in its brutal literal significance we wholly reject and loathe the French maxim: "The lover completes the wife," and yet if we know the true facts of nature we must confess that there is a profound inner truth in it. No woman comes to her full womanly empire and charm who has not felt in what Dr T—— calls "her passional nature" the arousing power of more than one man. But Oh how important to her

1. Poet and critic of literature and society in Victorian England (1822–88).
2. Pen name of J. M. W. van der Poorten Swartz (1858–1915), popular Anglo-Dutch novelist.
3. English philosopher of the theory of evolution (1820–1903).

purity, her honor her inner self-respect that she shall (again quoting Dr
T——) "distinguish between passion and love." So that instead of guiltily
saying, "I fear I love that man" she shall say within herself with *no* sense
of guilt—"How that man's masculinity stirs me"—say it above all to
her husband. Now all this, which I am saying so clumsily needs saying
powerfully; needs to be taught by that most potent method of expression
open to man—a great novel. *You* can write it. You alone. You are free
from decadency. Your mind and heart are healthful, free, clean, sympathetic. Give us a great hearted manly *man*—give us a great natured
woman for his wife. Give us the awakening of her whole nature, let her
go to the *utmost* short of *actual* adultery—shew that her danger is in
her ignorance of the great distinctions of which Dr T—— speaks. Shew
us how such a husband can save such a wife and turn the influence of
sex to its intended beneficial end. I trust I need not say that my suggestion
that she go *very very* far is not for the sake of scenes of passion, but that
readers may be helped whose self respect is shipwrecked or near it because
they have gone far and are saying "I might as well go all the way."

Let me give you this from real life. A wife of three years, mother of
one babe found her "passional nature" (Dr T——'s word) disturbed,
excited, by a certain man of her circle. She at last desperately said to
her husband, "Pray dont invite Capt —— any more." He said nothing
then, but the light flashed upon him, and he remembered how his
beautiful darling had been either unwontedly warm and tender, or irritable and unreasonable, after she had been dancing or dining with
Capt —— Fortunately he was a *man* and not what my husband calls
a "Turk." So he was very loving and tender in those days until one night
when she lay lovingly in his arms he said "Sweetheart, dont some men
make you passionate? Of course I know it *must* be so. You would not
be the grand little woman you are if it were not so."

"Oh Phil" she said—"aren't we women horrid that it should be so?
And then he told her what (I agree with Dr T——) all husbands ought
to tell their wives—that *passion* is not sin—that between being made
passionate *by* the presence of a virile man, and feeling passion *for* him
is a distance as wide as space. Then she saw it and Oh *such* a burden
of causeless self reproach rolled away. "Oh Phil" she said, "I never felt
a moment's wish to *sin* with *any* man. But when I dance with a fine
fellow, or sit by one, and I know he is looking down into my bosom, I
feel what I have supposed was a very guilty glow all through—have felt
conscious of my sex—have felt pleased and animated—and have—oh
made it easy for them to look—but I *never* wished to sin with them."

And she told him it was Captain —— who most affected her that
way. And then, woman like, she was frightened at her avowal, and
wondered if in his heart her husband did not despise her.

Not long after that he told her that some of his friends were coming
to play at cards, and he said "Now sweetheart I want you to be simply
ravishing when you preside at a little late supper. Have something

very nice for us about midnight. You need not come down till then."

Whereupon he invited Capt ———— and two other men whom he knew perfectly well were quite in the Captain's class in effect upon his dear wife.

About half-past eleven he went to her room, laughingly made her change her gown for the very *most* décolleté one she had; and when later she came to the library where the men were to speak to them before supper—lo! there was her Captain! They had a merry supper, the "glow" came of course, but now she yielded to it unafraid and unashamed. She had never seen her husband happier, and at last he sent her up to the nursery with the Captain to shew him her dimpled two year old baby boy asleep. The other gentlemen begged to go but her husband said No—he was not going to have a mob of noisy men disturbing his baby. Oh how her heart sang the praises of her husband as she went, and she was not afraid of herself nor of the Captain, strong as the "glow" was when she bent over the little bed, and knew that the Captain was looking far less at the little sleeping babe than at her pretty charms.

I have made a long and stupid story of what *you* would have packed into one of your brief paragraphs—those paragraphs which are like sunlight and like flowers.

Wont you write us a brave book which will really interpret our sister women to themselves. When "Sir George Tressady"[4] was appearing serially a few of us hoped Sir George was going to be a husband indeed to his little wife. How near they were to it that night in the carriage. She was proud of his handsome well set up figure, of his abilities, his character. He (Prig to the last) could only see that her gown was too low!

If I can do anything for you pray command me. I know publishers, translators, &c, &c.

I shall go to Montreux in December at latest, but the address at the beginning will always find me.

With every best wish,
Janet Scammon Young

TELEGRAPHIC ADDRESS
"LANGHAM, LONDON"

LANGHAM HOTEL,
LONDON.
5 Oct. 99.

My dear Lady Janet:

It is commonplace to say that I am indebted to you for a great pleasure in the loan of that remarkable book "The Awakening." I have read it twice—once at a sitting when I ought to have been asleep, and again

---

4. Novel (1896) by Mrs. Humphry (Mary Augusta) Ward (1851–1920), prolific English writer best known for her *Robert Elsmere* (1888).

more deliberately in my brougham. Doubtless it will be published over here, but I am having my bookseller get two copies of the American edition—one for Crestwood and one for town. It is easily the book of the year. The ending reminds one of "The Open Question,"[5] but how vastly superior in power, ethic and art is this newer book.

You accuse "Kate Chopin" (a pen name I suppose) of an unnecessary tragedy. My dear Lady Janet, the authoress took the world as it is, as all art must—and 'twas inevitable that poor dear *Edna*, being noble, and having Pontellier for husband, and Arobin for lover, and average women for friends, should die.

My wrath is not toward "Kate Chopin" at all. That which makes "The Awakening" legitimate is that the author deals with the commonest of human experiences. You fancy *Edna's* case exceptional? Trust an old doctor—most common. It is only that *Edna* was nobler, and took that last clean swim. The others live. Not all meet *Arobin* or *Robert*. The essence of the matter lies in the accursed stupidity of men. They marry a girl, she becomes a mother. They imagine she has sounded the heights and depths of womanhood. Poor fools! She is not even awakened. She, on her part is a victim of the abominable prudishness which masquerades as modesty or virtue. Every great and beautiful fact of nature has a vile counterfeit. The counterfeit of goodness is self righteousness—of true modesty, prudishness. The law, spoken or implied, which governs the upbringing of girls is that passion is disgraceful. It is to be assumed that a self respecting female has it not. In so far as normally constituted womanhood *must* take account of *something* sexual, it is called "love." It was inevitable, therefore, that *Edna* should call her feeling for *Robert* love. It was as simply & purely passion as her feeling for *Arobin*. "Kate Chopin" would not admit that. Being (I assume) a woman, she too would reserve the word love for *Edna's* feeling for *Robert*.

The especial point of a wife's danger when her beautiful, God given womanhood awakes, is that she will save her self-respect by imagining herself in love with the awakener. She should be taught by her husband to distinguish between passion and love. Then she is safe, invulnerable. Even if, at the worst she "falls"—she will rise again.

It is inevitable, natural, and therefore clean and harmless, that a normal, healthfully constituted married woman will be stirred in her passional being by the men between whom and herself there is that mysterious affinity of the real nature of which we know nothing. If she calls that stirring of her nature "love" she is lost. If she knows perfectly well that it is passion; if she esteems and respects her passional capacity as she does her capacity to be moved by a song or a sunset, or a great poem, or a word nobly said—she is safe. She knows what that thing *is*. She is no more ashamed of it than of her responsiveness to any other

---

5. *The Open Question: A Tale of Two Temperaments*, by C. E. Raimond (New York and London: Harper, 1899). Raimond is a pen name of Elizabeth Robins (1865–1952), American actress known for her portrayal of Ibsen roles in London during the 1890s.

great appeal. She knows that it does not touch her wife-life, her mother-life, her true self-hood. It is not "naughty."

A wise husband (there are some) is at no point so loving and tenderly wise as at this point. A cad or a cur is (God save the mark) *jealous*. If his wife is weak she quails, and hides from men, or shelters herself in a pretended indifference. If she is strong she resents the monstrous insult of his suspicion. I am happier over nothing in my professional life than that I have helped *many* men at this point—many men, many women. I have said to more than one man: "Your wife's nature is stirring: lovingly help her. Let her see that you know it and like it: and that you distinguish perfectly between her *heart*, her wifely loyalty, and her body—make her distinguish too.

But I weary you. This book has stirred me to the soul. *Edna* is like a personal friend. She is not impure. The art, the local colour, the distinctness of characterisation of even the minor personages are something wonderful.

Thanking you again, dear Lady Janet,

I am as ever yours faithfully

Dunrobin Thomson

My house is closed—I am here till Oct 15 when Betty comes back with Lucy.

Chopin's "Retraction"†

The Awakening

BY KATE CHOPIN

Having a group of people at my disposal, I thought it might be entertaining (to myself) to throw them together and see what would happen. I never dreamed of Mrs. Pontellier making such a mess of things and working out her own damnation as she did. If I had had the slightest intimation of such a thing I would have excluded her from the company. But when I found out what she was up to, the play was half over and it was then too late.

St. Louis, Mo.,
May 28, 1899

Kate Chopin

---

† From "Aims and Autographs of Authors," *Book News* 17 (July 1899): 612. In response to adverse criticism of the novel, Chopin published this "tongue-in-cheek" note.

Essays in Criticism

PERCIVAL POLLARD

[The Unlikely Awakening of a Married Woman]†

* * * "The Awakening" asked us to believe that a young woman who had been several years married, and had borne children, had never, in all that time, been properly "awake." It would be an arresting question for students of sleep-walking; but one must not venture down that bypath now. Her name was Edna Pontellier. She was married to a man who had Creole blood in him; yet the marrying, and the having children, and all the rest of it, had left her still slumbrous, still as innocent of her physical self, as the young girl who graduates in the early summer would have us believe she is. She was almost at the age that Balzac[1] held so dangerous—almost she was the Woman of Thirty—yet she had not properly tasted the apple of knowledge. She had to wait until she met a young man who was not her husband, was destined to tarry until she was under the influence of a Southern moonlight and the whispers of the Gulf and many other passionate things, before there began in her the first faint flushings of desire. So, at any rate, Kate Chopin asked us to believe.

The cynic was forced to observe that simply because a young woman showed interest in a man who was not her husband, especially at a fashionable watering-place, in a month when the blood was hottest, there was no need to argue the aforesaid fair female had lain coldly dormant all her life. There are women in the world quite as versatile as the butterfly, and a sprouting of the physical today need not mean that yesterday was all spiritual.

However, taking Kate Chopin's word for it that Edna had been asleep, her awakening was a most champagne-like performance. After she met Robert Lebrun the awakening stirred in her, to use a rough simile, after the manner of ferment in new wine. Robert would, I fancy, at any Northern summer resort have been sure of a lynching; for, after a trifling encounter with him, Edna became utterly unmanageable. She neglected

† From *Their Day in Court* (New York and Washington: Neale Publishing, 1909) 41–45. Footnotes are by the editor of this Norton Critical Edition.
1. Honoré de Balzac (1799–1850), a master of the French novel (see above, p. 171, n. 6). In 1841 he published a novel called *La Femme de Trente Ans* [The Woman of Thirty].

her house; she tried to paint—always a bad sign, that, when women want to paint, or act, or sing, or write!—and the while she painted there was "a subtle current of desire passing through her body, weakening her hold upon the brushes and making her eyes burn."

*   *   *

All this, mind you, with Robert merely a reminiscence. If the mere memory of him made her weak, what must the touch of him have done? Fancy shrinks at so volcanic a scene. Ah, these sudden awakenings of women, of women who prefer the dead husband to the quick, [2] of women who accept the croupier's [3] caresses while waiting for hubby to come up for the week-end, and of women who have been in a trance, though married! Especially the awakenings of women like Edna!

We were asked to believe that Edna was devoid of coquetry; that she did not know the cheap delights of promiscuous conquests; though sometimes on the street glances from strange eyes lingered in her memory, disturbing her. Well, then those are the women to look out for—those women so easily disturbed by the unfamiliar eye. Those women do not seem to care, once they are awake, so much for the individual as for what he represents. Consider Edna. It was Robert who awoke her. But, when he went away, it was another who continued the arousal. Do you think Edna cared whether it was Robert or Arobin? Not a bit. Arobin's kiss upon her hand acted on her like a narcotic, causing her to sleep "a languorous sleep, interwoven with vanishing dreams." You see, she was something of a quick-change sleep-artist: first she slept; a look at Robert awakened her; Arobin's kiss sent her off into dreamland again; a versatile somnambulist, this. Yet she must have been embarrassing; you could never have known just when you had her in a trance or out of it.

How wonderful, how magical those Creole kisses of Arobin's must have been, if one of them, upon the hand, could send Edna to sleep! What might another sort of kiss have done? One shivers thinking of it; one has uncanny visions of a beautiful young woman all ablaze with passion as with a robe of fire. Arobin, however, had no such fears. He continued gaily to awake Edna—or to send her to sleep; our author was never clear which was which!—and it was not long before he was allowed to talk to her in a way that pleased her, "appealing to the animalism that stirred impatiently within her." One wonders what he said! It was no long before a kiss was permitted Arobin. "She clasped his head, holding his lips to hers. It was the first kiss of her life to which her nature had really responded. It was a flaming torch that kindled desire."

Ah, these married women, who have never, by some strange chance, had the flaming torch applied, how they do flash out when the right moment comes! This heroine, after that first flaming torch, went to her finish with lightning speed. She took a walk with Arobin, and paused,

2. The living.
3. A croupier is one who stands second, usually used in reference to one who runs a gambling table.

mentally, to notice "the black line of his leg moving in and out so close to her against the yellow shimmer of her gown." She let the young man sit down beside her, let him caress her, and they did not "say good-night until she had become supple to his gentle seductive entreaties."

To think of Kate Chopin, who once contented herself with mild yarns about genteel Creole life—pages almost clean enough to put into the Sunday school library, abreast of Geo. W. Cable's[4] stories—blowing us a hot blast like that! Well, San Francisco, and Paris, and London, and New York had furnished Women Who Did; why not New Orleans?

* * *

It may seem indelicate, in view of where we left Edna, to return to her at once; we must let some little time elapse. Imagine, then, that time elapsed, and Robert returned. He did not know that Arobin had been taking a hand in Edna's awakening. Robert had gone away, it seems, because he scrupled to love Edna, she being married. But Edna had no scruples left; she hastened to intimate to Robert that she loved him, that her husband meant nothing to her. Never, by any chance, did she mention Arobin. But, dear me, Arobin, to a woman like that, had been merely an incident; he merely happened to hold the torch. Now, what in the world do you suppose that Robert did? Went away—pouff!—like that! Went away, saying he loved Edna too well to—well, to partake of the fire the other youth had lit. Think of it! Edna finally awake—completely, fiercely awake—and the man she had waked up for goes away!

Of course, she went and drowned herself. She realised that you can only put out fire with water, if all other chemical engines go away. She realised that the awakening was too great; that she was too aflame; that it was now merely Man, not Robert or Arobin, that she desired. So she took an infinite dip in the passionate Gulf.

Ah, what a hiss, what a fiery splash, there must have been in those warm waters of the South! But—what a pity that poor Pontellier, Edna's husband, never knew that his wife was in a trance all their wedded days, and that he was away at the moment of her awakening! * * *

DANIEL S. RANKIN

[Influences Upon the Novel]†

* * * What is most curious and valuable to consider, is the relationship between Kate Chopin's life and her study of the feminine mind

---

4. Cable, a contemporary of Kate Chopin, also wrote novels and stories of Creole life.
† From *Kate Chopin and Her Creole Stories* (Philadelphia: U of Pennsylvania P, 1932) 173–75. This first biography of Chopin, though containing a number of inaccuracies, is invaluable in its collection of remembrances from Chopin contemporaries. Footnotes are by the editor of this Norton Critical Edition.

in *The Awakening*. The author's imagination, as a very young girl, through the zeal and the story-telling propensity of her greatgrandmother, had been saturated with a keen interest in woman's nature, and its mysterious vagaries. This curiosity never dimmed.

I believe *The Awakening* had its origin in these story-telling days of impressionable youth. I have no doubt Kate Chopin's sympathies in the stories told her by Madame Victoria Charleville were with Madame Chouteau.[1] One review suggested that her sympathies in *The Awakening* were with Edna (the *Los Angeles Times*, June 25, 1899). I believe they were.

More important than the consideration of the influence of curiosity aroused in youth, is the endeavor to discriminate and discover the literary influences that engendered *The Awakening*. The novel may be similar to D'Annunzio's *Triumph of Death*,[2] Edna may be "la femme de trente ans" whose dangerous attractions Marcel Proust admirably displayed,[3] but it is also possible to decide that Kate Chopin was influenced by Beardsley's hideous and haunting pictures, with their disfiguring leer of sensuality,[4] yet carrying a distinguishing strength and grace and individuality.

An exposition of an author as nothing but a synthesis of influences, strong and sharply defined as links in a chain, does more credit to an investigator's industry and intimate acquaintance with fiction than to a sense of perspective, and to what I must call, for want of a more comprehensive phrase, a knowledge of literary psychology. Kate Chopin was an original genius. Her story may be similar to any number of novels, but all suggestion of direct literary descent in method or manner of treatment is false. Literary influences are deceptive at best, and in the case of Kate Chopin no single author can be said to have contributed the weightiest influential impetus to *The Awakening*. She was a great reader, a contemporary mind. She absorbed the atmosphere and the mood of the ending of the century, as that ending is reflected in Continental European art and literature. Perhaps in St. Louis she was closest in touch with the tendencies of the century's ending—in music, poetry, fiction. She was not imitative in the narrow sense of being completely under the sway of any one writer, but the range of her debts is wide:

1. Victoria Verdon Charleville (1780–1863), Kate O'Flaherty's maternal great-grandmother, was a contemporary of the first settlers of St. Louis and delighted in telling the young Kate stories and legends about the founding of the city. Marie Thérèse Chouteau, the subject of one of these stories, left her husband after the birth of their son Auguste and formed an unsanctioned but widely approved union with Pierre Laclède, the founder of St. Louis, by whom she had four children.
2. Gabriele D'Annunzio (1863–1938), Italian novelist, author of *Triumph of Death*, a novel about extramarital love that ends with the death of the lovers in the sea.
3. "The woman of thirty." Odette de Crecy Swan in *Remembrance of Things Past*, by Marcel Proust (1871–1922), may be the woman alluded to. More likely is that Rankin took the idea from Pollard, who more precisely attributes the phrase to Balzac. See above, p. 179, n. 1.
4. Rankin is incorporating the idea and the phraseology of the review that appeared in the *Los Angeles Sunday Times*. See p. 169.

Flaubert, Tolstoi, Turgénieff, D'Annunzio, Bourget, especially de Maupassant,[5] all contributed to her broad and diverse culture.
The Awakening follows the current of erotic morbidity that flowed
strongly through the literature of the last two decades of the nineteenth
century. The end of the century became a momentary dizziness over
an abyss of voluptuousness, and Kate Chopin in St. Louis experienced
a partial attack of the prevailing artistic vertigo. The philosophy of Schopenhauer, the music of Wagner, the Russian novel, Maeterlinck's
plays—all this she absorbed.[6] The Awakening in her case is the result
—an impression of life as a delicious agony of longing.
   In The Awakening under her touch the Creole life of Louisiana glowed
with a rich exotic beauty. The very atmosphere of the book is voluptuous,
the atmosphere of the Gulf Coast, a place of strange and passionate
moods.
   The mania for the exotic that fed upon evocations of a barbaric
past—Salome's dance, Cleopatra's luxury, the splendor and cruelty of
Salammbo's Carthage[7]—gave energy to the creation in this country of
two works dealing with southern Louisiana, Lafcadio Hearn's[8] Chita
and Kate Chopin's The Awakening. These books owe nothing to each
other. They are derived from a common source.
   The Awakening is exotic in setting, morbid in theme, erotic in motivation.
   Kate Chopin felt most profoundly and expressed most poignantly in
The Awakening facts about life which to her were important, facts which
easily might be overlooked, she thought. Being a woman she saw life
instinctively in terms of the individual. She took a direct, personal,
immediate interest in the intimate personal affairs of Edna's daily life
and changing moods. But the questions arise, "Is it at all important?
Did Kate Chopin by her art reveal a fresh beauty or vision or aspiration?"
In all earnestness she meant The Awakening to be something more than

5. Gustave Flaubert (1821–80), French novelist whose Madame Bovary has been thought by a
   number of critics, the first of whom was Willa Cather, to be the model for Chopin's novel.
   Leo Tolstoy (1828–1910), Russian novelist best known for his War and Peace and Anna
   Karenina. He wrote a novel originally entitled The Awakening that was published serially in
   The Cosmopolitan; the title was changed to The Resurrection when it was published in book
   form (Rankin, p. 177). Ivan Turgénieff (Turgenev), Russian novelist (1818–83) best known
   for his Fathers and Children. Paul Bourget (1852–1935), French psychological novelist. Guy
   de Maupassant (1850–1893), French writer whom Chopin particularly admired; she translated
   four of his short pieces. He wrote a short sketch also entitled "The Awakening."
6. Arthur Schopenhauer (1788–1860), German philosopher known for his dark vision of the
   human condition. Richard Wagner (1813–83), German composer of elaborate operas based
   on Nordic and Teutonic mythology. Maurice Maeterlinck (1862–1949), Belgian writer best
   known for his symbolic dramas. Rankin is not suggesting any specific influence, but rather
   the excesses that were thought to be characteristic of the end of the century.
7. Salome, a biblical figure who danced for Herod and demanded the head of John the Baptist
   as a reward. Oscar Wilde's play (1894) on the subject suggests Salome's romantic attachment
   to the Baptist. Cleopatra, queen of Egypt from 69 B.C. to 30 B.C. figures in plays by Shakespeare
   and Dryden and in George Bernard Shaw's Caesar and Cleopatra (1900). Salammbo (1862)
   is a novel by Flaubert set in ancient Carthage.
8. American journalist and novelist (1850–1904), whose Chita (1887) concerns a young Creole
   girl who survives a mid-century hurricane on Grand Isle.

literature, more than the mere art of writing, more than a pleasant help for the passing of leisure hours!

The reader, following Edna as she walks for the last time down to the beach at Grand Isle—well, what does he feel? Merely that human nature can be a sickening reality. Then the insistent query comes—*cui bono?*[9]

* * *

The theme was not an easy subject to treat, for morbid states of mind and motives need endurance and a resistant restraint on the author's part. Kate Chopin's extraordinary tact enabled her to produce a book which tells the truth without offense, with detachment, and with just that gleam of humor which makes even the nasty digestible, illuminates the agreeable and gives a grace of movement to the whole. But was the theme deserving of the exquisite care given it?

CYRILLE ARNAVON

[An American *Madame Bovary*]†

If we are to appreciate this American *Madama Bovary*, we have to analyze the personality of the main character, Edna, to find the human value and psychological truth in her tragedy. To be able to form an opinion, we would have to go back to an age in which a flourishing romanticism, literary in origin, was deliberately carried over into real life. A woman, idle, little enough occupied with her children, and frequently neglected by a husband absorbed in his business affairs, would feel strongly tempted to indulge in the particular kind of daydreaming which Jules de Gaultier[1] has called *bovarysme*. The story of Edna's childhood forms an important part of the novel. She had lost her mother, was far more sensitive than her sisters, and projected her sentimental and sensual longings on men whom she had scarcely even seen. Then she was unthinkingly married to a much older man, as was customary in those days, because he was attracted by her exceptional beauty, and although she had two children, she felt that the idea of motherhood seemed somehow external to her. We find her during one torrid tropical summer in which discipline is relaxed, all social obligations are more or less forgotten or disregarded, and the barriers behind which the higher

9. The expression, meaning "what's the use?", was first used in relation to the novel by Frances Porcher. See above, p. 162, n. 1.
† From "Introduction" to *Edna* (Paris, 1953), trans. Bjorn Braaten and Emily Toth, in *The Kate Chopin Miscellany*, Per Seyersted and Emily Toth, eds. (Natchitoches: Northwestern State UP, 1979) 168–88. Reprinted by permission of Northwestern State University Press. Footnotes are by the editor of this Norton Critical Edition.
1. French philosopher (1858–1942), author of *Bovarysm: La psychologie dans l'oeuvre de Flaubert*, trans. Gerald M. Spring (Paris: [Cerf.], 1892).

classes seek protection are withdrawn. We see Edna at age twenty-nine, incarnating the feminine beauty ideal of that age: ample curves, beautiful arms and white neck (and, already, an incipient double chin). We learn something about the kinds of clothing that were the fashion in those days: immense skirts, enormous hats, gauze veils, sunshades for use on the beach, and a profusion of rustling garments.[2] There were long siestas, and the women's long conversations about intimate matters, discussed with a frankness unknown to Edna, who was always hampered by Puritan inhibitions in her dealings with others.

*   *   *

In any case, there seems to be insufficient justification for Edna's "romantic" suicide, and this is the main weakness of this fine novel. Edna's situation is far from hopeless, either morally or materially. Robert Lebrun leaves her, he says, because he loves her. In other words, their love affair has not come to an end; rather, one would say there is a chance of reconciliation. Léonce Pontellier, who is absent, leaves her in peace. And has not she herself often pointed out that she does not really love him, although he enables her to lead a pampered existence? Is she a victim of her nerves? Possibly, but there is nothing in her behavior so far that suggests a characteristic inclination toward suicide. When we consider the hopeless infatuation of *Madame Bovary*, we find this psychological weakness in Kate Chopin's novel doubly striking.

*   *   *

In any case, it is a fact that around 1900, there were a number of literary examples of suicide as the ultimate escape, generally as a result of idleness and disenchantment. Ivan Strannik[3] (Gabrielle Rosenthal), who deals with this subject in *L'Appel de L'Eau* (1901), certainly had not read *The Awakening*, but in her novel, in which Russia provides the rather exotic background, the heroine is disappointed in her married life and conceives an ideal love for a romantic young actor who usually plays the lover's part. Then she meets a seducer, and subsequently shows signs of mental instability. She is examined by a psychiatrist, and finally drowns herself.

Certain curious similarities in the plots of both novels are less surprising than the poetic and nostalgic atmosphere, virtually the same in both books. Dolly, like Edna, has had a difficult childhood and has suffered greatly because of the constraints and hypocrisies of social life. In both novels, we observe a kind of "naturism," sometimes expressed in a very stilted, rhetorical style and sometimes in a style too simple to be really genuine. This naturism, fundamentally, is a very romantic nature religion of the heart, a plea for the rights of the senses, voicing their demands with unusual force against rigorous prohibitions.

2. See above, pp. 126–36.
3. Pseudonym of Anna Mitrofanovna Anichkova, novelist and critic of Russian literature and author of *L'Appel de L'Eau*.

We have no right to assume, especially according to Kate Chopin's biographer,[4] that her novel is autobiographical. We are told that her marriage was perfectly happy at home and that she led an exemplary life. Nevertheless, the analogies between her situation and that of Edna Pontellier at the beginning of *The Awakening* escape no one. Consciously or unconsciously, Edna's tragedy is presented in a dramatic and tragic form, an extension of the conflict in the innermost recesses of her mind, where the normal and the abnormal can be said to exist side by side. Mentally unbalanced, Edna provides an example of a psychosis with a direct bearing on her external life and her behavior.

* * *

Although Kate Chopin's applied symbolism depends on an aestheticism that does not really impress us, one remains, nevertheless, convinced that this portrayal of a woman is on the whole correct. We are, of course, aware that in Kate Chopin's psychology and dramatic art there are some weaknesses that leave us somewhat confused. To her translator, Edna's story seems firmly anchored in a common experience shared by all those who have made a careful study of real life—an experience providing material for any solid piece of work, whether it be a poem, play, or novel. *The Awakening* is something more than a mere curiosity in American literature, and it is something more than just a welcome novel about woman. Yet for some unknown reason, it never found its way into the library catalogues and contemporary manuals written for the benefit of later generations.

This tragic novel goes far beyond the conscious intentions of Kate Chopin, who originally meant to describe the dullness of the life of a bourgeoise who, for our convenience, she placed in New Orleans. We have already used the word *symbolism*; but a clear symbolism, a completely intellectual reconstruction, remains on the level of a witicism or intellectual game. Without, however, making our interpretation too limited by using a too systematic terminology that Kate Chopin could not possibly have known, we can easily see a kind of regressive fixation in Edna Pontellier and, through her, in her creator. The presence of a youthful and fairly attractive father is possibly the root of this psychosis. The attraction to the sea, which from her early childhood has been represented by the blue fields of Kentucky (significant because there do not seem to be any large expanses of water where Edna grew up), corresponds to a longing (often the result of a trauma) to return to the mother's womb.

Likewise, Edna's inexplicable suicide, which seems to stem from her negative attitude toward life, is in reality a flight from sexual experience. The reader will remember that Edna, with her strict Puritan upbringing and resulting repressions and inhibitions, once confided in Adèle Ra-

4. Daniel Rankin.

tignolle. Since early adolescence, her gestures and descriptions of herself reveal, she possessed a very ardent temperament. She had felt attracted to men who for some reason or other were inaccessible: the cavalry officer, the engaged man, the actor. Subsequently, she displays an affection for her brilliant and headstrong fellow vacationer Adèle Ratignolle which neither she herself nor Kate Chopin was able to explain. She let herself be married, primarily as a reaction against her own family and the atmosphere prevailing in her home.

The writer leaves no doubt that Edna's marriage to Pontellier was never satisfying. Indeed, her attitude towards her two sons can be said to be that of a discontented woman. After a few years, she is no longer her husband's wife except in name; and with Arobin, she experiences a second failure because she can not help thinking about Robert. Arobin, detached at first, becomes more and more enthralled by Edna's physical attraction. The explanation for Edna's failure may be that complex characters like her can be attracted by only a very limited number of people, as was convincingly demonstrated by Dr. Marañon with regard to Amiel.[5]

As for Robert Lebrun, the existence of social taboos against a relationship which is the only kind that would have satisfied Edna, causes the relationship to end because of outside pressures. And the attraction the water holds for her, symbolizing a return to a pre-natal existence, becomes gradually stronger. Something similar had happened during her vacation in Grand Isle, a period in which she felt more dissatisfied than usual. One is left with a feeling that if she had not refused Arobin for Robert's sake—in itself a logical consequence of Arobin's erotic behavior—and if Robert had not most inopportunely vanished, Edna would in time have surmounted her psychological difficulties. Might not her trusted physician, Mandelet, better at curing souls than healing bodies, have succeeded in exorcising the evil spirits that were haunting her? Perhaps he would. Indeed, at the very moment when she throws herself into the water (end of Chapter XXXIX), Edna has not yet altogether given up hope. But this hope of recovery, which would probably have proved illusory if she had only consulted the old family doctor and no one else, would very likely have been fulfilled if she had been able to consult Dr. Freud.[6]

It is strange and at the same time suggestive that the general construction of the book and, even more, certain seemingly insignificant details like the attraction exercised by the water, integral to Edna's fictional personality, should seem, even to an ordinary reader, to accord very well with a number of observations and interpretations which are now

5. See Gregario Marañon, *Amiel: un estudio sobre la timidez* (Madrid: Espasa-Calpe, 1932). The book is a study of Henri-Frederic Amiel's *Fragments d'un journal intime* (Paris, 1883–87, 1923, 1927).
6. Sigmund Freud (1856–1939), Austrian founder of modern psychoanalysis.

common knowledge. If a psychoanalyst were to read this text carefully, he might perhaps be able to see what is autobiographical and what is not. But this brief account, restricted to a few selected hypotheses, may perhaps suffice to convince a literary critic or even an ordinary reader that there is something worth remembering in Edna Pontellier's pathetic story. One may have read ten or twenty novels of this type without retaining anything except a very blurred outline of the various plots, because the whole presentation was too stylized. On the other hand, greater and weightier works like those modelled upon Flaubert's novel, such as the story told by Kate Chopin, a lucid and sensitive woman who seems very close to us today, although she lived nearly a hundred years ago—that story, though heavily influenced by aestheticism, could assume a permanent value both as a warning and as a confession.

KENNETH EBLE

[A Forgotten Novel]†

* * * The claim of the book upon the reader's attention is simple. It is a first-rate novel. The justification for urging its importance is that we have few enough novels of its stature. One could add that it is advanced in theme and technique over the novels of its day, and that it anticipates in many respects the modern novel. It could be claimed that it adds to American fiction an example of what Gide[1] called the *roman pur*, a kind of novel not characteristic of American writing. One could offer the book as evidence that the regional writer can go beyond the limitations of regional material. But these matters aside, what recommends the novel is its general excellence.

It is surprising that the book has not been picked up today by reprint houses long on lurid covers and short on new talent. The nature of its theme, which had much to do with its adverse reception in 1899, would offer little offense today. In a way, the novel is an American *Bovary*, though such a designation is not precisely accurate. Its central character is similar: the married woman who seeks love outside a stuffy, middle-class marriage. It is similar too in the definitive way it portrays the mind of a woman trapped in marriage and seeking fulfillment of what she vaguely recognizes as her essential nature. The husband, Léonce Pontellier, is a businessman whose nature and preoccupations are not far

† From "A Forgotten Novel: Kate Chopin's *The Awakening*," *Western Humanities Review* 10 (Summer 1956): 261–69. Reprinted by permission. Footnotes are by the editor of this Norton Critical Edition.
1. Andre Gide (1869–1951), French writer and critic. The phrase *roman pur*, the "pure novel," distinguishes the work from other forms of the genre such as *roman à thèse*, the "novel with a purpose."

different from those of Charles Bovary. There is a Léon Dupuis in Robert
Lebrun, a Rodolphe Boulanger in Alcée Arobin. And too, like *Madame
Bovary*, the novel handles its material superbly well. Kate Chopin herself
was probably more than any other American writer of her time under
French influence. Her background was French-Irish; she married a
Creole; she read and spoke French and knew contemporary French
literature well; she associated both in St. Louis and Louisiana with
families of French ancestry and disposition. But despite the similarities
and the possible influences, the novel, chiefly because of the independent character of its heroine, Edna Pontellier, and because of the intensity of the focus upon her, is not simply a good but derivative work.
It has a manner and matter of its own.

Quite frankly, the book is about sex. Not only is it about sex, but the
very texture of the writing is sensuous, if not sensual, from the first to
the last. Even as late as 1932, Chopin's biographer, Daniel Rankin,
seemed somewhat shocked by it. He paid his respects to the artistic
excellence of the book, but he was troubled by "that insistent query—
cui bono?" He called the novel "exotic in setting, morbid in theme,
erotic in motivation." One questions the accuracy of these terms, and
even more the moral disapproval implied in their usage. One regrets
that Mr. Rankin did not emphasize that the book was amazingly honest,
perceptive and moving.

*   *   *

Kate Chopin, almost from her first story, had the ability to capture
character, to put the right word in the mouth, to impart the exact gesture,
to select the characteristic action. An illustration of her deftness in
handling even minor characters is her treatment of Edna's father. When
he leaves the Pontelliers' after a short visit, Edna is glad to be rid of him
and "his padded shoulders, his Bible reading, his 'toddies,' and ponderous oaths." A moment later, it is a side of Edna's nature which is
revealed. She felt a sense of relief at her father's absence; "she read
Emerson until she grew sleepy."

Characterization was always Mrs. Chopin's talent. Structure was not.
Those who knew her working habits say that she seldom revised, and
she herself mentions that she did not like reworking her stories. Though
her reputation rests upon her short narratives, her collected stories give
abundant evidence of the sketch, the outlines of stories which remain
unformed. And when she did attempt a tightly organized story, she often
turned to Maupassant and was as likely as not to effect a contrived
symmetry. Her early novel *At Fault* suffers most from her inability to
control her material. In *The Awakening* she is in complete command
of structure. She seems to have grasped instinctively the use of the
unifying symbol—there the sea, sky and sand—and with it the power
of individual images to bind the story together.

The sea, the sand, the sun and sky of the Gulf Coast become almost a presence themselves in the novel. Much of the sensuousness of the book comes from the way the reader is never allowed to stray far from the water's edge. A refrain beginning "The voice of the sea is seductive, never ceasing, clamoring, murmuring, . . ." is used throughout the novel. It appears first at the beginning of Edna Pontellier's awakening, and it appears at the end as the introduction to the long final scene, previously quoted. Looking closely at the final form of this refrain, one can notice the care with which Mrs. Chopin composed this theme and variation. In the initial statement, the sentence does not end with "solitude," but goes on, as it should, "to lose itself in mazes of inward contemplation." Nor is the image of the bird with the broken wing in the earlier passage; rather there is a prefiguring of the final tragedy: "The voice of the sea speaks to the soul. The touch of the sea is sensuous, enfolding the body in its soft close embrace." The way scene, mood, action and character are fused reminds one not so much of literature as of an impressionist painting, of a Renoir[2] with much of the sweetness missing. Only Stephen Crane,[3] among her American contemporaries, had an equal sensitivity to light and shadow, color and texture, had the painter's eye matched with the writer's perception of character and incident.

The best example of Mrs. Chopin's use of a visual image which is also highly symbolic is the lady in black and the two nameless lovers. They are seen as touches of paint upon the canvas and as indistinct yet evocative figures which accompany Mrs. Pontellier and Robert Lebrun during the course of their intimacy. They appear first early in the novel. "The lady in black was reading her morning devotions on the porch of a neighboring bath house. Two young lovers were exchanging their heart's yearning beneath the children's tent which they had found unoccupied." Throughout the course of Edna's awakening, these figures appear and reappear, the lovers entering the pension, leaning toward each other as the water-oaks bent from the sea, the lady in black, creeping behind them. They accompany Edna and Robert when they first go to the Chênière, "the lovers, shoulder to shoulder, creeping, the lady in black, gaining steadily upon them." When Robert departs from Mexico, the picture changes. Lady and lovers depart together, and Edna finds herself back from the sea and shore, and set among her human acquaintances, her husband; her father; Mme. Reisz, the musician, "a homely woman with a small wizened face and body, and eyes that glowed"; Alcée Arobin; Mme. Ragtinolle; and others. One brief scene from this milieu will further illustrate Mrs. Chopin's conscious or unconscious symbolism.

---

2. Pierre-Auguste Renoir (1841–1919), French impressionist painter.
3. American novelist and short-story writer (1871–1900), best known for *The Red Badge of Courage* (1895). His *The Open Boat* (1898) is a realistic account of four men who escape in a small dinghy from a shipwreck off the Florida coast.

The climax of Edna's relationship with Arobin is the dinner which is to celebrate her last night in her and her husband's house. Edna is ready to move to a small place around the corner where she can escape (though she does not phrase it this way) the feeling that she is one more of Léonce Pontellier's possessions. At the dinner Victor Lebrun, Robert's brother, begins singing, "Ah! si tu savais!" a song which brings back all her memories of Robert. She sets her glass so blindly down that she shatters it against the carafe. "The wine spilled over Arobin's legs and some of it trickled down upon Mrs. Highcamp's black gauze gown." After the other guests have gone, Edna and Arobin walk to the new house. Mrs. Chopin writes of Edna, "She looked down, noticing the black line of his leg moving in and out so close to her against the yellow shimmer of her gown." The chapter concludes:

> His hand had strayed to her beautiful shoulders, and he could feel the response of her flesh to his touch. He seated himself beside her and kissed her lightly upon the shoulder.
> "I thought you were going away," she said, in an uneven voice.
> "I am, after I have said good night."
> "Good night," she murmured.
> He did not answer, except to continue to caress her. He did not say good night until she had become supple to his gentle, seductive entreaties.

It is not surprising that the sensuous quality of the book, both from the incidents of the novel and the symbolic implications, would have offended contemporary reviewers. What convinced many critics of the indecency of the book, however, was not simply the sensuous scenes, but rather that the author obviously sympathized with Mrs. Pontellier. More than that, the readers probably found that she aroused their own sympathies.

It is a letter from an English reader which states most clearly, in a matter-of-fact way, the importance of Edna Pontellier. The letter was to Kate Chopin from Lady Janet Scammon Young, and included a more interesting analysis of the novel by Dr. Dunrobin Thomson, a London physician whom Lady Janet said a great editor had called "the soundest critic since Matthew Arnold."[4] "That which makes The Awakening legitimate," Dr. Thomson wrote, "is that the author deals with the commonest of human experiences. You fancy Edna's case exceptional? Trust an old doctor—most common." He goes on to speak of the "abominable prudishness" masquerading as "modesty or virtue," which makes the woman who marries a victim. For passion is regarded as disgraceful and the self-respecting female assumes she does not possess passion. "In so far as normally constituted womanhood must take account of something sexual," he points out, "it is called love." But marital love and passion

4. See above, pp. 173–78, for the complete letters.

may not be one. The wise husband, Dr. Thomson advises, seeing within his wife the "mysterious affinity" between a married woman and a man who stirs her passions, will help her see the distinction between her heart and her love, which wifely loyalty owes to the husband, and her body, which yearns for awakening. But more than clinically analyzing the discrepancy between Victorian morals and woman's nature, Dr. Thomson testifies that Mrs. Chopin has not been false or sensational to no purpose. He does not feel that she has corrupted, nor does he regard the warring within Edna's self as insignificant.

Greek tragedy—to remove ourselves from Victorian morals—knew well eros[5] was not the kind of love which can be easily prettified and sentimentalized. Phaedra's struggle with elemental passion in the Hippolytus[6] is not generally regarded as being either morally offensive or insignificant. Mrs. Pontellier, too, has the power, the dignity, the self-possession of a tragic heroine. She is not an Emma Bovary, deluded by ideas of "romance," nor is she the sensuous but guilt-ridden woman of the sensational novel. We can find only partial reason for her affair in the kind of romantic desire to escape a middle-class existence which animates Emma Bovary. Edna Pontellier is neither deluded nor deludes. She is woman, the physical woman who, despite her Kentucky Presbyterian upbringing and a comfortable marriage, must struggle with the sensual appeal of physical ripeness itself, with passion of which she is only dimly aware. Her struggle is not melodramatic, nor is it artificial, nor vapid. It is objective, real and moving. And when she walks into the sea, it does not leave a reader with the sense of sin punished, but rather with the sense evoked by Edwin Arlington Robinson's Eros Turannos:[7]

> . . . for they
> That with a god have striven
> Not hearing much of what we say,
> Take what the god has given;
> Though like waves breaking it may be,
> Or like a changed familiar tree,
> Or like a stairway to the sea
> Where down the blind are driven.

How wrong to call Edna, as Daniel Rankin does, "a selfish, capricious" woman. Rather, Edna's struggle, the struggle with eros itself, is farthest removed from capriciousness. It is her self-awareness, and her awakening into a greater degree of self-awareness than those around her can comprehend, which gives her story dignity and significance.

Our advocacy of the novel is not meant to obscure its faults. It is not

5. Passionate love, after the Greek god Eros.
6. Euripides' play, in which Phaedra, wife of Theseus, is made to fall passionately in love with Hippolytus by Aphrodite, who is angry because Hippolytus has scorned the love of women.
7. Poem about a woman's life-experience with eros, from The Man Against the Sky (1916), by Edwin Arlington Robinson (1869–1935), American poet.

perfect art, but in total effect it provokes few dissatisfactions. A sophisticated modern reader might find something of the derivative about it. Kate Chopin read widely, and a list of novelists she found interesting would include Flaubert, Tolstoy, Turgenev, D'Annunzio, Bourget, Goncourt and Zola.[8] It is doubtful, however, that there was any direct borrowing, and *The Awakening* exists, as do most good novels, as a product of the author's literary, real, and imagined life.

How Mrs. Chopin managed to create in ten years the substantial body of work she achieved is no less a mystery than the excellence of *The Awakening* itself. But, having added to American literature a novel uncommon in its kind as in its excellence, she deserves not to be forgotten. *The Awakening* deserves to be restored and to be given its place among novels worthy of preservation.

MARIE FLETCHER

[The Southern Woman in Fiction]†

* * * Kate Chopin's most ambitious work is *The Awakening*, a novel which tells of the awakening of Edna Pontellier from the easy comfort of a marriage of convenience to a realization of what she considers to be the deeper needs of her soul. Edna, a Kentucky Presbyterian, has impetuously and somewhat rebelliously married the Louisiana Creole, Léonce Pontellier. It is suggested that the marriage was purely an accident, a decree of Fate, for it is "his absolute devotion" and "the violent opposition of her father and her sister Margaret to her marriage with a Catholic" that led Edna to accept Léonce. But as subsequent developments in the novel reveal, Edna's first "rebellion" was only one of many. Indeed, her entire life is a flight from one kind of confinement after another.

In an account of a summer vacation on Grand Isle, Mrs. Pontellier is sharply contrasted with the other New Orleans matrons so that the qualities of Creole wives and mothers are emphasized. She is definitely not one of the "mother women" who prevail on the island:

> It was easy to know them, fluttering about with extended, protecting wings when any harm, real or imaginary, threatened their brood. They were women who idolized their children, worshiped their husbands, and esteemed it a holy privilege to efface themselves as individuals and grow wings as ministering angels.

8. For identifications of these authors, see above, p. 183, n. 5, p. 182, n. 2, p. 168, n. 1, p. 23, n. 9, and p. 166, n. 1.
† From "The Southern Woman in the Fiction of Kate Chopin," *Louisiana History* 7 (Spring 1966): 117–32. Reprinted by permission. Author's footnotes deleted.

One of these mothers, Adele Ratignolle, is "the embodiment of every womanly grace and charm." With her beauty "flaming and apparent," she is like "the bygone heroines of romance and the fair lady of our dreams." She has spun-gold hair hanging loose, sapphire blue eyes, lips like cherries or other delicious crimson fruit, soft white skin, slender hands and arms. The fact that she is growing a little stout does not detract from her poise and grace. Her exquisite hands draw attention as she threads her needle or adjusts her gold thimble to sew on night-drawers for her children. Even when she visits, Adele takes her sewing with her; and though Edna is not concerned about winter garments for her sons, in order not to appear unamiable, she cuts a pattern for their drawers. Unlike the French ladies, she cannot devote herself exclusively to her husband and children. She hugs her sons passionately one moment and then forgets them the next; she is even gratified by their occasional absence. Edna is willing to give her time and her money but not her inner self to her family.

Mrs. Pontellier, intimately associated with a group of Creoles for the first time, is impressed forcibly by their "entire absence of prudery. Their freedom of expression was at first incomprehensible to her, though she had no difficulty in reconciling it with a lofty chastity which in the Creole woman seems to be inborn and unmistakable." A book openly read and discussed by the others, Edna feels compelled to read only in secret. Like most Creole women, Madame Ratignolle has a baby about every two years. During this summer she talks constantly about her "condition," though her pregnancy—her fourth in seven years—is in no way apparent and no one would have known about it had she not persisted in making it a topic of conversation. Even the young Creole Robert Lebrun joins in until he notices the color mount into Mrs. Pontellier's face. After that, when she arrives, he even stops the amusing stories he often tells the married women.

Always "self-contained," Edna "was not accustomed to an outward and spoken expression of affection, either in herself or in others," and hardly knows how to accept the spontaneous caresses of her French associates. In fact, one reason she grew fond of her husband was her "realizing with some unaccountable satisfaction that no trace of passion or excessive and fictitious warmth colored her affection, thereby threatening its dissolution."

* * *

She is not like the Creole women in being able to continue as a long-suffering, self-sacrificing, faithful, and loyal wife and mother when love is gone. She is also unable—perhaps because of her Protestant rigidity, anarchic individualism, pride, and conscience—to live on and enjoy the fuller, happier life of which her "awakening" has made her aware. For love, of which she is now capable, is also a threat to selfhood, which she still cannot surrender. The easy-going, relaxed Creole women, with their South European Catholic background, function as norms against which to contrast Edna's little drama of revolt first against the life for which her ancestry and rearing designed her and then her final escape from the consequences of repudiating this life and learning about a more complete existence. Her suicide is the last in a series of rebellions which structure her life, give it pathos, and make of the novel a study in contrasting cultures (as well as an interpretation of the "new woman").

* * * the Creole girl lives to become a Creole wife; she should marry once, and, once married, she should be a devoted and dutiful wife even though her husband and her life in general may prove anything but ideal. With their assumption that marriage is of supreme importance, these women see no happiness, actually no real existence, without marriage; and most of them are wed young. To satisfy her strong maternal instinct, it was assumed that a woman should by all means have children to complete the family. If she is unable to marry or if she marries and has no children, she feels the lack very deeply.

Though the heroines of Kate Chopin's local color fiction have some of the characteristics of the traditional lady, changes are already appearing. However, Edna Pontellier, a Southerner, though a Kentucky Protestant rather than a Creole Roman Catholic, is the only one of the heroines who finds and likes personal independence. The irony is that to keep from relinquishing it she has to commit suicide. Sexually awakened as she is, she cannot bear to live on as the wife of Léonce Pontellier; Robert Lebrun does not really want her; and with Alcée Arobin there is no feeling of companionship, only sexual satisfaction about which she has a sense of guilt because of her feeling that she has betrayed Robert.

The most unchanging quality in Southern heroines is the ideal of chastity. In spite of her realism, or perhaps because of it, Kate Chopin, throughout her work, upholds the Creole belief in the purity of womanhood and those other aspects of the feminine mystique and Southern cult of family which follow from it. There is "modern" honesty in her treatment of human situations, such as Edna Pontellier's awakening, her need for fulfillment, and her inability to live on with her husband in a hypocritical relationship. Emotional realism notwithstanding, Mrs. Chopin's fictional treatment of French Louisiana is illustrative of the truth of the old adage, well known amongst them, that the more some things change, the more they stay the same.

LARZER ZIFF

From *The American 1890s*†

* * * The community about which she [Chopin] wrote was one in which respectable women took wine with their dinner and brandy after it, smoked cigarettes, played Chopin sonatas, and listened to the men tell risqué stories. It was, in short, far more French than American, and Mrs. Chopin reproduced this little world with no specific intent to shock or make a point, as did, for instance, Frederic, who was straining after a specific effect when he posed his Celia Madden[1] at the piano with a cigarette. Rather, these were for Mrs. Chopin the conditions of civility, and, since they were so French, a magazine public accustomed to accepting naughtiness from that quarter and taking pleasure in it on those terms raised no protest. But for Mrs. Chopin they were only outward signs of a culture that was hers and had its inner effects in the moral make-up of her characters. Though she seldom turned her plot on these facts, she showed that her women were capable of loving more than one man at a time and were not only attractive but sexually attracted also.

The quality of daily life in Kate Chopin's Nachitoches is genial and kind. People openly like one another, enjoy life, and savor its sensual riches. Their likes and their dislikes are held passionately, so that action bears a close and apparent relation to feeling. In setting a character, Mrs. Chopin writes, "Grégoire loved women. He liked their nearness, their atmosphere; the tones of their voices and the things they said; their ways of moving and turning about; the brushing of their garments when they passed him by pleased him."[2] This open delight in the difference between the sexes was not a mentionable feeling until Mrs. Chopin brought to American literature a setting in which it could be demonstrated with an open geniality.

* * *

Like *Madame Bovary*, *The Awakening* is about the adulterous experiments of a married woman, and while Mrs. Chopin did not have to go to Flaubert for the theme, she obviously was indebted to him for it as well as for the masterful economy of setting and character and the precision of style which she here achieved. Sarah Orne Jewett had also been an admirer of *Madame Bovary* and had defended Flaubert's theme

---

† From *The American 1890s: Life and Times of a Lost Generation* by Larzer Ziff (New York: Viking, 1966) 297–305. Copyright © 1966 by Larzer Ziff. Used by permission of Viking Penguin, a division of Penguin Books USA Inc.
1. Innocent Irish-Catholic girl in the 1896 novel *The Damnation of Theron Ware*, written by Harold Frederic (1856–1898) [*Editor*].
2. *Bayou Folk* (Boston: Houghton Mifflin, 1894), p. 86.

by saying that "a master writer gives everything weight."[3] But she had drawn quite a different moral from the novel. Miss Jewett wrote of Emma Bovary. "She is such a lesson to dwellers in country towns, who drift out of relation to their surroundings, not only social, but the very companionship of nature, unknown to them."[4] Emma Bovary is a foolish, bored woman, while Mrs. Chopin's Edna Pontellier is an intelligent, nervous woman, but Edna's salvation is not to be found in drifting back into relation with her environment. Rather, the questions Mrs. Chopin raises through her are what sort of nature she, twenty-eight years of age, married to a rich man and the mother of two children, possesses, and how her life is related to the dynamics of her inner self. Sarah Jewett counseled sublimation; Kate Chopin pursued self-discovery and counseled not at all.

*   *   *

The Awakening was the most important piece of fiction about the sexual life of a woman written to date in America, and the first fully to face the fact that marriage, whether in point of fact it closed the range of a woman's sexual experiences or not, was but an episode in her continuous growth. It did not attack the institution of the family, but it rejected the family as the automatic equivalent of feminine self-fulfillment, and on the very eve of the twentieth century it raised the question of what woman was to do with the freedom she struggled toward. The Creole woman's acceptance of maternity as totally adequate to the capacities of her nature carried with it the complements of a fierce chastity, a frankness of speech on sexual matters, a mature ease among men, and a frank and unguilty pleasure in sensual indulgence. But this was not, ultimately, Edna Pontellier's birthright, and she knew it. She was an American woman, raised in the Protestant mistrust of the senses and in the detestation of sexual desire as the root of evil. As a result, the hidden act came for her to be equivalent to the hidden and true self, once her nature awakened in the open surroundings of Creole Louisiana. The new century was to provide just such an awakening for countless American women, and The Awakening spoke of painful times ahead on the road to fulfillment.

Kate Chopin sympathized with Edna, but she did not pity her. She rendered her story with a detachment akin to Flaubert's. At one point Edna's doctor says, "Youth is given up to illusions. It seems to be a provision of Nature; a decoy to secure mothers for the race. And Nature takes no account of moral consequences, of arbitrary conditions which we create, and which we feel obliged to maintain at any cost." These appear to be the author's sentiments. Edna Pontellier is trapped

---

3. Sarah Orne Jewett, Letters, ed. by Annie Fields (Boston, 1911), p. 86. [Jewett (1849–1909) wrote short stories set in Maine, the best-known volume of which is The Country of the Pointed Firs (1896)—Editor.]
4. Ibid., pp. 82–3.

between her illusions and the conditions which society arbitrarily establishes to maintain itself, and she is made to pay. Whether girls should be educated free of illusions, if possible, whether society should change the conditions it imposes on women, or whether both are needed, the author does not say; the novel is about what happened to Edna Pontellier. * * *

GEORGE ARMS

[Contrasting Forces in the Novel]†

* * * Basically she [Chopin] writes as a non-intrusive author but principally presents her material with a sense of constant contrast, partly in the whole social situation, partly in Edna, but essentially as the author's way of looking at life. In the first of her two editorializing chapters she speaks of this contrast: "In short, Mrs. Pontellier was beginning to realize her position in the universe as a human being, and to recognize her relations as an individual to the world within and about her." Into the next chapter she extends this observation by remarking, "At a very early period she had apprehended instinctively the dual life —that outward existence which conforms, the inward life which questions." Yet Mrs. Chopin is unwilling to present Edna as simply struggling between two opposites, later remarking that her emotions "had never taken the form of struggles." On occasion the polarity reappears, as when the author writes that the husband could not see that his wife "was becoming herself and daily casting aside that fictitious self which we assume like a garment with which to appear before the world." In a much more adolescent fashion Edna speaks: "By all the codes which I am acquainted with, I am a devilishly wicked specimen of the sex. But some way I can't convince myself that I am."

On the whole, as she reveals herself, her aimlessness impresses us more than her sense of conflict. Early in the novel, recalling an incident from her childhood, Edna first interprets it as running away from the gloomy Presbyterianism of her father, but then goes on to say that her walk on that Sunday morning was "idly, aimlessly, unthinking and unguided." Thus Edna appears not so much as a woman who is aware of the opposition of two ideals but rather as one who drifts—who finally, even in death, is drifting when she again recalls having wandered on the blue-green meadow as a little girl. In the second editorial chapter, the author again considers the conflicts in Edna's life, but at this stage

† From "Kate Chopin's The Awakening in the Perspective of Her Literary Career," in Essays on American Literature in Honor of Jay B. Hubbell, ed. Clarence Gohdes (Durham: Duke UP, 1967) 215–28. Reprinted with permission of the publisher.

the contrasts have become a series of "multitudinous emotions." Edna is sensitive to many states of mind as the author describes her after the consummation of her affair with Arobin: irresponsibility, shock, her husband's and Robert's reproach, but not shame and not remorse, though regret that she has yielded from erotic longing rather than from love. Still, there is an "understanding" that hints of a polarity: "She felt as if a mist had been lifted from her eyes, enabling her to look upon and comprehend the significance of life, that monster made up of beauty and brutality."

At the time of Edna's suicide she thinks of many things, yet in the final paragraph the images that come to her are all those of her childhood. One is that of a cavalry officer whom she had romantically loved when he visited her father. When she married, the author observes that "she felt she would take her place with a certain dignity in the world of reality, closing the portals forever behind her upon the realm of romance and dreams." And upon Robert's leaving for Mexico, "she recognized anew the symptoms of infatuation" of her earlier life, but the recognition "did not lessen the reality, the poignancy of the revelation by any suggestion or promise of instability." Thus one of the oppositions which the author develops throughout the novel is that of romance and reality, and she suggests that Edna remains a figure of romantic ideals in spite of her acting with a sexual freedom that the common reader would call realistic or even naturalistic. Part of Edna's romanticism derives from a sense of fate, as the comment late in the book suggests: "She answered her husband with friendly evasiveness,—not with any fixed design to mislead him, only because all sense of reality had gone out of her life; she had abandoned herself to Fate, and awaited the consequences with indifference." As so often in the novel, Mrs. Chopin made specific preparation by noting that marriages "masquerade as the decrees of Fate." So one can summarize that instead of identifying herself with Edna's actions, Mrs. Chopin tends to regard them as romantically motivated rather than as realistically considered. Yet, as if to say that there are other kinds of romanticism, the author introduces Adele Ratignolle, Edna's friend who is completely in love with her husband, in this fashion: "There are no words to describe her save the old ones that have served so often to picture the bygone heroine of romance and the fair lady of our dreams."

In all, the author presents these contrasts suggestively rather than systematically. Perhaps if she takes any stand at all it is to favor individualism against social obligation, for she writes of Edna, "Every step which she took toward relieving herself from obligations added to her strength and expansion as an individual." Yet even here she leaves the question open. What does the author mean when she writes that after her father and husband leave on trips, "Then Edna sat in the library after dinner and read Emerson until she grew sleepy"? Eble interprets this as a reaction against the father's Presbyterianism, and such it may be; but to grow sleepy over a Transcendental individualist also hints that Edna's individualism lacks philosophical grounding.

This sleepiness from reading Emerson leads to the contrast, implicit in the title. In treating Edna's awakening, the author shows irony and even deviousness. We look upon Edna's awakening as archetypal in marking her passage from death to rebirth, but we may also look upon her awakening as not a rebirth but as another kind of death that is self-sought. Amusingly enough, the author, quite consciously I am sure, allows Edna to do an inordinate amount of sleeping throughout the novel, in spite of her underlying vitality. She first appears "with some appearance of fatigue" (admittedly after she has been swimming); that night she is "fast asleep," and her weariness is noted many times, especially when she falls in love with Robert, though at one time she only sleeps fitfully. When she first openly seeks out Robert and takes him— again amusingly—to Sunday morning mass, she is so drowsy at the service that she has to leave, and sleeps the whole of the rest of the morning and afternoon at a nearby house, with Robert remarking at the end, "You have slept precisely one hundred years." Again, when she celebrates her decision to break with her husband at a dinner party, "the old ennui" overtakes her. It is almost as if the author were saying: here is my heroine who at the critical points of her progress toward an awakening constantly falls asleep.

An even grimmer irony, of course, is in her awakening to an erotic life not through Robert, whom she truly loves, but through Alcée, whom she uses merely as a convenience. Though Edna recognizes this, she hardly does so in the sense that the novel does. We are told that "Alcée Arobin's manner was so genuine that it often deceived even himself," but also that "Edna did not care or think whether it were genuine or not." We cannot help suspecting that Edna simplifies and melodramatizes her view of herself far more than the author does. After Robert's return, she exclaims to him, "It was you who awoke me last summer out of a life-long, stupid dream. Oh! you have made me so unhappy with your indifference. Oh! I have suffered, suffered!" Almost compulsively she is soon saying the same thing to the family doctor, who earlier had seen her as an "animal waking up in the sun" and now cautions her about the illusions of youth:

> "Yes," she said. "The years that are gone seem like dreams—if one might go on sleeping and dreaming—but to wake up and find—oh! well! perhaps it is better to wake up after all, even to suffer, rather than to remain a dupe to illusions all one's life."

Finally, the underlying awareness of contrasting forces in the novel is exhibited in its use of children. Edna has two boys of four and five. With them she has little intimacy, and her husband accuses her of neglecting them, as does her mother-in-law—an accusation endorsed by the author, who early in the story announces, "In short, Mrs. Pontellier was not a mother-woman." Again we are somewhat perplexed as to whether or not the author approves of Edna's attitude toward her children. I suppose that those who look upon the novel as a defense of the New Woman would feel that Mrs. Chopin regards freedom from children as a necessary basis for complete freedom. But again I am doubtful, for Mrs. Chopin delights in the contraries which are present in Edna's response toward her boys.

Perhaps Edna most fully expresses her attitude in a conversation with Madame Ratignolle midway in the book:

> "I would give up the unessential; I would give my money, I would give my life for my children; but I wouldn't give myself. I can't make it more clear; it's only something which I am beginning to comprehend, which is revealing itself to me."

This passage will be recalled for us at the time of Edna's death, but in the meantime we observe her constantly returning to her children as a kind of penance whenever she displays most markedly her love outside of marriage. When she suspects that Robert goes to Mexico to avoid her, she shows an unusual intimacy with her children by telling them a bedtime story. She had already coddled and caressed one of her sons immediately after her day spent with Robert. After her second night with Alcée she visits her children in the country—one would think more as an act of penance than of affection. Just after Edna had fully admitted her love for Robert to a friend, she sent her children "a huge box of bonbons."

When Robert finally returns to New Orleans and Edna declares her love for him, she is called away from their reunion to attend the birth of another child of Adele Ratignolle. After the birth, which is not an easy one, Adele's parting injunction is: "Think of the children, Edna. Oh think of the children! Remember them!" From this scene she returns to discover that Robert has not waited for her, but instead has left a note, bidding her "Good-by—because I love you." The next day she goes to Grand Isle to drown herself, saying in the meanwhile again and again: "To-day it is Arobin; to-morrow it will be some one else. It makes no difference to me, it doesn't matter about Léonce Pontellier—but Raoul and Etienne!" Immediately afterward, she thinks back to her earlier conversation with Adele in which she had declared that she would give up everything for her children, including her life, but not "herself." This final opposition then leads directly to her death: "The children appeared before her like antagonists who had overcome her; who had overpowered and sought to drag her into the soul's slavery for the rest of her days. But she knew a way to elude them." Though she does not think of these things, the author tells us, when she walks toward the beach, her thoughts revert to the children and her husband as she tires in her swim toward death: "They were a part of her life. But they need not have thought that they could possess her, body and soul."

While the motivation from the children has been amply anticipated, its final realization produces something of a shift. Perhaps one might go so far as to say that the children, used in this way, somewhat flaw the novel. We recall that many of Mrs. Chopin's short stories first appeared in *Harper's Young People's Magazine*, the *Youth's Companion*, and also in *Vogue*, with the uneasy feeling that the author is still writing in a juvenile vein or from the conventional angle of a woman's magazine. Yet this difficulty might be answered by recognizing that the children stand for a stable society and the permanency of an unbroken home. Perhaps it would even be better to treat them as bringing another contrast into the story. Like those contrasts of purpose and aimlessness, of romance and realism, and of sleep and awakening, this one is not of absolute opposition but is complex and even blurred. As my argument has suggested, precisely this complexity may be what Mrs. Chopin is trying to achieve. She presents a series of events in which the truth is present, but with a philosophical pragmatism she is unwilling to extract a final truth. Rather, she sees truth as constantly re-forming itself and as so much a part of the context of what happens that it can never be final or for that matter abstractly stated. * * *

PER SEYERSTED

[Kate Chopin and the American Realists]†

* * * Cyrille Arnavon is thus no longer alone in elevating Kate Chopin from the group of local colorists to that of the American pioneer writers of the 1890's, the group which comprises such authors as Crane, Garland, Norris, and Dreiser.[1] It is therefore fitting to look at works like *Maggie*, *Rose of Dutcher's Coolly*, *McTeague*, and *Sister Carrie*, all written in that formative decade of American literature, and compare their approach to certain fundamental issues with that of *The Awakening*. If we turn to the treatment of sexuality in Garland's novel, for example,

---

† From *Kate Chopin: A Critical Biography* (Baton Rouge: Louisiana State UP, 1969) 190–96. Reprinted by permission of the author. Except as noted, all footnotes are by the editor of this Norton Critical Edition.
1. Theodore Dreiser (1871–1945), prolific naturalist novelist, best known for his *Sister Carrie* (1900) and *An American Tragedy* (1925). "Crane": see above, p.190, n. 3. "Garland": Hamlin Garland (1860–1940) wrote novels depicting the hardships of farm life in the Middle West. "Norris": Frank Norris (1870–1902) is best known for his *The Octopus* (1901), one of a number of novels examining economic and social realities.
   See also Cyrille Arnavon, "Les Débuts du Roman Réaliste American et l'Influence Française," in *Romanciers Américains Contemporains*, Henri Kerst, ed. (*Cahiers des Langues Modernes*, I Paris, 1946), pp. 9–35; and the introduction to Arnavon's French translation of the novel: *Edna* (Paris, 1953), pp. 1–22 (above, pp. 184–88).

we find that his Rose, a farmer's daughter, views all aspects of animal reproduction as natural matters. We might then perhaps expect her to see sex in humans as equally natural, a view undoubtedly held by Edna. But though she is courted by "wholesome," "clean" men—one of them observes that human procreation is "not as yet a noble business"—she feels "revulsion" when she realizes how their presence stirs up desire in her "pure wholesome awakening womanhood." While men are "sordid and vicious, . . . polygamous by instinct, insatiable as animals," women are virtuous by nature, Garland declares, and Rose sublimates her "brute passion" into a desire to become a great poet."[2]

That man's erotic and other drives are brutal is of course one of the tenets of naturalism, and Garland's illustration of it is mild compared to that of the others of the quartet. Norris, for example, whose theme in *McTeague* is how greed leads to murder, compares his hero to an evil beast who takes a "panther leap" and kisses Trina, the heroine, "grossly, full on the mouth," and who delights his wife and himself with biting and beating her.[3] Though Kate Chopin saw brute selfishness as the dominant principle of the world, she rarely used the imagery of man as a warring animal, and, more specifically, she never attached anything brutish to physical passion. Moreover, she lets Edna make absolutely no attempt to suppress her amatory impulses.

In fact, not only does Mrs. Chopin treat sex at least as amorally as any of the other four writers, but she also describes it more openly than they do. Their heroines—Maggie, Rose, Trina, and Carrie—are all rather sexless compared to Edna, and their descriptions of sexual matters in general are tame. This is perhaps most surprising in Dreiser, who is otherwise so elaborate and who wants us to believe that Carrie is dangerously attractive to men, and in Norris, who had made sex the main theme of his unfinished *Vandover and the Brute*. Garland is comparatively daring when he lets Rose feel desire and when he speaks of her "splendid curve of bust," but he allows her no more than a kiss on the hand.[4] It is hard to understand that this book was locally banned; yet this reaction frightened the author, who thereafter fully adhered to R. W. Gilder's[5] genteel literary code. *The Awakening*, meanwhile, is suffused with sex, and we witness how Alcée arouse Edna and how she in turn sets Robert on fire with a voluptuous kiss. On this point of physical attraction and contact, Kate Chopin gave not only a fuller, but also a more convincing picture than any other serious American novelist had done.

2. Hamlin Garland, *Rose of Dutcher's Coolly* (Chicago, 1895), pp. 59, 62, 121, 147, 288, 294, 364 [*Seyersted's note*].
3. Frank Norris, *McTeague* (New York, 1899), pp. 30–31, 300, 310 [*Seyersted's note*].
4. Garland, *Rose*, p. 245 [*Seyersted's note*].
5. Editor of *Scribner's Monthly* (1870–81) and *The Century Magazine* (1881–1909), Gilder was a strong influence in establishing what he considered standards of moral wholesomeness in the popular and literary magazines at the end of the century.

A fact which significantly sets off *The Awakening* from *Maggie, Rose, McTeague,* and *Sister Carrie,* is that Edna has children and the other heroines do not. This points to a fundamental difference in emphasis: Kate Chopin concentrates mainly on the biological aspects of woman's situation, while the other writers are more concerned with the socio-economic forces shaping her life. When Edna stands back from society and questions its rules for woman's existence, the other women move with the procession in their fight for wealth, rank, or physical survival. Common to all Edna's four counterparts is their admiration of those who are well dressed. Maggie and Carrie are more easily seduced because of their suitors' stylishness, which they equate with power and standing. Both Rose and Carrie[6] are allured by the life of the rich, and their "imagination," as it is called, repesents a desire to succeed and move up in the world. Dreiser speaks in one breath of Carrie's "emancipation" and her "more showy life." For Edna, who is the only one of these five women to start near the top, emancipation means something quite different; as she moves to a smaller house, she has "a feeling of having descended in the social scale, with a corresponding sense of having risen in the spiritual."

When Carrie leaves Hurstwood, on the other hand, it is not her inner integrity she is thinking of, but her outer or material progress. She arrives at the attitude which long dominates Rose, that is, she does not want a husband and children to impede her climb on the ladder. As the two women rise, both judge themselves against their betters in society. Rose is particularly influenced by a woman doctor who tells her to think first of her career. Garland, who had once let a heroine demand "the right to be an individual human being first and a woman afterwards," is ostensibly in favor of female emancipation; the doctor leaves out the promise of obedience in her marriage ceremony, and Rose is told by her suitor that he expects her to be as "free and as sovereign" as himself and to follow her profession. But the author could not quite free himself from accepted ideas: The doctor insists that though she is ambitious in her career, she "could bear to give it all up a hundred times over, rather than [her] hope of being a mother," and Rose revels in "doing wifely things" for her friend the moment he has proposed, just as she suddenly finds it much more important that he appreciates her as a woman than that he praises her poetry.[7]

In Crane's version of the relationship between man and woman, Maggie's swaggering seducer asserts his "reassuring proprietorship" while she shows a dependent air: "Her life was Pete's." Norris' view is also

---

6. Garland, *Rose*, p. 299; Theodore Dreiser, *Sister Carrie* (New York, 1900), pp. 58, 126. Jessie Ogden of Henry B. Fuller's *The Cliff-Dwellers* (New York, 1893) is an example of a contemporary American heroine who has a child; when she neglects it, it is in order to rise socially, not spiritually [*Seyersted's note*].

7. Hamlin Garland, "A Spoil of Office" in *Arena*, V (March, 1892), 515; *Rose*, pp. 330, 380, 395 [*Seyersted's note*].

uncomplicated when he lets Trina be subdued and conquered by McTeague's "sheer brute force" and declares that she "belongs" to him, body and soul, "forever and forever," because "the woman [worships] the man for that which she yields up to him." Norris here seems to have been influenced by the Darwinian idea of the female selecting the strongest suitor[8] (which fits in with general male conceptions), and he also accepts the concomitant unromantic view of the love of an aroused heroine when he writes: "The Woman is awakened, and, starting from her sleep, catches blindly at what first her newly opened eyes light upon. It is a spell, a witchery, ruled by chance. . . ." *McTeague* thus for a moment parallels *The Awakening*, but Trina's "love of submission," on the other hand, is utterly unthinkable in the self-asserting Edna.[9]

Kate Chopin's novel stands up well when compared to these four important works in the canon of early American realism or naturalism. *Maggie* is a stereotype seduction-story which is only saved by Crane's irony and general artistic mastery; *Rose* has much of a moralistic, sentimental romance in spite of Garland's attempts to make it into a serious *Bildungsroman*,[1] and *McTeague* has not a little of the melodramatic, particularly in the conclusion of its Zolaesque motif. *The Awakening*, on the other hand, has a fundamental seriousness which goes beyond that of these three works, and this and other qualities unite it more closely with *Sister Carrie* than with any of the other books.

Kate Chopin and Theodore Dreiser have in common a directness and a complete honesty in their descriptions of Edna's and Carrie's violations of what both writers considered society's "arbitrary scale" of morals. Unable to see their heroines as sinners, they braved public opinion by refusing to let the two repent, and they had the further audacity to present their stories with no trace of moralism and without apology. There are no villains in the two works. A seducer like Arobin appeals to the reader; Hurstwood achieves a certain dignity even in his downfall, and Adèle, who represents everything that Edna opposes, is portrayed with sympathy and understanding.

We have here two unillusioned authors each writing about a heroine pursuing a chimera; the magnet drawing Carrie is the golden radiance on the distant hill tops, and the illusion firing Edna is the idea that she can achieve the ecstasy of an all-encompassing love. Both writers see their protagonists as wisps in the wind among the forces that move us, but with a difference. Though Dreiser at one point speaks in terms of evolutionary optimism and Kate Chopin sees man as basically unimprovable, there are greater changes, certainly a greater spiritual evolution, in Edna than in Carrie.

8. See Charles Darwin, *The Descent of Man, and Selection in Relation to Sex*, eds. John Tyler Bonner and Robert M. May (Princeton: Princeton UP, 1981) 262.
9. Stephen Crane, *Maggie: A Girl of the Streets* (New York, 1893), pp. 106, 107; Norris, *McTeague*, pp. 84, 88, 89, 183, 309 [*Seyersted's note*].
1. A novel of "education," traditionally of a young boy arriving at manhood.

The reason is that Dreiser, reflecting a mostly socio-economic determinism, endows Carrie with less free will than that found in Edna. What freedom Carrie has she uses to act out the changing roles which she copies from those one step ahead of her. True, she achieves outer independence, but she is unthinkable without the society which provides her with models. As symbolized by the rocking-chair, she has scarcely moved at the end of the novel; she is basically unchanged, ever looking to the next hill, her eyes still largely unopened to the real emptiness of her longings.

Edna, meanwhile, is awakened to a spiritual independence in general and to a realization of the nature of reality in particular. Of these two solitary souls, the outwardly successful Carrie gains little more than the finery without which she, like her first lover, is merely "nothing";[2] when the apparently defeated Edna takes off her clothes, on the other hand, it symbolizes a victory of self-knowledge and authenticity as she fully becomes herself.

Carrie's blind, irresistible fight to get ahead has an unquestionable universality, and there is a similar quality in Edna's open-eyed choice to defy illusions and conventions. Different as these two novels are in form and theme—one terse in its concentration on inner reality, the other full of details on the outer show—both give a sense of tragic life, conveying something of the human condition.

What unites these five works from the 1890's is that they all, in one way or another, represent their authors' will to renew American literature. In subject matter or approach, they had enough of the new realism or naturalism to shock the Iron Madonnas.[3] Refusing to idealize life in the old manner, these writers all took a step forward in what Howells[4] called truthful treatment of material.

Kate Chopin parallels the naturalists in her view of basic urges as imperative, but differs from them in that she lets Edna decide her own destiny in an existentialist way. *The Awakening* also differs from *Maggie* and *McTeague* in that there is nothing of the sordid in it. Yet we note that while Norris and Crane became less iconoclastic in their subsequent work, Mrs. Chopin moved on to the increased openness of "The Storm."[5] After science had robbed her of some of her early beliefs, she may at times have wanted to join one of her heroines who decided to "go back into the dark to think" because "the sight of things" confused her. However, whereas Maupassant's reaction to the new knowledge was sadness rather than exhilaration—"tous ces voiles levés m'attristent," as

2. Dreiser, *Sister Carrie*, p. 4 [*Seyersted's note*].
3. A phrase used to describe the female audience of late-nineteenth-century fiction.
4. William Dean Howells (1837–1920), influential critic and novelist, proponent of literary realism; edited *The Atlantic Monthly* from 1871 to 1881, served on the editorial board of *Harper's*. His best-known novel is *The Rise of Silas Lapham* (1885).
5. See Per Seyersted, ed., *The Complete Works of Kate Chopin* (Baton Rouge: Louisiana State UP, 1969) 2.592–96.

he expressed it[6]—Kate Chopin was sad only at the thought of woman's position, while being exhilarated at the opportunity of portraying life truthfully. Though she did not aim at exposing false respectability, her work is in certain respects a forerunner of such later eye-openers as *Spoon River Anthology, Winesburg, Ohio,* and *Main Street.*[7]

Mrs. Chopin was at least a decade ahead of her time. During the years following America's silencing of her, "Edith Wharton's genteel satire and Ellen Glasgow's moral searchings were the strongest fare that it could take," as Robert E. Spiller has observed.[8] Kate Chopin can be seen not only as one of the American realists of the 1890's, but also as a link in the tradition formed by such distinguished American women authors as Sarah Orne Jewett, Mary E. Wilkins Freeman, Willa Cather,[9] and the two just mentioned. One factor uniting these writers is their emphasis on female characters. Another is their concern with values, but here we see a difference between the St. Louisian and the others in that she is less interested than they are in preserving these values. As exemplified in Mrs. Todd of *The Country of the Pointed Firs,* for instance, woman is a rock guarding the old qualities, the men being either weak or dead. To Mrs. Chopin, woman is no more of a rock than is man, being neither better nor worse than he. Mrs. Wharton and Miss Glasgow may have attacked certain aspects of the aristocracies they sprang from, but they also wanted to preserve some of their values. Kate Chopin, on the other hand, was no celebrant of the aristocratic qualities of her own distinguished background.

The one value that really counted with her was woman's opportunity for self-expression. She knew that there are many *Woman's Kingdoms.*[1] She was sensitive, intelligent, and broad enough in her outlook to see the different basic needs of the female and the various sides of her existence and to represent them with impartiality. Her work is thus no feminist plea in the usual sense, but an illustration—rather than an assertion—of woman's right to be herself, to be individual and independent whether she wants to be weak or strong, a nest-maker or a soaring bird.

6. Maupassant, as quoted in Edward D. Sullivan, *Maupassant: The Short Stories* (London, 1962), p. 57 [*Seyersted's note*]. "All these lifted veils sadden me."
7. Edgar Lee Masters's *Spoon River Anthology* (1915), Sherwood Anderson's *Winesburg, Ohio* (1919), and Sinclair Lewis's *Main Street* are all works of realism with a satiric edge that made them controversial books, especially in the locales they depict.
8. Robert E. Spiller, et al., eds., *Literary History of the United States,* II (New York, 1948), 1197 [*Seyersted's note*]. Edith Wharton (1862–1937), American novelist of manners and morals in New York society. Ellen Glasgow (1847–1945), American author of nineteen novels, many of which are set in Virginia.
9. See p. 197, n. 3; Mary Wilkins Freeman (1852–1930) wrote short stories and a novel of life in New England; Willa Cather (1876–1947), best known for her *Death Comes for the Archbishop* (1927), wrote a number of studies of southwest immigrant settlers.
1. The title of a novel by Dinah Maria Mulock Craik, published in New York in 1869, from which Chopin copied an antifeminist passage into her diary. See Seyersted, *Kate Chopin,* p. 29. See also Showalter, below, p. 312, n. 2.

GEORGE M. SPANGLER

[The Ending of the Novel]†

* * * one can easily and happily join in the praise that in recent years has been given to *The Awakening*—one can, that is, until one reaches the conclusion of the novel, which is unsatisfactory because it is fundamentally evasive. Other commentators, it should be noted here, have been as affirmative about the conclusion as they have been about the novel as a whole. Though Edmund Wilson merely notes that the ending has "the same sensuous beauty as all the rest," other writers have not confined their praise to the esthetic. Berthoff, for example, finds Edna's suicide "psychologically, sensually, convincing," "matter-of-course, unarguable"; and Kauffmann sees it as "the confrontation of resultant consequences without plot contrivance or escape."[1] Ziff, in some detail, argues for the psychological coherence and, by implication, the rightness of the suicide; and Eble comments on Mrs. Chopin's "complete command of structure," including, presumably, the conclusion. What, in the narrowest sense, happens in the final pages, which seem so right to five readers and so unsatisfactory to at least one?

After finding Robert's farewell note and spending a sleepless night in her home, Edna takes a boat to the resort, now in its off-season, where the novel and her attraction to Robert began. She arranges with the caretaker for a room and for dinner in the evening, and then, deciding to go swimming, borrows some towels. There is no hint that suicide is her intention. As she walks toward the beach thinking of nothing in particular, the reader learns of her thoughts during the previous night. Primary was her fear of a succession of lovers and the effect such a future would have on her children: "To-day it is Arobin; tomorrow it will be some one else. It makes no difference to me, it doesn't matter about Léonce Pontellier— but Raoul and Etienne!" In her despondency (which "had never lifted"), her children "appeared before her like antagonists who had overcome her; who had overpowered and sought to drag her into the soul's slavery for the rest of her days. But she knew a way to elude them." However, "she was not thinking of these things" as she walks to the beach, decides against a bathing suit ("How strange and awful it seemed to stand naked under the sky! How delicious!"), and begins her walk into the sea. As she goes farther and farther out, "her arms and legs growing tired," she thinks

---

† From "Kate Chopin's *The Awakening*: A Partial Dissent," *Novel* 3 (Spring 1970): 249–55. Reprinted with permission. Footnotes are by the editor of this Norton Critical Edition.
1. Edmund Wilson, *Patriotic Gore: Studies in the Literature of the American Civil War* (New York: Oxford UP, 1962) 151. Warner Berthoff, *The Ferment of Realism* (New York: Free Press, 1965) 89. Stanley Kauffmann, "The Really Lost Generation," *New Republic* 155 (3 Dec. 1966): 38. Other essays noted are included in part in this collection.

again of her husband and children ("they need not have thought that they could possess her, body and soul"); of Robert ("He did not know; he did not understand. He would never understand"); and, in the final lines, of her childhood in Kentucky.

And what is wrong with this conclusion? Its great fault is inconsistent characterization, which asks the reader to accept a different and diminished Edna from the one developed so impressively before. Throughout the novel the most striking feature of Edna's character has been her strength of will, her ruthless determination to go her own way. In thought and act she has rejected unequivocally the restraints of conventional morality, social custom and personal obligation to her husband and children (through most of the novel the children are visiting their grandmother). Yet in the final pages, Mrs. Chopin asks her reader to believe in an Edna who is completely defeated by the loss of Robert, to believe in the paradox of a woman who has awakened to passional life and yet quietly, almost thoughtlessly, chooses death. Having overcome so much in the way of frustration, Edna is destroyed by so little. As well, the reasonings and feelings attributed to her as motivation at the end do not bear scrutiny. Her brief affair with Arobin hardly proves the certainty of a host of future lovers, but it has clearly shown her what is missing from her life; and since she has long been indifferent to convention and domestic ties, she could well expect to find someone less shoddy than Arobin and less scrupulous than Robert. Equally perplexing is the sudden concern for her children, who previously have seemed to matter little as long as they were out of the way. Increasingly strong, practical and sure of herself and her needs through most of the novel, Edna suddenly collapses, and what the reader gets in the way of explanation does not follow from what he has witnessed before. Once capable of leaving her husband, relegating her children, establishing her own home, earning money with her painting, accepting one lover, pursuing another—at the end she is unable to endure Robert's tender note of rejection.

What happened was that Mrs. Chopin provided a conclusion for a novel other than the one she wrote, a conclusion for a novel much more conventional and much less interesting than *The Awakening*. Specifically it is a conclusion for an ordinary sentimental novel, not for a subtle psychological treatment of female sexuality. If the rest of the novel existed only at the sentimental, romantic level, then Edna's suicide would be conventionally appropriate and acceptable: a woman surrenders her chastity and death is the consequence. In such a novel Robert would be the single great love of her life, a great romantic passion, finally doomed and destructive. But despite its conclusion *The Awakening* is not such a novel; indeed its relation to the conventional sentimental novel is not apparent until the final pages. For Mrs. Chopin was concerned not with seduction and retribution, but with woman's passional nature and its relation to self, marriage and society. Yet at the end she transformed a character who has embodied these complex issues into one who simply dies from disappointed, illicit love. In a word, a complex psychological novel is converted into a commonplace sentimental one. Possible reasons for such an unfortunate change, which also mars a number of Mrs. Chopin's short stories, are not difficult to discover. With her conclusion the author managed to provide both pathos and poetic justice, pathos to please her sentimental readers and justice to satisfy her moralistic ones. The shift toward the sentimental and pathetic is implicit in the image of "a bird with a broken wing" which Edna, just before her death, sees "reeling, fluttering, circling, disabled down, down to the water." Nearly a hundred pages before, Edna's confidant used the image of the crippled bird to suggest what happens to those who, lacking great strength, would "soar above the level plain of tradition and prejudice." When the image recurs at the end, the reader no doubt is expected to see Edna as such a person. But of course she is not: whatever destroys Edna, it is not tradition and prejudice, not environmental pressure—except, perhaps, that of the tradition of the sentimental novel. The sentimental is also present in a different and rather special form. Just as the reader of Mrs. Wharton's[2] House of Mirth may well conclude that Lily Bart's death is the result of Selden's conventionality so he can hardly avoid the suggestion in The Awakening that Edna dies because Robert is so foolishly scrupulous—the conventionality of both men of course being a mask to hide a severe deficiency of masculine force. The result in both novels is, unfortunately, the special pathos, the feminine self-pity, expressed in the words of the ballad, "hard is the lot of all womankind," and of course in countless magazine stories aimed at a feminine audience.

The moralistic explanation for the conclusion is just as obvious, though far less evident in the tone and diction of the concluding pages: Edna has sinned in thought and deed against accepted sexual morality, and for the average reader in 1899, her sin required that she suffer and die. But if Mrs. Chopin had hoped to avoid the kind of trouble Dreiser was soon to have with Sister Carrie,[3] she was to be disappointed. The reviewers were hostile to her subject, the book was withdrawn from the libraries in St. Louis, her native city, and she was denied membership in the St. Louis Fine Arts Club because of the scandal.

If then, the conclusion Mrs. Chopin chose for The Awakening allows for pathos and poetic justice to please the sentimental and moralistic— a dubious accomplishment indeed—it also leads to a painful reduction in Edna's character. For in the final pages Edna is different and di-

2. Edith Wharton (1862–1937), whose House of Mirth (1905) ends with the suicide of Lily Bart. See Cynthia Griffin Wolff, "Lily Bart and the Beautiful Death," American Literature 45 (May 1974): 16–41.
3. Either ignored by influential reviewers or vigorously condemned, Sister Carrie (by Theodore Dreiser [1871–1945]) was a commercial failure when it was published in 1900 by reluctant publishers. When it was reissued in 1907, it was more widely and favorably reviewed. Thereafter the novel appeared in numerous editions and was sold to RKO Pictures in 1940.

minished: she is no longer purposeful, merely willful; no longer liberated, merely perverse; no longer justified, merely spiteful. And the painful failure of vision (or, more likely, of nerve) implicit in the change prevents a very good, very interesting novel from being the extraordinary masterpiece some commentators have claimed it is.

JOHN R. MAY

Local Color in *The Awakening*†

Kate Chopin appeals subtly to all of the reader's senses, and her descriptions are delicate impressionistic touches on her canvas of New Orleans and Grand Isle. In her use of color she is similar to Stephen Crane,[1] yet somehow the strokes of her brush are less jarring. Leonce Pontellier watches his wife and Robert Lebrun approach the cottage: "He fixed his gaze upon a white sunshade that was advancing at a snail's pace from the beach. He could see it plainly between the gaunt trunks of the water-oaks and across the stretch of yellow camomile. The gulf looked far away, melting hazily into the blue of the horizon." When Edna goes with Arobin to the "pigeon-house" after her farewell party, she notices "the black line of his leg moving in and out so close to her against the yellow shimmer of her gown." The garden that Edna visits in the suburbs of New Orleans is "a small, leafy corner, with a few green tables under the orange trees."

The Gulf breeze that reaches the Lebrun cottages is "soft and languorous . . . , charged with the seductive odor of the sea." After the Lebrun party, as the guests leave for the beach, there are "strange, rare odors abroad—a tangle of the sea smell and of weeds and damp, new-plowed earth, mingled with the heavy perfume of a field of white blossoms somewhere near." "The everlasting voice of the sea" breaks "like a mournful lullaby upon the night."

As the story progresses there is an increasing emphasis on tactile imagery. When Victor ceremoniously apologizes for offending Edna, the touch of his lips is "like a pleasing sting to her hand." During her reunion with Robert, Edna notices the "same tender caress" of his eyes. Edna's "soft, cool, delicate kiss" is a "voluptuous sting," penetrating Robert's whole being. When Edna leaves Adele after the birth of her child, the air is "mild and caressing, but cool with the breath of spring and the night."

It is the personification of the sea, though, that dominates all the

† From "Local Color in *The Awakening*," *The Southern Review* 6 (Fall 1970): 1031–40. Reprinted by permission of the author.
1. See above, p. 190, n. 3 [*Editor*].

imagery. The sea is undoubtedly the central symbol of the novel; like all natural symbols it is basically ambiguous. Initially, though, it embodies for Edna all of the sensuousness of her new environment. The early passage describing the voice and touch of the sea becomes a poetic refrain when repeated at the close of the story. The sea presides over the dawn of Edna's awakening as it does over the night of her fate; but it is not just another sea, as Seyersted seems to imply.[2] The images attempt to capture the mystery and enchantment of the semitropical summer Gulf: "The voice of the sea is seductive; never ceasing, whispering, clamoring, murmuring, inviting the soul to wander for a spell in abysses of solitude; to lose itself in mazes of inward contemplation. The voice of the sea speaks to the soul. The touch of the sea is sensuous, enfolding the body in its soft, close embrace."

When the description appears again in the final chapter, the words "for a spell" have been dropped and the first sentence ends with "solitude." The second sentence is not repeated. The effect of the repetition is to suggest that the end for Edna was indeed the beginning of her awakening. The omissions emphasize the finality of her solitude; she gives herself to the sea only because she has already lost herself in a maze of self-contemplation.

The full symbolism of the novel is complex, yet Kate Chopin proves herself at all times to be the master of it. Supporting the rhythmic movement of the narrative from Grand Isle to the Creole quarter of New Orleans and back to Grand Isle are the basic symbols of sea and city. Even though the Lebrun cottges at Grand Isle the summer the novel begins are occupied exclusively by Creoles, there is a more relaxed atmosphere at the beach than in the winter of the city—because there one must "observe *les convenances*." The tension between freedom and restraint is evident in the use of the symbols.

Paralleling the significance of sea and city in the temporal sequence of the narrative is Edna's remembrance of the contrast between the Kentucky meadow and the Presbyterian household of her youth. She recalls the summer day when as a child she ran from the Sunday prayer service that her father always conducted "in a spirit of gloom." The meadow seemed like an ocean to her as she walked through it, "beating the tall grass as one strikes out in the water." "My sunbonnet obstructed the view," she tells Adele; "I could see only the stretch of green before me, and I felt as if I must walk on forever, without coming to an end of it. . . . Sometimes I feel this summer as if I were walking through the green meadow again; idly, aimlessly, unthinking and unguided."

The lady in black, the young lovers, and the mother-women represent the actual limits imposed by the Creole environment; as symbols they specify the restraint of the city. The lady in black is either "walking

2. *Kate Chopin: A Critical Biography* (Baton Rouge: Louisiana State University Press, 1969), p. 151.

demurely up and down, telling her beads," or "reading her morning devotions." The young lovers lean upon each other like "water-oaks bent from the sea," "exchanging their vows and sighs" and showing an inclination "to linger and hold themselves apart." Yet it is the mother-women who seem to prevail: "It was easy to know them, fluttering about with extended, protecting wings when any harm, real or imaginary, threatened their precious brood. They were women who idolized their children, worshiped their husbands, and esteemed it a holy privilege to efface themselves as individuals and grow wings as ministering angels." By reason of her marriage and children, Edna rightfully belongs to this group; but she is not and cannot be a mother-woman.

In the criticism of the novel to date, no one has commented on the symbolic stages of Edna's rebellion against the restraints of Creole society—a withdrawal into solitude that poses as a quest for freedom. The sequence also adds irony to the final meaning of the sea. I refer here to the significance of the home on Esplanade Street, the "pigeon-house" around the corner, the garden in the suburbs, and finally the sea. The Pontellier home on Esplanade is a perfect microcosm of the restraints of the Creole city. There Edna must be mistress of the household, receive callers on Tuesday afternoons, and be the perfect mother-woman. Yet, even while still there, Edna stops receiving callers, abandons the household to the erratic performance of the servants, and severs ties with her family. She refuses to attend her sister's wedding; and when her father terminates his shopping trip to New Orleans, which is also an abortive mission of persuasion, Edna is "glad to be rid of . . . his wedding garments and his bridal gifts, . . . his padded shoulders, his Bible reading, his 'toddies' and his ponderous oaths." At the farewell party, Edna's appearance suggests "the regal woman, the one who rules, who looks on, *who stands alone*" (my emphasis). The "pigeon-house," which Edna moves into in her husband's absence, the first stage of her actual physical withdawal from Creole society, is just large enough to satisfy her needs. She knows that she will "like the feeling of freedom and independence." Seyersted's preoccupation with sexual freedom leads him at this point to ignore the obvious reference to the size of the place in relation to the home on Esplanade and to suggest that "it is to be a place of cooing love."[3]

After her disappointing reunion with Robert, Edna becomes the prey of alternating moods of hope and despondency. Robert does not return to see her during the days that follow. "Each morning she awoke with hope, and each night she was a prey to despondency." Then one night Arobin asks her to drive with him out to the lake. Her realization that it has become "more than a passing whim with Arobin to see her and be with her" leads to a second and more significant stage in her with-

3. Ibid., p. 159.

drawal. We are told that "there was no despondency when she fell asleep that night; nor was there hope when she awoke in the morning." Significantly, the very next scene takes place in a garden in the suburbs— a place "too modest to attract the attention of the people of fashion, and so quiet as to have escaped the notice of those in search of pleasure and dissipation."

The final stage of Edna's withdrawal is, of course, the return to Grand Isle and the sea. It is the day after Robert has left her the note which says: "I love you. Good-by—because I love you." Despondency has returned to her and has not left. Now, at the beach, there is "no living thing in sight." "Absolutely alone," Edna removes her "unpleasant, pricking garments" and swims out into the water. The sea which at first spoke sensuously to Edna of freedom has become finally the symbol of her liberation—but, also, ironically, of her complete withdrawal from society, her total isolation. It is curious that, as she swims on, Edna is drawn back in her memory to the days of her youth. She hears the voices of her father and sister, the barking of a chained dog, the clanging spur of the cavalry officer, and the hum of the bees. Seyersted, consistent as always with his critical motif, sees these final lines as "a parable on the female condition."[4] He ignores the voices and the barking dog to note the symbol of male dominance in the clanging spurs and the generative symbolism of the bees. The meaning of Edna's recollections is, at best, ambiguous. Although the sea and the meadow were associated earlier, she remembers now instead the sounds of her Presbyterian home. The gradual diminution of sound may indicate simply that her strength is gone, but it may also suggest ironically that Edna is returning home—defeated.

In what sense, then, has Edna been awakened by the alien Creole environment? I have already suggested that an explanation of her awakening simply in terms of a growing awareness of her sexual needs is too facile an interpretation of this rather complex novel. On a much deeper level Edna awakens to the reality of her own nature in relation to life. In seeking to possess Robert and be possessed by him, she has allowed herself to be duped by the sensuous freedom of the environment into thinking that she can satisfy her deepest human longings. Robert himself represents the unattainable, the possibilities that life offers, but never actualizes. During her farewell party on Esplanade Street, Edna experiences "the acute longing which always summoned into her spiritual vision the presence of the beloved one, overpowering her at once with a sense of the unattainable." It is longing which summons Robert as its symbol.

While still at Grand Isle, where her "awakening" begins, Edna is disturbed by dreams that leave "only an impression on her half-awakened

4. Ibid., p. 160.

senses of something unattainable." She pities Adele Ratignolle because of the "colorless existence" that Adele leads as a mother-woman, one "in which she would never have the taste of life's delirium," although Edna wonders at the time what she means by "life's delirium." The irony here, and Edna clearly awakens to this realization, is that life's delirium is never attainable. There are days when she feels as if life is passing her by, "leaving its promise broken and unfulfilled," yet others when she is "led on and *deceived* by fresh promises" (my emphasis). Once when Edna is with Robert at Grand Isle and again when she returns from Adele's at the end of the novel, she has the sensation of striving to overtake her thoughts.

Life itself creates the longing within her, but it never fulfills its promise. Edna is not simply a dreamer, a romantic, because it was life that offered her the promise of the sad-eyed cavalry officer, the engaged young men, and the great tragedian. The fulfillment though was only the frustration of Leonce Pontellier, Alcée Arobin, and Robert Lebrun. Life among the Creoles promised familiarity, open expression of affection, and freedom from moral rigor, but then only as a mother-woman, a lady in black, or an innocent young lover.

It is nature and man that conspire to frustrate human longing. "As if a mist had been lifted from her eyes," Edna awakens to "the significance of life, that monster made up of beauty and brutality." Clearly, beauty and brutality correspond to vision and reality, promise and fulfillment. When, finally, Edna assists Adele in childbirth, it is, "with an inward agony, with a flaming, outspoken revolt against the ways of Nature." Doctor Mandelet, sensing the honest questions that Edna wants to ask, attempts an answer: "The trouble is . . . that youth is given up to illusions. It seems to be a provision of Nature; a decoy to secure mothers for the race. And Nature takes no account of moral consequences, or arbitrary conditions which we create, and which we feel obliged to maintain at any cost."

If Edna opens her eyes to the tyranny of life, she also becomes aware of her own nature. She is "a solitary soul," as Kate Chopin's original title for the novel indicated.[5] Nature has made her independent, willful, and selfish. When she moves from the home on Esplanade, she resolves "never again to belong to another than herself." She assures Robert, "I give myself where I choose." And when Doctor Mandelet asks if she is going abroad with her husband, Edna answers: "I'm not going to be forced into doing things. . . . I want to be let alone." Realizing that she is "wanting a good deal," she adds, "I don't want anything but my own way."

In reality, the Creole setting has simply provided a climate of psychological relaxation sufficient to allow Edna's true nature to reveal

5. Daniel S. Rankin, *Kate Chopin and Her Creole Stories* (Philadelphia: University of Pennsylvania Press, 1932), p. 171.

itself. Thus, because Edna is what she is, the longing for freedom has become the assertion of independence. The possibility of an open break with tradition has led simply to withdrawal from life. And the atmosphere of familiarity has revealed her radical incapacity to deal with anyone except on her own terms.

When Edna recalls that the friends of her youth had been of the self-contained type, the author notes: "She never realized that the reserve of her own character had much, perhaps everything, to do with this." Even Leonce Pontellier did not realize what was happening to his wife, "that she was becoming herself and daily casting aside that fictitious self which we asume like a garment with which to appear before the world." Only Mlle Reisz and Adele Ratignolle seemed to sense, though vaguely, what was actually happening. Mlle Reisz had warned Edna, "The bird that would soar above the level plain of tradition and prejudice must have strong wings." Thus, expectedly, when Edna walks to the beach at Grand Isle for the last time, a bird with a broken wing hovers above her, "reeling, fluttering, circling disabled down, down to the water." And Adele had pleaded with Robert, "Let Mrs. Pontellier alone. . . . She is not one of us."

Edna Pontellier's final revolt against nature, when she swims to her death in the sea, is certainly not an eventuality that the reader is unprepared for. Her innate sense of independence and her desire to assert her freedom, despite nature's refusal to satisfy her longing, have led her "step by inexorable step,"[6] in Stanley Kauffmann's phrase, to withdraw from life. The stages of her withdrawal into the solitude of complete isolation are symbolized, as we have seen, by the retreat from the home on Esplanade to the "pigeon-house," the garden, and the sea. The ultimate realization that she has awakened to is that the only way she can save herself is to give up her life. She cannot accept the restrictions that nature and man have conspired to impose upon her, the perpetual frustration of desire that living entails. And so, paradoxically, she surrenders her life in order to save herself.

Although it is difficult—perhaps presumptuous—to write with assurance about the essence of local color, it seems safe to say that a local color novel is one in which the identity of the setting is integral to the very unfolding of the theme, rather than simply incidental to a theme that could as well be set anywhere. *The Awakening* is clearly of the former type. The greater freedom of the new environment—with all of its characteristic sensuousness—has tempted Edna to reach for the unattainable because, in contrast with the severity of her Kentucky background, the summer at Grand Isle actually deluded her into thinking that her deepest longings could be satisfied. By the time she awakens to the cruel illusion nurtured by life in her new environment, her inde-

6. Stanley Kauffmann, "The Really Lost Generation, *The New Republic*, CLV (December 3, 1966), 38.

pendent and selfish temperament—which supported her vain efforts—
has led her irrevocably into abysses of solitude.

LEWIS LEARY

[Kate Chopin and Walt Whitman]†

* * * Through much of the novel like an obbligato refrain runs the-
voice of the sea—"the everlasting voice of the sea," that "broke like a lullaby" on her consciousness. When Edna is first introduced, returning
from bathing in the sea with Robert, her husband's attitude toward her is
defined by the remark, "You are burnt beyond recognition"; he looks at
his wife "as one looks at a valuable piece of property which has suffered
some damage." Four chapters later, when Robert invites her to go bathing
again, the sea's "sonorous murmur reached her like a loving but imperative entreaty": the sea is "delicious," her companion tells her; "it will not
hurt you." The voice of the sea invites the soul "to lose itself in mazes of
inward contemplation. . . . The touch of the sea is sensuous, enfolding
the body in its soft, close embace." These words that appear first in Chapter 6 are repeated almost exactly in the final chapter, as are these also:
"The voice of the sea is seductive; never ceasing, clamoring, murmuring,
inviting the soul to wander for a spell in the abysses of solitude."

Echoes of the poetry of Whitman[1] can be recognized in these recurrent
murmurings of the sea, especially of his "Out of the Cradle Endlessly
Rocking," in which the sea whispers the strong and "delicious" word
death. Mrs. Chopin seems to have known Whitman's poetry well and
to have had confidence that her readers did also, as is suggested in her
quotation from Whitman's "Song of Myself" in her story "A Respectable
Woman," where the quotation depends for its force on the reader's
adding to the apparently innocent lines "Night of south winds—night
of the large few stars! / Still nodding night—" the sensuous words
which Whitman precedes and follows them: "Press close bare-bosom'd
night . . . " and "mad naked summer night." Indeed the whole of *The
Awakening* is pervaded with the spirit of Whitman's "Song of Myself."
Edna Pontellier is awakened to her self, until with Whitman she might
finally say, "I exist as I am, that is enough." As she who early in the
novel shrinks almost prudishly from physical contact with other people

† Reprinted by permission of Louisiana State University Press from *Southern Excursions: Essays
on Mark Twain and Others* (Baton Rouge: Louisiana State UP, 1971) 169–74. Copyright ©
1971 by Louisiana State University Press. Footnotes are by the editor of this Norton Critical
Edition.
1. Walt Whitman (1819–1892), American poet whose *Leaves of Grass*, first published in 1855,
generated controversy because of its unorthodox form and subject matter. The poetry was in
free verse and at times employed frank sexual imagery.

is awakened to the joy of touch, a reader may be reminded of Whitman's "Is this then the touch? quivering me to new identity." And the end of the novel is suggested in lines from Section 22 of "Song of Myself":

> You sea! I resign myself to you also—I guess what you mean.
> I behold from the beach your crooked inviting fingers,
> I believe you refuse to go back without feeling of me,
> We must have a turn together, I undess, I hurry out of sight
> of the land,
> Cushion me soft, rock me in billowy drowse.

Not only does the sea sound an anticipatory refrain; incidents and characters early introduced in the novel often seem emblematic or teasingly suggestive of what will happen later. Some may find it significant that this narrative of self-discovery begins with the voice of an impertinent parrot and with a mockingbird "whistling his notes out upon the breeze with maddening persistence," and that it ends drowsily with "the hum of bees, and the musky odor of pinks." Others may wonder why Edna sleeps so often and so soundly, or whether her appetite for food and her shrugging off of niceness in eating are related, or supposed to be related, to other appetites. The silent woman clothed in black who appears six times in the first fifteen chapters may seem an ominous portent, as may also the pair of anonymous young lovers who roam the seaside, their courtship interrupted by children at play, much as Edna's adventuring toward freedom is disturbed—but how much?—by her concern for children. "I would give my life for my children," she says at one time; "but I wouldn't give myself." The significance of the Spanish girl Mariequita, who appears just before Robert Lebrun flees to Mexico and who appears again just before the final scene of the novel, is worthy of contemplation, as are the implications intended in the carefree and self-indulgent character of Victor Lebrun.

Bird images will be found throughout the novel, sometimes presented with quiet irony, as when Edna, seeking more freedom than her husband's house affords, takes a house of her own and calls it her "pigeon-house," allowing a reader then to recall that the pigeon of the kind she thought of was a domesticated, often a captive bird. The bird with the broken wing which, "reeling, fluttering, circling," is the only witness to Edna's final encounter with the sea may remind a reader that Mademoiselle Reisz had warned Edna earlier that "a bird that would soar above the level plain of tradition and prejudice must have strong wings," and is prefigured also (the ending of the novel may be discovered to be prefigured) in the vision which Edna has in Chapter 9 "of a man standing beside a desolate rock on the seashore. He was naked. His attitude was one of hopeless resignation as he looked toward a distant bird winging his flight away from him."

Things like this do not seem accidental. Almost every incident or reference in *The Awakening* anticipates an incident or reference that follows it or will remind a reader of something that has happened before. Other characters appear only in their relation to Edna Pontellier. Only such elements of background are introduced as contribute to her awakening. The narrative focus remains on her, as "blindly following whatever impulse moved her," she stumbles on finally "as if her thoughts had gone ahead of her. She is timid at first, almost cold: no trace of passion . . . colored her affection for her husband"; she is not accustomed to outward and spoken expression of affection. But as she is aroused by love outside of marriage, and by passion outside of love, she seems finally, not so much an enlightened woman, as "a beautiful, sleek animal waking up in the sun," uncaged and vulnerable.

Everything fits—the imagery and the reasons, gradually revealed, of the awakening. Among Mrs. Chopin's American contemporaries only Henry James and perhaps Sarah Orne Jewett[2] had produced fiction more artfully designed; there is a simpleness and a directness in *The Awakening* which has inevitably reminded readers of Flaubert's *Madame Bovary*, and an economy and mastery of incident and character which seem to forecast the lucid simplicity of Willa Cather's *Death Comes for the Archbishop*,[3] so different in theme, but comparable in technique. Few words are wasted; nothing is incomplete: it is a book about Edna Pontellier, and about her only.

To keep focus sharply on Edna, Mrs. Chopin needed somewhat to blur the supporting characters, revealing just enough about them to enable a reader to recognize their function. Most of them are familiar fictional types, familiarly realized: the kindly family doctor; the husband with a proprietary attitude toward his wife, a vacillating concern for his children, who enjoys weekend card games, and cares greatly for appearances; the irresponsible insolence of Victor Lebrun, which contrasts with the almost storybook concept of gallantry held by his brother; the misanthropy of Mademoiselle Reisz; and the almost professional charm of Alcée Arobin. Conventional characters like Madame Ratignolle, "a mother woman," are described in conventional, romantic terms: "There are no words to describe her," says Mrs. Chopin, "save the old ones that have served so often to picture the bygone heroine of romance and the fair lady of our dreams." Her hair is "spun gold," and her eyes "like nothing but sapphires; two lips that pouted, that were so red that one could only think of cherries or some other delicious fruit in looking at them. . . . Never were hands more exquisite than hers, and it was a joy to look at them when she threaded her needle or adjusted her gold thimble to her middle finger as she sewed on the little night drawers or fashioned a bodice or a bib."

Madame Ratignolle is "a sensuous Madonna," happily pregnant,

---

2. See above, p. 197, n. 3. "James": master of the novel and short story (1843–1916), creator of a number of memorable female heroes.
3. *Death Comes for the Archbishop* (1927) concerns the struggles of two French clergymen in the New Mexico territory. Cather (1876–1947) wrote an early review of *The Awakening*. See above, pp. 170–72.

motherly wise, and mindful of the future: in summer she prepares garments for the winter to come. Edna, obsessively concerned with herself, is careless about the future. Her thoughts are of herself, her concerns are her vague desires. But of all the characters she alone is described with precision, not in clichés but as an individual whose "graceful severity of poise and movement" made her "different from the crowd." She is not another mother woman, like those who "idolized their children, worshipped their husbands, and esteemed it a holy privilege to efface themselves as individuals." her eyes "were a yellowish brown, the color of her hair. . . . Her eyebrows were a shade darker. . . . They were thick and horizontal, emphasizing the depth of her eyes. . . . The lines of her body were long, clean and symmetrical; it was a body which occasionally fell into splendid poses; there was no suggestion of the trim stereotyped fashion plate about it."

Surrounded by other characters, most of whom are typical, Edna Pontellier gradually emerges as an understandable, though perhaps not completely admirable, individual reality. Whether she is weak and willful, a woman wronged by the requirements of society, or a self-indulgent sensualist, finally and fundamentally romantic, who gets exactly what she deserves—these are not considerations that seem to have concerned Mrs. Chopin. *The Awakening* is not a problem novel. If it seems inevitably to invite questions, these are subsidiary to its purpose, which is to describe what might really happen to a person like Edna Pontellier, being what she was, living when she did, and where.

Mrs. Chopin has presented a compelling portrait of a trapped and finally desperate woman, a drama of self-discovery, of awakening and doom, a tragedy perhaps of self-deceit. No questions are required, no verdict is given. Here is Edna Pontellier, a woman. She is awakened to possibilities for self-expression which, because she is what she is or because circumstances are what they are or because society is what it is, cannot be realized. Her awakening, only vaguely intellectual, is disturbingly physical. But wronged or erring, she is a valiant woman, worthy of place beside other fictional heroines who have tested emancipation and failed—Nathaniel Hawthorne's Hester Prynne, Gustave Flaubert's Emma Bovary, or Henry James's Isabel Archer.[4] Readers are likely to find something of themselves in her.

---

4. Henry James's novel *Portrait of a Lady* (1881) concerns the fortunes of Isabel Archer, an American girl whose "awakening" occurs in Europe. See also p. 170, n. 1. In Hawthorne's *The Scarlet Letter* (1850) Hester Prynne suffers the scorn of her community for having borne a child by a man who is not her husband.

JULES CHAMETZKY

[Edna and the "Woman Question"]†

* * *

The condemnation, in its time, of *The Awakening* as shocking and immoral does not surprise us now, when we reflect on the reception given *Sister Carrie* only a year later because of its presumedly amoral attitude toward departures from genteel standards of sexual propriety.[1] What does surprise one is the modernity, in numerous small and large ways, of Mrs. Chopin's insights into "the woman question." It is not so much that she advocates women's libidinal freedom or celebrates the force of the body's prerogatives—our post-Freudian age has won those battles (or should have). Nor is she terribly explicit about the mechanics of sex, in the contemporary way. What Kate Chopin shows so beautifully are the pressures working against woman's true awakening to her condition, and what that condition is.

From the opening images of a parrot in its cage and the marriage ring on the woman's finger, to the final images that flash before the drowning heroine—clanging spurs of a cavalry officer and "the hum of bees, and the musky odor of pinks"—the struggle is for the woman to free herself from being an object or possession defined in her functions, or owned, by others. Despite her middle-class advantages—money and the freedom to pursue a talent—Edna Pontellier, the heroine, is finally unable to overcome by herself the strength of the social and religious conventions and the biological mystique that entrap her.

Along the way, nevertheless, she is vouchsafed a glimpse of life as an autonomous self. She knows the joy of being able to say she would "never again belong to another than myself." Her young children, however, present a great problem. She says that she might die for her children, but would not give up her essential selfhood for them. This sentiment seems admirable but it is somewhat ambiguous, for at the end, in a muddled way, it is precisely the image of the children and her uncertainty about the nature of her role toward them that prove her undoing. Unconcerned herself about her new, freer attitude toward illicit sex, she fears the effects it will have upon her children when they learn about it. Mrs. Chopin had shown earlier how the husband uses the children and the mother's presumed duties

---

† From "Our Decentralized Literature," *Jarbuch fur Amerikastudien* (1972): 56–72, part of a longer essay on George Washington Cable, Abraham Cahan, Charles W. Chestnutt, and Kate Chopin, portions of which also appear in Chametzky's *Our Decentralized Literature: Cultural Mediations in Selected Jewish and Southern Writers* (Amherst: U of Massachusetts P, 1986). Copyright © 1986 by The University of Massachusetts Press.

1. See above, p. 210, n. 3 [*Editor*].

toward them as a means of control and subjugation of the woman, but she is, finally, at a loss as to how to break through to newer and more humane conventions—a legitimate and recognizable dilemma. More startling to contemporaries must have been Edna's sentiments after her fall into adultery, and with a most unworthy lover. Whatever the conflicting emotions that assail her, she says, "there was neither shame nor remorse."

Edna's struggle toward a new state of awareness and independent being is to some extent understood and encouraged by only one other woman in the book—the pianist Mme. Reisz. But this strange woman's encouragement takes the form of urging a kind of self-sufficiency that is as selfless as the marriage vows: if Edna is serious about her work as an artist, then she must give herself to it entirely—a renunciation, really, of the flesh and conventional human relationships. That, of course, is an answer, but no answer to the woman's question posed in this book: how to be free in one's self and for one's self but still meaningfully connected to others. Posed in this way, the question, of course, applies to everyone. What makes it peculiarly related to the woman question in *The Awakening* is Mrs. Chopin's unwillingness to make her heroine's situation easier by removing from her selfness the burden and possibility of motherhood. As indicated earlier, Mrs. Chopin stumbles ambiguously on this question, as indeed we still do.

Awakened by a realization of her sensuous self, Edna Pontellier grows in self-awareness and autonomy. But it is a lonely and isolated autonomy that exacts a terrible price. Like Kate Chopin herself, who broke through to new perceptions and honesty as an artist, Mrs. Pontellier, in the context of her time and milieu, found no firm ground beneath her, either in theory or practice, and she went under.

* * *

DONALD A. RINGE

[Romantic Imagery]†

* * * *The Awakening* posits a double world, one within and one without. Early in the book, Edna Pontellier feels contradictory impulses impelling her, impulses that at first serve to bewilder her, but which also reveal that she is "beginning to realize her position in the universe as a human being, and to recognize her relations as an individual to

† From "Romantic Imagery in Kate Chopin's *The Awakening*," *American Literature* 43 (January 1972): 580–88. Durham: Duke University Press, copyright 1972. Reprinted with permission of the publisher. Some of the author's footnotes have been omitted.

the world within and about her." As with Emerson's theory,[1] moreover, it is through the eyes that these worlds meet and influence each other, the outer world perceived and colored by the unique nature that lies within, and the inner world brought to its self-awareness by the influences that enter from the world without. Thus, when Edna returns from Chênière Caminada on the fateful Sunday she spends there with Robert Lebrun, she begins to perceive a new self "in some way different" from her old one. Though Edna does not yet fully suspect what is happening, the author makes abundantly clear that a process is occurring that closely resembles the transcendentalist theory of self-discovery: "she was seeing with different eyes and making the acquaintance of new conditions in herself that colored and changed her environment."

The process is triggered, moreover, by an experience that Edna has in the ocean, an experience described by Kate Chopin through imagery that has deep romantic roots. As W. H. Auden has pointed out in *The Enchafèd Flood*, the sea plays an important role in romantic iconography. It is "the place where there is no community," where "the individual . . . is free from both the evils and the responsibilities of communal life." It is the place, moreover, where "decisive events, the moments of eternal choice . . . occurs."[2] In *The Awakening*, the sea serves precisely this purpose, for it is in the Gulf that Edna experiences the crisis that determines her development throughout the rest of the book. As in much romantic art, however, the sea serves here a double purpose for the individual: it invites "the soul to wander for a spell in abysses of solitude; to lose itself in mazes of inward contemplation." In other words, it can turn the soul's attention outward to the infinity suggested by the endless expanse of encircling horizon and sky—to confront the universe alone—or it can cause, as it does to Pip in *Moby-Dick*, an "intense concentration of self" that can hardly be endured.[3]

Edna experiences both of these feelings on the night she learns to swim. When she pulls herself through the water for the first time, "a feeling of exultation [overtakes] her," as if she has received "some power of significant import . . . to control the working of her body and her soul." She turns away from shore "to gather in an impression of space and solitude, which the vast expanse of water, meeting and melting with the moonlit sky, conveyed to her excited fancy," and as she swims out into the Gulf, she seems "to be reaching out for the unlimited in which to lose herself." The expansive feeling of striving toward the infinite is

1. The author is referring to Emerson's theory of correspondence. See *The Works of Ralph Waldo Emerson* (Boston and New York: Houghton Mifflin, 1883) 1.13–80 [Editor].
2. W. H. Auden, *The Enchafèd Flood; or The Romantic Iconography of the Sea* (New York, 1967), pp. 15, 13.
3. Herman Melville, *Moby-Dick; or The Whale*, eds. Luther S. Mansfield and Howard P. Vincent (New York, 1952), p. 412. We must not assume, of course, that *Moby-Dick* itself lies behind *The Awakening*, but that both Herman Melville and Kate Chopin drew upon a common tradition of romantic imagery.

not to last, however, for when she turns to look at the shore, which seems to her now to be far away, a "flash of terror" strikes her, a "quick vision of death [smites] her soul," and she hurries back to her waiting husband and friends. The fear of death, of a threat to the self, clearly reveals the intensification of self-awareness that the experience has given her—an awakening of the self as important, perhaps, as any other in the novel. For from this point on, Edna develops a growing self-awareness from which there is no turning back.

The process, however, is not complete until she returns to New Orleans. This is the romantic "city" which, as Auden has pointed out, is the symbolic opposite of the sea. It is community, with all the demands that the social organization makes upon the individual, and which the self sometimes finds hard to accept after the expansive experience on the sea or, we may add, the innocent interlude on the "happy island," a third romantic symbol[4] which, in Edna's case, is Grand Isle. It is not surprising, then, that in keeping with the romantic imagery through which the book is developed, Edna's rebellion should become complete when she returns to society. She refuses to take seriously the social forms through which the community functions, but instead determines to go her own way, independent of both her family and the society in which they live. By this time, even Léonce, her husband, sees that Edna is "not herself," that is, not her old self. As Kate Chopin puts it, "he could not see that she was becoming herself and daily casting aside that fictitious self which we assume like a garment with which to appear before the world."

But if Edna's real self is revealed as a result of this process, we may legitimately ask what that real self is like. It is one that insists upon its own inviolability, that will brook no interference from others. Indeed, Edna carries this insistence upon her own integrity almost to an extreme. As she tells Adèle Ratignolle at one point, she would be willing to give up what she considers the unessential for her children—her money or even her life—but she would not give up herself. "Nobody has any right," she believes, to force her to do anything, and she frankly admits to Doctor Mandelet, "I don't want anything but my own way. That is wanting a good deal, of course, when you have to trample upon the lives, the hearts, the prejudices of others—but no matter . . ." Though Edna usually exempts the children—at least partially and hesitantly—from her sweeping statements on her individual inviolability, she is indeed willing to sacrifice everyone else to the demands of her sole self. As a consequence, her characteristic state in the latter half of the novel is solitude. For the most part, she is alone.

Kate Chopin compares and contrasts Edna's state with a number of others in the book, developing her theme through the polarities of self-

---

4. Auden, *The Enchafèd Flood*, p. 20. That Grand Isle may serve this familiar function in *The Awakening* seems clear from the innocent relationships that the characters maintain there until Edna's awakening drives Robert away to Mexico.

absorption (Madame Reisz) and willing surrender of self to another (Adèle and Alphonse Ratignolle). In Madame Reisz, the consequences of insisting on the self alone are clearly developed. Though she is indeed a fine artist, she is also self-assertive, imperious, and disposed "to trample upon the rights of others." She is venomous, disagreeable, and rude. Small wonder, then, that she is more often than not alone. By contrast, the Ratignolles are a prime example of two individuals who, like right hand and left, heart and soul, have indeed become one. "The Ratignolles understood each other perfectly. If ever the fusion of two human beings into one has been accomplished on this sphere it was surely in their union." Chopin, of course, makes no explicit judgment on these two ways of life, but it is apparent that Edna lies between the two extremes.

Yet another contrast is symbolized by a recurring detail that appears in the depiction of life on Grand Isle. Throughout this part of the novel, a pair of lovers and a lady in black, who is usually saying her rosary or reading her prayer book, are frequently seen in the background. As symbolic figures, they cannot perhaps be assigned precise meanings. But the two lovers are indeed so lost in each other as to be almost completely oblivious to what is going on around them. There is surely no self-assertion here. Nor does there seem to be any in the lady in black who, in praying to her God, is surrendering herself to the Deity. Both the couple and the lady in black represent a strong contrast to Edna, who never really achieves the loss of self in love for another, and who is never portrayed as submitting herself to worship God in communion with others. She is pictured instead as running away from the Presbyterian service as a girl, and as leaving the Catholic mass with "a feeling of oppression" on Chênière Caminada.

Edna stands apart from all these people, even those, like Madame Reisz, whom she most resembles. She vacillates between the polar positions, reaching out to her children on occasion, and even to her old friend Adèle, who calls for her during her labor. But she turns away from all of them eventually, and takes pleasure most often in being alone. Edna, moreover, is hardly consistent in her behavior, for she is unwilling to allow others the same freedom she demands for herself. Though she insists that she will not be possessed by anyone, it is clear that she wishes to possess Robert. She wants to hold on to him when he decides to leave for Mexico, and she accuses him of selfishness when he will not submit to her demands. Indeed, when she returns from Adèle Ratignolle's confinement expecting to find Robert waiting for her, "she could picture at that moment no greater bliss on earth than *possession* of the beloved one. His expression of love had already *given him to her* in part" (italics mine). She demands of others what none may demand of her; she wishes to possess, who will not herself be possessed.[5]

5. Unlike the Creole husbands, moreover, who never feel jealous, Edna becomes jealous almost as soon as she perceives that she loves Robert, and the emotion recurs later—a clear sign of her desire for possession.

Edna's reaching out to others is either brief and transitory (as with Adèle and the children) or colored by a selfish motive (as with Robert). Indeed, as the story develops, one begins to suspect that Edna's self is by its very nature a solitary thing, that she is utterly incapable of forming a true and lasting relationship with another. The men to whom she is attracted before her marriage are either such as might inflame a youthful imagination (the cavalry officer and the tragedian), or the kind she is told she must not covet (the young man who is engaged to the lady on a neighboring plantation). Forbidden fruit seems to appeal to her most, a sign, perhaps, of a certain perverseness in her character. She married Léonce Pontellier partly at least because her family was opposed to him, and one suspects that the appeal of Alcée Arobin—and even of Robert Lebrun—derives from the fact that she knows she should not become involved with them.[6] The result is that she either ends up as a possession—and both Léonce and Alcée treat her as one[7]—or she is herself overwhelmed with the desire to possess another. Both relationships are, of course, thoroughly destructive.

Edna's final awakening, her ultimate self-discovery, reveals an inner nature that is devoid of hope. After she learns that Robert has left her for good, she lies awake throughout the night, a sense of despondency that never lifts overwhelming her spirit. She faces the truth about herself, that for her no lasting union with anyone is possible. Though she may want Robert with her now, she "realized that the day would come when he, too, and the thought of him would melt out of her existence, leaving her alone." Ever her children appear to her as enemies, as "antagonists who had overcome her; who had overpowered her and sought to drag her into the soul's slavery for the rest of her days." Since Edna cannot give herself to anyone, but instead remains aloof from any true relationship with another, she is doomed to stand completely alone in the universe, a position that is clearly symbolized by the final episode in the book: her solitary swim far out into the emptiness of the Gulf.

The sea is presented here in language almost identical with that of the passage quoted above. A very important clause, however, is omitted. In the former passage, the dual nature of the sea experience is suggested, the outward expansion into the infinite, and the intensification of self-awareness that can also result from finding oneself alone in the apparently limitless sea. Here, the second aspect of the experience is not included. By now, Edna has explored herself completely and has penetrated to her true nature, solitary and aloof though it may be. The seductive voice of the sea, therefore, can only incite her spirit "to wonder in abysses of solitude." This Edna does, swimming on and on, pleased with the

---

6. Note too that one of the few women she associates with in New Orleans is Mrs. Highcamp, whom her husband had advised her not to encourage socially.
7. This relationship is suggested by parallel scenes. Once his affair with Edna is established, Arobin settles down to smoke a cigar and read his newspaper in her house, in much the same way Léonce does in the first chapter of the book.

thought that she is escaping the slavery represented to her imagination in the form of Léonce and the children. But the price she pays for her escape is death. In defending her self against the threat of community, she loses it in the infinity suggested by the expanse of the sea.[8] Read in these terms, Kate Chopin's The Awakening is a powerful romantic novel.[9] It develops the theme of self-discovery so important in the works of the transcendentalists and does it in terms of imagery that is thoroughly appropriate to its presentation. Unlike the transcendentalists, however, Kate Chopin allows her character no limitless expansion of the self. She presents her, rather—in terms suggesting Melville—as a solitary, defiant soul who stands out against the limitations that both nature and society place upon her, and who accepts in the final analysis a defeat that involves no surrender. Chopin herself makes no explicit comment on Edna Pontellier's actions. She neither approves nor condemns, but maintains an aesthetic distance throughout, relying upon the recurring patterns of imagery to convey her meaning. It is not the morality of Edna's life that most deeply concerns her, nor even the feminist concept so obviously present in the book. It is, rather, the philosophic questions raised by Edna's awakening: the relation of the individual self to the physical and social realities by which it is surrounded, and the price it must pay for insisting upon its absolute freedom.

RUTH SULLIVAN AND STEWART SMITH

[Narrative Stance]†

* * *

The novel dramatizes the irony that the awakening which Edna most desires is to sleep and dream, to merge with a warm body, to be indulged, and to be fed, drives related to her early motherlessness and to a need for compensation. The latent wish to be fed is communicated in the novel through one of its dominant images: food. Almost every significant occurrence in Edna's life is associated with food. Because Mr. Pontellier often sends his wife huge boxes of candies and liqueurs, the women on

---

8. Edna's death by drowning seems consistent with the sea imagery through which much of the theme is developed. According to Auden, once the island is left behind, "the only possible place of peace for the romantic is under the waters." The Enchafèd Flood, p. 24.
9. I am aware, of course, that both The Awakening and the whole local color school to which Kate Chopin is said to belong are usually classified as late nineteenth-century realism. That realistic detail is not inconsistent with romantic imagery, however, is amply illustrated by so thoroughly romantic a book as Moby-Dick.
† From "Narrative Stance in Kate Chopin's The Awakening," Studies in American Fiction 1 (1973): 62–75. Reprinted by permission of Studies in American Fiction and Northeastern University. The author's footnotes have been omitted.

Grand Isle consider him an excellent husband. Meanwhile, he neglects returning to have dinner with his family and forgets the bonbons he promised his sons. One of the Pontellier's most serious quarrels takes place over dinner and concerns supervision of the cook. Two other marriages are assessed in the novel, one as sterile (the Highcamp's), one as ideal (the Ratignolle's), and in both instances the couples demonstrate the qualities of their marriages over dinner with Edna. Dr. Mandelet's diagnostic visit occurs at dinner and Edna celebrates her farewell to her husband and her old way of life with a spectacular banquet. It is immediately after this banquet that she first commits adultery. Mlle Reisz offers Edna chocolates on Grand Isle and hot chocolate and brandy in New Orleans; all such offerings are somehow connected with the absent Robert. Robert himself is almost always tied to food, from the most trivial kind of association, such as the buns and coffee he and Edna hurriedly take for breakfast the morning of their visit to the *Chênière*, through more important events, such as the announcement about his leaving for Mexico made during dinner at Madame Lebrun's. When Mlle Reisz shows Edna a letter telling of Robert's return, Edna joyfully sends a huge box of candy to her sons. When Robert does return, Edna prevails upon him to stay for dinner; and on the occasion of his avowal of love, Edna had shortly before met him accidentally in a small garden where she was dining. Robert's rejection seems to leave her literally hungry, for the next morning she arrives at Grand Isle and, on her way to her death, says to Victor, "What time will you have dinner? . . . I am very hungry." And once more, "I hope you have fish for dinner."

Edna's motherlessness makes appropriate the abundance of images connecting food with love and its loss; motherlessness also seems to account for the double irony that a woman who wishes to awaken should nevertheless wish so often to sleep and dream, and that one who wants to find herself should be described as happily losing herself: "the voice of the sea is seductive . . . inviting the soul . . . to lose itself in inward contemplation." "As she swam she seemed to be reaching out for the unlimited in which to lose herself." "She discovered many a sunny sleepy corner, fashioned to dream in. And she found it good to dream and to be alone and unmolested." At Madame Antoine's she sleeps refreshingly to a lullaby of murmurs: "the voices were only part of the other drowsy, muffled sounds lulling her senses."

The imagery of food, sleep, dreaming, and self-loss seem to culminate in a latent desire to merge with a warm body. In fact, Chopin makes that need for fusion a refrain in her novel:

> The voice of the sea is seductive; never ceasing, whispering, clamoring, murmuring, inviting the soul to wander for a spell in abysses of solitude; to lose itself in mazes of inward contemplation.

The voice of the sea speaks to the soul. The touch of the sea is sensuous, enfolding the body in its soft, close embrace.

Part of this passage is repeated when Edna commits suicide by allowing herself to sink, naked as a newborn (she casts aside her swim suit and "felt like some new-born creature,") into the "soft, close embrace" of that "sensuous" sea. Earlier, the "voice of the everlasting sea" is described as being like a lullaby: "It broke like a mournful lullaby upon the night." Edna's final act is indeed to lose herself, to surrender like a sleepy child to her mother's song and her warm embrace.

In *The Awakening*, then, Chopin dramatizes two almost contradictory views of her heroine, one of them critical and the other sympathetic and admiring. This narrative technique must affect an interpretation of the theme of the novel and should discourage hasty identifications between Kate Chopin and her work. Readers distort the meaning of the novel if they conclude that the author is identified with, say, the sympathetic part of her narrative stance when actually, of course, the author speaks through both. The effect of such a technique in this novel is to present simultaneously two essentially different and incompatible ideals about how people should conduct their lives. The partisan narrative stance speaks for a romantic vision of life's possibilities; the alternate stance for a realistic understanding and acceptance of human limits.

When it is sympathetic, the narrative perspective regards Edna Pontellier as a woman who seeks more than the "freedom" involved in release from social convention, and more even than finding out who she is so she might affirm that. She wants intensity of experience. It does not matter whether she suffers pain or feels ecstasy as long as she can feel deeply. Edna does not admire or want for herself the domestic harmony of Adèle Ratignolle in her happy wife and motherhood.

The little glimpse of domestic harmony which had been offered her gave her no regret, no longing. It was not a condition of life which fitted her, and she could see in it but an appalling and hopeless ennui. She was moved by a kind of commiseration for Madam Ratignolle,—a pity for that colorless existence which never lifted its possessor beyond the region of blind contentment, in which no moment of anguish ever visited her soul, in which she would have the taste of life's delirium.

Temperance, sanity, and rationality are not for Edna, who wants to explore the unknown and forbidden rather than to accept the safe security of her considerate husband in his comfortable mansion. Edna wants to be free to do, but even more, to feel.

This stance sympathizes with Edna's romantic values. In fact, like a fond parent who not only praises his child's virtues but gilds them, the partisan view claims for Edna not only romantic virtues but others that Edna seems neither to have nor to value. For instance, though Edna does not want to be rational, the sympathetic stance nevertheless claims that her awakening means not only full sensuous awareness but conscious understanding as well.

The alternate part of the narrative perspective displays less sympathy for Edna's journey into the underworld of instinctual impulses and does not seem to understand the need an overly-civilized woman might feel for reckless self-abandon. In effect, this view affirms that while making contact with one's instinctual self is good, such contact must somehow be brought into relationship with the demands of the adult world. Impulsiveness, self-indulgence, refusal to accept responsibility, flagrant unconventionality, society will punish, probably severely. Besides, conscience eventually punishes offenses against unconsciously held moral convictions no matter what indulgence reason may presently grant. Edna may refuse motherhood, reject her husband, and become sexually promiscuous, but eventually her unrecognized guilt will demand terrible retribution. The alternate vision also seems to say that "freedom" can be found not in uninhibited instinctual expression but in reason and in recognition of one's own capacities and limits as well as the limits imposed by the environment. Edna can be free only if she consciously recognizes her need for intensity of experience and wishes to find this through sexual adventure. Then she might find a suitable place in which, and people with whom, to realize these desires. She would not be blindly driven to self-destruction or to acts of aggression against her children and husband.

To some readers, the sympathetic view speaks so movingly that they do not hear the sober realism also richly represented in the novel. *The Awakening* portrays neither the feminist's heroine nor an impulsive, somewhat shallow self-deceiver; it portrays both in unresolved tension. Perhaps, then, this complex narrative technique encourages its readers to project their own fantasies into the novel and to see Edna as they wish to see her. One might say that the realistic narrative view appeals most to the reader's adult self; the partisan, to the child, or to the self that would reach beyond its grasp no matter what the tragic consequences.

CYNTHIA GRIFFIN WOLFF

[Thanatos and Eros]†

* * * An astonishing proportion of that part of the novel which deals with Edna's sojourn at Grand Isle is paced by the rhythm of her basic needs, especially the most primitive ones of eating and sleeping. If one were to plot the course of Edna's life during this period, the most reliable indices to the passage of time would be her meals and her periods of sleep. The importance of these in Edna's more general "awakening" can be suggested if we examine the daylong boat trip which she makes with Robert.

There is an almost fairy-tale quality to the whole experience; the rules of time seem suspended, and the mélange of brilliant sensory experiences—the sun, the water, the soft breeze, the old church with its lizards and whispered tales of pirate gold—melts into a dreamlike pattern. It is almost as if Edna's fantasy world had come into being. Indeed, there is even some suggestion that after the event, she incorporates the memory of it into her fantasy world in such a way that the reality and the illusion do, in fact, become confused. Later on in the novel when Edna is invited to tell a true anecdote at a dinner party, she speaks "of a woman who paddled away with her lover one night in a pirogue and never came back. They were lost amid the Baratarian Islands, and no one ever heard of them or found trace of them from that day to this. It was pure invention. She said that Madame Antoine had related it to her. That, also, was in invention. Perhaps it was a dream she had had. But every glowing word seemed real to those who listened."

Yet even this jewel-like adventure with Robert is dominated by the insistence of the infantile life-pattern—sleep and eat, sleep and eat. Edna's rest had been feverish the night prior to the expedition: "She slept but a few hours," and their expedition begins with a hurried breakfast. Her taste for sight-seeing, even her willingness to remain with Robert, is so overwhelmed by her lassitude that she must find a place to rest and to be alone. Strikingly, however, once she is by herself, left to seek restful sleep, Edna seems somewhat to revive, and the tone shifts from one of exhaustion to one of sensuous, leisurely enjoyment of her own body. "Left alone in the little side room, [she] loosened her clothes, removing the greater part of them. . . . How luxurious it felt to rest thus in a strange, quaint bed, with its sweet country odor of laurel lingering about the sheets and mattress! She stretched her strong limbs

† From "Thanatos and Eros: Kate Chopin's *The Awakening*," *American Quarterly* 25 (October 1973): 449–71. Copyright 1973. Reprinted by permission.

that ached a little. She ran her fingers through her loosened hair for a while. She looked at her round arms as she held them straight up and rubbed them one after the other, observing closely, as if it were something she saw for the first time, the fine, firm quality and texture of her flesh." Powerfully sensuous as this scene is, we would be hard put to find genital significance here. Reduced to its simplest form, the description is of a being discovering the limits and qualities of its own body—discovering, and taking joy in the process of discovery. And having engaged in this exploratory "play" for a while, Edna falls asleep.

The manner of her waking makes explicit reference to the myth of the sleeping beauty. " 'How many years have I slept?' she inquired. 'The whole island seems changed. A new race of beings must have sprung up, leaving only you and me as past relics.' " Robert jokingly falls in with the fantasy: " 'You have slept precisely one hundred years. I was left here to guard your slumbers; and for one hundred years I have been out under the shed reading a book.' " In the fairy tale, of course, the princess awakens with a kiss, conscious of love; but Edna's libidinal energies have been arrested at a pre-genital level—so she awakens "very hungry"—and her lover prepares her a meal! "He was childishly gratified to discover her appetite, and to see the relish with which she ate the food which he had procured for her." Indeed, though the title of the novel suggests a re-enactment of the traditional romantic myth, it never does offer a complete representation of it. The next invocation is Arobin's kiss, "the first kiss of her life to which her nature had really responded"; but as we have seen earlier, this response is facilitated, perhaps even made possible, by the fact that her emotional attachment is not to Arobin but to the Robert of her fantasy world. The final allusion to an awakening kiss is Edna's rousing of Robert; and yet this is a potentially genital awakening from which both flee.

Edna's central problem, once the hidden "self" begins to exert its inexorable power, is that her libidinal appetite has been fixated at the oral level. Edna herself has an insistent preoccupation with nourishment; on the simplest level, she is concerned with food. Her favorite adjective is "delicious": she sees many mother-women as "delicious" in their role; she carries echoes of her children's voices "like the memory of a delicious song"; when she imagines Robert she thinks "how delicious it would be to have him there with her." And the notion of something's being good because it might be good to "eat" (or internalize in some way) is echoed in all of her relationships with other people. Those who care about her typically feed her; and the sleep-and-eat pattern which is most strikingly established at the beginning of the novel continues even to the very end. Not surprisingly, in the "grown-up world" she is a poor housekeeper, and though Léonce's responses are clearly petty and self-centered, Edna's behavior does betray incompetence, especially when we compare it (as the novel so often invites us to) with the nurturing capacities of Adèle.

It is not surprising that the most dramatic gesture toward freedom that Edna makes is to move out of her husband's house; yet even this gesture toward "independence" can be comprehended as part of an equally powerful wish to regress. It is, after all, a "tiny house" that she moves to; she calls it her "pigeon house," and if she were still a little girl, we might call it a playhouse.

The decision to move from Léonce's house is virtually coincidental with the beginning of her affair with Arobin; yet even the initial stages of that affair are described in oral terms—Edna feels regret because "it was not love which had held this cup of life to her lips." And though the relationship develops as she makes preparations for the move, it absorbs astonishingly little of Edna's libido. She is deliberately distant, treating Arobin with "affected carelessness." As the narrator observes, "If he had expected to find her languishing, reproachful, or indulging in sentimental tears, he must have been greatly surprised." She is "true" to the fantasy image of Robert. And in the real world her emotional energy has been committed in another direction. She is busy with elaborate plans—for a dinner party! And it is on this extravagant sumptuous oral repast that she lavishes her time and care. Here Edna as purveyor of food becomes not primarily a nourisher (as Adèle is) but a sensualist in the only terms that she can truly comprehend. One might argue that in this elaborate feast Edna's sensuous self comes closest to some form of expression which might be compatible with the real world. The dinner party itself is one of the longest sustained episodes in the novel; we are told in loving detail about the appearance of the table, the commodious chairs, the flowers, the candles, the food and wines, Edna's attire—no sensory pleasure is left unattended. Yet even this indulgence fails to satisfy. "As she sat there amid her guests, she felt the old ennui overtaking her; the hopelessness which so often assailed her, which came upon her like an obsession, like something extraneous, independent of volition. It was something which announced itself; a chill breath that seemed to issue from some vast cavern wherein discords wailed." Edna, perhaps, connects this despair to the absence of Robert. "There came over her the acute longing which always summoned into her spiritual vision the presence of the beloved one, overpowering her at once with a sense of the unattainable." However, the narrator's language here is interestingly ambiguous. It is not specifically *Robert* that Edna longs for; it is "the presence of the beloved one"—an indefinite perpetual image, existing "always" in "her spiritual vision." The longing, so described, is an immortal one and, as she acknowledges, "unattainable"; the vision might be of Robert, but it might equally be of the cavalry officer, the engaged young man, the tragedian—even of Adèle, whose mothering attentions first elicited a sensuous response from Edna and whose own imminent motherhood has kept her from the grand party. The indefinite quality of Edna's longing thus described has an ominous tone, a tone made even more ominous by the rising specter of those "vast caverns" waiting vainly to be filled.

Perhaps Edna's preoccupation with the incorporation of food is but one aspect of a more general concern with incorporating that which is external to her. Freud's hypotheses about the persistence in some people of essentially oral concerns makes Edna's particular problem even clearer.

Originally the ego includes everything, later it separates off an external world from itself. Our present ego-feeling is, therefore, only a shrunken residue of a much more inclusive—indeed, an all-embracing—feeling which corresponded to a more intimate bond between the ego and the world about it. If we may assume that there are many people in whose mental life this primary ego-feeling has persisted to a greater or less degree, it would exist in them side by side with the narrower and more sharply demarcated ego-feeling of maturity, like a kind of counterpart to it. In that case, the ideational contents appropriate to it would be precisely those of limitlessness and of a bond with the universe . . . the 'oceanic' feeling.[1]

A psychologically mature individual has to some extent satisfied these oral desires for limitless fusion with the external world; presumably his sense of oneness with a nurturing figure has given him sustenance sufficient to move onward to more complex satisfactions. Yet growth inevitably involves some loss. "The feeling of happiness derived from the satisfaction of a wild instinctual impulse untamed by the ego is incomparably more intense than that derived from sating an instinct that has been tamed."[2] To some extent all of us share Edna's fantasy of complete fulfillment through a bond with the infinite; that is what gives the novel its power. However, for those few people in whom this primary ego-feeling has persisted with uncompromising force the temptation to seek total fulfillment may be both irresistible and annihilating.

Everywhere and always in the novel, Edna's fundamental longing is postulated in precisely these terms. And strangely enough, the narrator seems intuitively to understand the connection between this longing for suffusion, fulfillment, incorporation, and the very earliest attempts to define identity.

But the beginning of things, of a world especially, is necessarily vague, tangled, chaotic, and exceedingly disturbing. How few of us ever emerge from such a beginning! How many souls perish in its tumult!

The voice of the sea is seductive; never ceasing, whispering,

---

1. Sigmund Freud, "Civilization and Its Discontents," in *The Standard Edition of the Complete Works*, James Strachey, ed. (London: Hogarth Press, 1971), 21:71.
2. Ibid., p. 160.

clamoring, murmuring, inviting the soul to wander for a spell in abysses of solitude; to lose itself in mazes of inward contemplation. The voice of the sea speaks to the soul. The touch of the sea is sensuous, enfolding the body in its soft, close embrace.

Ultimately, the problem facing Edna has a nightmarish circularity. She has achieved some measure of personal identity only by hiding her "true self" within—repressing all desire for instinctual gratification. Yet she can see others in her environment—the Creoles generally and Adèle in particular—who seem comfortably able to indulge their various sensory appetites and to do so with easy moderation. Edna's hidden self longs for resuscitation and nourishment; and in the supportive presence of Grand Isle Edna begins to acknowledge and express the needs of that "self."

Yet once released, the inner being cannot be satisfied. It is an orally destructive self, a limitless void whose needs can be filled, finally, only by total fusion with the outside world, a totality of sensuous enfolding. And this totality means annihilation of the ego.

Thus all aspects of Edna's relationship with the outside world are unevenly defined. She is remarkably vulnerable to feelings of being invaded and overwhelmed; we have already seen that she views emotional intimacy as potentially shattering. She is equally unable to handle the phenomenal world with any degree of consistency or efficiency. She is very much at the mercy of her environment: the atmosphere of Mademoiselle Reisz' room is said to "invade" her with repose; Mademoiselle Reisz' music has the consistent effect of penetrating Edna's outer self and playing upon the responsive chords of her inner yearning; even her way of looking at objects in the world about her becomes an act of incorporation; "she had a way of turning [her eyes] swiftly upon an object and holding them there as if lost in some inward maze of contemplation or thought." Once she has given up the pattern of repression that served to control dangerous impulses, she becomes engaged in trying to maintain a precarious balance in each of her relationships. On the one hand she must resist invasion, for with invasion comes possession and total destruction. On the other hand she must resist the equally powerful impulse to destroy whatever separates her from the external world so that she can seek union, fusion and (so her fantasies suggest) ecstatic fulfillment.

In seeking to deal with this apparently hopeless problem, Edna encounters several people whose behavior might serve as a pattern for her. Mademoiselle Reisz is one. Mademoiselle Reisz is an artist, and as such she has created that direct avenue between inner and outer worlds which Edna seeks in her own life. Surely Edna's own attempts at artistic enterprise grow out of her more general desire for sustained ecstasy. "While Edna worked she sometimes sang low the little air, 'Ah, si tu savais!' "

Her work is insensibly linked with her memories of Robert, and these
in turn melt into more generalized memories and desires. The little
song she is humming "moved her with recollections. She could hear
again the ripple of the water, the flapping sail. She could see the glint
of the moon upon the bay, and could feel the soft, gusty beating of the
hot south wind. A subtle current of desire passed through her body,
weakening her hold upon the brushes and making her eyes burn." In
some ways, Edna's painting might offer her an excellent and viable
mode for coming to terms with the insistent demands of cosmic yearning.
For one thing, it utilizes in an effective way her habit of transforming
the act of observing the external world into an act of incorporation: to
some extent the artist must use the world in this way, incorporating it
and transforming it in the act of artistic creation. Thus the period during
which Edna is experimenting with her art offers her some of the most
satisfying experiences she is capable of having. "There were days when
she was very happy without knowing why. She was happy to be alive
and breathing when her whole being seemed to be one with the sunlight,
the color, the odors, the luxuriant warmth of some perfect Southern
day. . . . And she found it good to dream and to be alone and unmolested."

Yet when Edna tells Mademoiselle Reisz about her efforts, she is
greeted with skepticism: " 'You have pretensions,' " Mademoiselle Reisz
responds. " 'To be an artist includes much; one must possess many
gifts—absolute gifts—which have not been acquired by one's own effort.
And moreover, to succeed, the artist must possess the courageous soul.
. . . The brave soul. The soul that dares and defies.' " One implication
of Mademoiselle Reisz' half-contemptuous comment may well be the
traditional view that the artist must dare to be unconventional; and it is
this interpretation which Edna reports later to Arobin, saying as she
does, however, " 'I only half comprehend her.' " The part of Mademoiselle Reisz' injunction that eludes Edna's understanding concerns
the sense of purposiveness which is implied by the image of a courageous
soul. Mademoiselle Reisz has her art, but she has sacrificed for it—
perhaps too much. In any case, however, she has acknowledged limitations, accepted some and grappled with others; she is an active agent
who has defined her relationship to the world. Edna, by contrast, is
passive.

The words which recur most frequently to describe her are words like
melting, drifting, misty, dreaming, shadowy. She is not willing (perhaps
not able) to define her position in the world because to do so would
involve relinquishing the dream of total fulfillment. Thus while Mademoiselle Reisz can control and create, Edna is most comfortable as
the receptive vessel—both for Mademoiselle Reisz' music and for the
sense impressions which form the basis of her own artistic endeavor.
Mademoiselle Reisz commands her work; Edna is at the mercy of hers.
Thus just as there are moments of exhilaration, so "there were days

when she was unhappy, she did not know why,—when it did not seem worth while to be glad or sorry, to be alive or dead; when life appeared to her like a grotesque pandemonium and humanity like worms struggling blindly toward inevitable annihilation. She could not work on such a day, nor weave fantasies to stir her pulses and warm her blood." Art, for Edna, ultimately becomes not a defense against inner turmoil, merely a reflection of it.

Another possible defense for Edna might be the establishment and sustaining of a genuine genital relationship. Her adolescent fantasies, her mechanical marriage, her liaison with Arobin and her passionate attachment to the fantasy image of Robert all suggest imperfect efforts to do just that. A genital relationship, like all ego-relationships, necessarily involves limitation; to put the matter in Edna's terms, a significant attachment with a real man would involve relinquishing the fantasy of total fulfillment with some fantasy lover. In turn, it would offer genuine emotional nourishment—though perhaps never enough to satisfy the voracious clamoring of Edna's hidden self.

Ironically, Adèle, who seems such a fount of sustenance, gives indications of having some of the same oral needs that Edna does. Like Edna she is preoccupied with eating, she pays extravagant care to the arrangement of her own physical comforts, and she uses her pregnancy as an excuse to demand a kind of mothering attention for herself. The difference between Edna and Adèle is that Adèle can deal with her nurturing needs by displacing them onto her children and becoming a "mother-woman." Having thus segregated and limited these desires, Adèle can find diverse ways of satisfying them; and having satisfied her own infantile oral needs, she can go on to have a rewarding adult relationship with her husband. Between Adèle and M. Ratignolle there is mutual joining together: "The Ratignolles understood each other perfectly. If ever the fusion of two human beings into one has been accomplished on this sphere it was surely in their union." The clearest outward sign of this happy union is that the Ratignolles converse eagerly and clearly with each other. M. Ratignolle reports his experiences and thoughts to his' wife, and she in turn "was keenly interested in everything he said, laying down her fork the better to listen, chiming in, taking the words out of his mouth." Yet this picture of social and domestic accord is indescribably dismaying to Edna. She "felt depressed rather than soothed after leaving them. The little glimpse of domestic harmony which had been offered her, gave her no regret, no longing."

Again, what has capitulated is the fantasy of complete and total suffusion; the Ratignolles have only a union which is as perfect as one can expect "*on this sphere*" (italics added). Yet the acme of bliss which Edna has always sought "was not for her in this world." Edna wishes a kind of pre-verbal union, an understanding which consistently surpasses words. Léonce is scarcely a sensitive man (that is, as we have seen, why she chose to marry him). Yet Edna never exerts herself to even such efforts at communication with him as might encourage a supportive emotional response. She responds to his unperceptive clumsiness by turning inward, falling into silence. Over and over again their disagreements follow the pattern of a misunderstanding which Edna refuses to clarify. At the very beginning of the novel when Léonce selfishly strolls off for an evening of gambling, Edna's rage and sense of loneliness are resolutely hidden, even when he seeks to discover the cause of her unhappiness. "She said nothing, and refused to answer her husband when he questioned her." Perhaps Léonce could not have understood the needs which Edna feels so achingly unfulfilled. And he is very clumsy. But he does make attempts at communication while she does not, and his interview with the family doctor shows greater concern about Edna's problems than she manages to feel for his.

The attachment to Robert, which takes on significance only after he has left Grand Isle, monopolizes Edna's emotions because it does temporarily offer an illusion of fusion, of complete union. However, this love affair, such as it is, is a genuinely narcissistic one; the sense of fusion exists because Edna's lover is really a part of herself—a figment of her imagination, an image of Robert which she has incorporated into her consciousness. Not only is her meeting with Robert after his return a disappointment (as we have seen earlier); it moves the static, imaginary "love affair" into a new and crucial stage; it tests, once and for all, Edna's capacity to transform her world of dreams into viable reality. Not surprisingly, "some way he had seemed nearer to her off there in Mexico."

Still she does try. She awakens him with a kiss even as Arobin had awakened her. Robert, too, is resistant to genuine involvement, and his initial reaction is to speak of the hopelessness of their relationship. Edna, however, is insistent (despite the interruption telling her of Adèle's accouchement). " 'We shall be everything to each other. Nothing else in the world is of any consequence. I must go to my friend; but you will wait for me? No matter how late; you will wait for me, Robert?' " And at this point, Edna seems finally to have won her victory. " 'Don't go; don't go! Oh! Edna, stay with me,' he pleaded. . . . Her seductive voice, together with his great love for her, had enthralled his senses, had deprived him of every impulse but the longing to hold her and keep her." And at this moment, so long and eagerly anticipated, Edna leaves Robert!

Robert's own resolve weakens during the interval, and it would be all too easy to blame Edna's failure on him. Certainly he is implicated. Yet his act does not explain *Edna's* behavior. "Nothing else in the world is of any consequence," she has said. If that is so, why then does she leave? No real duty calls her. Her presence at Adèle's delivery is of virtually no help. The doctor, sorry for the pain that the scene has caused Edna, even remonstrates with her mildly for having come. " 'You shouldn't have been there, Mrs. Pontellier. . . . There were a dozen women she might have had with her, unimpressionable women.' " To have stayed with Robert would have meant consummation, finally, the joining of her dreamlike passion to a flesh and blood lover; to leave was to risk losing that opportunity. Edna must realize the terms of this dilemma, and still she chooses to leave. We can only conclude that she is unconsciously ambivalent about achieving the goal which has sustained her fantasies for so long. The flesh and blood Robert may prove an imperfect, unsatisfactory substitute for the "beloved" of her dreams; what is more, a relationship with the real Robert would necessarily disenfranchise the more desirable phantom lover, whose presence is linked with her more general yearning for suffusion and indefinable ecstasy.

The totality of loss which follows Edna's decision forces a grim recognition upon her, the recognition that all her lovers have really been of but fleeting significance. "To-day it is Arobin; to-morrow it will be some one else. . . . It makes no difference to me. . . . There was no one thing in the world that she desired. There was no human being whom she wanted near her except Robert; and she even realized that the day would come when he, too, and the thought of him would melt out of her existence, leaving her alone." Her devastation, thus described, is removed from the realm of romantic disappointment; and we must see Edna's final suicide as originating in a sense of inner emptiness, not in some finite failure of love. Her decision to go to Adèle is in part a reflection of Edna's unwillingness to compromise her dream of Robert (and in this sense it might be interpreted as a flight from reality). On the other hand, it might also be seen as a last desperate attempt to come to terms with the anguish created by her unfulfilled "Oceanic" longing. And for this last effort she must turn to Adèle, the human who first caused her to loosen the bonds of repression.

The pre-eminence of Adèle over Robert in Edna's emotional life, affirmed by Edna's crucial choice, is undeniably linked to her image as a nurturing figure and, especially here, as a mother-to-be. In this capacity she is also linked to Edna's own children—insistent specters in Edna's consciousness; and this link is made explicit by Adèle's repetition of the cryptic injunction to "think of the children."

Now in every human's life there is a period of rhapsodic union or fusion with another, and this is the period of early infancy, before the time when a baby begins to differentiate himself from his mother. It is the haunting memory of this evanescent state which Freud defines as "Oceanic feeling," the longing to recapture that sense of oneness and suffused sensuous pleasure—even, perhaps, the desire to be reincorporated into the safety of pre-existence. Men can never recreate this state of total union. Adult women can—when they are pregnant. Most pregnant women identify intensely with their unborn children, and through that identification in some measure re-experience a state of complete and harmonious union. "The biologic process has created a unity of mother and child, in which the bodily substance of one flows into the other, and thus one larger unit is formed out of two units. The same thing takes place on the psychic level. By tender identification, by perceiving the fruit of her body as part of herself, the pregnant woman is able to transform the 'parasite' into a beloved being. Thus, mankind's eternal yearning for identity between the ego and the nonego, that deeply buried original desire to reachieve the condition once experienced, to repeat the human dream that was once realized in the mother's womb, is fulfilled."[3] Adèle is a dear friend, yes; she is a nurturing figure. But above all, she is the living embodiment of that state which Edna's deepest being longs to recapture. Trapped in the conflict between her desire for "freedom," as seen in her compulsive need to protect her precarious sense of self, and her equally insistent yearning for complete fulfillment through total suffusion, Edna is intensely involved with Adèle's pregnancy.

Edna's compulsion to be with Adèle at the moment of delivery is, in the sense which would have most significance for her, a need to view individuation at its origin. For if pregnancy offers a state of total union, then birth is the initial separation: for the child it is the archetypal separation trauma; for the mother, too, it is a significant psychic trauma. It is the ritual re-enactment of her own birth and a brutal reawakening to the world of isolated ego. "To make it the being that is outside her, the pregnant mother must deliver the child from the depths of herself. . . . She loses not only it, but herself with it. This, I think, is at the bottom of that fear and foreboding of death that every pregnant woman has, and this turns the giving of life into the losing of life."[4] Edna cannot refuse to partake of this ceremony, for here, if anywhere, she will find the solution to her problem.

Yet the experience is horrendous; it gives no comfort, no reassuring answer to Edna's predicament. It offers only stark, uncompromising truth. Adèle's ordeal reminds Edna of her own accouchements. "Edna began to feel uneasy. She was seized with a vague dread. Her own like experiences seemed far away, unreal, and only half remembered. She recalled faintly an ecstasy of pain, the heavy odor of chloroform, a stupor which had deadened sensation, and an awakening to find a little new life to which she had given being." This is Nature's cruel message. The fundamental significance to Edna of an awakening is an awakening to separation, to individual existence, to the hopelessness of ever satisfying the dream of total fusion. The rousing of the sensuous being had led Edna on a quest for ecstasy; but the ecstasy which beckoned has become in the end merely an "ecstasty of pain," first in her protracted struggle to retain identity and finally here in that relentless recognition of inevitable separation which has been affirmed in the delivery, "an awakening to find a little new life." Edna is urged to leave, but she refuses.

3. Helene Deutsch, *The Psychology of Women* (New York: Grune and Stratton, 1971), 2:139.
4. Ibid., p. 79.

"With an inward agony, with a flaming, outspoken revolt against the ways of Nature, she witnessed the scene of torture." In this world, in life, there can be no perfect union, and the children whom Adèle urges Edna to remember stand as living proof of the inevitability of separation. Edna's longing can never be satisfied. This is her final discovery, the inescapable disillusionment; and the narrator calls it to our attention again, lest its significance escape us. " 'The years that are gone seem like dreams,' " Edna muses, " 'if one might go on sleeping and dreaming—but to wake up and find—' " Here she pauses, but the reader can complete her thought—"a little new life." " 'Oh! well! perhaps it is better to wake up after all, even to suffer rather than to remain a dupe to illusions all one's life.' "

One wonders to what extent Edna's fate might have been different if Robert had remained. Momentarily, at least, he might have roused her from her despondency by offering not ecstasy but at least partial satisfaction. The fundamental problem would have remained, however. Life offers only partial pleasures, and individuated experience.

Thus Edna's final act of destruction has a quality of uncompromising sensuous fulfillment as well. It is her answer to the inadequacies of life, a literal denial and reversal of the birth trauma she has just witnessed, a stripping away of adulthood, of limitation, of consciousness itself. If life cannot offer fulfillment of her dream of fusion, then the ecstasy of death is preferable to the relinquishing of that dream. So Edna goes to the sea "and for the first time in her life she stood naked in the open air, at the mercy of the sun, the breeze that beat upon her, and the waves that invited her." She is a child, an infant again. "How strange and awful it seemed to stand naked under the sky! how delicious! She felt like some new-born creature, opening its eyes in a familiar world that it had never known." And with her final act Edna completes the regression, back beyond childhood, back into time eternal. "The touch of the sea is sensuous, enfolding the body in its soft, close embrace."

SUZANNE WOLKENFELD

Edna's Suicide:
The Problem of the One and the Many†

The recent critical controversy as to the meaning and value of Kate Chopin's *The Awakening* is epitomized in the range of responses to Edna's suicide. This finale constitutes the critical crux of the novel, not

† Reprinted by permission of the author. Footnotes are by the author and refer only to materials not included in this Norton Critical Edition.

only in that it is central to the interpretation of Edna's character and the theme of the story; but also because it is joined with the issue of Chopin's attitude to her protagonist and the artistic integrity of her work. It is primarily through the interpretation of the pattern of imagery by which Edna's suicide is dramatized, and of the tone of the narrative voice, that each critic decides whether or not to take the final swim with Edna and determines Chopin's complicity in the act.

The most emphatic affirmations of Edna's suicide are found in the criticism of Per Seyersted and Kenneth Eble. Each proclaims the nobility of Edna's achievements and the heroic grandeur of her final gesture. Seyersted, approaching the story through feminist and existentialist perspectives, sees Edna's death as motivated by an uncompromising desire for "spiritual emancipation." Her suicide is "the crowning glory of her development from the bewilderment which accompanied her early emancipation to the clarity with which she understands her own nature and the possibilities of her life as she decides to end it."[1] Eble, distinguishing Edna from such deluded romantics as Emma Bovary, places her with classical figures who "struggle with elemental passion." Her suicide, seen as an immersion in Eros, gives her "the power, the dignity, the self-possession of a tragic heroine." Both Seyersted and Eble acclaim the artistry of Chopin and assert her sympathy for Edna.

Donald A. Ringe and George Arms, each focusing on Edna's romanticism, present more qualified views of the significance of her suicide and question the assumption of Chopin's sympathy for her protagonist. Ringe relates Edna's romanticism to the transcendentalist theme of self-discovery and perceives her suicide as the consequence of her realization of her essentially solitary nature. Stressing Chopin's philosophic concern with the relation of the individual to external reality, he evaluates Edna's final act as "a defeat that involves no surrender." Arms, despite the basic realism of Edna's sexual emancipation, sees her as a figure motivated by romantic ideals, who "drifts" aimlessly into death. Noting the irony that pervades Chopin's treatment of Edna, he distinguishes between the romantic heroine and the realistic writer.

Daniel S. Rankin represents the negative pole of reaction in his verdict on the work as "exotic in setting, morbid in theme, erotic in motivation." Edna's suicide is a testimony to the fact that "human nature can be a sickening reality." He identifies Chopin with Edna and judges the writer as an impressionable victim of romantic literature.

George M. Spangler also presents a forceful indictment of the conclusion, not as does Rankin in terms of moral perversity, but on purely aesthetic grounds. He regards Edna's suicide as a pathetic defeat that is inconsistent with the depiction of her previous strength and achievements

1. Per Seyersted, *Kate Chopin: A Critical Biography* (Baton Rouge: U of Louisiana P, 1969) 134–63.

and accuses Chopin of a lapse from psychological subtlety into banal sentimentality.

Cynthia Griffin Wolff, acknowledging Chopin's insight into human nature, sees her depiction of Edna as a penetrating account of psychological disintegration. Wolff analyzes Edna's experiences in the contexts of Laing and Freud and defines her as a schizoid personality whose erotic development has been arrested at the oral stage. Her suicide is a regressive act coming from "a sense of inner emptiness" and a failure to fulfill in real life her infantile yearnings for fusion.

Between the positive and negative responses to Edna's suicide stand the views of Kenneth M. Rosen and Ruth Sullivan and Stewart Smith. Rosen insists on a purposeful ambiguity in which the sea is seen as symbolizing both life and death.[2] Sullivan and Smith argue not for ambiguity but for ambivalence in Chopin's presentation of Edna through two distinct and irreconcilable points of view. The reader's response to Edna's suicide depends on whether he is compelled by the voice that indulges a romantic vision of life's possibilities or by the contrasting voice that insists on accommodation to the limitations of reality.

Those critical views that distinguish between the realism of Chopin and the romanticism of Edna and question the value of her suicide reflect most closely the meaning and spirit of *The Awakening*. The vision of life that emerges from the novel constitutes an affirmation of the multiple possibilities of fulfillment, an affirmation made with a clear and profound grasp of the problematic nature of reality. Chopin's attitude to Edna involves the same mixture of irony and respect that marks her treatment of the other characters in the story. Her sympathy, and perhaps even identification, with Edna are most evident in her dramatization of Edna's struggle to face the realities of life and her partial achievements of selfhood. But ultimately Chopin places Edna's suicide as a defeat and a regression, rooted in a self-annihilating instinct, in a romantic incapacity to accommodate herself to the limitations of reality.

This approach has affinities with the interpretations of Donald A. Ringe and George Arms and corresponds at points to the psychoanalytic study by Cynthia Griffin Wolff. But Ringe and Arms do not probe Edna's romanticism far enough to the psychological core, and Wolff tends to impose a clinically schematic pattern that sometimes distorts Chopin's use of imagery and implicitly raises the question of the author's control over her material. A reading that remains faithful to the psychological implications of Chopin's imagery in terms of her own apprehension of reality will illuminate most fully the meaning of Edna's suicide.

The editorial commentary that Chopin introduces at the point of Edna's first intuition of her passion for Robert provides the key to the

2. Kenneth M. Rosen, "Kate Chopin's *The Awakening*: Ambiguity as Art," *Journal of American Studies* 5 (August 1971): 197–200.

author's thematic intention and to the central symbol in which it is embodied:

> In short, Mrs. Pontellier was beginning to realize her position in the universe as a human being, and to recognize her relations as an individual to the world, within and about her. . . . But the beginning of things, of a world especially, is necessarily vague, tangled, chaotic, and exceedingly disturbing. How few of us ever emerge from such beginning! How many souls perish in its tumult!
>
> The voice of the sea is seductive; never ceasing, whispering, clamoring, murmuring, inviting the soul to wander for a spell in abysses of solitude; to lose itself in mazes of inward contemplation.
>
> The voice of the sea speaks to the soul. The touch of the sea is sensuous, enfolding the body in its soft, close embrace.

What Chopin defines here are the two paths open to Edna from the point at which her instinctual nature is roused. Ideally, Edna's growth could bring her to self-awareness and community with the external world. But aware of the complex and vulnerable nature of the human psyche, Chopin emphasizes the perils that attend Edna's awakening. She stresses the universal temptation to yield to the primitive lure of the unconscious, to return to the primal sea in which body and soul are one. This symbolic invocation of the seductive sea that calls one to the ecstasy of immersion corresponds to Freud's conception of the Oceanic feeling of absolute fusion of the infantile ego.[3]

Chopin repeatedly underlines Edna's particular susceptibility to the infantile yearning for regression and subtly weaves the patterns of imagery that will culminate in her final surrender. The struggle within Edna between the desire for selfhood in relationship with others and the longing for self-annihilation is enacted in the scene of her first swim. Stirred to passion by the music she has heard, she achieves her first mastery over the ocean and swims out far in a spirit of self-assertion. But her instinctual intoxication also makes her open to the regressive urge: "As she swam she seemed to be reaching out for the unlimited in which to lose herself."

Edna's regressive instincts are embodied in the series of fantasies of unattainable lovers that dominated her early life. The infantile core of her romanticism is revealed in the childhood memory reawakened by the sight of the "water stretching so far away." She recalls walking through a meadow of grass, feeling that she "must walk on forever, without coming to the end of it." She connects this experience of the infinite in "that ocean of waving grass" to her first passionate infatuation with a visiting cavalry officer.

Her uncertainty about her response to the incident—"I don't remem-

---

3. See Wolff (above, pp. 231–41), for a fuller treatment of Freud's conception of the infantile ego and its relationship to the character of Edna.

ber whether I was frightened or pleased"—suggests her ambivalence to her romantic yearnings. Sensing the impossibility of fulfilling such passions "in this world," Edna marries a man she does not love, "closing the portals forever behind her upon the realm of romance and dreams."

When Robert arouses these fantasies once again, Edna determines not to love hopelessly in secret but to turn the phantom lover into reality, to take "possession of the beloved one." Through Robert she hopes to actualize her romantic need for Oneness in the act of sexual consummation.

Through her dramatization of the Sleeping Beauty motif, Chopin reveals the conflict between the basic reality of Edna's erotic desire for Robert and the impossibility of her romantic quest for fusion. When Edna awakens from a long sleep at Chênière, she sees Robert as the Prince who has waited "one hundred years" to achieve his bride. The fact that she finds herself "very hungry" reflects her longing for a new life of sensuous satisfaction. Wolff's interpretation of this hunger as an indication that Edna's "libidinal energies have been arrested at a pregenital level" contradicts Chopin's use of food imagery as a positive symbol of life's nourishment.[4] Edna's problem is that she believes she can attain the final, unlimited union of the fairy-tale lovers. Robert's departure forces her to face the fact that real life is quite different from the idealized realm of the fairy tale.

Edna does achieve the existential integrity to value her painful coming to consciousness:

> The years that are gone seem like dreams—if one might go on sleeping and dreaming—but to wake and find—Oh! well! perhaps it is better to wake up after all, even to suffer, rather than to remain a dupe to illusions all one's life.

She not only awakens to knowledge of external reality but succeeds in penetrating the core of her inner nature. She confronts the shattering truth that even had Robert stayed, he could never have ultimately satisfied her need for "one thing":

> There was no one thing in the world that she desired. There was no human being whom she wanted near her except Robert; and she even realized that the day would come when he, too, and the thought of him would melt out of her existence, leaving her alone.

Edna does not possess the strength to live her life alone and is therefore driven to seek the solitary security of death. Her view of her children as enemies who seek "to drag her into the soul's slavery for the rest of her days" is the hysterical response of a woman who, compelled by the

4. Wolff (above, pp. 232–34) imposes a Freudian context in interpreting Edna's preoccupation with food as an indication of her infantile nature. Chopin uses food imagery to represent Edna's desire for life in contrast to her regressive desire for death by her request for fish for dinner before she starts her final walk down to the sea.

instinct to return to the unbroken bond with her mother, must perforce renounce her own motherhood.

Edna's suicide is not a conscious choice reached through her achievement of self-awareness. She was "not thinking" as "she walked down to the beach." In the grip of the unconscious she responds to the call of the sea: "The voice of the sea is seductive, never ceasing, whispering, clamoring, murmuring, inviting the soul to wander in abysses of solitude." Her act of stripping off her clothes is not a gesture of self-liberation but rather a regression to the animality of infancy: "She felt like some new-born creature. . . ." Her experience of rebirth is directed not forward to new life but backward to the womb. Her final memories before her death represent a return to childhood, to her first fantasy lover, and to her walk in the meadow of infinity:

> Edna heard her father's voice and her sister Margaret's. She heard the barking of an old dog that was chained to the sycamore tree. The spurs of the cavalry officer clanged as he walked across the porch. There was the hum of bees, and the musky odor of pinks filled the air.

Edna finds her union with the One in the sea. Chopin affirms the many possibilities for satisfaction to be found on the land. In her portraits of Adèle Ratignolle and Mademoiselle Reisz, she suggests the multiplicity of roles open to women. Adèle, the "mother-woman," the dutiful wife, embodies the fertility of nature and the harmony of marital union. Her forays into art are all family oriented: She continually sews clothes for her children and keeps up her music as "a means of brightening the home and making it attractive." She is raised above the level of mere bovine domesticity by her charm, her amiability, and the generosity of her nurturing capacities. She is counterpointed by Mademoiselle Reisz, the artist who is isolated by her unamiable and imperious disposition. The "artificial violets" that she perpetually wears in her hair reflect her discordance with nature. But she is strong enough to live alone on her own terms, giving enough to secure the friendship of Robert and later of Edna, and capable through her music of inspiring passion.

The richness of Chopin's vision of life comes from her awareness of the many paths to self-realization from which to choose, each one involving compromise and renunciation. Her realism is inherent in her refusal to endorse the sentimentality of a fairy-tale resolution or the feminist fatalism of presenting Edna as the victim of an oppressive society. Chopin, as wife, as mother of six children, and as writer, is herself an affirmation of the many modes of living a woman can attain—each limited, each problematic, each real.

In a personal essay on her writing, published in the same year as *The Awakening*, Chopin affords us a glimpse of her personal life:

... I write in the morning, when not too strongly drawn to struggle
with the intricacies of a pattern, and in the afternoon, if the temptation to try a new furniture polish on an old table leg is not too
powerful to be denied; sometimes at night, though as I grow older
I am more and more inclined to believe that night was made for
sleep. . . . I am completely at the mercy of unconscious selection.
To such an extent is this true, that what is called the polishing up
process has always proved disastrous to my work, and I avoid it,
preferring the integrity of crudities to artificialities.[5]

In this image of a writer who prefers at times to "polish" a piece of
furniture rather than a work of art, who balances her commitment to
writing with an indulgence to her moods and physical needs, one sees
a woman who has learned to mediate between the inner and outer worlds,
between fantasy and reality.

MARGO CULLEY

Edna Pontellier: "A Solitary Soul"†

One sees that dead, vacant look steal sometimes over the rarest, finest of
women's faces—in the very midst, it might be, of their warmest summer's
day; and then one can guess at the secret of intolerable solitude that lies
beneath the delicate laces and brilliant smile.
                              —Rebecca Harding Davis,
                              Life in the Iron Mills (1861)

The Awakening, an existential novel about solitude, is distinguished
from most of such fiction by its female protagonist. Because of her sex,
Edna Pontellier experiences not only dread in the face of solitude, but
also delight. As a woman, she has had so little sense of a self alone that
new-found solitude suggests entirely new arenas and modes of activity.
Solitude also brings a confrontation with the ultimate aloneness—
death—and thus the threat of extinction of the fragile, newborn self.
When dread of solitude possesses Edna, she seeks, as she has sought
from her youth, the deliverance of the imagination; her sexual awakening
now leads her to seek the deliverance of the flesh. When she understands
that both these deliverers will fail her, she embraces death with the same
mixture of dread and delight as when she first discovered her solitude.

Daniel S. Rankin states, "In 1899 Herbert S. Stone and Co. of Chicago published *The Awakening*, a novel the author intended to name
A Solitary Soul." One early reviewer suggests that the title we know was

5. *St. Louis Post Dispatch* 26 Nov. 1899, pt. 4: 1. Reprinted in Per Seyersted, ed., *The Complete Works of Kate Chopin* (Baton Rouge: Louisiana State UP, 1969) 721–23.
† Reprinted by permission of the author.

furnished by "intelligent publishers."[1] In any case, when Chopin added the title *The Awakening* to her notebook, she did not cancel *A Solitary Soul*, as she usually did when changing a title; and Per Seyersted suggests she may have wished to retain it as a subtitle.

In 1895 Chopin published a translation of a Guy de Maupassant sketch called "Solitude." In this piece two friends talk after leaving a high-spirited dinner party and walk into the night. One reflects: "For a long time I have endured the anguish of having discovered and understood the solitude in which I live. And I know that nothing can end it; nothing! Whatever we may do or attempt, despite the embraces and transports of love, the hunger of the lips, we are always alone. I have dragged you out into the night in the vain hope of a moment's escape from the horrible solitude which overpowers me. But what is the use! I speak and you answer me, and still each of us is alone; side by side but alone."[2] With images of drowning and the night, he continues his description of his solitude: "You may think me a little mad, but since I have realized the solitude of my being I feel as if I were sinking day by day into some boundless subterranean depths, with no one near me, no other living soul to clasp my out-stretched, groping hands. There [are] noises, there are voices and cries in the darkness. Behold, I strive to reach them, but I can never discover where they come in the darkness, this life which engulfs me." The speaker continues that the illusion which love brings—that he is not alone—is the cruelest of all, for " . . . after each embrace the isolation grows, and how pungent it is. And after the rapturous union which must, it would seem, blend two souls into one being, how, more than ever before, do you feel yourself alone—alone!" In another essay of de Maupassant which Chopin translated, the speaker also awakens from the illusion that he is not alone to the reality of his solitude. In this essay, though the dreams and illusions have persisted for a long time, they have ultimately fled; it is the sketch entitled "Suicide."

What we feel most keenly about Edna is her remoteness from those about her—her husband, her children, her two female friends, her two male friends. And her solitude is underscored by the dramatic action of the novel as the significant persons in her life repeatedly leave her alone. At the end of the first chapter, Léonce Pontellier leaves Edna for his club; at the end of the third chapter, he leaves her for his business: he leaves her after a quarrel later in the novel, again the next morning for his business, and then, finally, for New York—not to appear again in the novel. Similarly, Robert leaves Edna repeatedly: he leaves her to herself after the evening of the moonlight swim, and again on the

---

1. Daniel S. Rankin, *Kate Chopin and Her Creole Stories* (Philadelphia: U of Pennsylvania P, 1932) 171 and 173n.
2. Guy de Maupassant, "Solitude," trans. Kate Chopin, *St. Louis Life* 13 (December 28, 1895): 30. The quotations following appear on the same page.

Chênière Caminada. He leaves her penultimately in going to Mexico, and finally with "Good-by—because I love you." Edna's children are also removed from her for the major action of the novel. The key scenes in the novel are the scenes where Edna is alone: alone on the porch weeping in chapter two; alone in her daring swim; alone in the hammock that evening; alone on Chênière Caminada; alone after Léonce leaves for New York; alone in the pigeon house; and, finally, alone in death. The word *alone* resounds like a refrain in the text, occurring some two dozen times.

On the evening of the swim, Edna listens to Mademoiselle Reisz play the piano. One piece moves her especially; Edna secretly calls it "Solitude." Later at the beach she feels like a child who "walks for the first time alone." She enters the water: " . . . intoxicated with her newly conquered power, she swam out alone." She swims, turning her face "seaward to gather in an impression of space and solitude" and returns to say, "I thought I should have perished out there alone." This climactic scene of learning to swim—where the waves of the music, the sea, and the passion seem to become one—captures the ambivalence Edna experiences toward her solitude. The solitude is "intoxicating," as it is when she is left alone on Chênière Caminada to sleep: "She looked at her round arms as she held them straight up and rubbed them one after the other, observing closely, as if it were something she saw for the first time, the fine, firm quality and texture of the flesh." Also when she is alone after Léonce's departure for New York, the solitude transports her: "A feeling that was unfamiliar but very delicious came over her. She walked all through the house, from one room to another, as if inspecting it for the first time." It is in these moments of exhilaration that Edna discovers her body, her freedom, her will, her self. But just as childbirth for the nineteenth-century woman occurred in the shadow of death, the birth of Edna's new life, occurring as it does in the "abyss of solitude" which is the sea, brings with it its attendant vision of death.

Edna connects the ocean with a memory from her childhood: " . . . a meadow that seemed as big as the ocean to the very little girl walking through the grass, which was higher than her waist. She threw out her arms as if swimming when she walked, beating the tall grass as one strikes out in the water. . . . 'I could see only the stretch of green before me, and I felt as if I must walk on forever, without coming to the end of it. I don't remember whether I was frightened or pleased.' " Likely she was both. She tells of her first deliverance from that vast expanse: "At a very early age—perhaps it was when she traversed the ocean of waving grass—she remembered that she had been passionately enamored of a dignified and sad-eyed cavalry officer who visited her father in Kentucky." The cavalry officer is followed by another young gentleman and by the "face and figure of a great tragedian." The tragedian is undoubtedly Edwin Booth, who began "to haunt her imagination and stir her senses." His portrait is in her room and "when alone she some-times picked it up and kissed the cold glass passionately."

Edna's marriage to Léonce ends this life of fancy until Robert loves her and then leaves for Mexico, thus taking his place among the pres-ences in her imagination which deliver her from her solitude. When she feels most alone, she summons Robert to her as she had summoned the romantic figures before him. In the midst of her high-spirited dinner party Edna "suggested the regal woman, the one who rules, the one who looks on, who stands alone." The next paragraph tells us of her characteristic deliverance from this solitary position: "But as she sat there amid her guests, she felt the old ennui overtaking her; the hopelessness which so often assailed her, which came upon her like an obsession, like something extraneous, independent of volition. It was something which announced itself; a chill breath that seemed to issue from some vast cavern wherein discords wailed. There came over her the acute longing which always summoned into her vision the presence of the beloved one, overpowering her at once with a sense of the unattainable."

The unattainable quality of the vision is its essence. Robert's return to Edna is doomed, for his actual presence can never match the fantasy; and she knows even the fantasy will fail her. Just before she dies, she realizes this: "There was no human being whom she wanted near her except Robert; and she even realized that the day would come when he, too, and the thought of him would melt out of her existence, leaving her alone."

Alcée Arobin has offered Edna another escape from solitude, the deliverance of the flesh. Victor, who is associated with Arobin in his escapades with women, becomes transformed into a Bacchanalian figure, with a garland of roses on his black curls, his cheeks "the color of crushed grapes," well flushed with wine. Observing him, a dinner guest quotes the first two lines from this Swinburne sonnet:[3]

A Cameo

There was a graven image of Desire
    Painted with red blood on a ground of gold
    Passing between the young men and the old,
And by him Pain, whose body shone like fire,
And Pleasure with gaunt hands that grasped their hire,
    Of his left wrist, with fingers clenched and cold,
    The insatiable Satiety kept hold,
Walking with feet unshod that pashed the mire.
The senses and the sorrows and the sins,
    And the strange loves that suck the breasts of Hate

---

3. Bernard J. Koloski also points out this source in "The Swinburne Lines in *The Awakening*," *American Literature* 45 (1974): 608–10.

Till lips and teeth bite in their sharp indenture,
Followed like beasts with flaps of wings and fins.
Death stood aloof behind a gaping grate,
Upon whose lock was written Peradventure.

Placed thus, the allusion to the rather brutal Swinburne poem about the insatiety of fleshly desire and the final victory of time and death over passion, foretells the impossibility of such deliverance for Edna. Again, just before her death, she realizes the futility of this route: "To-day it is Arobin; to-morrow it will be someone else."

Having dismissed both possibilities of deliverance from her solitude, and unable to sustain the delight it brings her, Edna embraces death whose voice she has heard in her aloneness: "The voice of the sea is seductive, never ceasing, whispering, clamoring, murmuring, inviting the soul to wander in the abysses of solitude." She watches the Icarian figure fall from its lonely flight to its lonely death and "there beside the sea, absolutely alone, she cast the unpleasant, pricking garments from her. . . ."

Chopin's study of "A Solitary Soul" is particularly poignant because the soul is a female soul, characteristically defined as someone's daughter, someone's wife, someone's mother, someone's mistress. To discover solitude in the midst of this connectedness is surely among the most painful of awakenings, because the entire social fabric sustains the dream and the illusion. As Edna says to the doctor before her death: "The years that are gone seem like dreams—if one might go on sleeping and dreaming—but to wake up and find— Oh! well! perhaps it is better to wake up after all, even to suffer, rather than remain a dupe to illusions all one's life."

We feel the tragedy of Edna Pontellier because we see so many brave moments of delight she takes in her solitary self. We glimpse the ecstasy of the discovery of the power of the self and the refusal to adjure it. To Madame Ratignolle she says, "I would give up my life for my children; but I wouldn't give up myself." Having resolved "never again to belong to another than herself," she tells Robert: "I am no longer one of Mr. Pontellier's possessions to dispose of or not. I give myself where I choose. If he were to say 'Here, Robert, take her and be happy; she is yours,' I should laugh at you both." But Edna cannot sustain these moments of resolve and when her two deliverers, the imagination (Robert) and the flesh (Arobin), have failed her, she begins to understand something of what Mademoiselle Reisz's presence and words have told her about the price of solitude, and thinking that Mademoiselle would have laughed, perhaps sneered, she swims out alone.

NANCY WALKER

[Feminist or Naturalist?]†

* * *

The novel is best read with an eye to its social and literary contexts. Whatever feminist beliefs Kate Chopin held, she makes it clear that Edna Pontellier is largely unaware of—and certainly unconcerned wtih—the reasons for her actions and that her awakening is a realization of her sensual nature, not of her equality or freedom as an individual Cynthia Griffin Wolff, in a recent article, attempts to analyze the novel from a psychological standpoint in order to show that Chopin did not intend to write a feminist tract.[1] I propose that the proof is simpler and that much of Chopin's portrait of Edna depends upon the Louisiana Creole setting she chose and the naturalistic literary convention of her day.

Creole society was in some ways unlike any other in the United States. Occupying the southern half of Louisiana (and parts of Alabama and eastern Missouri), the Creoles were the descendants of French and Spanish colonists of the eighteenth century. Some of them became very wealthy as sugar cane planters; others were less successful economically, but all were bound by Catholicism, strong family ties, and a common language (French) into a cultural subgroup which had little in common with—indeed, was often in conflict with—Anglo-American society. The cultural patterns of the Creoles have been romanticized by local colorists, including Chopin, in her short stories, but some basic characteristics may be agreed upon.

Clement Eaton states that "the Creoles, to a greater degree than the Anglo-Americans, lived a life of sensation and careless enjoyment. They loved to dance, gamble, fish, attend feasts, play on the fiddle and to live without much thought of the morrow."[2] There are several reasons for this reputation for an easygoing attitude. One is Catholicism. The pre-Lenten celebrations known as Mardi Gras, and the Sunday after-Mass holiday spirit were shocking to visitors trained to the gloom of Calvinism. New Orleans was called a Southern Babylon because of the quadroon and octoroon mistresses supported openly by Creole men. Quadroons, having one-quarter Negro blood, were of course considered fully Negro by society (cf. the quadroon servants in *The Awakening*), and it is probable that the mother of a quadroon girl was pleased—and

† From "Feminist or Naturalist: The Social Context of Kate Chopin's *The Awakening*," *Southern Quarterly* 17 (1979): 95–103. Reprinted by permission.
1. See above, pp. 231–41 [*Editor*].
2. Clement Eaton, *The Civilization of the Old South*, ed. Albert D. Kirwan (Lexington: U of Kentucky P, 1968), p. 83.

economically relieved—to have her daughter become the mistress of a wealthy white man.

Another reason for the reputed carpe diem[3] philosophy no doubt is that the Creoles did not move westward in search of larger pieces of land, as did most colonists. They were content to remain in the vicinity of New Orleans, and made up about a third of its population in 1860. (About forty-five percent of the white population of the state then lived in New Orleans, which had until shortly before been the state capital.)[4] This lack of what the rest of the country would call "industry" did have its detrimental effects, for the same parcel of land had to be subdivided repeatedly among heirs, making it increasingly difficult for a single individual to benefit from the plantation system.

Since much of what we know of Creole culture comes from observers who were chiefly impressed with notable differences from their own environments, it is difficult to draw an accurate picture of these people. It is also difficult to ascertain how much change had taken place by the time Kate Chopin lived in southern Louisiana in the 1870s; but since she had grown up in St. Louis, another area of Creole settlement, in the 1850s and 1860s, her description is probably a reliable one.

A close reading of the novel reveals that Chopin has not placed her heroine in a rigidly moralistic environment. Relatively unaffected by the puritanical mores of much of American society, the Creoles among whom Edna finds herself are openly sensual people. Ernest Earnest, referring to "The Storm," an unpublished story written after *The Awakening*, says, "The characters are all Creoles and therefore outside the Puritan tradition."[5] Warner Berthoff refers to "the languor, sensuality, frankness, and erotic sophistication of Creole manners."[6] And Larzer Ziff says of Chopin:

> The community about which she wrote was one in which respectable women took wine with their dinner and brandy after it, smoked cigarettes, played Chopin sonatas, and listened to the men tell risque stories. It was, in short, far more French than American, and Mrs. Chopin reproduced this little world with no specific intent to shock or make a point. . . . Rather, these were for Mrs. Chopin the conditions of civility. . . . People openly like[d] one another, enjoy[ed] life, and savor[ed] its sensual riches.[7]

Hence, Edna is not behaving in a shocking, inexplicable manner in the novel; she is not flaunting the mores of the society she finds herself in. Rather, by succumbing to the sensuality of the Creoles, she is denying what she has been raised to believe, so that in some ways the novel deals

3. "Seize the day" or "live for the moment" [Editor].
4. Eaton, p. 99.
5. Ernest Earnest, *The American Eve in Fact and Fiction, 1775–1914* (Urbana: University of Illinois Press, 1974), p. 262.
6. Warner Berthoff, *The Ferment of Realism: American Literature, 1884–1919* (New York: The Free Press, 1965), p. 88.
7. See above, p. 196 [Editor].

with the clash of two cultures. She is a Kentucky Presbyterian by birth and has been thrown into a very different culture by virtue of her marriage to Leonce Pontellier.

* * *

It is important to note that Edna Pontellier initially finds it difficult to participate in the easy intimacy of the Creoles.

> A characteristic which distinguished [the Creoles] and which impressed Mrs. Pontellier most forcibly was their entire absence of prudery. . . . Never would Edna Pontellier forget the shock with which she had heard Madame Ratignolle relating to old Monsieur Farival the harrowing story of one of her *accouchements*, withholding no intimate detail. . . . A book had gone the rounds of the *pension*. When it came her turn to read it, she did so with profound astonishment. She felt moved to read the book in secret and solitude, though none of the others had done so—to hide it from view at the sound of approaching footsteps.

Even the simplest gestures of affection are foreign to her, and she becomes confused when Madame Ratignolle touches her hand during a conversation. "She was not accustomed to an outward and spoken expression of affection, either in herself or others." She describes herself as "self-contained," and remains largely so until the end of the novel, in the sense that she espouses no doctrine or set of principles outside herself. However, she does become a fully sexual being.

Edna's sexual awakening begins with the flirtations of Robert Lebrun, but it is apparent that this, too, is a part of the society in which Edna finds herself. No one is surprised that Robert is attentive to her—in fact, it is expected, even by Edna's husband. When Edna leaves Mass and goes to Madame Antoine's with Robert, she says, upon awakening from her nap, "I wonder if Leonce will be uneasy!" And Robert replies, "Of course not; he knows you are with me." When Robert leaves for Mexico:

> Everyone seemed to take for granted that she missed him. Even her husband, when he came down the Saturday following Robert's departure, expressed regret that he had gone. "How do you get on without him, Edna?" he asked. "It's very dull without him," she admitted.

Before this point, Chopin has told us that "the Creole husband is never jealous; with him the gangrene passion is one which has been dwarfed by disuse." The relationship between Edna and Robert is, of course, expected to have limits. At one point, realizing that the situation could go beyond acceptable boundaries, Adele Ratignolle warns Robert: "She is not one of us; she is not like us. She might make the unfortunate blunder of taking you seriously."

The warning is too late. Edna has realized by this point the feelings that she is capable of having for a man, and although Robert does the "gentlemanly" thing by going away, Edna translates her sexual feelings into love for him. And during the rest of the novel, she does not flee from her marriage, her children, and her social obligations; rather, she runs *toward* the promise of sexual fulfillment in the person of Robert. But *run* is the wrong word, for there is nothing frantic about Edna; in fact, she resembles a sleepwalker much of the time, not aware on an intellectual level of what she is doing.

It is on this point—Edna's lack of intellectual understanding of her actions—that setting, theme, and style converge. Chopin has caused Edna to be hypnotized by the sensuous Creoles, by the warmth and color of Grand Isle. In the process, Edna has experienced a sexual awakening, and because of its suddenness and power, she is not really in control of herself. To demonstrate this, Chopin uses the style of the naturalists in depicting a fated character. Echoing Crane's "None of them knew the color of the sky," in "The Open Boat,"[8] are numerous references to Edna which indicate a somnambulistic state: "she did not know why," "she was not aware," "she did not realize." It is significant, for example, that the first time she resists her husband's wishes, when he orders her to come inside in chapter eleven, Chopin writes, "She *could not at the moment have done other* than denied and resisted" (italics mine).

Evidence of this lack of command over her own feelings and actions continues to accumulate throughout the novel. Sailing to the Cheniere for Mass the day following the incident mentioned above, "Edna felt as if she were being borne away from some anchorage which had held her fast." This statement has been interpreted as meaning that she wants to be freed from her marriage. However, there are two reasons why this cannot be true. One is the passive nature of the statement: she is "being borne" by something other than her own will. More importantly, she has no thought of her husband or her marriage at this point in the novel; Chopin has merely provided words for an emotional state. The "anchorage" is emotional sterility; she feels free to respond to Robert's attentions. When she does "leave" Leonce, it is not so much a conscious action as a series of unplanned, unconnected moves. When she tells Mademoiselle Reisz, for example, that she is going to move into a house of her own, she has "only thought of it this morning," and when Mademoiselle asks for a reason,

> Neither was it quite clear to Edna herself; but it unfolded itself as she sat for a while in silence. Instinct had prompted her to put away her husband's bounty in casting off her allegiance.

In giving herself over to emotion, Edna has allowed her decisions to be made below the conscious level, so that they surprise even her, and she

8. See above, p. 190, n. 3 [Editor].

gives little thought to the consequences. When Edna writes what will be her last letter to her husband, Chopin remarks that "all sense of reality had gone out of her life; she had abandoned herself to Fate, and awaited the consequences with indifference." She has begun living for the day in the Creole manner. And, like that of a new convert, her devotion to this way of life is often extreme, causing Madame Ratignolle to remark, "In some way you seem to me like a child, Edna. You seem to act without a certain amount of reflection which is necessary in this life."

The last scene of the novel, that of Edna's suicide, reveals the same pattern of behavior. Significantly, the final chapter opens with Victor Lebrun's description to Mariequita of the dinner he had attended at Edna's, full of the sensual detail of flowers, golden goblets, and beautiful women. The young Creole, with his exaggerated account, thus sets the scene for Edna's final immersion into sensuality—the sea. She has not determined to commit suicide; in fact, on her way to the beach she talks with Victor about what will be served for dinner upon her return. And when she realizes that she hasn't the strength to swim back, the last images in the novel are serene, sensual ones; "the hum of bees, and the musky odor of pinks." In effect, Edna drifts into death because she does nothing to stop it; in this action, as in preceding ones, she has not controlled her own destiny.

Kate Chopin has written an important novel, and not the smallest factor in its importance is the author's open acceptance of the sensual nature of women, especially considering the era in which the novel was written. But the novel is also important as an examination of cultural patterns, and especially the collision of two cultures. Edna's awakening to sensuality—in which Chopin includes music, color, and food— occurs as a direct result of exposure to a society which valued these pleasures much more openly and unashamedly than did the one Edna had been reared in. Encouraged to develop her sense of freedom in enjoyment, Edna does so, with results that damage her marriage and eventually lead to her death. In addition, Chopin writes *The Awakening* from the perspective of a naturalist, giving Edna little control over her own destiny, and it is important to note that she is controlled by her own emotions, not by men or society. She has less "open-eyed choice" than Dreiser's Carrie.[9] There is, in Chopin's novel, no stance about women's liberation or equality; indeed, the other married women in the novel are presented as happy in their condition. Perhaps those who read the novel as a feminist document are also affected by a clash of cultures: their own and that which the novelist inhabited.

9. Carrie Meeber, female hero of Theodore Dreiser's novel *Sister Carrie* (1900). See also above, p. 202, n. 1 [*Editor*].

ELIZABETH FOX-GENOVESE

[Progression and Regression in Edna Pontellier]†

* * *

In important respects, *The Awakening* may be read as a variant of the female *bildungsroman* or novel of female initiation.[1] But it cannot neatly be fit to either model. The ending, which overshadows the rest of the novel, inescapably shapes our assessment of the text. Chopin, moreover, remains simultaneously preoccupied with the tension between female destiny as a truth of nature and female destiny as a social truth. Her open critique of male privilege and power is shadowed by a more tentative and ambiguous exploration of female influence over other women. If *The Awakening* sets forth a quest for a possible female identity, it remains nuanced in its evaluation of the decisive forces that shape such an identity. And, as it plays with male and female influences, so does it weave a complex pattern of progression and regression in the course of the woman who seeks to escape the institutional context of female life.

Unlike many other novels, *The Awakening* does not present marriage as the external symbol of female identity formation. From the early days of the novel, marriage had figured as a conventional resolution of the female quest for self. If many novelists, both male and female, had oversentimentalized marriage or refused to look at the real price it extracted from women, some who accepted the convention had, nonetheless, understood that marriage must be taken to unite the natural and social, the subjective yearnings and objective possibilities of female existence. Female adolescence, in one novel after another, constitutes a quest for self or a strugle to assume willingly the appropriate social role that invariably ends in marriage. The emphasis falls not on the inescapable limitations of female destiny. Romantic love may constitute a myth, but it also functions as the codifier of female aspiration, desire, and even self-assertion. And, within the conventional possibilities of the novel, female love normally ended in marriage or death.

By the time Chopin wrote *The Awakening*, the constitutive assumptions of this tradition were being widely questioned. She had not merely read the major European realist and naturalist novelists, but had shown serious interest in Darwin, Schopenhauer,[2] and many others preoccupied with the deep strains of struggle and tragedy inherent to the human

---

† From "Kate Chopin's *The Awakening*," *Southern Studies* 18 (1979): 261–90. Except as noted, all footnotes are by the editor of this Norton Critical Edition.
1. See Elaine Ginsburg, "The Female Initiation Theme in American Fiction," *Studies in American Fiction*, III (Spring 1975), 27–37, and Patricia Meyer Spacks, *The Female Imagination* (New York, 1975). [*Fox-Genovese's note*].
2. See above, p. 183, n. 6. "Darwin": Charles Darwin (1809–82), best-known exponent of the theory of evolution.

condition. In notable respects, *The Awakening* belongs to the same sensibility that generated Ibsen's plays—especially, but not only, *A Doll's House*. For if *The Awakening* shares with *A Doll's House* a profound concern with the self-experience and self-representation of women in patriarchal marriages, it also resonates with the complex picture of female psychology that informs *Hedda Gabler*.[3] It is impossible to read Edna's story as the simple victory of patriarchy over a fragile female soul—or, it is impossible so to read it unless one understands patriarchy as an exceptionally complex set of social and psychological relations that depend upon the complicity of women.

*   *   *

Indisputably, Edna's awakening consists, at least partially, in her growing rejection of the prescribed social role of woman, namely the acquiescent creature of her designated lord and guardian. Edna's first appearance as an intrusion on her husband's vision seemingly underscores this perspective. Chopin, however, weakens her own focus on this patriarchal dominion by having the possessive glance fall upon Edna while sharing the intimacy of her sunshade with a male attendant. To be sure, the licensing of a mild flirtation might indicate the strength of the patriarchal system rather than its weakness. But Chopin further whittles away at the foundations of male supremacy by placing Leonce himself within an unambiguously domestic space, the Lebrun compound owned and run by Madame Lebrun. Mr. Pontellier was disturbed in his newspaper reading by the clamour of a parrot. "He had been seated before the door of the main house. The parrot and the mockingbird were the property of Madame Lebrun, and they had the right to make all the noise they wished. Mr. Pontellier had the privilege of quitting their society when they ceased to be entertaining." He retreats, accordingly, to the cottage occupied for the summer by his wife and children. He is merely down for a weekend visit. The cottages are connected to the main house, in which everyone eats together, by a bridge. The newspaper is a day old. Grand Isle is clearly established as its own world, different from that of hot news, market reports, and the other concerns of the masculine, public space.

If *The Awakening* begins with a domestic space carved out from the masculine world, it ends with an oceanic maternal space that negates the entire world. The point, however, is to seize the dynamic of Edna's progress from one space to the other. Chopin leaves no doubt that the world as it is affords numerous models of female being and numerous opportunities for female assertion. Edna's problem results from the ways in which these models and opportunities fail, or fail to satisfy, her. Women are at least as important to her as are men. But the narrative of Edna's relations with and dependence upon other women pursues a

3. *A Doll's House* (1879) and *Hedda Gabler* (1890) are plays by Henrik Ibsen (1826–1906), Norwegian dramatist, author of many other realist social dramas.

more subterranean course than does that of her infatuation with Robert and her rebellion against the social structures she sees as incarnated by her husband. *The Awakening* is densely peopled with socially adapted women. And the social requires underscoring. Madame Lebrun, Madame Ratignolle, Mlle. Reisz, Mrs. Highcamp, Mrs. Merriman, the shadowy and sinister lady in black, even Edna's sisters, all live. They have all found a social space adequate to their existence. As has the briefly-mentioned Miss Mayblount who, "no longer in her teens, . . . looked at the world through lorgnettes and with the keenest interest. It was thought and said that she was an intellectual; it was said of her that she wrote under a *nom de guerre.*" And she came to Edna's farewell/coming-out party with a male companion, Mr. Gouvernail, whose name suggests that Miss Mayblount had shared her unconventional, but apparently stable, existence not with some patriarchal governor, but with one whose modest function was to serve as a rudder.

The point is that the patriarchal world depicted in *The Awakening* provides considerable space for a variety of female being. Men may set the public terms of female existence, but they do not seem capable of crushing the female spirit. Chopin even hints at Edna's unconscious awareness of these complexities when she has her dream "of Mr. Highcamp playing the piano at the entrance of a music store on Canal Street, while his wife was saying to Alcée Arobin, as they boarded an Esplanade streetcar: 'What a pity that so much talent has been neglected! but I must go.'" In other words, Chopin is exploring a complex interaction between men and women, between public and private spaces, in the construction of personal—but especially female—identity. Commentators frequently call attention to the passage in which Edna reflects, " 'By all the codes which I am acquainted with, I am a devilishly wicked specimen of the sex. But some way I can't convince myself that I am. I must think about it.' " Edna's words to Alcée Arobin are taken to attest her lack of guilt for her unsanctioned behavior. But they can also be taken to mean that the codes allow for considerable personal variation and that Edna has difficulty feeling her subjectivity as a function of a social role.

*   *   *

From early in the novel, Chopin establishes that Edna is not one of the "mother-women," not one of those female creatures who live only for and through husbands and children. Critics frequently applaud that dimension of Edna's personality as proof of her incipient independence, her willingness to live for herself. Chopin doubtless intended Edna's rejection of motherhood as a totally self-determining vocation to express her own impatience with women's internalization of the social restrictions under which they lived. Thus, when Edna affirms that she would sacrifice everything for her children—money, her life, whatever—but not the essential, she surely speaks for a serious criticism of an overly-sentimentalized view of motherhood. Chopin does not leave matters there. Motherhood cannot be reduced to a social convention, however much society attempts to do so. Motherhood also has something to do with bringing forth life—an experience that Chopin herself supremely valued—and with accepting one's place in the succession of generations. Edna never received that nurture from her own mother that would have permitted her to nurture others and then move on. She remains tied to an unsatisfied maternal longing that forces her either to subordinate herself to, or to divorce herself from, her own children. Chopin embeds her critique of women's social subordination in the complexities of Edna's personal immaturity.

The love Edna seeks transcends any social possibility. Had she been content to settle for a satisfying, sensuous affair, she could have been satisfied with a relationship such as that she had with Alcée. Chopin presents that affair as rousing and meeting Edna's sensual needs. Had she sought self-realization through her work, she could have pursued her increasingly successful career. Hardly a great artist, Edna nonetheless was succeeding in selling her paintings and in taking pleasure in the mastery of her craft. The needs that drive her, however, spring from deeper sources and seem to permit no assuaging short of delirium. And Chopin clearly indicates that the love for Robert derives in large part from the repressed longing for the mother who died before helping Edna to become a woman.

The disturbing and sinister figure of Mlle. Reisz haunts Edna's story much as the woman in black haunts the steps of the young lovers in the early scenes at Grand Isle. Mlle. Reisz fills a complex function in the novel. Her role as counterpart to Madame Ratignolle is highlighted by the juxtaposition between the white of Madame Lebrun and the black of the other lady in the opening sections of the book. As Madame Ratignolle is married, beautiful, sensual, fair, and beneficently maternal, Mlle. Resiz is single, homely, ascetic, dark, and malevolently maternal. As an artist, Mlle. Reisz stands for the possibility of female independence. Her life may be austere and frugal, but it is her own. And her unappealing external frame harbors a rare musical talent. Her music, indeed, seduces and entwines Edna, blending into, even as it seems to articulate, the nameless, shapeless longing that consumes and fires Edna's soul.

Mlle. Reisz first appears at Grand Isle where she is called upon to play for the assembled guests. Her performance draws together the threads of the transformation that Edna is beginning to undergo. Having always loved the music of the pianist, in particular her rendition of a Chopin *Impromptu*, Edna finds herself participating in it in a new way. Previously, the pianist's playing had evoked pictures in her mind: One piece, which Edna privately named "Solitude" brought into her imagination the picture of a man "standing beside a desolate rock on the seashore. He was naked. His attitude was one of hopeless resignation as he looked toward a distant bird winging its flight away from him." At the novel's close, Edna herself, perched on the edge of the ocean, will shed her clothing and recreate this picture. On this particular evening, however, she waited in vain for the pictures to materialize. "She saw no pictures of solitude, of hope, of longing, or of despair. But the very passions themselves were aroused within her soul, swaying it, lashing it, as the waves daily beat upon her splendid body. She trembled, she was choking, and the tears blinded her."

Thenceforth, the dour little pianist is closely associated with Edna's passion for Robert. After her return to the city, Edna goes in search of Mlle. Reisz, for whom no one seems to have an address. Eventually, she finds her through Madame Lebrun. Having found her in a small set of rooms at the top of a building, she begs permission to return often to hear Mlle. Reisz's playing. As Arnavon pointed out, Mlle. Reisz's rooms are the only space in the novel from which one looks out over the quays and warehouses of New Orleans: Her vision encompasses the business life of the city.[4] But Edna goes not for what lies outside the rooms but what they contain. The music becomes her drug, her potion. And her favorite theme is that of Isolde.[5] Chopin's treatment of music as romantic love potion prefigures that of Thomas Mann,[6] even as it echoes Schopenhauer.

The female space of Mlle. Reisz includes none of the normal womanly attributes. Significantly, she must go out to eat or to bring in food. No material nurturance here. But for spiritual nurturance, she offers not merely music but talk of Robert and—wonder of wonders—letters from Robert over which Edna can cry as she listens to the strains of the piano. Mlle. Reisz is a seductress. Appearing to offer Edna that which she most craves, she contributes to binding her to a hopeless passion. She casts a spell as surely as any evil fairy from an ancient tale. If Madame Ratignolle stimulates and lures Edna with her warm, embracing body, Mlle. Reisz winds the threads of her power around Edna's soul. Robert writes to Mlle. Reisz. Mlle. Reisz turns his letters over to Edna. She mediates their love and, in mediating, encourages it in the paths of fantasy, longing, and that soul-engulfing death of drugged escape.

*   *   *

4. Cyrille Arnavon, "Introduction" to Edna in Per Seyersted and Emily Toth, eds., A Kate Chopin Miscellany (Oslo: Universitetsforlaget, and Natchitoches: Northwestern State UP, 1979). In fact, Arnavon writes: "one sees the river and the ships from the window of Mademoiselle Reisz (the pianist), but there is no real description of the town."
5. See above, p. 61, n. 8.
6. German-born winner of the Nobel Prize for Literature in 1929, Mann (1875–1955) is best known for his novel The Magic Mountain (1924). Forced by the Nazis to leave Germany, he became a naturalized U.S. citizen in 1944.

Edna's quest for her mother through a sequence of impossible and unattainable loves lies at the core of *The Awakening*, but does not exhaust its subject matter. The theme of longing and regression coexists throughout with the serious critique of bourgeois patriarchalism. For reasons of her own, however, Chopin resists either the clear editorial judgment or the clear invitation to an identification with Edna that would permit a firm statement about the message of the novel. Antinomies balance each other so neatly that the center remains deadlocked. The possible reasons for this strategy are numerous and most likely reinforce rather than compete with each other.

Although Chopin's personal biography cannot be advanced as an interpretive key to the text, personal motivations may have contributed to the complex and unresolved structure of the text. Taking the ending as central, we may ask from what perspective could the ending be read as satisfying. And one answer is from Chopin's personal perspective. It requires no extraordinary effort to recognize important bits of Chopin herself in Mlle. Reisz, Madame Ratignolle, and Edna. A successful writer, who had been very happily married, mother of six children, by all accounts content in her life, Chopin had also lost her husband and the mother with whom she had been unusually intimate.[7] In writing *The Awakening*, Chopin may easily have been killing off a part of herself—a residual adolescent dependency—even as she played with criticizing a society that had, by and large, treated her well.

Whether or not some such motivation prompted Chopin's writing of her novel, the novel assuredly sets forth a series of conflicts between individual female identity and social structure that it never elucidates. In *The Awakening*, Chopin offers the reader a range of clues about Edna's preoccupation with and repression of the loss of her mother. In this respect, Chopin adopts a splendidly clever strategy. She tells a story of a young woman who awakens to the injustices of her society and to her own sexuality, who rebels against patriarchal restrictions, and who attempts to realize her inner being through sensuality, love, and art. The tale should be a straightforward indictment of a society's treatment of women. But Chopin laces this account with unmistakeable indications that her heroine suffered from unusual psychological weaknesses. And she musters a galaxy of women who adapt perfectly well to the unjust social order in a variety of different roles. Suddenly, the indictment of the social system becomes an individual case history—and the case history of an aberrant individual at that. We are dealing with personal pathology—with a proclaimed "outsider"—not with social or sexual injustice at all. But Chopin cannot bring herself to undercut the feminist thrust of her novel entirely: She simply weds it indissolubly to the portrait of a psychological regression. The two narratives must be read together, for the grounds for choosing one rather than the other do not exist.

7. Seyersted, *Kate Chopin*; Rankin, *Kate Chopin*; Seyersted, *Miscellany*, 47–99.

The narrative voices of *The Awakening* are, respectively, institutional and personal voices. Edna's subjective experience provides the critique of social institutions: the reality of social institutions provides the critique of Edna's subjectivity. In this way, Chopin avoids a fully candid look at the interrelations between the personal and the institutional. Chopin was a genuinely institutional and essentially conservative person herself, even if one deeply aware of the hypocrisies and waste attached to social forms.[8] She was not likely to let a searching critique lead her to conclude that the social order of the bourgeois South required the institutional subordination of women. Nor would she have been comfortable with the view that the freedom of women dictated the substantial reform of prevailing social institutions. The spirit of rebellion burned within her, but did not dominate her life. By wedding that restlessness to female adolescence she simultaneously tied it to the roles, both positive and negative, passed on from mothers to daughters and denuded it of social import. In *The Awakening*, she explored her own knowledge that a person who wished to be free could not aspire to become a woman— in the sense that her society constructed womanhood—and that a girl who wanted to become a woman had to kill her deepest wishes to be free.

Chopin accepted the institutional compromise and, in so doing, had to tie the impulse to freedom to the longings, fantasies, and loves of early adolescence—to a state of mind that could and should be outgrown with the assumption of natural and social womanhood. Her position resembled that of those slaveholders who flourished between the Revolution and the nullification controversy.[9] Deploring slavery, they nonetheless cherished a Southern way of life that depended upon slavery for its continued existence. Thus Chopin, deploring the subordination of women, cherished a society for which challenging the prevailing sexual division of labor would have challenged the foundations of the social structure.

PAULA A. TREICHLER

[Language and Ambiguity]†

The central narrative of Kate Chopin's novel *The Awakening* can be said to concern Edna Pontellier's struggle to define herself as an active

---

8. *Ibid.*
9. The belief that "states' rights" include the power to nullify federal law.
† From "The Construction of Ambiguity in *The Awakening*: A Linguistic Analysis," in *Women in Language in Literature and Society*, eds. Sally McConnell-Ginet, Ruth Borker, and Nelly Furman (New York: Praeger, 1980) 239–57. Reprinted by permission of Praeger Publishers, an imprint of Greenwood Publishing Group, Inc., Westport, CT. Some of the author's footnotes have been omitted.

subject, and to cease to be merely the passive object of forces beyond her control.[1] But the precise nature of this struggle, as well as its emotional and psychological dimensions, is less easily articulated. One textual counterpart to this complexity is the ongoing syntactic interplay between active and passive voice which parallels, and not infrequently undermines, the overt narrative. The relationship between formal grammatical patterns and obvious narrative meaning shapes our understanding of Edna's changing consciousness and serves as an index to its vicissitudes. The verb "awaken," from which the novel's title and central metaphor derive, formally complicates in a similar way the active and passive elements of Edna's experience. Both transitive and intransitive, it can take a grammatical object but does not have to: someone can awaken, can be awakened, can awaken someone else. The title of the novel, a noun, is structurally unspecified and can draw on all these possibilities. Similarly, the novel's personal pronouns are revealing: one could argue that *The Awakening* charts Edna Pontellier's growing mastery of the first person singular, and that when this "I" has been created, the book has successfully completed its mission and comes to an end.

* * *

The first part of the book establishes contradictions and dualities, presumably to parallel what the narrative tells us about Edna—the "contradictory subtle play of features," her "dual life." She is continually baffled by her behavior and feelings, and fluctuates between apparent self-knowledge and apparent self-deception. Her perceptions are hedged in modals and conditional structures, negatives, and relative clauses. Any sense of guiding consciousness is undercut by verbal signals of doubt and hesitation. The caged birds that open the novel establish immediately the sense of constrained potential that marks these first chapters. When Edna does experience "a first breath of freedom," it is compared to wine and intoxication, images of deceptive euphoria that suggest only an illusory loss of restraint. The first sentence of Chapter VI, the short chapter that establishes the "voice of the sea" refrain, offers us similar complications: "Edna Pontellier could not have told why, wishing to go to the beach with Robert, she should in the first place have declined, and in the second place have followed in obedience to one of the two contradictory impulses which impelled her." Not only are we *told* that Edna's own behavior baffles her, the sentence itself is a wordy puzzle through which we must work our way, in suspense to the heart—"one

1. As Cynthia Griffin Wolff, "Thanatos and Eros" (p. 449), writes, most critics see the novel "as growing out of an existential confrontation between the heroine and some external, repressive force"; others see the struggle as largely internal. The forces against which Edna is seen to struggle include familial and social demands, Victorian culture, the constraints of marriage and of a male-dominated society and civilization, Romantic myths and illusions, the restraints of Creole society, interpersonal relationships, her "emotionally impoverished childhood" (Sullivan and Smith), maternity, matrimony, her female need for dependency, "her passional nature's drive for fulfillment" (Spangler), eros, death and sleep.

of the two contradictory impulses." The repeated modals and negatives, the mixture of active and passive voice, the almost clinical vocabulary, discourage Edna's too-close scrutiny of these "impulses"—and discourage us as well. This last point is important. For while the contradictory verbal signals underscore both Edna's own doubts and the contradictions we are told her character includes, they also thwart our own tendencies, as readers, to respond to the narrative from a single perspective.

But the verbal complications I have been describing fall away on the night Edna learns to swim, an event that integrates both modes of syntactic presentation and triumphantly celebrates a unity of emotions and will. The evening begins with the family entertainment at which Mademoiselle Reisz is asked to play the piano. Edna's unexpectedly passionate response to the music transcends the stolid domestic texture of the evening; to her own astonishment, the customary gentle, poetic images are absent, and in their place "the very passions themselves were aroused within her soul, swaying it, lashing it, as the waves daily beat upon her splendid body. She trembled, she was choking, and the tears blinded her." The response is an escalated version of her earlier crying, and again she is described as being at the mercy of forces beyond her control. But not only are these forces more concrete here, the figurative parallel between passions and waves (and soul and body) gives way at once to real waves as the guests walk down to the beach and Edna learns to swim.

She has been trying to learn to swim all summer, but "a certain ungovernable dread hung about her when in the water, unless there was a hand nearby that might reach out and reassure her." Like the earlier oppression that filled her, "ungovernable dread" has "hung about her"—another globally vague picture which admits no guiding consciousness and shows Edna paralyzed and impotent, the passive recipient of instructions from others. Now there is a change:

> But that night she was like the little tottering, stumbling, clutching child, who of a sudden realizes its powers, and walks for the first time alone, boldly and with over-confidence. She could have shouted for joy. She did shout for joy, as with a sweeping stroke or two she lifted her body to the surface of the water.

We find our way through the cluster of adjectives and commas to Edna's triumph: animated and active herself, engaged and roused, she can transform a figure of speech into a real shout of joy. The grammatical shift from "could have" to "did"—like the shift from the little child to Edna herself—signals real changes in her behavior and understanding. Her shout fuses body and consciousness.

Similarly, the passage fuses the contrasting verbal patterns I have described. It begins with "she," but the simile that follows deflects us momentarily from Edna herself with its explicit comparison of her to a child. Both the pronoun "that" and the definite article "the" give the images a still, emblematic quality that characterizes the entire scene. The participles—"stumbling," "tottering," "clutching"—are concrete and visual, and though they suggest faltering and vulnerability, they are intransitive, thus active, not passive. The digression has added suspense: the child "of a sudden realizes its powers" and walks "boldly and with over-confidence"; now Edna's action breaks through the mentalistic language of this symbolic picture, as though the "she" that began the sentence has gathered power that is now released. "She could have shouted for joy. She did shout for joy. . . ." This is one of the most unambivalent expressions of active force in the book: Edna passes from the metaphorical to the actual and offers a verbal model, in miniature, for what the story is about. The passage ends in the wholly immediate and concrete, "as with a sweeping stroke or two she lifted her body to the surface of the water."

Like the scene as a whole, the passage makes clear that swimming has both sensual and spiritual dimensions, and its risks are both sexual and political: "She wanted to swim far out, where no woman had swum before." Edna's experience of the water is immediately, passionately sensuous, but its spiritual and political dimensions are continually affirmed: "A feeling of exultation overtook her, as if some power of significant import had been given her to control the working of her body and her soul." We may dwell for a moment on this sentence, which not only relates the swimming experience to both body and soul explicitly but also formally fuses the passive and active elements of Edna's situation. "Exultation," in the first clause, is the familiar abstract noun: as a replacement for "oppression," only the nature of the emotion has changed; formally, Edna remains in the sentence the passive object of abstract forces beyond her control. But then the burden of responsibility shifts when the power is given to her: though still the recipient of this gift, the "her" which is the object of "given" is also the subject of the infinitive "to control." The grammatical simultaneity of "her" as object and subject is equivalent to the fluctuating and sometimes paradoxical images that interlace subject and object, self and other, container and contained, inner and outer. For a moment at least, Chopin creates a perfect verbal merging between the forces that act on Edna from outside her and the imperatives of her own self, between the abstractions of consciousness and the concrete language of her physical world. Nowhere does the narrative voice achieve a fuller sense of integration than in this passage: "She turned her face seaward to gather in an impression of space and solitude, which the vast expanse of water, meeting and melting with the moonlit sky, conveyed to her excited fancy. As she swam she seemed to be reaching out for the unlimited in which to lose herself."

The celebratory language and physical beauty of the scene, however, should not make us forget the threat, signalled first by the description of the little child who walks "with over-confidence" and echoed in words like "reckless," "intoxicated," and "overestimating her strength." Though she may wish "to swim far out," she can in fact only manage a short distance; unaccustomed even to this exertion, she is overcome by exhaustion and a vision of death, and can barely swim back to shore. This experience, together with other features of the scene, deliberately invokes the earlier "voice of the sea" refrain and its sinister promises:

> The voice of the sea is seductive; never ceasing, whispering, clamoring, murmuring, inviting the soul to wander for a spell in abysses of solitude; to lose itself in mazes of inward contemplation. The voice of the sea speaks to the soul. The touch of the sea is sensuous, enfolding the body in its soft, close embrace.

This passage conceals in poetic metaphor the threat which emerges suddenly when Edna, in the swimming scene, experiences both a vision of death and a real danger of drowning. Seduced by the sea's space and solitude, Edna seeks to lose herself in its mazes. The sea may speak to the soul, but its seduction of the body is a more literal and risky enfolding.

The swimming scene gives substance to what has only been metaphorical suggestion; it is the turning point in the novel which offers us, in a rush, a sudden access to Edna's possibilities and an expanded vision of her situation. (We did not know until this scene, for example, that Edna had even been trying to learn to swim.) This conversion of metaphor to experience gives the scene its power. The confusion and hesitance of Edna's earlier behavior fall away as she takes her life, literally, into her own hands. In the scene that follows, speaking to Robert and then to her husband, she uses the first person pronoun with far greater authority than before, describing her feelings and her will. As a reading experience, the swimming scene is a triumph. For Edna, in perfect and dangerous solitude, an "I" has been created.

* * *

Chopin achieves her effects by building up, over time, a network of images, words, verbal refrains, and grammatical textures, often through simple and quite artificial repetition, until the language we remember is continually energizing the language on the page. This growing resonance of language and imagery makes complex and sensuous what is essentially straightforward prose. In the closing chapters of *The Awakening*, this cumulative density is apparent, and contributes to the drama and sense of narrative completion that the reading experience creates.

Chopin's central metaphor of waking and sleeping, for example, depends on more than a hundred references to literal and metaphorical awakening, sleeping, and dreaming. At first the words themselves tempt us to make some fairly conventional equations: sleep means blindness, inertia, passivity, death; awakening means energy, activity, vision, life. Nothing in the prose denies us these meanings. But gradually, as they are linked to specific words, images, and narrative developments, the novel's unique associations supplant the personal and literary associations we have brought to it. By the time we reach the final scenes, most of the key words have occurred before and resonate with a verbal history internal to the text. This process of cumulative association—this intricate and increasingly paradoxical interweaving of meanings—radically changes their impact. Whatever we accept as the meaning of the novel must take into account this process of transformation.

The process can be briefly sketched. In an early scene, Edna is literally awakened by her husband. The night she learns to swim, her sleep is "troubled and feverish, disturbed with dreams" that leave fleeting impressions the next day upon "her half-awakened senses." Her sensuality is later said to be awakened by Arobin, while Edna attributes her awakening to Robert. Elsewhere her awakening seems self-generated. The ambiguous structure of the word "awakening" encompasses these definitions, permitting Edna to be awakened, to awaken someone else (as she awakens Robert), or simply to awaken spontaneously (as she does on p. 36). Critics have noted that the act of awakening (like sleeping) figures both literally and symbolically in the novel (see Wheeler or Wolff, for example),[2] and most of the key scenes, in fact, play upon these events. But the density and complexity of verbal reference are critical. Repeated references make clear Edna's "awakening sensuousness"; yet after Arobin kisses her hand, she feels like a woman who "realizes the significance of [unfaithfulness] without being wholly awakened from its glamour." She is simultaneously, in other words, awakening *to* sensuality and awakening *from* it. Because in Chopin, the individual line or paragraph is inevitably subordinate to the cumulative verbal effect, such paradoxical usage thwarts any single perspective or definition.

When Edna meets Robert in the garden and returns with him for the final time to her little house, the imagery of sleeping, awakening and dreaming intensifies. " 'Robert,' " Edna asks him as he sits in shadow, "as if in a reverie," " 'Are you asleep?' " This same question opened the intricate, political battle of wills between Edna and her husband the night she learned to swim. Here, it opens and exchange between Edna and Robert which parallels the earlier scene and clarifies Chopin's position in this novel on relationships between women and men. When Edna leans down and kisses Robert, she takes control of her life (as she did with Arobin) and shatters his evasive reticence; at first it seems that what she earlier characterized as a "delicious, grotesque impossible dream" is coming true, for Robert confesses his own " 'wild dream of your some day becoming my wife.' " But in shock and surprise Edna replies " 'Your wife!' " and in this exclamation reveals the vast distance that separates her earlier consciousness from that which now tells Robert, " 'You have been a very, very foolish boy, wasting your time dreaming

2. Otis Wheeler, "The Five Awakenings of Edna Pontellier," *Southern Review* 11 (1975): 118–28; for Wolff, see above, pp. 231–32 [*Editor*].

of impossible things when you speak of Mr. Pontellier setting me free! I am no longer one of Mr. Pontellier's possessions to dispose of or not. I give myself where I choose.' "

Edna explicitly rejects her role as a possession and an object, and it is significant that she refers to her husband formally as "Mr. Pontellier"; for it was as "Mrs. Pontellier" that the novel introduced her and almost at once referred to her as both an object and a possession. Her statement at this point recalls her inward determination, earlier, "never to belong to another than herself"; but now she expresses herself aloud, and it is her new language, perhaps, that frightens Robert as much as what she says. It was in this language that she confronted him in an earlier scene and demonstrated the same mastery of the first person singular pronoun: " 'I suppose this is what you would call unwomanly; but I have got into a habit of expressing myself. It doesn't matter to me, and you may think me unwomanly if you like.' " In contrast to this language of the self are numerous references to literal and figurative voices in the novel which for Edna become increasingly unimportant as her own language emerges. By the time the doctor offers meaningful conversation—to "talk of things you never have dreamt of talking about before"—it is a language Edna no longer speaks.

Robert turns pale during Edna's assertion of independence, but she does not yet recognize that they are at cross-purposes—that her insistence and initiative have at last shattered his vaguely self-congratulatory indecisiveness and, in fact, terrified him. " 'It was you,' " she goes on, " 'who awoke me last summer out of a life-long, stupid dream.' " Robert himself has been treated as a part of this dream until now, and so the sudden description of her whole life as a *stupid* dream (and of Robert's dream as a waste of time) confirms that, for Edna, the meaning of the word "dream" has changed: what was "delicious" fantasy is now rejected as delusion.

Chopin introduced the metaphor of sleeping and awakening by rooting it in reality when Edna was awakened by her husband. Now Edna is called away to be with Adele Ratignolle during childbirth, and as she sits at her bedside, the central metaphor is once more transformed into literal reality:

> Edna began to feel uneasy. She was seized with a vague dread. Her own life experiences seemed far away, unreal, and only half remembered. She recalled faintly an ecstasy of pain, the heavy odor of chloroform, a stupor which deadened sensation, and an awakening to find a little new life to which she had given being, added to the great unnumbered multitude of souls that come and go.

This passage is of critical narrative importance, for together with Edna's response to the birth process itself and her exchange with Doctor Mandelet, it makes clear that for women the birth of children is a central and inescapable issue. It is a philosophical as well as a physiological fact, for Edna having just declared her love for Robert, comprehends with vivid clarity the inescapable link between sexual fulfillment, childbirth, and responsibility for those "little lives." In the passage, multiple verbal connections come together: for example, the phrase "heavy odor of chloroform" binds an earlier fragment "heavy with sleep" to Arobin's "narcotic" presence and to the "heavy odor of jessamine" at Edna's dinner party; earlier, when Arobin and Robert have both left, Edna "stayed alone in a kind of reverie—a sort of stupor"; the stupor which deadens sensation recalls the Ratignolles' marriage of "blind contentment." The drugged stupor of childbirth, its deadened sensations, resolves in women's terms the conventional paradox that out of death comes life. But the passage also gives specific reality to the sense of alien forces that has governed Edna's awakening consciousness: her original experience of "indescribable oppression" is in fact clearly described here. The "vague dread" that seizes her recalls her earlier "vague anguish," the "ungovernable dread" she experienced in the water, and the "vague dread" that has filled Adele: in *The Awakening*, the source of this dread, the source of the oppression, lies in the reality of the female body. This reality is the source, in turn, of life's compelling illusions.

Edna's revelation leaves her "stunned and speechless with emotion," for its corollary is that her own sexual awakening is as deluded as her previous life has been; it is merely part of the "stupid life-long dream." Dazed, speaking as much to herself as to Doctor Mandelet, she completes the vision: " 'The years that are gone seem like dreams—if one might go on sleeping and dreaming—but to wake up and find—oh! well! perhaps it is better to wake up after all, even to suffer, rather than to remain a dupe to illusions all one's life.' " The deliciousness of the dream is at the root of its deceptive power. The "cup of life" that sexual passion holds out is nature's narcotic, which both intoxicates and drugs—" 'a decoy,' " as the doctor says, " 'to secure mothers for the race.' " Edna accepts responsibility for her vision. " 'One has to think of the children some time or other,' " she says, speaking in the abstract but at once shifting to the first person: " 'I don't want anything but my own way. . . . Still, I shouldn't want to trample upon the little lives.' " The change of pronoun signals the self's recognition of responsibility, though not necessarily, as most readings have had it, for her own children; she is no more a "mother-woman" than she has ever been. Rather, she sees the inevitability of the connection, and the "unnumbered multitude" of young lives that result from the illusion of sexual fulfillment. These are "the realities" with which Edna has at last come "face to face"; this is the "alien force" that threatens to invade her.

Characteristically, Edna does not accept this vision without a struggle; her consciousness attempts one last evasion by reviving earlier dreams. "Numb with the intoxication of expectancy" (the language continues to link passion with pregnancy and death), she hopes Robert will have fallen asleep so that she can "awaken him with a kiss" and "arouse him with her caresses." "She could picture at that moment no greater bliss on earth than possession of the beloved one." But as the vocabulary itself should tell us, none of this is to be. Instead, we learn how dense the language has become when Edna finds the house empty and reads Robert's farewell note (" 'I love you. Good-by—because I love you' "):

> Edna grew faint when she read the words. She went and sat on the sofa. Then she stretched herself out there, never uttering a sound. She did not sleep. She did not go to bed. The lamp sputtered and went out. She was still awake in the morning, when Celestine unlocked the kitchen door and came in to light the fire.

This "awakening," for Edna, is final. Her faintness momentarily invokes her customary tendency to dream and sleep, but not for long. Unlike the first awakening scene, here she does not cry nor succumb at last to sleep. In perfect solitude and silence, her mind is entirely occupied with itself. The threatening external forces have been internalized within her own body: the language of childbirth underlies the "vast cavern wherein discords wailed." Though the passage holds us fast to Edna's literal behavior, it is no longer purely concrete; its structures are invaded with meaning. In the terms that the book has created, to be alive is to sleep and to dream; out of the deathlike stupor of childbirth comes life, but conversely, to awaken, as Edna has done, is to die. When her consciousness fully awakens, it undoes itself. The passage doubles as a retrospective catalogue of her consciousness and a preparation for the decision she is making.

* * *

SANDRA M. GILBERT

[The Second Coming of Aphrodite]†

* * * I want to argue that *The Awakening* is a female fiction that both draws upon and revises *fin de siècle*[1] hedonism to propose a feminist and matriarchal myth of Aphrodite/Venus[2] as an alternative to the masculinist and patriarchal myth of Jesus. In the novel's unfolding of this implicit myth, the dinner party scene is of crucial importance, for here,

† From "The Second Coming of Aphrodite: Kate Chopin's Fantasy of Desire," *Kenyon Review* 5 (Summer 1983): 42–66. Versions of this essay have also appeared in "Introduction," "*The Awakening*" *and Selected Short Stories*, ed. Sandra Gilbert (New York: Penguin, 1984) and in Sandra M. Gilbert and Susan Gubar, *No Man's Land: The Place of the Woman Writer in the Twentieth Century*, vol. 2 (New Haven: Yale UP, 1989).
1. End of the century [*Editor*].
2. The goddess of love. In one account of her birth, she sprang from the ocean foam, engendered by the blood of Uranus (god of the sky), who had been castrated by his son Cronus [*Editor*].

as she presides over a Swinburnian[3] Last Supper, Edna Pontellier definitely (if only for a moment) "becomes" the powerful goddess of love and art into whose shape she was first "born" in the Gulf near Grand Isle and in whose image she will be suicidally borne back into the sea at the novel's end. Thus when Victor, the dark-haired young man who was ritually draped and garlanded at the climax of the feast, tells his friend Mariequita that "Venus rising from the foam could have presented no more entrancing a spectacle than Mrs. Pontellier, blazing with beauty and diamonds at the head of the board," he is speaking what is in some deep sense the truth about Kate Chopin's heroine.

To see *The Awakening* in these terms is not, of course, to deny that it is also the work most critics and readers have thought it is: a "Creole Bovary," a feminist "critique of the identity of 'mother-women,' " a New Orleans version of "the familiar transcendentalist fable of the soul's emergence, or 'lapse' into life," "a eulogy on sex and a muted elegy on the female condition," a turn-of-the-century "existentialist" epiphany, and "a tough-minded critique of the Victorian myths of love."[4] Taken together, all of these definitions of the novel articulate the range of political, moral, and philosophical concerns on which Chopin meditates throughout this brief but sophisticated work. What unifies and dramatizes these often divergent matters, however, is the way in which, for all its surface realism, *The Awakening* is allusively organized by Kate Chopin's half-secret (and perhaps only half-conscious) but distinctly feminist fantasy of the second coming of Aphrodite.

* * *

The oceanic imagery embedded in Chopin's description of Edna's response to Mlle. Reisz's music is neither casual nor coincidental; rather it suggests yet another agency through which Mme. Le Brun's predominantly female summer colony on Grand Isle awakens and empowers this Creole Bovary. For Chopin's Aphrodite, like Hesiod's[5] is born from the sea, and born specifically because the colony where she comes to consciousness is situated, like so many places that are significant for women, outside patriarchal culture, beyond the limits of the city where men make history, on one of those magical shores that mark the margin where nature intersects with culture. Here power can flow from outside, from the timelessness or from, in Mircea Eliade's phrase, the "Great Time"[6] that is free of historical constraints; and here, therefore, the sea

3. After the style of Algernon Swinburne (1837–1909), English poet whose sensuous lyricism challenged prevailing Victorian sensibilities. See also above, pp. 250–51 [Editor].

4. Willa Cather, see above, pp. 170–72. Helen Taylor, Introduction to *The Awakening* (London: The Woman's Press, 1978), p. xviii. Warner Berthoff, *The Ferment of Realism: American Literature, 1884–1919* (New York: The Free Press, 1965), p. 89; Seyersted, *Kate Chopin*, p. 161; Stanley Kauffmann, "The Really Lost Generation," *The New Republic*, 155 (December 1966), 37–38. Otis B. Wheeler, "The Five Awakenings of Edna Pontellier," *The Southern Review*, 11 (1975), 118–28.

5. Hesiod, Greek epic poet, born c. 700 B.C. Aphrodite's birth is recorded in his *Theogony*. See above, n. 2 [Editor].

6. See Mircea Eliade, *The Myth of the Eternal Return, or Cosmos and History*, trans. Willard R. Trask, Bollingen Series, 46 (Princeton: Princeton University Press, 1954).

can speak in a seductive voice, "never ceasing, whispering, clamoring, murmuring, inviting the soul to wander for a spell in abysses of solitude; to lose itself in mazes of inward contemplation."

It is significant, then, that not only Edna's silent dialogue with Mlle. Reisz but also her confessional conversation with Adèle Ratignolle incorporates sea imagery. Reconstructing her first childhood sense of self for her friend, Edna remembers "a meadow that seemed as big as the ocean" in which as a little girl she "threw out her arms as if swimming when she walked, beating the tall grass as one strikes out in the water." Just as significantly she speculates that, as she journeyed through this seemingly endless grass, she was most likely "running away from prayers, from the Presbyterian service, read in a spirit of gloom by my father that chills me yet to think of." She was running away, that is, from the dictations and interdictions of patriarchal culture, especially of patriarchal theology, and running into the wild openness of nature. Even so early, the story implies, her quest for an alternative theology, or at least for an alternative mythology, had begun. In the summer of her awakening on Grand Isle, that quest is extended into the more formalized process of learning not to run but to swim.

Edna's education in swimming is, of course, obviously symbolic, representing as it does both a positive political lesson in staying afloat and an ambiguously valuable sentimental education in the consequences of getting in over one's head. More important, however, is the fact that swimming immerses Edna in an *other* element—an element, indeed, of otherness—in whose baptismal embrace she is mystically and mythically revitalized, renewed, reborn. That Chopin wants specifically to emphasize this aspect of Edna's education in swimming, moreover, is made clear by the magical occasion on which her heroine's first independent swim takes place. Following Mlle. Reisz's evocative concert, "someone, perhaps it was Robert, thought of a bath at that mystic hour and under that mystic moon." Appropriately, then, on this night that sits "lightly upon the sea and land," this night when "the white light of the moon [has] fallen upon the world like the mystery and softness of sleep," the previously timid Edna begins for the first time to swim, feeling "as if some power of significant import had been given her" and aspiring "to swim far out, where no woman had swum before." Her new strength and her new ambition are symbolically fostered by the traditionally female mythic associations of moonlight and water, as well as by the romantic attendance of Robert Le Brun and the seemingly erotic "heavy perfume of a field of white blossoms somewhere near." At the same time, however, Chopin's description of the waves breaking on the beach "in little foamy crests . . . like slow white serpents" suggests that Edna is swimming not only with new powers but into a kind of alternative paradise, one that depends upon deliberate inversions and conversions of conventional theological images, while her frequent reminders that this sea is a *gulf* reinforce our sense that its waters are at

least as metaphysical as those of, say, the Golfo Placido in Conrad's
Nostromo.[7] Thus, even more important than Edna's swim are both its
narrative and its aesthetic consequences, twin textual transformations
that influence and energize the rest of Chopin's novel. For in swimming
away from the beach where her prosaic husband watches and waits,
Edna swims away from the shore of her old life, where she had lingered
for twenty-eight years, hesitant and ambivalent. As she swims, moreover,
she swims not only toward a female paradise but out of one kind of
novel—the work of Eliotian or Flaubertian "realism" she had previously
inhabited[8]—and into a new kind of work, a mythic/metaphysical romance that elaborates her distinctively female fantasy of paradisiacal
fulfillment and therefore adumbrates much of the feminist modernism
that was to come within a few decades.

In a literal sense, of course, these crucial textual transformations can
be seen as merely playful fantasies expressed by Robert and Edna as part
of a "realistically" rendered courtship. I am arguing, though, that they
have a metaphorical intensity and a mythic power far weightier than
what would appear to be their mimetic function,[9] and that through this
intensity they create a ghostly subtextual narrative that persists with
metaphorical insistence from Edna's baptismal swimming scene in chapter ten through her last, suicidal swim in chapter thirty-nine. For when
Edna says "I wonder if any night on earth will ever again be like this
one," she is beginning to place herself in a tale that comes poetically
"true." Her dialogue with Robert, as the two return from their moonlit
midnight swim in the Gulf, outlines the first premises of this story. "It
is like a night in a dream," she says. "The people about me are like
some uncanny, half-human beings. There must be spirits abroad to-
night." Robert's reply picks up this idea and elaborates upon it. It is "the
twenty-eighth of August," he observes, and then explains, fancifully,
that

> on the twenty-eighth of August, at the hour of midnight, and if
> the moon is shining—the moon must be shining—a spirit that has
> haunted these shores for ages rises up from the Gulf. With its own
> penetrating vision the spirit seeks some one mortal worthy to hold
> him company, worthy of being exalted for a few hours into realms
> of the semicelestials. His search has always hitherto been fruitless,
> and he has sunk back, disheartened, into the sea. But tonight he
> found Mrs. Pontellier. Perhaps he will never wholly release her

---

7. Ukrainian-born of Polish parents, Joseph Conrad (1857–1924) was best known for his *Heart
   of Darkness* (1902). He became a British subject in 1886 and wrote and published his many
   novels in English, including *Nostromo* (1904) [*Editor*].
8. Two giants of realistic fiction in nineteenth-century Europe, the English novelist George Eliot
   (1819–80) and the French novelist Gustav Flaubert (1821–80) were almost exact contemporaries. Eliot is best known for her novel *Middlemarch: A Study of Provincial Life* (1871–72),
   and Flaubert for his *Madame Bovary* (1857), the novel that most directly influenced *The
   Awakening*. See above, pp. 170–72 and 184–88 [*Editor*].
9. The idea that art "imitates" or "mirrors" life [*Editor*].

from the spell. Perhaps she will never again suffer a poor, unworthy earthling to walk in the shadow of her divine presence.

Fanciful as it seems, however, this mutual fantasy of Edna's and Robert's is associated, first, with a real change in their relationship, and then, with a real change in Edna. Sitting on the porch in the moonlight, the two fall into a erotic silence that seems to be a consequence of the fiction they have jointly created: "No multitude of words could have been more significant than those moments of silence, or more pregnant with the first-felt throbbings of desire." And the next day, when Edna awakens from her night of transformative dreaming, she finds herself "blindly following whatever impulse moved her, as if she had placed herself in alien hands for direction, and freed her soul of responsibility."

The scenes that follow—Edna's waking of Robert in chapter twelve, their voyage in the same chapter to the Chenière Caminada, their attendance at church in chapter thirteen, Edna's nap at Madame Antoine's cottage again in chapter thirteen, and their return to Grand Isle in chapter fourteen—constitute a wistful adult fairytale that lies at the heart of this desirous but ultimately sardonic fantasy. Journeying across the Gulf to Mass on the nearby island of Chenière Caminada—the island of live oaks— Edna and Robert find themselves in the Fellini-esque[1] company of the lovers, the lady in black, and a barefooted Spanish girl (apparently Robert's sometime girlfriend) with the allegorical name of Mariequita. Yet despite all this company Edna feels "as if she were being borne away from some anchorage which had held her fast, whose chains had been loosening," and together with Robert she dreams of "pirate gold" and of yet another voyage, this one to the legendary-sounding island of "Grande Terre," where they will "climb up the hill to the old fort and look at the little wriggling gold snakes and watch the lizards sun themselves." When she finally arrives at the "quaint little Gothic church of Our Lady of Lourdes," therefore, she is not surprisingly overcome by "a feeling of oppression and drowsiness." Like Mariequita, the Church of Our Lady of Lourdes is named for the wrong goddess, and Edna inevitably struggles—as she did when "running away from prayers" through the Kentucky meadow—to escape its "stifling atmosphere . . . and reach the open air."

Everything that happens after she leaves the church further implies that she has abandoned the suffocation of traditional Christian (that is, traditional patriarchal) theology for the rituals of an alternative, possibly matriarchal but certainly female religion. Attended by the ever-solicitous Robert, she strolls across the "low, drowsy island," stopping once— almost ceremonially—to drink water that a "mild-faced Acadian" is drawing from a well. At "Madame Antoine's cot," she undresses, bathes,

---

1. After the Italian filmmaker Federico Fellini (b. 1920). Using symbolic characters, his films explore dreamlike fantasies of isolation and desire [Editor].

and lies down "in the very center of [a] high, white bed," where like a
revisionary Sleeping Beauty, she sleeps for almost a whole day. When
she awakens, for the fifth or sixth but most crucial time in this novel of
perpetual "awakening," she wonders, "How many years have I slept?
. . . The whole island seems changed. A new race of beings must have
sprung up . . . and when did our people from Grand Isle disappear from
the earth?" Again she bathes, almost ceremonially, and then she eats
what appear to be two ritual meals. First she enters a room where she
finds that though "no one was there . . . there was a cloth spread upon
the table that stood against the wall, and a cover was laid for one, with
a crusty brown loaf and a bottle of wine beside the plate." She bites "a
piece from the brown loaf, tearing it with strong, white teeth" and drinks
some of the wine. Then, after this solitary communion, she dines à
deux with Robert, who serves her "no mean repast." Finally, as the sun
sets, she and Robert sit—again ceremonially—at the feet of fat, matriarchal Madame Antoine, who tells them "legends of the Baratarians
and the sea," so that as the moon rises Edna imagines she can hear "the
whispering voices of dead men and the click of muffled gold."

Having bathed, slept, feasted, communed, and received quasireligious
instruction in an alternate theology, she seems definitively to have entered a fictive world, a realm of gold where extraordinary myths are real
and ordinary reality is merely mythical. Yet of course the pagan fictive
world Edna has entered is absolutely incompatible with the fictions of
gentility and Christianity by which her "real" world lives. Metaphorically
speaking, Edna has become Aphrodite, or at least an ephebe[2] of that
goddess. But what can be—must be—her fate? Shadowing her earlier
"realism" with the subtextual romance she has developed in these chapters of swimming and boating, sleeping and eating, Chopin devotes the
rest of her novel to examining with alternate sadness and sardonic verve
the sequence of struggles for autonomy, understandings and misunderstandings, oppressions and exaltations, that she imagines would have
befallen any nineteenth-century woman who experienced such a fantastic transformation. If Aphrodite—or at least Phaedra[3]—were reborn
as a fin-de-siècle New Orleans housewife, says Chopin, Edna Pontellier's
fate would be her fate.

*   *   *

To take the last point first, I want to emphasize how important it is
for us to remember that Chopin was a woman of the nineties, a writer
of the fin de siècle. What did it mean, though, to be a woman, a female
artist, of the fin de siècle, with all that such a faintly exotic, voluptuously
apocalyptic French phrase implied? Superficially, at least, the fin de
siècle meant, for literary women as for literary men, a kind of drawing-

2. A youth in the service of the goddess; originally, a young man in ancient Greece eighteen to
   twenty years old and entered into military service [Editor].
3. Daughter of Minos, king of Crete, wife of Theseus, Phaedra became infatuated with her step-
   son Hippolytus, and when he rejected her, she accused him of having raped her and then
   hanged herself. The outraged Theseus arranged to have his son (by Hippolyta) killed [Editor].

room sophistication—smoking Turkish cigarettes, subscribing to *The Yellow Book*,[4] reading (and translating) French fiction, all of which Kate Chopin did, especially in the St. Louis years of her widowhood, which were the years of her major literary activity. More centrally, the *fin de siècle* was associated, for women as for men, with artistic and intellectual revolutionaries like Beardsley and Wilde, together with their most significant precursors—Swinburne, Pater, Whitman, Wagner, Baudelaire.[5] For women, however, the nineties also meant the comparatively new idea of "free love" as well as the even newer persona of "The New Woman."[6] In addition, to be a woman of the nineties meant to have come of age in a new kind of literary era, one whose spirit was, if not dominated by literary women, at least shared and shaped by female imaginations. For it was only in the nineteenth century, after all, that women entered the profession of literature in significant numbers.

Such a sharing of the literary terrain had, however, double and mutually contradictory consequences. On the one hand, a number of male writers consciously or unconsciously perceived this commercial as well as aesthetic strengthening of the female imagination as a threatening cultural event. Belated heirs of a long patrilineage, they feared that with the entrance of women into high culture, history's originatory male center might no longer hold; lawless and unsponsored, the female imagination might fragment or even ruin civilization. On the other hand, women writers for the first time experienced the validation of a literary matrilineage. The earliest heiresses of a brief but notably enlivened cultural past, they now felt empowered to imagine a powerful future. At the same time, though, they had to contend against the male anxieties that saw them as the ruinous daughters of Herodias,[7] rousing terrible winds of change and presaging apocalypse.[8]

Given these cultural developments, it became inevitable that a work

4. An illustrated quarterly periodical published in England between 1894 and 1897, *The Yellow Book* published many of the avant garde writers and artists of the day, including Aubrey Beardsley (see n. 5 below), who was one of its founding editors [*Editor*].
5. All these artists and writers challenged the social and aesthetic norms of their day: Aubrey Beardsley (1872–98), English illustrator and writer, whose black-and-white line drawings were widely criticized in the 1890s as gloomy and unwholesome; Oscar Wilde (1854–1900), Irish poet and playwright best known for *The Importance of Being Earnest* (1895), and notorious for his imprisonment for "homosexual offenses" in 1895; Walter Pater (1839–94), English essayist and critic known as an elegant stylist and associated with an "art for art's sake" aesthetic; Walt Whitman (1819–92), American poet whose *Leaves of Grass* offended many in its form and subject matter; Richard Wagner (1813–83), German composer whose monumental operas based on Germanic legends earned him popular acclaim and critical censure; Charles Baudelaire (1821–67), French poet whose *Flowers of Evil* (1857) led to prosecution and fines for "offenses to public morals." (Flaubert, upon the publication of *Madame Bovary*, was tried for similar offenses and was acquitted.) [*Editor*].
6. A term widely used from the mid-1890s until after World War I to describe women of newfound social, economic, and sexual independence [*Editor*].
7. Salome, daughter of Herodias, danced before King Herod and won his promise to grant her whatever she asked. Prompted by her mother, she asked for the head of John the Baptist, who had criticized Herodias's second marriage to her uncle [*Editor*].
8. Oscar Wilde's *Salome* (1894) and W. B. Yeats's "Nineteen Hundred and Nineteen" are only two of the many works that focus on a desirous female as a sign of imminent apocalypse. For further discussion of this figure, see Mario Praz, *The Romantic Agony* (London and New York: Oxford University Press, 1970).

like *The Awakening* would enter into a complicated dialectic with contextual works by both male and female artists. If we once again compare Chopin's novel to its most obvious precursor, for instance—Flaubert's *Madame Bovary*—we can see that where the French writer dramatizes what he considers the destructive power of the female imagination. Chopin struggles to articulate what is positive in that power, never copying Flaubert (the way Cather and others thought she did) but always responding to him. Thus, for Flaubert, water is, as D. L. Demorest noted in 1931, "the symbol of Venus the delectable" (as it is for Chopin) but what this means in Flaubert's case is that throughout *Madame Bovary* "images of fluidity" dissolve and resolve to "evoke all that is disastrous in love." Emma's girlish sentimentality, for instance, is represented in what the writer himself called "milky oceans of books about castles and troubadours" while the final destructive horror of her imagination pours as black liquid, a sort of morbid ink, from her dead mouth, as if she were vomiting the essential fluid which had inscribed the romantic fictions that killed her and would eventually destroy her uxorious husband. Such Flaubertian images slowly filter the very idea of the fluid female imagination—the idea, that is, of female fluency—through what Sartre called "a realism more spiteful than detached" (and it is possible to speculate that they are general defensive strategies against the developing cultural power of women as well as specific defenses by which Flaubert armored himself against Louise Colet, a woman of letters on whom he felt helplessly dependent, defenses—to quote Sartre again— "in the diplomacy of Flaubert with regard to this pertinacious poetess"[9]). Whatever the source of Flaubert's anxieties, however, Chopin vigorously defends herself and other literary women against such Flaubertian defenses, for she consistently revises his negative images of female "fluency" to present not a spitefully realistic but a metaphysically lyric version of the seductive mazes of the sea from which her Venus is born, substituting the valorizations of myth for the devaluations of realism.

But of course Chopin was aided in this revisionary struggle by aesthetic strategies learned from other precursors, both male and female. Surely, for example, she learned from Whitman and Swinburne, both of whom she much admired, to see the sea the way she did—as, implicitly, "a great sweet mother" uttering "the low and delicious word 'death' " even while rocking her heroine in life-giving "billowy drowse." In a sense, in fact, her Edna Pontellier is as much a cousin of the twenty-eight-year-old "twenty-ninth bather" in Whitman's "Song of Myself" as she is a niece of Flaubert's Emma Bovary. "Handsome and richly dressed," Edna, like Whitman's woman, has had "twenty-eight years of womanly

---

9. D. L. Demorest, ["Structures of Imagery in *Madame Bovary*], in the Norton Critical Edition of *Madame Bovary*, p. 280; Flaubert, letter to Louise Colet, 3 March 1852, *ibid.*, p. 311; Jean-Paul Sartre, ["Flaubert and *Madame Bovary*: Outline of a New Method], *ibid.*, p. 303, fn 3.

life, and all so lonesome," hiding "aft the blinds of the window," and now, "dancing and laughing," she comes along the beach to bathe in the waters of life. Yet again, much as she had learned from Whitman, Chopin swerves from him, less radically than, but almost as significantly as, she had from Flaubert, to create a woman who does not enter the sea to "seize fast" to twenty-eight young men but rather to seize and hold fast to herself. Similarly, she swerves from Swinburne to create an ocean that is not simply an other—a "fair, green-girdled mother"—but also a version of *self*, intricately veined with "mazes of inward contemplation" and sacramental precisely because emblematic of such subjectivity. [1]

In this last respect, indeed, the sea of Chopin's *Awakening* has much in common with the mystically voluptuous ocean Emily Dickinson imagines in a love poem like "Wild Nights—Wild Nights!" For when Dickinson exclaims, "Rowing in Eden— / Ah, the Sea! / Might I but moor—Tonight— / In Thee!" (Johnson 249), [2] she is imagining an ocean of erotic energy that will transform and transport her, an ocean that exists *for* her and in some sense *is* her. More, in identifying this sea with Eden, she is revising the vocabulary of traditional Christian theology so as to force it to reflect the autonomy and urgency of female desire. Such a revision is of course exactly the one that Chopin performed throughout *The Awakening*. Thus where the Extreme Unction[3] that Flaubert intones over the corpse of Emma Bovary (stroking the oil of reductive metaphor over her no longer impassioned eyes, nostrils, lips, hands, and feet) functions as a final, misogynistic exorcism of the ferocity of the imagining and desirous woman, Kate Chopin's redefined sacraments of bread and wine or crimson cocktails function, like Dickinson's, to vindicate female desire in yet another way. For in creating a heroine as free and golden as Aphrodite, a "regal woman" who "stands alone" and gives herself where she "pleases," Chopin was exploring a vein of revisionary mythology allied not only to the revisionary erotics of free love advocates like Victoria Woodhull and Emma Goldmann[4] but also to the feminist theology of women like Florence Nightingale, who believed that the next Christ might be a "female Christ," and Mary Baker Eddy, who argued that because "the ideal woman corresponds to life

1. See Swinburne, "The Triumph of Time," line 257; Whitman, "Out of the Cradle Endlessly Rocking," line 168, and "Song of Myself," line 452, lines 199–224; and "The Triumph of Time," line 265. Portions of this last poem do, however, foreshadow the denouement of *The Awakening*: disappointed in love, the speaker dreams of suicide by drowning, and imagines himself first casting off his clothes and then being reborn in the sea (lines 281–88).
2. Emily Dickinson (1830–86), major nineteenth-century American poet, author of over a thousand poems published mostly after her death. Thomas H. Johnson, *The Poems of Emily Dickinson*, 3 vols. (Cambridge: Belknap, 1955), is the definitive edition of her works [*Editor*].
3. In the Catholic church, the annointing of the dying with oil, "the last rites" [*Editor*].
4. Anarchist, writer and lecturer (1869–1940), who fought against capitalism, militarism, and the sexual exploitation of women; Goldmann's autobiography, *Living My Life*, was published in 1931. "Woodhull": suffragist, editor, and lecturer (1838–1927), known for her views on "free love," spiritualism and worker's rights [*Editor*].

and to Love . . . we have not as much authority for considering God masculine as we have for considering Him feminine, for Love imparts the clearest idea of Deity."[5] Finally, therefore, Chopin's allusive sub-textual narrative of the second coming of Aphrodite becomes an important step in the historical female struggle to imagine a deity who would rule and represent a strong female community, a woman's colony transformed into a woman's country.

To be sure, men from Wagner (in *Tannhäuser*) to Baudelaire (writing on Wagner), Swinburne (in "Lais Veneris," "Sapphics," and, by implication, his version of "Phaedra"), Beardsley (in "Under the Hill"), and Pierre Louÿs (in *Aphrodite* and *Song of Bilitis*)[6] had begun to examine the characteristics of the goddess of love, who had in the past, as Paul Friedrich points out in his useful study of *The Meaning of Aphrodite*, often been "avoided" by poets and scholars because they found her female erotic autonomy both "alarming" and "alluring."[7] But for the most part even these revolutionary nineteenth-century artists used Aphrodite the way Flaubert used Emma Bovary—to enact a new anxiety about female power. For Chopin, however, as for such feminist descendants as Isadora Duncan and H. D.,[8] Aphrodite/Venus becomes a radiant symbol of the erotic liberation that turn-of-the-century women had begun to allow themselves to desire.

The source of Aphrodite's significance for this revisionary company of women is not hard to discern. Neither primarily wife (like Hera), mother (like Demeter), nor daughter (like Athena),[9] Aphrodite is, and has her sexual energy, for herself, her own grandeur, her own pleasure. As Friedrich observes, moreover, all her essential characteristics—her connections with birds and water, her affinity for young mortal men, her nakedness, her goldenness, and even her liminality, as well as her erotic sophistication—empower her in one way or another.[1] Her dove- or swan-drawn chariot enables her to travel between earth and sky, while her sea-birth places her between earth and sea. Naked yet immortal, she moves with ease and grace between the natural and the super-natural, the human and the inhuman, nature and culture. Golden and decked in gold, she is associated with sunset and sunrise, the liminal hours of transformative consciousness—the entranced hours of awakening or

---

5. Florence Nightingale, *Cassandra* (Old Westbury, New York: The Feminist Press, 1979), p. 53; Mary Baker Eddy, *Science and Health with Key to the Scriptures* (Boston: First Church of Christ Scientist, 1875), p. 517.
6. Pierre Louÿs (1870–1925) was a French novelist and poet, author of novels of courtesan life in ancient Alexandria. See above, p. 277, n. 4 [*Editor*].
7. Paul Friedrich, *The Meaning of Aphrodite* (Chicago: University of Chicago Press, 1978), p. 1.
8. Both Isadora Duncan (1878–1927), American dancer, and H. D. (Hilda Doolittle) (1886–1961), poet and novelist, used classical themes in their work [*Editor*].
9. Daughter of Zeus, who sprang from his head fully clothed in armor at her birth. "Hera": sister and wife of Zeus, greatest of the Greek goddesses; "Demeter": goddess of the earth, and mother of Persephone [*Editor*].
1. Friedrich, *Aphrodite, passim*, but esp. pp. 33–35, 132–48.

drowsing—that mediate between night and day, dream and reality. Almost inevitably, then, she is the patron goddess of Sappho, whom that paradigmatic literary feminist Virginia Woolf called "the supreme head of song"[2] and whose lyric imagination famously fostered and was fostered by unique erotic freedom. Inevitably, too, she became a crucial image of female divinity in the increasingly feminist years of the *fin de siècle,* and almost as inevitably Kate Chopin (perhaps half-consciously, perhaps consciously) made her a model for a "regal" sea-borne, gold-clad, bird-haunted woman whose autonomous desire for freedom, and for a younger man, edged her first out of a large patriarchal mansion into a small female cottage and then across the shadowline that separates the clothing of culture from the nakedness of nature.

It is no coincidence, after all, that Kate Chopin imagined her Venus rising from the foam of a ceremonial dinner party in 1899, the same year that another American artist, Isadora Duncan, was beginning to dance the dances of Aphrodite in London salons while the feminist classicist, Jane Ellen Harrison, who would soon recover the matriarchal origins of ancient Greek religion, chanted Greek lyrics in the background. Within a few years, Duncan, haunted by her own birth "under the star of Aphrodite," was to sit "for days before the *Primavera,* the famous painting of Botticelli"[3] and create a dance "in which I endeavoured to realise the soft and marvelous movements emanating from it; the circle of nymphs and the flight of the Zephyrs, all assembling about the central figure, half Aphrodite, half Madonna, who indicates the procreation of spring in one significant gesture."[4] Musing on the "sweet, half-seen pagan life, where Aphrodite gleamed through the form of the gracious but more tender Mother of Christ," this prophetess of the beauty of female nakedness was struggling, as Chopin had, to see the power of the pagan through the constraints of the Christian and the triumph of the female through the power of the pagan. She was striving, as H. D. would, to "relight the flame" of "Aphrodite, holy name," and of "Venus, whose name is kin / to venerate, / venerator." And she was laboring, as Chopin had, to define the indefinable mythic essence of "a familiar world that [she] had never known."

2. Virginia Woolf, *A Room of One's Own* (New York: Harcourt Brace, 1929), p. 69.
3. Sandro Botticelli (1445–1510), among the greatest painters of the Italian Renaissance. His *Primavera* depicts the Three Graces and other mythological figures in the Garden of Venus. He also painted a *Birth of Venus* (1485). [Editor].
4. See Jill Silverman, "Introduction to 'Andre Levinson on Isadora Duncan,' " *Ballet Review* 6, no. 4 (1977–78), 4. Silverman notes that Harrison also "guided the young dancers through the Greek collections at the British Museum," and adds that "Harrison's . . . glorification of matriarchal structures in archaic Greek . . . undoubtedly influenced the early development of Duncan's art" (*loc. cit.*); see also Isadora Duncan, *My Life* (New York: Liveright, 1927), p. 114. Another connection between Duncan and Chopin is suggested by Elizabeth Kendell, who points out that the dancer's mother, Mary Dora Grey Duncan, was a "bold-minded St. Louis Irish girl about the same age as . . . Kate Chopin." "Before the World Began," *Ballet Review* 6, no. 4 (1977–78), 24.

LEE R. EDWARDS

[Sexuality, Maternity, and Selfhood]†

* * * *The Awakening* explicitly connects the imposition of limits on female sexual indulgence with the special relationship between women's sexuality and, not parenthood, but specifically maternity.

            * * *

Chopin's title provides the image which controls Edna's psychic life throughout the book. The plot demonstrates how the process of Edna's waking into an awareness of her body's life alters the psychic and social structures that orient her in the world: "She was seeing with different eyes and making the acquaintance of new conditions in herself that colored and changed her environment." Unfortunately, this alteration serves merely to move her from the anesthetized world of the comic heroine, unsatisfactory despite—or because of—"her husband's kindness and . . . uniform devotion," into the equally unsatisfactory world of the fairy tale or romance.[1] For Edna's involvement with Robert, like her more disturbing if less complex relationship with the rakish Alcée Arobin, is rooted in childhood's infatuations with remote, fantastic figures. Edna believes that the warmth aroused by these men—a cavalry officer, a tragic actor, and a young man already engaged to someone else—could never blaze in reality; her marriage to Léonce signals her acceptance of the chilly deadliness of life.

    Chopin embodies Edna's ambivalent feelings towards both her own denied sensuality and the sanctioned structures of repression in an extremely rich, almost dreamlike fragment of memory brought to the surface of consciousness by Edna's encounter with Robert in the summer by the sea. In this fragment, Edna feels her way back to her early childhood in Kentucky. She remembers " 'a meadow . . . as big as the ocean' " and a " 'very little girl walking through the grass, which was higher than her waist. She threw out her arms as if swimming when she walked, beating the tall grass as one strikes out in the water.' " Edna surmises that the early encounter took place on a Sunday morning when she ran " 'from the Presbyterian service, read in a spirit of gloom by my father that chills me yet to think of.' " This part of the memory is echoed in the main body of the fiction when Edna flees the church service to which Robert has taken her and finds refuge in Madame Antoine's providentially provided house. There she goes to sleep and wakens to discover Robert waiting for her. The final significant motif in this highly

---

† From *Psyche as Hero: Female Heroism and Fictional Form* (Middletown: Wesleyan UP, 1984) 123–26, 130–32. Reprinted by permission of University Press of New England.
1. For a further discussion of this point, see Ringe, above, pp. 222–27 [*Editor*].

charged recollection emerges in Edna's description of herself as wearing a sunbonnet that " 'obstructed the view' " so that she " 'could see only the stretch of green before me, and . . . felt as if I must walk on forever, without coming to the end of it.' " Edna's struggle throughout *The Awakening* concerns her efforts to cast off this obstruction, metaphorically associated also with parasols and all manner of restrictive or "protective" clothing, in order to stand fully exposed to the sun's light and to the revelation of her consciousness. Léonce first voices his objections to what he experiences as a change in Edna and hostility towards himself by telling her she is " 'burnt beyond recognition,' " by which he means that she is "a valuable piece of personal property which has suffered some damage." The motif of Edna's awakening is associated with a return to her earliest childhood in order to bring the sunlight of adult awareness to bear on a mode of existence which her Presbyterian upbringing has forced into repression.[2] The mysterious and somewhat sinister "lady in Black," counting her rosary and haunting the equally shadowy pair of young lovers—"the lovers, shoulder to shoulder creeping; the lady in black gaining steadily upon them"—suggests similar tensions existed even in the much less repressed life Edna shared with the Creoles on Grand Isle.

Edna's inability to cast her awakening into social terms is directly related to her seduction by the childish forms already established to contain her sensual impulses. This failure rests partly with her and partly with Robert—her inspiration, her collaborator, but a man whose arrested capabilities are finally as shocked by his encounter with Edna as hers are by her involvement with him. Both regard their own person and the other as characters in a predetermined fairy tale. She, like the young and mortal Psyche, is the sleeping princess; he, like Amor, is the charming prince.[3] When Edna awakens to find Robert after her flight from church, she remarks, " 'How many years have I slept? . . . The whole island seems changed. A new race of beings must have sprung up, leaving only you and me as past relics. How many ages ago did . . . our people from Grand Isle disappear from the earth?' " Robert responds in kind: " 'You have slept precisely one hundred years. I was left here to guard your slumbers.' "

If this structure liberates in some ways, it confines in others. Edna's existence as the princess requires Robert to be the prince. When, unwilling to take on the burdens of this role, Robert flees to Mexico (perhaps in a similar indulgence of romantic possibility denied by the obligations of the adult world), Edna feels stranded. Tortured "with the biting conviction that she had lost that which her impassioned, newly awakened

---

2. This point is also pursued, although with a differing interpretation of its ultimate significance, in Wolff, "Thanatos and Eros," above, pp. 231–41.
3. Wolff's "Thanatos and Eros" once again offers a wonderful reading of this scene, limited, however, by Wolff's conviction that Edna never gets beyond her longing for a prince to satisfy her needs.

being demanded," she feels that Robert's absence leaves "a void and wilderness behind her." Meaning has leached from the world. "The street, the children, the fruit vender, the flowers growing there under her eyes, were all part and parcel of an alien world which had suddenly become antagonistic." Whatever options this period of isolation provides for Edna, it leaves her need for a combined intimacy and sensuousness unsatisfied. It is only when Robert returns, prepared to do what the fairy tale requires and marry Edna, that she realizes this plot suffers from the same restrictiveness as the one in which she is already involved in her life with Léonce. When Robert reveals his " 'wild dream' " of Edna's becoming his wife, his recollection of " 'men who had set their wives free,' " Edna is indignant:

> "You have been a very, very foolish boy, wasting your time dreaming of impossible things when you speak of Mr. Pontellier setting me free! I am no longer one of Mr. Pontellier's possessions to dispose of or not. I give myself where I choose. If he were to say, 'Here, Robert, take her and be happy; she is yours,' I should laugh at you both."

* * *

When Edna finally discovers that even with Robert, the structures of sexual relationships ill fit the evanescence of desire, the implications of this revelation are devastating. Edna's love for Robert makes her wish to see him as unique and herself as faithful. But the attraction between herself and Alcée Arobin forces her to acknowledge that sensuality, once roused, is inherently promiscuous. Edna has also misjudged Robert, who reveals himself to be as conventional as Léonce. Robert's love for Edna includes a wish to marry her, and he cannot understand that marriage is, at best, irrelevant to the qualities Edna most values in their relationship. If merging with Robert means marriage, marriage—to Edna—means death. The wish to merge is only a screen for the wish to die. Isolation and sexual abstinence is the only viable alternative, but Edna cannot endure a solitary life. She is not strong enough to live under the austere tutelage of Mademoiselle Reisz. She cannot submit her newly discovered feelings to the discipline of work, or alter their forms or functions by the application of imaginative vision. By the end of the book she knows that " 'to-day it is Arobin; tomorrow it will be someone else. It makes no difference to me.' " There is "no human being whom she wanted near her except Robert; and she even realized that the day would come when he, too, and the thought of him would melt out of her existence, leaving her alone." Edna finds this knowledge too much to bear. If she cannot give in to Robert's wish for marriage, neither can she carry on without him.

At the same time that she acknowledges her spiritual solitude, Edna must also admit that she is not literally alone. Her presence at the

Ratignolles' home when Madame Ratignolle is giving birth compels her "with an inward agony, with a flaming, outspoken revolt against the ways of Nature" always to " 'think of the children. . . . Remember them!' " * * * Edna is trapped in the awareness that succumbing to sexual desire moves one from the private realm of feeling to the public realm of production and that children can demand the mother's life, even if they cannot claim the woman's soul. As Edna walks down to the waters of the Gulf, the children appear before her "like antagonists who had overcome her; who had overpowered and sought to drag her into the soul's slavery for the rest of her days. But she knew a way to elude them." Suicide: a way indeed.

Edna's hope that individual consciousness could be combined with sensual union is unfulfilled. The sun is not " 'hot enough to have warmed the very depths of the ocean.' " The flight from the controlling norms—morality, marriage, maternity—that began on a Sunday in childhood when, running from church, she found herself in a grassy meadow, blue-green like the sea, ends with Edna's vision of a "bird with a broken wing . . . reeling, fluttering, circling disabled down, down to the water." Adèle Ratignolle's plea that Edna " 'think of the children' " is countered, but not conquered, by the memory of Mademoiselle Reisz's derisive summation: " 'And you call yourself an artist! What pretensions, Madame! The artist must possess the courageous soul that dares and defies.' " The moment at which Edna stands "for the first time in her life . . . naked in the open air, at the mercy of the sun" is ironically, bitterly, the moment that precedes her death.

* * *

PATRICIA S. YAEGER

[Language and Female Emancipation]†

* * * *The Awakening*'s most radical awareness is that Edna inhabits a world of limited linguistic possibilities, of limited possibilities for interpreting and re-organizing her feelings, and therefore of limited possibilities for action. In Edna's world what sorts of things are open to question and what things are not? Although Edna initially attempts to move into an arena in which she can begin to explore feelings which lie outside the prescribed social code, finally she can only think about herself within that code, can only act within some permutation of the subject-object relations her society has ordained for her.

† From " 'A Language Which Nobody Understood': Emancipatory Strategies in *The Awakening*," *Novel* (Spring 1987): 197–219. Reprinted with permission.

If this is so, can we still define *The Awakening* as one of the grand subversive novels, as a novel belonging to a great tradition of emancipatory fiction? We can make such claims for *The Awakening* only if Chopin has been successful in inventing a novelistic structure in which the heroine's very absence of speech works productively, in which Edna's silence offers a new dialogic ground from which we can measure the systematic distortions of her old ground of being and begin to construct a new, utopian image of the emergence of women's antithetical desires. Does Chopin's novel offer such utopian structures?

* * *

In the scene in *The Awakening* where Edna returns to the beach from her unearthly swim, it is Robert Lebrun who speaks for her, who frames and articulates the meaning of her adventure, and the plot he invents involves a mystical, masculine sea-spirit responsible for Edna's sense of election, as if romance were the only form of elation a heroine might feel. Edna repudiates Robert's story: " 'Don't banter me,' she said, wounded at what appeared to be his flippancy." And yet Robert's metaphors quickly become Edna's own:

> Sailing across the bay to the *Chênière Caminada*, Edna felt as if she were being borne away from some anchorage which had held her fast, whose chains had been loosening—had snapped the night before when the mystic spirit was abroad, leaving her free to drift whithersoever she chose to set her sails. Robert spoke to her incessantly . . .

The tension between Edna's imagined freedom and Robert's incessant speech is palpable, but unlike the speech of Edna's husband, Robert's words invite dialogue: " 'I'll take you some night in the pirogue when the moon shines. Maybe your Gulf spirit will whisper to you in which of these islands the treasures are hidden—direct you to the very spot, perhaps.' 'And in a day we should be rich!' she laughed. 'I'd give it all to you, the pirate gold and every bit of treasure we could dig up.' " Not only is Robert's vision one that Edna can participate in and help to create, but it is also like a fairy-tale: romantic, enticing, utopian. As a "utopia" Robert's vision is not at all emancipatory; it offers only the flip side, the half-fulfilled wishes of an everyday ideology.

> "How many years have I slept?" she inquired. "The whole island seems changed. A new race of beings must have sprung up, leaving only you and me as past relics. . . ."
> He familiarly adjusted a ruffle upon her shoulder.
> "You have slept precisely one hundred years. I was left here to guard your slumbers; and for one hundred years I have been out under the shed reading a book. The only evil I couldn't prevent was to keep a broiled fowl from drying up."

This comic repartee is charming: as Foucault explains in *The Order of Things*, utopias afford us special consolation. "Although they have no real locality there is nevertheless a fantastic, untroubled region in which they are able to unfold; they open up . . . countries where life is easy, even though the road to them is chimerical. . . . This is why utopias permit fables and discourse: they run with the very grain of language and are part of the fundamental dimension of the *fabula*.[1] What Robert Lebrun offers Edna is a continuing story, a mode of discourse which may be chimerical, but unlike Edna's talk with her husband is also potentially communal. This discursive mode cannot, however, invite its speakers to test the limits of their language; instead, it creates a pleasurable nexus of fancy through which Edna may dream. Freed from the repressive talk of her husband, Edna chooses another mode of oppression, a speech-world that offers space for flirtation that Edna finds liberating. But this liberation is also limiting, a form of stultification, and in exchanging the intoxicating sound of her own voice as she speaks on the beach for Robert's romantic voice, Edna Pontellier's growing sense of self is stabilized, frozen into a mode of feeling and consciousness which, for all its promise of sexual fulfillment, leaves her essentially without resources, without an opportunity for other internal dialogues.[2] We may see *The Awakening* as a novel praising sexual discovery and critiquing the asymmetries of the marriage plot, but we must also recognize that this is a novel in which the heroine's capacities for thought are shut down, a novel in which Edna's temptations *to think* are repressed by the moody discourse of romance. In fact, the novel's explicitly utopian constructs partake of this romance framework; they do not function transgressively. Does Chopin offer her heroine—or her reader—any emancipatory alternative?

*   *   *

On the evening when Edna first begins, consciously, to recognize her powers and wants "to swim far out, where no woman had swum before," her experience is one of multiple moods, of emotions which seem confused and inarticulate: "A thousand emotions have swept through me to-night. I don't comprehend half of them. . . . I wonder if any night on earth will ever again be like this one. It is like a night in a dream. The people about me are like some uncanny, half-human beings. There

---

1. Michel Foucault, *The Order of Things: An Archeology of the Human Sciences* (New York: Vintage, 1973), p. xviii.
2. Gilbert argues that Robert's telling of these "wistful adult fairy tale[s]" (above, p. 275) aids in reproducing a modern Aphrodite's birth from the foam—a birth in which Edna is "mystically and mythically revitalized." Gilbert imagines that Robert's words are without distorting power because she envisions Grande Isle as a women's world, a colony situated "outside partriarchal culture, beyond the limits of the city where men make history. . . . Here power can flow from outside . . . from the timelessness . . . that is free of historical constraints" (above, p. 272). The point of my essay is that these "historical constraints" invade Edna's fantasies of "timelessness" as insistently as they invade Mr. Pontellier's city life.

must be spirits abroad to-night." Sensing the extraordinary reach of her feelings, Lebrun answers in kind:

> "There are," whispered Robert. "Didn't you know this was the twenty-eighth of August?"
> "The twenty-eighth of August?"
> "Yes. On the twenty-eighth of August, at the hour of midnight, and if the moon is shining—the moon must be shining—a spirit that has haunted these shores for ages rises up from the Gulf. With its own penetrating vision the spirit seeks some one mortal worthy to hold him company, worthy of being exalted for a few hours into realms of the semi-celestials. His search has always hitherto been fruitless, and he has sunk back, disheartened, into the sea. But tonight he found Mrs. Pontellier. Perhaps he will never wholly release her from the spell. Perhaps she will never again suffer a poor, unworthy earthling to walk in the shadow of her divine presence."

While Robert Lebrun may have "penetrated her mood," he has also begun to alter its meaning. Edna's experience has been solitary and essentially mysterious; her swim has been a surpassing of limits, a mythic encounter with death—an experience suffused with metaphor, beyond comprehension. Robert's words do not begin to encompass its meaning, but he does attempt to communicate with her to understand her mood. And since Edna lacks an alternative register of language to describe her tumultuous feelings, Robert's conceit soon becomes her own; his language comes to stand for the nameless feelings she has just begun to experience. Just as Edna's initial awakening, her continuing journey toward self-articulation and self-awareness is initially eccentric and complex, so this journey is finally diminished and divided, reduced in the romantic stories that she is told and the romantic stories she comes to tell herself, to a simplistic narrative that falsifies the diversity of her awakening consciousness. From this perspective, the pivotal event of Chopin's novel is not Edna's suicide, nor her break with her husband, but her openness to Robert Lebrun's stories, her vulnerability to the romantic speech of the other which has, by the end of the novel, become her speech as well:

> "I love you," she whispered, "only you; no one but you. It was you who awoke me last summer out of a life-long, stupid dream. Oh! you have made me so unhappy with your indifference. Oh! I have suffered, suffered! Now you are here we shall love each other, my Robert. We shall be everything to each other. Nothing else in the world is of any consequence. I must go to my friend; but you will wait for me? No matter how late; you will wait for me, Robert?"

Edna's final retelling of her story is not an accurate self-portrait, but a radical betrayal of the "awakening" that emerges at the novel's beginning. This initial "awakening" does not involve the violent triangulation of adultery, romance, and erotic story-telling, but the exploration of a discontinuous series of images that are promisingly feminocentric. In fact, what is disturbing about Edna's last speech to Robert is its falsification of her story, its naming of Lebrun as author of her growth, as source of her awakening. For what this last speech denies is the essential strangeness of Edna's initial self-consciousness, the tantalizing world of unvoiced dreams and ideas that Edna encounters at the novel's inception. By the end of the novel Edna has drifted into a system of self-explanation that—while it seems to account for her experience—also falsifies that experience by giving it the gloss of coherence, of a continuous narrative line. Edna's thoughts at the beginning of the novel are much more confused—but they are also more heterogeneous and promising.

* * *

Given the power that Robert (and the romance plot itself) exerts over Edna's ordinary patterns of associative thinking, it is worth noting that Chopin's novel ends in a more heterogeneous zone, with Edna's attention turned neither toward Robert nor her husband and children, but toward her own past:

> She looked into the distance, and the old terror flamed up for an instant, then sank again. Edna heard her father's voice and her sister Margaret's. She heard the barking of an old dog that was chained to the sycamore tree. The spurs of the cavalry officer clanged as he walked across the porch. There was the hum of bees, and the musky odor of pinks filled the air.

This lyrical ending is as enigmatic as the novel's beginning; it might be read as a regression toward oral passivity: toward an infantile repudiation of the validity claims, the social responsibilities adult speech requires. But I would suggest this extralinguistic memory comes to Edna at the end of her life because it is in such a sequence of images, and not the language of Robert Lebrun, that Edna can find the most accessible path to her story—that even in death Edna is seeking (as she sought on the beach) a path of emancipation; she is seeking a register of language more her own.

At the end of the novel as Edna swims out to sea and tries to address Robert once more, she fails again; she finds herself trying to speak a language no one understands. " 'Good-by—because, I love you.' He did not know; he did not understand. He would never understand." The story that Edna has told herself about her affection for Robert is inadequate. Close to death, she turns her mind toward the blurred edge of her womanhood, and the novel ends as it has begun, with a medley of distinct and disconnected voices. Here they represent a point of possible origin; they trace that moment in time when, still experiencing the world as a multitude of sounds, Edna's attention begins to shift from the plural voices of childhood toward the socially anticipated fulfillment of her sexual rhythms, toward the obsessive "clang" of the cavalryman's spurs. Just as the novel begins with the parrot's strange speech, with an order of speaking that satirizes and escapes from the epistemological confines of the heroine's world, so Edna's own awakening begins with and returns at her death to the rich and painful lure of desires that are still outside speech and beyond the social order.

* * *

To argue that Edna lacks a language, then, is not only to say that culture has invaded her consciousness, has mortgaged her right to original speech, but that Edna's language is inadequate to her vital needs, that it is singular when it should be plural, masculine when it should be feminine, phantasmic when it should be open and dialectical. And what becomes clear by the novel's end is that Robert Lebrun has served as an iconic replacement for that which Edna cannot say; his name functions as a hieroglyph condensing Edna's complex desires—both those she has named and those which remain unnameable.

In *Powers of Horror* Julia Kristeva suggests that "phobia bears the marks of the frailty of the subject's signifying system," and Edna's love for Robert—although it is not phobic as such, reproduces this frailty as symptom; when Edna seeks nothing but the speech of her beloved, it makes her "signifying system" frail.[3] Edna Pontellier has no language to help her integrate and interrogate the diversity of her feelings; she experiences neither world nor signifying system capacious enough to accommodate her desires. But by the end of the novel these contradictory desires become noisy, impossible to repress. As Edna helps Adele Ratignolle through a difficult childbirth the romantic interlude that Edna has shared with Robert becomes faint; it seems "unreal, and only half-remembered," and once again language fails her. When Dr. Mandelet asks if she will go abroad to relax, Edna finds herself stumbling for words: " 'Perhaps—no, I am not going. I'm not going to be forced into doing things. I don't want to go abroad. I want to be let alone. Nobody has any right—except children, perhaps—and even then, it seems to me— or it did seem—' She felt that her speech was voicing the incoherency of her thoughts, and stopped abruptly." After watching Adele give birth and listening to her painful repetitions ("Think of the children, think of them"), Edna begins to re-experience the bodily sensations and feelings for her children that she has repressed; her extra-marital desires grow more tumultuous. Once more her sentences split with the weight of this conflict, and as Mandelet tries to put them together, as he offers to "talk of things you never have dreamt of talking about before," Edna

3. Julia Kristeva, *Powers of Horror: An Essay in Abjection*, trans. Leon S. Roudiez (New York: Columbia UP, 1982), p. 35.

refuses his kind and magian powers, just as, in childhood, she refused her father's chill summons to prayer. She gives herself, instead, to the "voice" of the sea, to that sibilance in which every name drowns. And her mind returns to what she can claim of her childhood, to the story she told Adele Ratignolle on the hot summer beach.

Kristeva has suggested that we consider "the phobic person as a subject in want of metaphoricalness," and I have suggested that the same becomes true of a woman in love, a woman who becomes the subject of her culture's romantic fantasies. "Incapable of producing metaphors by means of signs alone," Kristeva argues,

> [this subject] produces them in the very material of drives—and it turns out that the only rhetoric of which he is capable is that of affect, and it is projected, as often as not, by means of *images*. It will then fall upon analysis to give back a memory, hence a language, to the unnamable and namable states of fear, while emphasizing the former, which make up what is most unapproachable in the unconscious.[4]

I am not suggesting that Edna is in need of a Freudian or even a Kristevan analysis. I am suggesting instead that we can locate the power of the novel's final images in Edna's desire "to give back a memory, hence a language," to that within her which remains nameless.

> There is a fact which our experience of speech does not permit us to deny, the fact that every discourse is cast in the direction of something which it seeks to seize hold of, that it is incomplete and open, somewhat as the visual field is partial, limited and extended by an horizon. How can we explain this almost visual property of speaking on the basis of this object closed in principle, shut up on itself in a self-sufficient totality, which is the system of *langue*?[5]

The "voice" of the sea Edna tries to embrace is more than a harbinger of death, more than a sign of dark and unfulfilled sexuality; the novel's final images frame and articulate Edna's incessant need for some other register of language, for a mode of speech that will express her unspoken, but not unspeakable needs.

---

4. Kristeva, p. 37.
5. Jean-Francois Lyotard, *Le différend* (Paris: Minuit, 1983), p. 32. This translation is from Peter Dews' "The Letter and the Line: Discourse and Its Other in Lyotard," in *Diacritics* (Fall 1984), 41.

ANNA SHANNON ELFENBEIN

[American Racial and Sexual Mythology]†

Kate Chopin's *The Awakening* (1899) shocked its nineteenth-century readers by presenting without comment the adultery of Edna Pontellier, a wealthy, white American wife and mother adrift in Creole society. The shock was so great that the novel went unread for almost sixty years. Recent critics have tended to blame the literary double standard, which prohibited female authors at the turn of the century from broaching topics available to male authors, for the opprobrium Chopin suffered. But it was the cultural chauvinism of Chopin's contemporaries that was primarily responsible for their adverse reaction to *The Awakening*.

For much of Chopin's audience the troublesome issue of female desire was resolved through a racist conception of passion and purity according to which passion was projected onto "dark" women, while purity was reserved exclusively for "white" women. This conception manifests itself in the comments of early reviewers of *The Awakening*. W. M. Reedy, publisher of the *Mirror* and responsible for introducing some of Maupassant's provocative pieces to America, voiced the objections of many of his American confreres when he condemned Chopin for permitting her heroine, a "real American lady," to "disrupt the sacred institutions of marriage and American motherhood without repentance." Reedy was willing to accept a "woman sinner on American soil if she was a 'foreigner' "[1] or a member of the lower class, like Stephen Crane's Maggie, Frank Norris's Trina, or Theodore Dreiser's Carrie,[2] but not if she was white and upper-class, like Edna Pontellier.

Chopin's contemporaries were dismayed by *The Awakening* because its sexual realism assaulted American sexual-caste mythology. Profoundly subversive and courageous, the novel collapsed the traditional categories that had long segregated "dark" women and "white" women in American literature and advanced a new conception of female desire that was color-blind and democratic. Exploiting the complex social milieu available to her as a New Orleans author and deploying a multi-racial cast of female characters, who share to varying degrees Edna Pontellier's awakening sen-

---

† From "Kate Chopin's *The Awakening*: An Assault on American Racial and Sexual Mythology," *Southern Studies* 26.4 (Winter 1987): 304–12. Copyright © 1987. Permission for reprint granted by the author, Anna Shannon Elfenbein. Elfenbein develops these ideas further in *Women on the Color Line: Evolving Stereotypes and the Writings of George Washington Cable, Grace King, Kate Chopin* (Charlottesville: U of Virginia P, 1989).

1. Quoted by Per Seyersted, *Kate Chopin: A Critical Biography* (Baton Rouge, 1969), 114.

2. Edna Pontellier is unique because her creator was a woman and because she [Edna] is a white, upper-class wife and mother. Stephen Crane's Maggie, Hamlin Garland's Rose, Theodore Dreiser's Carrie, and Frank Norris's Trina manifest passion, but only Edna possesses an independent sense of herself as a sexual being; and she defies race, class, and sex conventions regarding woman's sexual nature.

suality, Chopin violated the expectations of her genteel readers by showing that sexual passion is no respecter of class or caste boundaries.

The complex social milieu Chopin depicted also distinguishes *The
Awakening* from Flaubert's *Madame Bovary*, to which it has frequently
been compared.[3] Instead of the bourgeois aspirations to social status of
an Emma Bovary, Chopin's Edna experiences ambivalence toward the
sensuality of the New Orleans Creoles. Her disorientation concerning
the behavior appropriate for privileged white women in Creole society
is perceived by Adèle Ratignolle, the exemplar of white Creole femininity, when she warns Robert Lebrun, who has been pursuing Edna
in a conventional Creole way, that Edna " 'is not one of us; she is not
like us. She might make the unfortunate mistake of taking you seriously.' " Edna does make this mistake, and because her status as a
privileged white woman depends upon her compliance with an elaborate
system of racial and sexual rules that constrict the sexual expression of
white women, her awakening and her noncompliance threaten a social
order she fails to understand. Constricted by class and caste bias and
her propensity to see everything only as it impinges on her own emotional
life, Edna's view of her world is not large enough to accommodate her
discovery of the common sexual ground of women's experience.

As Edna veers from the path charted for privileged white women, she
is contrasted with the other women characters in the novel, characters
who occupy an unchanging space in the patriarchal society Chopin
describes. Critics of the novel have of course discussed the contrast
between Edna and Adèle Ratignolle and Mademoiselle Reisz, a pianist,
noting that these women present mutually exclusive options for Edna.
They have also examined Chopin's ironic coupling of a pair of lovers
with a lady in black who tells her rosary while shadowing them and
Edna. However, in focusing on this dark lady, presumably a white
widow, and the lovers, they have neglected to note Chopin's implicit
comparison of Edna with women of color or ambiguous race who make
up the novel's gallery of "dark" women.[4] Peripheral and incompletely
realized as characters, these dark women in *The Awakening* add richness
and complexity to the novel, making it possible for Chopin in her
depiction of Edna, whose character is so much at odds with conventional
views of woman's nature, to subvert literary stereotype and popular prejudice. A matrix of diverse female types, "white" and "dark," surrounds
Edna, who sees other women only in the way convention dictates.

Although Chopin may have shared to a degree the racist assumptions

3. It is worth noting that Chopin's debt to Flaubert's *Madame Bovary* is less than has been
suggested by those who draw analogies between Edna Pontellier's situation and Emma Bovary's.
Significantly, Emma is surrounded by male characters, while Edna is surrounded by a gallery
of female types, white, black and racially mixed.
4. This critical neglect is merely one case in point of white solipsism. In *Ain't I a Woman: Black
Women and Feminism* (Boston: South End Press, 1981), Bell Hooks [Gloria Watkins] indicts
white critics in general for making black women invisible in their readings of literature.

of American culture of her period, the novel's realistic treatment of Edna's interaction with these women exposes the sex and caste prejudices of Creole society—a society itself the object of slur and stereotype in American society at large. In so doing, Chopin challenged the biases of the novel's contemporary detractors, who recognized too well the racial implications of the novel, and its current rediscoverers, who, in emphasizing the novel's depiction of sexism, see only a portion of the picture of a sexist, racist society that Chopin drew with compelling accuracy. At the center of this picture, Edna progresses toward discovery of "her position in the universe," but her way is doubly barred, for sexual *and* racial prohibitions block her as they block the other women in the novel.

Chopin's realism repeatedly captures the racism as well as the sexism of Edna's acquaintances. Swerving toward social satire in a dinner-table scene that reinforces our sense of the provinciality of her Creole characters, Chopin presents the diners' alarm and prurient interest when they learn that Robert Lebrun, the elder son of their hostess, plans to live and do business in Mexico. Any reader who has been privy to ethnic jokes in similar situations may squirm at Chopin's description of the round-table speculation that follows the news of Robert's departure, culminating in Adèle Ratignolle's request "that Robert . . . exercise extreme caution in dealing with the Mexicans . . . a treacherous people, unscrupulous and revengeful. She trusted she did them no injustice in thus condemning them as a race." The discussion concludes with the testimony of Victor Lebrun, who assures all who will listen that Mexicans, especially Mexican women, about whom he implies intimate knowledge, are happy, childlike people.

Victor, the younger son in the Lebrun family, embodies the racist and sexist prejudices of his society, asserting his importance by badgering the black women of the Lebrun household or by bragging of his sexual prowess. The "droll" stories he tells of his conquests and the demeaning treatment he accords the domestics who serve his family pass without notice in Edna's crowd, where such extremes of male self-assertion are sanctioned. Victor's behavior, an adolescent and therefore comic version of male practice in Edna's society, fuses sexual and racial exploitation, assorting Chopin's cast of women characters according to their conventional service functions. Edna fails repeatedly to hear Victor's "highly colored story" of adventures he "wouldn't want his mother to know." Presumably these adventures also take place with women whom he wouldn't want his mother to know.

Edna, Madame Lebrun, and the other white women in the novel accept the presence of such dark rivals as they do the services of dark menials without reflection and without criticizing the habits of their men. Madame employs a little black girl to "work the treadle" of her machine: "The Creole woman does not take any chances which may be avoided of imperiling her health." Edna, marked by her Presbyterian prudery as an outsider in the sensuous and expressive society of the Creoles, awakens too late to the absurdity of racial divisions of labor that do not protect white women from the biological perils women share. Deceived by the seeming candor of Creole society concerning sex, she recoils from Adèle Ratignolle's "harrowing story of one of her *accouchements*," which withheld "no intimate detail" from a mixed audience at table, and from Robert's "droll" stories related to an amused audience of married women. The meaning of Adèle's "harrowing" story and of Robert and his brother Victor's "droll" stories escapes Edna, who fails to understand, until too late, their applicability to her own situation as a woman. Edna's failure to see compounds her failure to hear. Her negative view of those whose stigmatized status she shares retards the intellectual and emotional development she requires for survival.

* * *

Edna's class consciousness and her incapacity for transcendence appear in her blindness to the quotidian presence of dark women in her world, blindness that establishes her inability to escape those patriarchal imperatives regarding sex and woman's place that her sensual nature leads her to violate. Edna's unthinking reliance on values that will ultimately require her suicide appears in her failure to perceive these women or their significance. Alienated from her role as a mother by the quadroon nurse, who cares for her two sons with "fictitious animation," and unable to take off her wedding ring or shatter a vase without being interrupted by a maid, who silently hands the ring back to her, Edna feels herself alone and exceptional. She wants "to swim far out, where no woman had swum before," but in the end she drowns herself like many other nineteenth-century heroines in no-exit situations.

Edna is not the only woman in *The Awakening* who fails to make common cause with other women. For the other women in the novel establish no more than the shallowest of female relationships. Ironically, it is Edna who feels the claims of sisterhood most acutely, forgoing the long-awaited consummation of her passion for Robert Lebrun to attend Adèle when her friend sends word that she is in labor. Watching Adèle, who is transformed by travail, her face "drawn and pinched, her sweet blue eyes haggard and unnatural," Edna confronts the facts of life that privileged women see only at rare moments. In contrast, Josephine, the attending "griffe" nurse or midwife, refuses "to take too seriously . . . a situation with which she [is] so familiar." Each woman is isolated in this experience that women share: Adèle, awaiting the male doctor, the audience for her grand performance, feels abandoned and neglected. Josephine works hard to maintain her professionalism and patience. Edna recoils from the scene of "torture" so reminiscent of her own experiences of childbirth, fleeing the labor room and later deciding, like other white heroines in Southern fiction, that "To-morrow would be time to think of everything."

The marked separation of the women in this scene underlines Chopin's consistent treatment of class and caste divisions among women in the novel, divisions she realistically portrays and implicitly calls into question. The staging of such separation is most evident in the foregoing scene, and in two other scenes in the novel that depict Mariequita, a peripheral but essential "dark" woman character whom Edna fatally misperceives. Mariequita's response mirrors Edna's, reflecting the class and caste antagonism that divides women from each other and from true self-knowledge. Although racism and sexism in Creole society and in the society in which Edna was born mandate a difference between women of Edna's class and Mariequita's caste, Chopin juxtaposes Edna and Mariequita, blurring the racial categories established by men to control the sexuality of women and exposing the flawed vision of these two victims of such distinctions.

It is no accident that Robert and Victor Lebrun, whose surname reinscribes their "dark" proclivities, court both Edna and Mariequita or that Mariequita appears at two crucial junctures in the story to underscore the unacknowledged importance of dark women in Edna's world. In the Chênière Caminada episode that juxtaposes the limiting facts of life and the romantic fantasies Edna and Robert weave for each other, Mariequita appears, "making 'eyes' " at Robert. Although Edna views Mariequita as stereotypically "dark" and carefree, it is Edna who is on a fool's errand and Mariequita who has business to transact. Separated from Mariequita by class, purpose, and language but *not*, quite obviously, by gender and sexuality, Edna is unable to understand Mariequita's amused banter in Spanish to Robert about the lovers in the boat. Edna's view of Mariequita is fragmented, focusing as it does on apparent irrelevancies such as the "sand and slime between her brown toes" rather than on the telling interaction between Robert and this young woman with whom he shares a language closed to Edna.

Later in this episode, Edna anatomizes her own body as she awakens to her sensuality and looks "at her round arms . . . as if [they] were something she saw for the first time." It is the whiteness of her skin, "the fine, firm quality and texture of her flesh," that is stressed here, as in an earlier episode when her husband Leonce looks at her tanning skin "as one looks at a valuable piece of personal property which has suffered some damage," and she responds by surveying her "hands, strong, shapely hands . . . drawing up her lawn sleeves about the wrists." The connection between Edna's badge of class, white skin, and her status as a married lady is forged here with a resigned closural gesture, as she "silently reach[s] out to [Léonce], and he, understanding, [takes] [her] rings from his vest pocket and drop[s] them into her open palm." Edna's fragmented body is not unified until the end of the novel, when she emerges "naked in the open air, at the mercy of the sun, the breeze that beat upon her, and the waves that invited her." At this moment, she, like Mariequita, stands barefoot in the sand, "the foamy wavelets curl[ing] up to her white feet, and coil[ing] like serpents about her ankles." The Chênière Caminada episode in which Mariequita first appears prepares for her reappearance in the final scene of the novel, linking Edna to a class of women conventionally assumed to differ from privileged women. This linkage is sustained through recurrent mention of dark women with flashing eyes who satisfy their desires without suffering the social ostracism Edna must suffer if she "swims out where no [white] woman had ever swum before." On the return from Chênière Caminada, Robert teaches Edna a romantic little air, *Ah! si tu savais!*—"Ah, if you knew what your eyes tell me!" Edna, who has dark and passionate eyes, parrots the words, failing to perceive the ironic connection between the lyrics of this refrain, Mariequita's eye-play, and the flashing eyes of other dark women in the novel. Although haunted by the melody, Edna refuses to confront the truth embodied in its lyrics until the end of the novel, when she flees her discovery of the impersonal and ephemeral nature of sexual passion.

Edna's first intuition of this truth comes when Robert returns from Mexico with a memento (aptly Freudian)—a finely embroidered tobacco pouch. When Edna, who has indulged in a brief consolation affair with Alcée Arobin, a notorious roué, questions Robert about this gift from his Vera Cruz "girl" and about the women of Mexico " 'with their black eyes and their lace scarfs,' " she betrays the limited range of her worldly experience. Robert's response shows his worldly wisdom, as does his blasé attitude toward the experience. Although Robert's experience contrasts with Edna's naivete, they both recognize the insignificance of the affairs they have enjoyed while apart. His callous assertion that the Vera Cruz girl " 'wasn't of the slightest importance' " and that " 'There are some people who leave impressions not so lasting as the imprint of an oar upon the water' " accords with Edna's claim that Alcée Arobin's photograph means nothing to her. The untimely interruption of this interchange by Alcée himself adds another voice to the tasteless, chauvinistic discussion of the dark women of Mexico, whom Alcée characterizes as " 'Stunning girls.' " Although Edna fails to see that her own status as an object of male possession is no different from that of women who serve as objects of male passion, she realizes that Robert, who shares a male language with Arobin that is as closed to her as was Mariequita's Spanish, "had seemed nearer to her off there in Mexico." Arobin's pointed request that Edna convey his regards to Mr. Pontellier when she writes puts her in her place, which differs from that of the dark women under discussion only in the strictly artificial or legal sense agreed upon by men.

The ability of men like Robert and Alcée to assert their mastery of women in such discussions confirms Edna's powerlessness to change her lot by allying herself with men. The end of the novel, which presents Mariequita once more, suggests Edna's powerlessness to change her lot by allying herself with women. When Edna walks as though catatonic past Mariequita and Victor to her death, she cannot really see Mariequita, nor can she be seen by her. Edna's hard-won understanding of her sexual nature thus remains bounded by race and class prejudices, which are signaled by the fact that here as in the beginning she is called "Mrs. Pontellier"[5] and by the fact that here as in the Chênière Caminada episode, she is unable to interact with Mariequita except by casting herself once more into the social role that she has sought to escape. Thus, she intrudes upon Victor and Mariequita and gives them orders for a supper she never intends to eat. In this, her last social act as Mrs. Pontellier, Edna betrays once more the conventional attitudes of her class, which dictate suicide, the socially correct choice for a respectable white woman who has strayed from her role as wife and mother. Through food, the emblem of her subjugation and her self-indulgence throughout the novel, Edna insists on service from Victor and Mariequita, the dark woman who will provide a plausible story to account for her "accidental drowning."

Held in reserve until this final scene and sketched once again with minimal but telling strokes, Mariequita responds to Edna according to convention. Even Edna's suspicious appearance at Grand Isle before the summer session cannot crack the class code that disables both women. Both are centered on themselves and must act out the roles they have been assigned, roles that satisfy neither but maintain the patriarchal order. Thus, Edna ignores Mariequita, addressing her remarks to Victor. And Mariequita feels jealous of Edna, believing the myth of a woman "who gave the most sumptuous dinners in America, and who had all the men in New Orleans at her feet." Such a belief, so at variance with the truth, suggests the romantic illusions that will survive Edna to perpetuate male control. Because Mariequita lives on to tell Edna's story —and to get it all wrong—and because Mariequita's story is so clearly the one Victor has told her to maintain his power over her, Edna's partial knowledge of the sexual realities concealed by romantic fictions dies with her.

The true story, Kate Chopin's story of Edna's awakening, however, remains to cancel those romantic fictions that lead Edna astray. The inevitable consequence of her initial belief in her ability to venture further than other women of her class and of the caste, and of the class consciousness she shares with other privileged women, Edna's suicide indicts both sexism and racism. For Edna, and Edna alone among the women in the world of the novel, awakens to the truth about her own

5. [See above, p. 269—Editor]. Paula A. Treichler notes that Edna achieves individuality in the course of the novel and becomes identified to the reader as Edna. Treichler asserts that by the final chapter Edna has fully achieved her identity, but "the real Edna is elsewhere." The use of Edna's married name in the final chapter, however, also suggests that in committing suicide Edna is behaving as she has been programmed to behave. She is following the only path open to women of her class who experience sexual passion outside of marriage.

sexuality and that of other women, a truth concealed by romantic, racist fictions. Through Edna's awakening and her suicide, through her "obstructed vision" of the sexual realities that impinge on the lives of all women, Chopin took her stand against the sexual stereotypes that deny women, including Edna and the other women in the novel, not only the freedom and the opportunity but even the ability to experience and express their diversity.

HELEN TAYLOR

[Gender, Race, and Region]†

* * *

There is clear evidence of Chopin's southern orthodox views on race. In 1894, when her collection *Bayou Folk* was published containing several stock portraits of (mainly comic) black figures, William Schuyler (a close friend of the author in St. Louis) wrote: "Her father's house was full of negro servants, and the soft creole French and patois and the quaint darkey dialect were more familiar to the growing child than any other form of speech. She also knew the faithful love of her negro 'mammy,' and saw the devotion of which the well-treated slaves were capable during the hard times of the war, when the men of the family were either dead or fighting in the ranks of the 'lost cause.' " Like Grace King,[1] Kate Chopin clearly expressed herself to close and sympathetic friends in terms of an affectionate nostalgia for the intimate black/white relations of childhood. Three years later, she wrote an essay in praise of Ruth McEnery Stuart,[2] whose "whole-souled darkies" she admired. Revealing her admiration for the fiction of Page and Harris,[3] she claims Stuart surpassed them "in the portrayal of that child-like exuberance which is so pronounced a feature of negro character, and which has furnished so much that is deliciously humorous and pathetic to our recent literature." For Chopin, as for Page and Stuart, literary black characters were best suited to provide peripheral amusement and

---

† Reprinted by permission of Louisiana State University Press from *Gender, Race and Region in the Writings of Grace King, Ruth McEnery Stuart, and Kate Chopin* (Baton Rouge: Louisiana State UP, 1989) 156–57, 183–87, 189, 193–95, 200–202. Copyright © 1989 by Louisiana State University Press.
1. New Orleans writer (1851–1932) of novels and short stories to whom Kate Chopin is often compared [*Editor*].
2. Popular turn-of-the-century Louisiana writer (1849–1917) of fiction set in the postbellum South [*Editor*].
3. Joel Chandler Harris (1848–1908), editor of the *Atlanta Constitution*, known for his Uncle Remus tales. "Page": Thomas Nelson Page (1853–1922), Virginia author whose fiction indulged a nostalgia for an aristocratic "Old South." His stories, published in the 1880s and 1890s, frequently used "Negro" dialect and explored Civil War themes [*Editor*].

pathos—the very elements of that Local Color from which Chopin always claimed she was eager to dissociate herself.[4]

When one examines the work for complex treatments of race, what emerges is a sentimental and anodyne view of Louisiana blacks and mulattoes, one that confirms their simplicity, fidelity to and love for whites, and constructs them as cheery figures acting out a pastoral subplot to the comic or tragic dramas of white communities. Like Stuart, Chopin provided stereotypical black characters and black dialect to satisfy that nationalist project of northern editors which she soon realized would provide a regular income. This meant that her short stories and sketches, set mainly in Louisiana's Cane River area, had to ignore the historical realities of extreme poverty and racial violence, its anachronistic plantation economy, and the tensions between poor whites and freedmen/women, and land-owning whites and free mulattoes. And she used the dialect of her subordinate black figures as Page and Stuart had done, to patronize and amuse. But from the beginning, her work featured black characters and motifs around the themes of slavery and emancipation: her first piece of writing used that very term—"Emancipation: A Life Fable"—about an animal escaping nervously but joyfully from its cage. Anne Goodwyn Jones suggests that throughout the fiction, Chopin used blacks "as an objective correlative for her feelings about oppression," and in terms of *female* oppression this seems to be the case, especially in the later works. As with other southern women writers, black suffering, slavery, and oppression are all linguistically and thematically appropriated for white women. The complexity of blacks' own lived experience is sacrificed.[5]

Part of the reason for this may well have been Chopin's strong identification with European, rather than American, realist writing. Her fiction is a response to European writings that focused on gender, rather than to those works by Stowe, Cable, and Twain[6] that foregrounded issues of race in relation to American history. Unlike Grace King, she did not identify herself as a southern cheerleader. Though using southern themes and characters, her texts work in opposition to, or dialogue with, European writers who shared her concern with questions of sexuality, bourgeois marriage, and woman's role—primarily in relation to women of Chopin's own race and class.

4. William Schuyler, *The Writer*, VII (1894), quoted in *Kate Chopin Miscellany*, 115–16; Kate Chopin, St. Louis *Criterion*, February 27, 1897, quoted in *Complete Works*, p. 711.

5. Kate Chopin, "Emancipation" (n.d. but, according to Seyersted, late 1869 or early 1870), in *Complete Works*, 37–38; Jones, *Tomorrow Is Another Day: The Woman Writer in the South, 1859–1936* (Baton Rouge: Louisiana State University Press, 1981), p. 151.

6. Mark Twain (Samuel L. Clemens) (1835–1910), realist writer best known for his *Adventures of Tom Sawyer* (1876) and *Adventures of Huckleberry Finn* (1884). "Stowe": Harriet Beecher Stowe (1811–96), author of *Uncle Tom's Cabin* (1852). "Cable": George Washington Cable (1844–1925), New Orleans-born writer of fiction set in Louisiana, best known for *Old Creole Days* (1879); a progressive on social issues, including race relations, Cable and his work were often criticized in the South, and he lived the last half of his life in Massachusetts, where he was a founder of the Northampton People's Institute [*Editor*].

* * *

The important ingredient in Chopin's development from a compromising critique of to a more iconoclastic and overtly critical attack on patriarchal values is her reading of European writing by male realists and feminists. This attraction and reference to Europe is mediated in *The Awakening* to a highly sophisticated degree, which partly explains the bewildered and furious condemnation of the book by puritanical American critics—a response that took aback its thoroughly Europeanized author. The hostile critical reception of *The Awakening* is a familiar story to scholars of eighteenth- and nineteenth-century women writers. Writers such as Mary Wollstonecraft, Madame de Staël, George Sand, and Charlotte Brontë[7] had all published novels with strong, self-determining heroines who spoke their minds and were assumed to speak those of their authors. Like Maria, Corinne, Lélia, and Jane Eyre, Edna Pontellier was condemned for her independence, defiance of society's rules and values, and most particularly for her expression of and joy in sexual passion. Willa Cather's review of *The Awakening*, published in the same year the novel appeared and typical of its reception, referred to the "trite and sordid" theme, and accused Edna of sharing with Emma Bovary a demand for "more romance out of life than God put into it" and for making "the passion of love . . . stand for all the emotional pleasures of life and art."[8] As Ellen Moers says, "if women writers do succeed with the expression or the dramatization of passion, if they do create an attractively erotic male character, their real-life experience at once becomes the only subject of critical discussion" (and in the two most extreme cases, de Staël was known as Corinne, Sand as Lélia, the latter even by her modern biographer André Maurois).[9]

Kate Chopin was no exception. What is interesting is the vehemence of the critical response, a response that indicates how much bolder was this treatment of illicit love by a woman writer than anything yet published in America. Though the "New Woman"[1] and adulterous wife were by then commonplace features of European fiction and drama, America's women writers, almost all firmly in a puritan Protestant tradition, avoided direct reference to female sexuality except as an expres-

7. English novelist (1816–55), whose *Jane Eyre* was published under the pseudonym "Currer Bell" in 1847. "Mary Wollstonecraft": English author (1759–97) of A *Vindication of the Rights of Woman* (1792) and a novel *Maria, or the Wrongs of Woman*, published posthumously. "Madame de Stael": French-born philosopher, critic, novelist, author of *Corinne* (1807); her famous salon became a center of intellectual and political activity. "George Sand": independent and prolific Paris-born novelist (1804–76), whose life and work laid claim to women's independence and sexual fulfillment; she published an average of two books a year from the 1830s until her death; Kate Chopin's only daughter was always known as "Leila" and may have been named after the hero of Sand's novel *Léila* (1833) [*Editor*].
8. See above, pp. 170–72.
9. Quoted in Sharon O'Brien, "The Limits of Passion: Willa Cather's Review of *The Awakening*," *Women and Literature*, III (1975), 11, 13, 14. Ellen Moers, *Literary Women* (Garden City: Doubleday, 1976), p. 144.
1. See above, p. 277, n. 6 [*Editor*].

sion of deviance (see, for instance, a work Chopin admired greatly, Mary Wilkins Freeman's[2] *Pembroke*, 1894). Kate Chopin herself, assumed to have been an unfaithful wife and negligent mother, suffered the fate of Mary Wollstonecraft rather than of George Sand; notoriety led not to fame but to cold silence, her novel dropped from libraries, polite company, and soon from print. Unlike Europeans, American genteel puritan critics had difficulty absorbing writing by women about sex. Chopin's creole links with French literature and culture, with European ways of thinking about sexual love, and especially with the long tradition of women's writing on love, marriage, and adultery, were to make a great difference both to the liberties she took in her writing and the ways she was received and misconstrued in her own country.

Edna Pointellier is by no means the *"femme de génie"*[3] depicted by de Staël, George Sand, or the Elizabeth Barrett Browning[4] of *Aurora Leigh*. But she echoes many elements of their works and creates interesting variations on their central feminist themes. Motifs from *Corinne* and especially *Lélia* recur in the novel to such an extent that the book cannot make sense when read just in the light of late nineteenth-century European naturalism and realism, and of male authors only. The comparison that is frequently made between *The Awakening* and *Madame Bovary*, seductive as it is, seems to me to locate Chopin's novel in a male tradition which, as I argued in relation to Maupassant, she was writing her way out of throughout her career. In her final novel, I believe she succeeded by returning to questions and themes raised by earlier women writers. The novel is usually read as an apolitical work, and even when a recent critic tried to rectify this he still asserted that, in this "political romance," "for roughly the first half of the novel Chopin subordinates the political implications of Edna's predicament to the solitude and tentative self-exploration that begins to occupy her heroine during the summer idyl on Grand Isle."[5] My analysis of the novel is an attempt to argue through the highly political subtext, demonstrating how the work makes an original contribution to women's writing about the Protestant/Catholic divide, about nationality and regionalism, and about patriarchal institutions and the "New Woman" in the 1890s South. These are all questions Chopin's foremothers had wrestled with, and which American women writers were aware of. Chopin's novel is the first to use mainly English and French feminist themes in an American and especially a southern context.

2. See above, p. 207, n. 9. Based on the history of her mother's family, *Pembroke* chronicles the broken engagement and ten-year separation of Charlotte Barnard and Barnabus Thayer. The novel is a gallery of New England character types [*Editor*].
3. "Woman of genius" [*Editor*].
4. Chopin wrote a few stories that feature women writers as protagonists, though the characters are usually seen ironically: for example, "Wiser than a God," "Miss Witherell's Mistake," and "Charlie." ["Browning": English poet (1806–61), whose *Aurora Leigh* (1857), a verse-novel exploring issues of literary authorship, widely influenced writers from Emily Dickinson to Virginia Woolf—*Editor*].
5. Lawrence Thornton, "*The Awakening*: A Political Romance," *American Literature*, 52 (1980), 52–53.

Several texts by English and French nineteenth-century women writers foreground the social and political differences between European
nations. Madame de Staël and Elizabeth Barrett Browning emphasize
the contrast between cold, northern Protestant England and warm,
southern Catholic Italy; Charlotte Brontë uses France (and French Belgium) as a symbolic site of revolution and moral and sexual laxity in
contrast with the bracing self-control and common sense of England.
Cora Kaplan writes of *Aurora Leigh*: "As in *Corinne*, and in so much
Protestant writing about Italy, classical architecture, Catholicism and
warm weather come to represent a blurred sensuality, missing in England, which opens the self to its permitted corollary, love."[6] For European women, and indeed for an American like Margaret Fuller,[7]
Italy—followed closely by France—stood for revolution in the widest
sense, and both Grace King and Kate Chopin felt stimulated and liberated when visiting France. For Margaret Fuller and Elizabeth Barrett
Browning, political revolution was exhilarating, while for Tory Protestant
Charlotte Brontë it was terrifying; but for many European women writers,
the farther south one moved, the more a woman could relax, feel free
to be herself, and relish sensual pleasures. This geographical transition
is also a metaphysical and emotional one—from the ascetic rigors of
Puritanism to the lavish "indulgent" rituals of the Catholic faith, away
from repression toward satisfaction of desire.

It is the complex dialectic between these contrasting attractions for
women—documented as it was in such well-known texts as *Corinne* and
Villette[8]—that Chopin borrows from European women's writing and
neatly transposes to Louisiana, by choosing a strictly reared, repressed
Presbyterian heroine from Kentucky who marries into the relaxed New
Orleans creole Catholic community that takes its vacations on a warm,
sensuous island in the Gulf of Mexico. This clash of cultures, sited
initially on Grand Isle and expressed mainly through the ripening friendship and understanding between Edna and creole "mother-woman"
Adèle Ratignolle, is seen very much in de Staël's terms. Corinne tells
Oswald of the difference between her Catholic and his Protestant faith
and practice:

> Yours is stern and serious, ours is bright and tender. . . . in Italy
> Catholicism has taken a character of gentleness and indulgence,
> while in England . . . the greatest strictness both in principles and
> morals. Our religion . . . breathes life into art, inspires poets, makes
> a part of all the joys of our life; whilst yours . . . has taken a
> character of moral austerity from which it will never depart. Ours
> speaks in the name of love; yours in the name of duty.

6. Kaplan, "Introduction" to *Aurora Leigh* by Elizabeth Barrett Browning (London: 1978), p.
   19.
7. American transcendentalist (1810–50), and author of *Woman in the Nineteenth Century* (1845);
   Fuller traveled, lived in, and wrote about Italy in the last years of her life [*Editor*].
8. *Villette* (1853), a novel by Charlotte Brontë set in Belgium, where Brontë had studied and
   taught school [*Editor*].

Ellen Moers records that Harriet Beecher Stowe felt "an intense sympathy" with Corinne but wrote that in America "feelings vehement and absorbing like hers become still more deep, morbid, and impassioned by the constant forms of self-government which the rigid forms of our society demand." Stowe, a Puritan New Englander, shied away from *Corinne*, but Chopin—raised a Catholic, and with strong fascination for literary locations associated with the exotic and sensual—found in the text a set of contrasts which would be employed in her own work.[9]

When she returned to her hometown after her husband's death, Kate Chopin was known as the "Corinne of St. Louis," and Ellen Moers suggests that she patterned her salon life on that of de Staël and other versions of this *femme de génie*, Margaret Fuller in Boston and George Eliot at the Priory.[1] She may also have heard from friends of the salon life established by the Howes in New Orleans,[2] taken up by women such as Grace King. But Corinne is not the most obvious model for Edna in *The Awakening*; the exceptional, independent artist was inappropriate for an 1890s American woman writer steeped in European naturalism. De Staël's disciple George Sand adopted a tone in *Lélia* (1833) that was more attractive to Chopin. The "threnody of sexual despair and bitter skepticism which made the *maladie du siècle* a female as well as a male disease" was ripe for intertextual reading by a *fin de siècle* novelist who was appropriating overwhelmingly male-created and male-oriented European and American romantic and realist themes and forms for herself. As Patricia Thomson has demonstrated, *Lélia*, of all Sand's novels, had huge popular success and *succès de scandale*, and was widely known and referred to by the very Victorian novelists Chopin had known from childhood. Several of Chopin's stories, and especially *The Awakening*, amount to a dialogue with and response to *Lélia*, and indeed to Sand herself, who clearly attracted Chopin because of her "introduction of passion as a major theme in the novel."[3]

* * *

I have emphasized the influence of European women's writing, since it seems clear that throughout her career Chopin used and reworked feminist themes associated with that exotic, remote site of the female libido, Europe. In many of her writings there are indications of the importance of literature in the construction of different kinds of femininity, and her own intertextual use of women's and men's European fiction forms part of such commentary.

9. Madame de Staël, *Corinne: or Italy* (London: 1911), 178; Moers, *Literary Women*, 205.
1. See Moers, *Literary Women* 184 [Editor].
2. As head of the Women's Department at the Cotton Centenniel Exposition in 1885, Julia Ward Howe (1819–1910), abolitionist, suffragist, and writer, with her daughter Maud Howe Elliott, became the center of much literary, cultural, and social life in New Orleans during the 1880s. See Taylor 38 [Editor].
3. Moers, *Literary Women*, 33; Patricia Thomson, *George Sand and the Victorians: Her Influence and Reputation in Nineteenth-Century England* (London, 1977). Thomson makes the point that for Victorian English Writers (and this also applies to Americans) "what each chose to concentrate on is as revealing of his personality as of her achievement" (1). She also notes that the first reviews—like those of *The Awakening*—called *Lélia* "a monster" and the book itself a "revolting romance" and a "regular topsyturvification of morality" (12, 19, 9).

* * *

A frequent feature of Chopin's fiction is the escape from gender definition by a female protagonist. *The Awakening* is no exception. Edna tries to discover what kind of woman she might be through refusal of "feminine" behavior and style. It is not surprising that, as she begins to find her freedom, she has more in common than before with her father; she shares his enthusiasm for the races and, when she goes there, talks like him. She begins to earn money from gambling and selling her paintings; walks everywhere alone and stays out late; at Mademoiselle Reisz's drinks brandy from a glass like a man; and takes the initiative in lovemaking with Robert, who (she suggests) thinks her "unwomanly." The novel can be read as an elaborate and subtle gloss on the notion of the "New Woman" of whom Chopin had heard and read much. As several critics have suggested, Chopin's impatience with organized women's clubs and the women's movement probably stemmed from her sense of the reductive nature of women's demands for freedom—seen in terms of suffrage, education, jobs, and so on—and *The Awakening* is an interesting contribution to the debate on the complexities of female growth and metamorphosis, especially in the South.

The night Edna has first admitted to loving Robert, she tells Arobin, "By all the codes which I am acquainted with, I am a devilishly wicked specimen of the sex." Chopin's use of the word *codes* is surprising here, but with its legal implications entirely apt. Edna knows well enough the meaning of her departures from the "codes" of acceptable female behavior, but increasingly she takes upon herself the role of lawbreaker. So completely has she succeeded that Robert, who has dreamed and agonized over the possibility of her divorcing Pontellier and marrying him, is dumbfounded at her scorn for his notion that she is the property of her husband. He, of course, is no lawbreaker and runs away, unwilling to compromise them both in the eyes of society.

In creole eyes, women who flout the codes governing female behavior are dangerous or mad. Arobin reports that the spinster Mademoiselle Reisz is widely thought to be "partially demented" (while to Edna she is "wonderfully sane"; Pontellier wonders if his wife's neglect of household management indicates she is "growing a little unbalanced mentally." This compares significantly with Corinne's wry thought when reading Nelvil's uncomprehending letter about Italy: "Perhaps the best way for a woman of superior mind to regain her coolness and dignity is to withdraw into herself as into an asylum."[4] To everyone who sees her, Edna Pontellier is physically transformed and indeed a *new woman*: her husband sees her as " 'not herself' "; Victor Lebrun remarks that she looks " 'ravishing' " and " 'doesn't seem like the same woman' "; and Dr. Mandelet recognizes her erotic awakening when he compares her to " 'some beautiful, sleek animal waking up in the sun.' " The

4. De Staël, *Corinne*, 97.

narrator, repudiating Pontellier's suspicion of madness, observes that Edna was simply "becoming herself and daily casting aside that *fictitious self which we assume like a garment with which to appear before the world*" (my emphasis). That fictitious self is socially defined and determined southern womanhood and ideal femininity, which Chopin knew had been reinforced and reified throughout nineteenth-century fiction.

Yet, new creature/woman as she undoubtedly becomes (and the animal imagery associated with her growth seems to suggest that monster which Ellen Moers, Adrienne Rich, Robin Morgan, and other women writers have associated with women's notion of change),[5] Edna recognizes how solitary and potentially destructive this reborn figure is. Her exhilaration at the casting off of responsibilities, unwanted duties, and codes is finally defeated by her loyalty and sense of "right." Though she tells Robert at a moment of intense desire, " 'We shall be everything to each other. Nothing else in the world is of any consequence,' " in the next breath she tells him she must go to attend Adèle's childbirth. Later, she claims to Dr. Mandelet that " 'nobody has any right—except children, perhaps.' " The most oppressive demands of patriarchal society (embodied during her final swim in thoughts of her sons, father, and the spur-clanging cavalry officer, as well as the scorn of the true rebel Mademoiselle Reisz) must be evaded if they cannot be defied. If women like Edna must always "witness the scene [of] torture" with only "an *inward* agony," "*speechless* with emotion" (my emphases), there is no way in which a woman may speak herself in such a society—except negatively.

In some ways, following the European tradition of Flaubert and Maupassant,[6] the novel is profoundly deterministic, demonstrating as it does the ways in which women—far more than men—are locked into socially prescribed roles and definitions. Ellen Moers argues that Madame de Staël uses *Corinne* to show that

> regional or national or what we call cultural values determine female destiny even more rigidly, even more inescapably than male. For as women are the makers and transmitters of the minute local and domestic customs upon which rest all the great public affairs of civilization . . . so women suffer more, in their daily and developing lives, from the influences of nationality, geography, climate, language, political attitudes, and social forms.[7]

To a certain extent, *The Awakening* shows Edna at the mercy of a patriarchal husband, a hot climate, a creole lifestyle, and the circumscribed expectations of a particular class of Louisiana women.

* * *

5. See Moers, *Literary Women* 90–110. Also Robin Morgan, *Monster* (New York: Random House, 1972). Adrienne Rich, *A Change of World* (New York: 1951) and *Diving Into the Wreck* (New York: Norton, 1973) [*Editor*].
6. See above, p. 183, n. 5 [*Editor*].
7. Moers, *Literary Women* 207.

Earlier I quoted Anne Goodwyn Jones's statement that Chopin used blacks as an objective correlative for her feelings about oppression. Throughout this book I have demonstrated the frequency of this "conceit" and have argued that it derives from a class- and race-bound perspective on blacks (and especially slaves) that is both dishonest and politically outrageous. Self-conscious as Chopin was about her use of imagery in other ways, and subtle as some of the regional allusions are to Louisiana's slave past, her analogy between bourgeois white marriage and slavery reveals the limitations of contemporary southern women's racist feminism. In *The Awakening*, it comes close to allying Chopin with the distasteful excesses of journalist Dorothy Dix, whose articles on Louisiana women frequently made this comparison:

> There comes a time in the life of almost every woman when she has to choose between a species of slavery and freedom, and when . . . she must hoist the red flag of revolt and make a fight for her rights. It counts for nothing that the oppressor is generally of her own household. . . . [We give in to our oppressors till we are] nothing more than bond slaves to the tyrant on our hearth.
> Chief and foremost among these oppressors are children.[8]

The Awakening is the novel that best brings together those concerns, analogies, and contrasts that made up white middle-class women's preoccupations in the postbellum decades. Its focus on marriage, its use of the slavery correlative, and the suggestive use of topographical and historical materials, mediated through European intertextual readings, all combine to produce a feminist regionalist work that nonetheless lapses into unexamined racism. And I suspect that the shock with which it was read by contemporary critics, and the startled disappointment its conclusion gives to modern readers, derive from a similar source. The novel appropriates male romantic concerns for women, concerned as it is with the problem of achieving full subjectivity through that "unmediated and eroticised relation to art and life" that it was presumptuous for an 1890s southern woman to desire. In her attempt to become a full subject, Edna negotiates her way through various versions of femininity, rejecting each model as she goes and refusing all definitions of what she should be—including that of artist (which is the crucial point at which the author departs from her protagonist). Julia Kristeva offers a suggestive way of explaining our profound disturbance at the novel's closure. She argues that the role women have in challenging phallic dominance lies in "assuming a *negative* function: reject everything finite, definite, structured, loaded with meaning, in the existing state of society. [This] places women on the side of the explosion of social codes: with revolutionary moments." Of course, Kristeva's "negative function" dangerously allies women with a kind of death. But Edna's suicide does symbolically "explode" codes in a revolutionary moment, hence her exhilaration as

8. See above, p. 148 [*Editor*].

she swims to her death and the romantic natural associations of the last line: "There was the hum of bees, and the musky odor of pinks filled the air."[9]

But the novel is by no means unequivocally triumphant. Its closure, which leaves so many readers uneasy, speaks the contradictory concerns and tensions of much of the late nineteenth-century regionalist fiction by Louisiana women. Better than any other text, perhaps, *The Awakening* brings together the romantic but deadly associations of the historic and mythic Gulf waters, the mingled voices of European and American naturalistic determinism and progressive or utopian feminism, and the hopelessness and joyous defiance of the "New Woman" who refuses political, social, and personal compromise.

Kate Chopin was disheartened at the critical reception of *The Awakening* and wrote little more before her death in 1904. As Thomas Hardy's[1] disgust with the critical reception of *Jude the Obscure* silenced him as a novelist, so Chopin appears to have recognized the limited imaginative capacity and generosity of contemporary critics and to have capitulated to the critical double standard. She had not consciously sought notoriety, though her experiences with publishers must have prepared her for the storm over her second novel. But as a southern woman with little taste for self-revelation and a strong bent for irony, she must have found hard to swallow the implicitly adverse judgments on her as a *woman*, identified as she immediately was with Edna Pontellier.

The Awakening and "The Storm," written before the novel but pragmatically never offered to an editor, were the logical conclusion of all Chopin's writing about women. Both celebrate woman as an infinitely desiring and versatile subject, and both demonstrate the power of erotic bliss in the creation of a new kind of woman. Chopin's departure from orthodox American and southern themes is usually read as an interesting kind of aberration, inspired by the English romantic poets and by Walt Whitman, and accomplished by individual genius. But as I have tried to show, most of Chopin's work made relatively conventional use of Local Color themes and techniques, and was as deeply embedded in southern racist ideology as the writings of Grace King and Ruth McEnery Stuart—though her project was very different. Her originality as a woman writer, as I see it, derives from her complex and subtle intertextual reworkings of European fictional works to produce a critique of the social meanings of southern womanhood. *The Awakening*, which

9. Kaplan, "Wild Nights: Pleasure/Sexuality/Feminism," in *Formations of Pleasure*, edited by Formations Editorial Collective, London, 1983, 27; Julia Kristeva, "Oscillation Between Power and Denial," in Elaine Marks and Isabelle De Courtivron, eds., *New French Feminisms: An Anthology* (New York, 1981), 166.
1. English novelist and poet (1840–1928), whose last novel, *Jude the Obscure* (1895), caused an uproar when published. Critics speculate that the harsh reaction to the novel was one factor in his abandoning fiction for poetry [*Editor*].

is thus the crucial text, is of considerable importance to this study since it embodies most of the regional and feminist concerns of southern women writers. Its unconsciously racist elements cannot be excused, but its feminist subtext manages to explore and explode the various meanings of femininity in the postbellum South.

ELIZABETH AMMONS

[Women of Color in *The Awakening*]†

* * *

The background of *The Awakening* is filled with nameless, faceless black women carefully categorized as black, mulatto, quadroon, and Griffe, distinctions which, significantly, do not even show up in Alice Dunbar-Nelson's book.[1] Also, Mexican American and Mexican women play crucial subordinate roles in *The Awakening*. Taken together, all of these women of color make Edna Pontellier's "liberation" possible. As menials they free her from work, from cooking to childcare. As prostitutes they service/educate the men in her world. Chopin is both in and out of control of this political story.

Compared to a Thomas Nelson Page or Thomas Dixon, Kate Chopin had liberal, enlightened views on the subject of race.[2] One of the ways

† From *Conflicting Stories: American Women Writers at the Turn Into the Twentieth Century* (New York and Oxford: Oxford UP, 1991) 74–75.

1. New Orleans-born Alice Dunbar-Nelson (1875–1935), widely published author of poems, short fiction, art and literary criticism, and essays on history and culture, stands as a transitional figure between African-American writers of an earlier generation (including her first husband, Paul Lawrence Dunbar) and the artists/writers of the Harlem Renaissance. Ammons has been discussing Dunbar-Nelson's *The Goodness of St. Rocque and Other Stories*. In her "People of Color in Louisiana," *Journal of Negro History* 1 (October 1916): 361, Dunbar-Nelson writes:

> The title of a possible discussion of the Negro in Louisiana presents difficulties, for there is no such word as Negro permissible in speaking of this State. The history of the State is filled with attempts to define, sometimes at the point of the sword, oftenest in civil or criminal courts, the meaning of the word Negro. By common consent, it came to mean in Louisiana, prior to 1865, slave, and after the war, those whose complexions were noticeably dark. As Grace King so delightfully puts it, "The pure-blooded African was never called colored, but always Negro." The *gens de couleur*, colored people, were always a class apart, separated from and superior to the Negroes, ennobled were it only by one drop of white blood in their veins. The caste seems to have existed from the first introduction of slaves. To the whites, all Africans who were not of pure blood were *gens de couleur*. Among themselves, however, there were jealous and fiercely-guarded distinctions: "griffes, briqués, mulattoes, quadroons, octoroons, each term meaning one degree's further transfiguration toward the Caucasian standard of physical perfection" (Grace King, *New Orleans, the Place and the People During the Ancien Regime* [New York, 1895] 333).

2. Discussion of the treatment of race in Chopin's work can be found in Seyersted, *Kate Chopin*, and in Anne Goodwyn Jones's excellent chapter on Chopin in *Tomorrow Is Another Day: The Woman Writer in the South, 1859–1936* (Baton Rouge: Louisiana State University Press, 1981), pp. 135–84. [See above, p. 299, n. 3. Thomas Dixon (1864–1946), North Carolina writer best known for *The Clansman* (1905), which was made into the movie *Birth of a Nation—Editor.*]

that she shows how despicable Victor Lebrun is, for example, is by providing glimpses of his racism—his contempt for black people in general, his verbal abuse of the black woman who insists on doing her job of opening the door when Edna knocks, his arrogant assumption of credit for the silver and gold cake which he orders two black women to create in his kitchen. It is also possible to argue that, as Edna awakens, black characters change from nameless parts of the scenery to individuals with names and voices. On Grand Isle the blacks who tend white women's children, carry messages, sweep porches, and crouch on the floor to work the treadle of Madame Lebrun's sewing machine (a child does this) so that Madame's health is not imperiled move through the narrative speechless and nameless. As the book progresses, however, individuals emerge: the "boy" Joe who works for the Pontelliers in the city, the "mulatresse" Catiche to whose tiny garden restaurant in the suburbs Edna repairs, the capable "Griffe" nurse who sees Madame Ratignolle through the birth of her baby. Yet as even these mentions betray, the individual people of color who do emerge from the background, as the book traces Edna's increasing distance from the rigid class- and gender-bound world of her marriage, are finally no more than types, human categories—unexamined representatives of the novel's repressed African American context. Minor white characters are not identified by the cups of Irish or French or German blood in them. In other words, even an argument that claims progression in the individualization of black characters has to face the fact that images of black people in *The Awakening*, a book about a woman trying to escape a limiting, caging assignment of gender that stunts her humanity and robs her of choices, are stereotypic and demeaning.

Deeper is the problem that the very liberation about which the book fantasizes is purchased on the backs of black women. If Edna's children did not have a hired "quadroon" to care for them night and day, it is extremely unlikely that she would swim off into the sunset at the end of *The Awakening* in a glorious burst of Emersonian free will. Edna's story is not universal, although most feminist literary criticism has failed to acknowledge the fact. It is the story of a woman of one race and class who is able to dream of total personal freedom because an important piece of that highly individualistic ideal (itself the product of the very capitalism that Edna in some ways gropes to shed) has already been bought for her. Though she does not see it, her freedom comes at the expense of women of other races and a lower class, whose namelessness, facelessness, and voicelessness record a much more profound oppression in *The Awakening* than does the surface story of Edna Pontellier. The great examined story of *The Awakening* is its heroine's break for freedom. The great unexamined story, one far more disturbing than the fiction privileged in the text, is the narrative of sororal oppression across race and class.

Toni Morrison argues in her groundbreaking essay "Unspeakable Things Unspoken: The Afro-American Presence in American Literature" that it is not the why but the how of racial erasure that constitutes the truly important question: "What intellectual feats had to be performed by the author or his critic to erase me from a society seething with my presence, and what effect has that performance had on the work?"[3] The answer to this question in *The Awakening* is in one way quite simple. The repression of black women's stories—and with them Edna's identity as oppressor as well as oppressed—plunges not just Edna but also Chopin into a killing silence from which neither returns. It is widely agreed that Kate Chopin did not write much after *The Awakening* because the hostile reviews of the novel devastated her. I am sure that is true. One might ask, however, after *The Awakening*, unless Chopin was willing to confront race, what was there to say? The book brilliantly spins the privileged white female fantasy of utter and complete personal freedom out to its end, which is oblivion—the sea, death. The fantasy itself deadends. (Willa Cather's irritation with the novel, which she criticized for its "over-idealization of love" and its shallowly "expecting an individual and self-limited passion to yield infinite variety, pleasure, and distraction," does not seem so cranky when viewed from this perspective.[4] Cut off from the large, urgent, ubiquitous struggle for freedom of African Americans in Chopin's America, a struggle hinted at but repeatedly repressed in the text, the utterly individualistic and solipsistic white female fantasy of freedom that *The Awakening* indulges in can only end in silence—in death.

* * *

ELAINE SHOWALTER

[Chopin and American Women Writers]†

* * * *The Awakening* belongs to a historical moment in American women's writing, and Chopin could not have written without the legacy of domestic fiction to work against, and the models of the local colorists and New Women writers with which to experiment. After the Civil War, the homosocial world of women's culture began to dissolve as

3. Toni Morrison, "Unspeakable Things Unspoken: The Afro-American Presence in American Literature," *Michigan Quarterly Review*, 28 (Winter 1989), 12.
4. See above, pp. 170–72 [Editor].
† From "*The Awakening*: Tradition and the American Female Talent," in *Sister's Choice: Tradition and Change in American Women's Writing* (Oxford: The Clarendon Press, 1991) 65–84. An earlier version of this essay appeared as "Tradition and the Female Talent: *The Awakening* as a Solitary Book," in *New Essays on "The Awakening*," ed. Wendy Martin (Cambridge and New York: Cambridge UP, 1988) 33–58. Reprinted with the permission of Cambridge University Press.

women demanded entrance to higher education, the professions, and the political world. The female local colorists who began to publish stories about American regional life in the 1870s and 1880s were also attracted to the male worlds of art and prestige opening up to women, and they began to assert themselves as the daughters of literary fathers as well as literary mothers.

* * *

Kate Chopin's literary evolution took her progressively through the three phases of nineteenth-century American women's culture and women's writing. Born in 1850, she grew up with the great best-sellers of the American and English sentimentalists. As a girl, she had wept over the works of Warner and Stowe[1] and had copied pious passages from the English novelist Dinah Mulock Craik's The Woman's Kingdom into her diary.[2] Throughout her adolescence, Chopin had also shared an intimate friendship with Kitty Garasché, a classmate at the Academy of the Sacred Heart. Together, Chopin recalled, the girls had read fiction and poetry, gone on excursions, and 'exchanged our heart secrets.'[3] Their friendship ended in 1870 when Kate Chopin married and Kitty Garasché entered a convent. Yet when Oscar Chopin died in 1883, his young widow went to visit her old friend and was shocked by her blind isolation from the world. When Chopin began to write, she took as her models such local colorists as Sarah Orne Jewett and Mary Wilkins Freeman,[4] who had not only mastered technique and construction but had also devoted themselves to telling the stories of female loneliness, isolation, and frustration.

Sandra Gilbert has suggested that local color was a narrative strategy that Chopin employed to solve a specific problem: how to deal with extreme psychological states without the excesses of sentimental narrative and without critical recrimination. At first, Gilbert suggests, 'local color' writing 'offered both a mode and a manner that could mediate between the literary structures she had inherited and those she had begun.' Like the anthropologists, the local colorist could observe vagaries of culture and character with 'almost scientific detachment.' Furthermore, 'by reporting odd events and customs that were part of a region's "local color" she could tell what would ordinarily be rather shocking or even melo-

1. Harriet Beecher Stowe (1811–96) and Susan Warner (1819–85), two of American's most popular writers at the mid-nineteenth century. Stowe's Uncle Tom's Cabin (1851–52) sold more books than any novel of the century, and Warner's Wide, Wide World (1850) also sold over a million copies. See Mary Kelley, Private Woman, Public Stage: Literary Domesticity in Nineteenth-Century America (New York and Oxford: Oxford UP, 1984) [Editor].
2. Dinah Mulock Craik (1826–87), one of the "second wave" of English Victorian novelists. She "specialized in tales of women's suffering and endurance." In Woman's Kingdom, one of a number of books for children that focused on the "joys of family life and the need for women to submit to their husband," the heroine Edna "almost succumbs to despair before she married a kindly doctor." From Elaine Showalter, "Dinah Mulock Craik and the Tactics of Sentiment: A Case Study in Victorian Female Authorship," Feminist Studies 2 (1975): 5, 7, 19–20 [Editor].
3. Per Seyersted, Kate Chopin: A Critical Biography (New York: Octagon Books, 1980), p. 18.
4. See above, p. 207, n. 9, and p. 197, n. 3 [Editor].

dramatic tales in an unmelodramatic way, and without fear of . . . moral outrage.'[5]

* * *

Much of the shock effect of *The Awakening* to the readers of 1899 came from Chopin's rejection of the conventions of women's writing. Despite her name, which echoes two famous heroines of the domestic novel (Edna Earl in Augusta Evans' *St Elmo*[6] and Edna Kenderdine in Dinah Craik's *Woman's Kingdom*), Edna Pontellier appears to reject the domestic empire of the mother and the sororal world of women's culture. Seemingly beyond the bonds of womanhood, she has neither mother nor daughter, and even refuses to go to her sister's wedding. For a generation which had grown up reading about Meg's wedding in *Little Women*,[7] this was shocking indeed.

Moreover, whereas the sentimental heroine nurtures others, and the abstemious local color heroine subsists upon meager vegetarian diets, Kate Chopin's heroine is a robust woman who does not deny her appetites. Freeman's New England nun[8] picks at her dainty lunch of lettuce leaves and currants, but Edna Pontellier eats hearty meals of paté, pompano, steak, and broiled chicken; bites off chunks of crusty bread; snacks on beer and Gruyère cheese; and sips brandy, wine, and champagne.

Formally, too, the novel has moved away from conventional techniques of realism to an impressionistic rhythm of epiphany and mood. Chopin abandoned the chapter titles she had used in her first novel, *At Fault* (1890), for thirty-nine numbered sections of uneven length, ranging from the single paragraph of section 28 to the sustained narrative of the dinner party in section 30. The sections are unified less by their style than by their focus on Edna's consciousness, and by the repetition of key motifs and images: music, the sea, shadows, swimming, eating, sleeping, gambling, the lovers, birth. Scenes of lyricism and fantasy, such as Edna's voyage to the Chenière Caminada, alternate with realistic, even satirical, scenes of Edna's marriage.

Most important, where previous works by American women largely ignored sexuality or spiritualized it through maternity, *The Awakening* is insistently sexual, explicitly involved with the body and with self-awareness through physical awareness. Although Edna's actual seduction by Arobin takes place in the narrative neverland between sections 31 and 32, Chopin brilliantly evokes sexuality through images and details. In keeping with the novel's emphasis on the self, several scenes suggest Edna's initial autoeroticism. Edna's midnight swim, which awakens the 'first-felt throbbings of desire,' takes place in an atmosphere of erotic

5. Sandra Gilbert, "Introduction" to *The Awakening and Selected Stories* (Hammondsworth: Penguin, 1984), p. 16.
6. An enormously popular novel about the moral reform of the male hero (St. Elmo) by a pious heroine, was published in 1867 by Augusta Jane Evans (Wilson) (1835–1909) [*Editor*].
7. Best-known novel (1868–69) of Louisa May Alcott (1832–88) [*Editor*].
8. The reference is to Mary Wilkins Freeman's *New England Nun* (1891) [*Editor*].

fragrance, 'strange, rare odors . . . a tangle of the sea-smell and of weeds and damp new-ploughed earth, mingled with the heavy perfume of a field of white blossoms.' A similarly voluptuous scene is her nap at Chenière Caminada, when she examines her flesh as she lies in a 'strange, quaint bed with its sweet country odor of laurel.' Edna reminds Dr Mandalet of 'some beautiful, sleek animal waking up in the sun,' and we recall that among her fantasies in listening to music is the image of a lady stroking a cat. The image both conveys Edna's sensuality and hints at the self-contained, almost masturbatory, quality of her sexuality. Her rendezvous with Robert takes place in a sunny garden where both stroke a drowsy cat's silky fur, and Arobin first seduces her by smoothing her hair with his 'soft, magnetic hand.'

Yet despite these departures from tradition, there are other respects in which the novel seems very much of its time. As its title suggests, *The Awakening* is a novel about a process rather than a program, about a passage rather than a destination. It is a transitional female fiction of the *fin de siècle*, a narrative of and about the passage from the homosocial women's culture and literature of the nineteenth century to the heterosexual fiction of modernism. Chopin might have taken the plot from a notebook entry Henry James made in 1892 about

> the growing divorce between the American woman (with her comparative leisure, culture, grace, social instincts, artistic ambition) and the male American immersed in the ferocity of business, with no time for any but the most sordid interests, purely commercial, professional democratic and political. This divorce is rapidly becoming a gulf.[9]

The Gulf where the opening chapters of *The Awakening* are set certainly suggests the 'growing divorce' between Edna's interests and desires and Leonce's obsessions with the stock market, property, and his brokerage business.

Yet in turning away from her marriage, Edna initially looks back to women's culture rather than forward to another man. As Sandra Gilbert has pointed out, Grand Isle is an oasis of women's culture, or a 'female colony':

> Madame Lebrun's pension on Grand Isle is very much a woman's land not only because it is owned and run by a single woman and dominated by 'mother-women' but also because (as in so many summer colonies today) its principal inhabitants are actually women and children whose husbands and fathers visit only on weekends . . . [and it is situated] like so many places that are significant for women, outside patriarchal cultures, beyond the limits and limi-

9. Henry James, November 26, 1892, quoted in Larzer Ziff, *The American 1890s* (New York: Viking, 1966), p. 275. [James (1843–1916), major American novelist, known for his complex style and structure and for his pioneering of psychological realism in the novel—*Editor.*]

tations of the city where men make history, on a shore that marks the margin where nature intersects with culture.[1]

Edna's awakening, moreover, begins not with a man, but with Adele Ratignolle, the empress of the 'mother-women' of Grand Isle. A 'self-contained' woman, Edna has never had any close relationships with members of her own sex. Thus it is Adele who belatedly initiates Edna into the world of female love and ritual on the first step of her sensual voyage of self-discovery. Edna's first attraction to Adele is erotic: 'the excessive physical charm of the Creole had first attracted her, for Edna had a sensuous susceptibility to beauty.' At the beach, in the hot sun, she responds to Adele's caresses, the first she has ever known from another woman, as Adele clasps her hand 'firmly and warmly' and strokes it fondly. The touch provokes Edna to an unaccustomed candor; leaning her head on Adele's shoulder and confiding some of her secrets, she begins to feel 'intoxicated.' The bond between them goes beyond sympathy, as Chopin notes, to 'what we might well call love.'

In some respects, the motherless Edna also seeks a mother surrogate in Adele and looks to her for nurturance. Adele provides maternal encouragement for Edna's painting and tells her that her 'talent is immense.' Characteristically, Adele has rationalized her own 'art' as a maternal project: 'she was keeping up her music on account of the children . . . a means of brightening the home and making it attractive.' Edna's responses to Adele's music have been similarly tame and sentimental. Her revealing fantasies as she listens to Adele play her easy pieces suggest the restriction and decorum of the female world: 'a dainty young woman . . . taking mincing dancing steps, as she came down a long avenue between tall hedges'; 'children at play.' Women's art, as Adele presents it, is social, pleasant, and undemanding. It does not conflict with her duties as a wife and mother, and can even be seen to enhance them. Edna understands this well; as she retorts when her husband recommends Adele as a model of an artist, 'She isn't a musician and I'm not a painter!'

Yet the relationship with the conventional Adele educates the immature Edna to respond for the first time both to a different kind of sexuality and to the unconventional and difficult art of Mademoiselle Reisz. In responding to Adele's interest, Edna begins to think about her own past and to analyze her own personality. In textual terms, it is through this relationship that she becomes 'Edna' in the narrative rather than 'Mrs. Pontellier.'

We see the next stage of Edna's awakening in her relationship with Mademoiselle Reisz, who initiates her into the world of art. Significantly, this passage also takes place through a female rather than a male mentor, and, as with Adele, there is something more intense than friendship

1. Gilbert, "Introduction," p. 25.

between the two women. Whereas Adele's fondness for Edna, however, is depicted as maternal and womanly, Mademoiselle Reisz's attraction to Edna suggests something more perverse. The pianist is obsessed with Edna's beauty, raves over her figure in a bathing suit, greets her as 'ma belle' and 'ma reine,' holds her hand, and describes herself as 'a foolish old woman whom you have captivated.' If Adele is a surrogate for Edna's dead mother and the intimate friend she never had as a girl, Mademoiselle Reisz, whose music reduces Edna to passionate sobs, seems to be a surrogate lover. And whereas Adele is a 'faultless madonna' who speaks for the values and laws of the Creole community, Mademoiselle Reisz is a renegade, self-assertive and outspoken. She has no patience with petty social rules and violates the most basic expectations of femininity. To a rake like Arobin, she is so unattractive, unpleasant, and unwomanly as to seem 'partially demented.' Even Edna occasionally perceives Mademoiselle Reisz's awkwardness as a kind of deformity, and is sometimes offended by the old woman's candor and is not sure whether she likes her.

Yet despite her eccentricities, Mademoiselle Reisz seems 'to reach Edna's spirit and set it free.' Her voice in the novel seems to speak for the author's view of art and for the artist. It is surely no accident, for example, that it is Chopin's music that Mademoiselle Reisz performs. At the *pension* on Grand Isle, the pianist first plays a Chopin prelude, to which Edna responds with surprising turbulence: 'the very passions themselves were aroused within her soul, swaying it, lashing it, as the waves daily beat upon her splendid body. She trembled, she was choking, and the tears blinded her.' 'Chopin' becomes the code word for a world of repressed passion between Edna and Robert that Mademoiselle Reisz controls. Later the pianist plays a Chopin impromptu for Edna that Robert has admired; this time the music is 'strange and fantastic— turbulent, plaintive and soft with entreaty.' These references to 'Chopin' in the text are on one level allusions to an intimate, romantic, and poignant musical *œuvre* that reinforces the novel's sensual atmosphere. But on another level, they function as what Nancy K. Miller has called the 'internal female signature' in women's writing, here a self-referential pun that alludes to Kate Chopin's ambitions as an artist and to the emotions she wished her book to arouse in its readers.[2]

* * *

Madame Ratignolle and Mademoiselle Reisz not only represented important alternative roles and influences for Edna in the world of the novel, but as the proto-heroines of sentimental and local color fiction, they also suggest different plots and conclusions. Adele's story suggests

2. Thanks to Nancy K. Miller of Barnard College for this phrase from her current work on the development of women's writing in France. I am also endebted to the insights of Carol Torsney of the University of West Virginia, and to the comments of other participants of my NEH Seminar on "Women's Writing and Women's Culture," Summer 1984.

that Edna will give up her rebellion, return to her marriage, have another baby, and by degrees learn to appreciate, love, and even desire her husband. Such was the plot of many late-nineteenth-century novels about erring young women married to older men, such as Susan Warner's *Diana* (1880) and Louisa May Alcott's *Moods* (1881). Mademoiselle Reisz's story suggests that Edna will lose her beauty, her youth, her husband, and children—everything, in short, but her art and her pride—and become a kind of New Orleans nun.

Chopin wished to reject both of these endings and to escape from the literary traditions they represented; but her own literary solitude, her resistance to allying herself with a specific ideological or aesthetic position, made it impossible for her to work out something different and new.

*   *   *

Can Edna, and Kate Chopin, then, escape from confining traditions only in death? Some critics have seen Edna's much-debated suicide as a heroic embrace of independence and a symbolic resurrection into myth, a feminist counterpart of Melville's Bulkington: 'Take heart, take heart, O Edna, up from the spray of thy ocean-perishing, up, straight up, leaps thy apotheosis!'[3] But the ending too seems to return her to the nineteenth-century female literary tradition, even though Chopin redefines it for her own purpose. Readers of the 1890s were well accustomed to drowning as the fictional punishment for female transgression against morality, and most contemporary critics of *The Awakening* thus automatically interpreted Edna's suicide as the wages of sin.

Drowning itself brings to mind metaphorical analogies between femininity and liquidity. As the female body is prone to wetness, blood, milk, tears, and amniotic fluid, so in drowning the woman is immersed in the feminine organic element. Drowning thus becomes the traditionally feminine literary death.[4] And Edna's last thoughts further recycle significant images of the feminine from her past. As exhaustion overpowers her, 'Edna heard her father's voice and her sister Margaret's. She heard the barking of an old dog that was chained to the sycamore tree. The spurs of the cavalry officer clanged as he walked across the porch. There was the hum of bees, and the musky odor of pinks filled the air.' Edna's memories are those of awakening from the freedom of childhood to the limitations conferred by female sexuality.

The image of the bees and the flowers not only recalls early descriptions of Edna's sexuality as a 'sensitive blossom,' but also places *The Awakening* firmly within the textual traditions of American women's writing, where it is a standard trope for the unequal sexual relations between women and men. Margaret Fuller, for example, writes in her

---

3. Ishmael memorializes his shipmate on *The Pequod* with these words in Herman Melville's *Moby-Dick* (1851) [*Editor*].
4. See Gaston Bachelard, "*L'eau et les reves*" (Paris, 1942), pp. 109–25.

journal: 'Woman is the flower, man the bee. She sighs out of melodious fragrance, and invites the winged laborer. He drains her cup, and carries off the honey. She dies on the stalk; he returns to the hive, well fed, and praised as an active member of the community.'[5] In post-Civil War fiction, the image is a reminder of an elemental power that women's culture must confront. The Awakening seems particularly to echo the last lines of Mary Wilkins Freeman's 'New England Nun,' in which the heroine, having broken her long-standing engagement, is free to continue her solitary life, and closes her door on 'the sounds of the busy harvest of men and birds and bees; there were halloos, metallic clatterings, sweet calls, long hummings.'[6] These are the images of a nature that, Edna has learned, decoys women into slavery; yet even in drowning, she cannot escape from their seductiveness, for to ignore their claim is also to cut oneself off from culture, from the 'humming' life of creation and achievement.

We can re-create the literary tradition in which Kate Chopin wrote The Awakening, but of course, we can never know how the tradition might have changed if her novel had not had to wait half a century to find its audience. Few of Chopin's literary contemporaries came into contact with the book. Chopin's biographer, Per Seyersted, notes that her work

> was apparently unknown to Dreiser, even though he began writing Sister Carrie just when The Awakening was being loudly condemned. Also Ellen Glasgow, who was at this time beginning to describe unsatisfactory marriages, seems to have been unaware of the author's existence. Indeed, we can safely say that though she was so much of an innovator in American literature, she was virtually unknown by those who were now to shape it and that she had no influence on them.[7]

Not until 1928, with the publications of Nella Larsen's Quicksand, did black women writers attempt to deal with the sexual ideology and repression facing a woman seeking independence.[8] Ironically, even Willa Cather, the one woman writer of the fin de siècle who reviewed The Awakening, not only failed to recognize its importance but also dismissed its theme as 'trite.'[9]

Edna's triumphant embrace of solitude had unexpected and unhappy

5. Margaret Fuller, "Life Without and Within," quoted in Bell G. Chevigny, The Woman and the Myth (Old Westbury, New York: Feminist Press, 1976), p. 349. See also Wendy Martin, An American Triptych: Anne Bradstreet, Emily Dickinson, Adrienne Rich (Chapel Hill: University of North Carolina Press, 1984), pp. 154–159.
6. "A New England Nun," in Mary Wilkins Freeman, The Revolt of Mother, ed. Michele Clark (New York: Feminist Press, 1974), p. 97.
7. Seyersted, Kate Chopin, p. 196.
8. Nella Larsen (1893–1964), novelist of the Harlem Renaissance, also known for the novel Passing (1929) [Editor].
9. See above, p. 170 [Editor].

consequences for Kate Chopin. A writer needs to cultivate solitude and independence, but literature depends on shared forms and representations of experience. Literary genres, like biological species, evolve because of significant innovations by individuals that survive through imitation and revision. Thus it can be a very severe set-back to a developing genre when a revolutionary work is taken out of circulation. Experimentation is retarded and repressed. The interruption of this process is most destructive for the literature of a minority group, since they are so often taxed with lacking originality and aesthetic boldness. Yet radical departures from literary convention are especially likely to be censured and suppressed within a minority tradition because they violate social as well as aesthetic expectations and stereotypes.

In many respects, *The Awakening* seems to comment on its own history as a novel, and to predit its own critical fate. The parallels between the experiences of Edna Pontellier, as she breaks away from the conventional feminine roles of wife and mother, and those of Kate Chopin, as she broke away from the conventions of literary domesticity, suggest that Edna's story may also be read as a parable of Chopin's literary awakening. Both the author and the heroine oscillate between two worlds, caught between contradictory definitions of femininity and creativity, and seeking whether to synthesize them or to go beyond them to an emancipated womanhood and an emancipated fiction. Edna's 'unfocused yearning' for an autonomous life is akin to Chopin's yearning to write works that go beyond female plots and feminine endings.

Edna Pontellier was no Margaret Fuller,[1] nor was meant to be; Chopin's view of her is ironic, and her death is not held up to us as the tragic loss of a great spirit. But the death of *The Awakening* was a tragic loss for Chopin's artistry. There are signs that it would have been a pivotal work in her career. While it was in press, she wrote one of her finest and most daring stories, 'The Storm,' which surpasses the novel in terms of its expressive freedom.[2] But her career was halted by the scandal, which may have also hastened her early death. At the turn of the century, Chopin, like Edith Wharton and Willa Cather, speaks for a painful transitional age in American women's writing.[3]

Yet we owe the rediscovery of Chopin's work not to American women writers but to male literary critics from France and Norway as well as from the United States. Chopin's editor Per Seyersted was the one who brought her work to the attention of a new feminist generation, while her French translator Cyrille Arnavon championed her as a stylist.[4] And while the novel has now firmly entered the academic canon, it has yet

1. See above, p. 303, n. 7.
2. Chopin, *The Complete Works*, II, 735.
3. Edith Wharton (1862–1937), major American writer, author of *The House of Mirth* (1905), *Ethan Frome* (1911), and *The Age of Innocence* (1920), among other novels. See above, p. 207, n. 9 [*Editor*].
4. See above, pp. 202–7 and pp. 184–87 [*Editor*].

to enter women's writing as a touchstone. In fact, the most significant contemporary rewriting of *The Awakening* is not by a woman novelist. It is rather Robert Stone's *Children of Light* (1986). Stone is on the surface a most unlikely writer to be influenced by Chopin. His literary reputation has been made as a post-Vietnam reporter of a violent, drugged-out America in the dying throes of its imperialist adventures. He won the National Book Award for *Dog Soldiers*, a novel of surrealistic doom which displayed his stunning gifts for dialog and his sense of apocalyptic fatality. These elements also appear in *Children of Light*, which reimagines Chopin's novel through the eyes of a Hollywood screenwriter who has been asked to write the script for a movie of *The Awakening*. The modern Edna is the movie star Lu Anne Verger, an actress who is alcoholic and schizophrenic, and who has lost custody of her child through a messy divorce. Through the role of Edna, Lu Anne hopes to redeem herself in a superb performance that will reveal her acting gifts, and give her life meaning. But it is too late; the years of pretense and narcissism have left her locked in her own hallucinations, unable to accept either friendship with other women or love from men. Like Edna, Lu Anne 'finds out who she is and it's too much and she dies.'[5]

Stone makes Lu Anne's suicide a symbol of the corruption of art and fantasy in *fin de siècle* America. But his dialog with Chopin is an important sign that contemporary American male writers are no longer living in a different country from women and never reading their work. While *Little Women* has remained a female myth, *The Awakening* has also become part of the texture of a masculine and mainstream art. That process must be troubling to some feminists, for when American women's writing passes into the mainstream, it ceases to be solitary, 'American,' or 'feminine.' But such rereadings, rewriting, and reinhabiting of women's texts are the only way that *The Awakening*, like other lost masterpieces by American women, is finally restored to us and takes its rightful place in our literary heritage.

5. Robert Stone, *Children of Light* (New York: Knopf, 1986), p. 132.

Kate Chopin:
A Chronology

1850   Catherine ("Kate") O'Flaherty born February 8 to Thomas O'Flaherty and Eliza Faris O'Flaherty in St. Louis, Missouri.

1855   Thomas O'Flaherty, Kate's father, dies in a railroad accident.

1855–68   Attends and graduates from Sacred Heart Academy, St. Louis.

1863   Victoire Verdon Charleville, Kate's great-grandmother, dies; George O'Flaherty, her half-brother, dies of typhoid while serving as a Confederate soldier; Kitty Gareshé, her closest friend, leaves for South Carolina when her family, supporters of the rebel cause, are driven out of St. Louis.

1870   Marries Oscar Chopin of Louisiana and, after a European honeymoon, moves to New Orleans.

1871–78   Gives birth to five sons.

1879   Moves to the village of Cloutierville, Natchitoches Parish, in northwest Louisiana. Gives birth to a daughter, Léila.

1882   Oscar Chopin dies suddenly of "swamp fever."

1884   Kate Chopin returns with her children to St. Louis.

1885   Her mother, Eliza Faris O'Flaherty, dies.

1889   Begins writing for publication.

1890   Publishes her first novel, *At Fault*.

1894   Publishes a collection of short stories, *Bayou Folk*, to enthusiastic reviews.

1897   Publishes a second collection of stories, *A Night in Acadie*, and continues to enjoy public acclaim for her literary achievement.

1898   Writes the short story "The Storm" but does not seek to publish it.

1899   Publishes *The Awakening* on April 22. Largely negative reviews of *The Awakening* appear in St. Louis and across the country during that spring and summer.

1900   Publisher rejects a collection of short stories, A Vocation and a Voice.

1904   Suffers a cerebral hemorrhage on August 20 after attending the St. Louis World's Fair. Dies two days later, on August 22; is buried in Calvary Cemetery, St. Louis.

Selected Bibliography

This bibliography does not include criticism excerpted in this volume.

KATE CHOPIN: WORKS

Seyersted, Per, ed. *The Complete Works of Kate Chopin*. 2 vols. Baton Rouge: Louisiana State UP, 1969.
Toth, Emily, ed. *A Vocation and a Voice: Stories by Kate Chopin*. New York: Penguin, 1990.
———, ed. *Kate Chopin's Private Papers*. Forthcoming.

BIOGRAPHY

Rankin, Daniel S. *Kate Chopin and Her Creole Stories*. Philadephia: U of Pennsylvania P, 1932.
Seyersted, Per. *Kate Chopin: A Critical Biography*. Baton Rouge: Louisiana State UP, 1969.
Toth, Emily. *Kate Chopin*. New York: William Morrow, 1990.

BIBLIOGRAPHY

Gannon, Barbara C. "Kate Chopin: A Secondary Bibliography." *American Literary Realism* 27. 1 (Spring 1984): 124–29.
Inge, Tonnette Bond. "Kate Chopin." In Maurice Duke, Jackson R. Bryer, and Thomas Inge, eds. *American Women Writers: Bibliographical Essays*. Westport: Greenwood Press, 1983. 47–69.

CRITICISM

Allen, Priscilla. "Old Critics and New: The Treatment of Chopin's *The Awakening*." In *The Authority of Experience: Essays in Feminist Criticism*, eds. Arlyn Diamond and Lee R. Edwards. Amherst: U of Massachusetts P, 1977. 224–38.
Bender, Bert. " 'The Teeth of Desire': *The Awakening* and *The Descent of Man*." *American Literature* 63. 3 (September 1991): 459–73.
Boren, Lynda S., and Sara de Saussure, eds. *Kate Chopin Reconsidered: Beyond the Bayou*. Baton Rouge: Louisiana State UP, 1992.
Brown, Dorothy H., and Barbara Ewell, eds. *Louisiana Women Writers: New Essays and a Comprehensive Bibliography*. Baton Rouge: Louisiana State UP, 1992.
Cantarow, Ellen. "Sex, Race, and Criticism: Thoughts of a White Feminist on Kate Chopin and Zora Neale Hurston." *Radical Teacher* 9 (1978): 30–33.
Cantwell, Robert. "*The Awakening* by Kate Chopin." *Georgia Review* 10 (Winter 1956): 489–94.
Casale, Ottavio Mark. "Beyond Sex: The Dark Romanticism of Kate Chopin's *The Awakening*." *Ball State University Forum* 19 (1978): 76–80.
Ewell, Barbara. *Kate Chopin*. New York: Ungar, 1986.
Franklin, Rosemary. "*The Awakening* and the Failure of Psyche." *American Literature* 56 (1984): 510–26.
Jones, Anne Goodwyn. *Tomorrow Is Another Day: The Woman Writer in the South 1859–1936*. Baton Rouge: Louisiana State UP, 1981.
Jones, Suzanne W. "Place, Perception and Identity in *The Awakening*." *Southern Quarterly* 25. 2 (Winter 1987): 108–19.

Justus, James H. "The Unawakening of Edna Pontellier." *Southern Literary Journal* 10 (1978): 107–22.

Koloski, Bernard. *Approaches to Teaching Chopin's "The Awakening."* New York: MLA, 1988.

Levine, Robert S. "Circadian Rhythms and Rebellion in Kate Chopin's *The Awakening.*" *Studies in American Fiction* 10.1 (Spring 1982): 71–81.

Louisiana Studies 14 (Spring 1975). Special issue.

Perspectives on Kate Chopin. Proceedings of the Kate Chopin International Conference. Northwestern State University, Natchitoches, Louisiana, 1989.

Rosen, Kenneth M. "Kate Chopin's *The Awakening*: Ambiguity as Art." *Journal of American Studies* 5 (August 1971): 197–99.

Schweitzer, Ivy. "Maternal Discourse and the Romance of Self-Possession in Kate Chopin's *The Awakening.*" *Boundary II* 17.1 (Spring 1990): 158–86.

Skaggs, Peggy. "Three Tragic Figures in Kate Chopin's *The Awakening.*" *Louisiana Studies* 14 (1975): 277–85.

Stange, Margrit. "Personal Property: Exchange Value and the Female Self in *The Awakening.*" *Genders* 5 (Summer 1989): 106–19.

Stone, Carole. "The Female Artist in Kate Chopin's *The Awakening*: Birth and Creativity." *Women Studies* 13.1–2 (1986): 23–32.

Thornton, Lawrence. *The Awakening*: A Political Romance." *American Literature* 52 (1980): 50–66.

Wheeler, Otis B. "The Five Awakenings of Edna Pontellier." *Southern Review* 11 (1975): 118–28.

Zlotnik, Joan. "A Woman's Will: Kate Chopin on Selfhood, Wifehood, and Motherhood." *The Markham Review* 3 (October 1968): 1–5.